CONTENTS

KU-039-034

Introduction

This book is our second of two that deals with the War of Independence in Dublin. It is also our fourth book of five whose subject matter is the momentous 1916–1923 period in Ireland's capital, seen through the eyes of those from both sides, and those caught between their struggle.

Our first work covering this war in the capital – *Killing at its Very Extreme: Dublin, October 1917–November 1920* (Mercier Press, 2020) – was itself a successor to our previous works: *When The Clock Struck in 1916: Close-Quarter Combat in the Easter Rising* (The Collins Press, 2015) and *Those of Us Who Must Die: Execution, Exile and Revival after the Easter Rising* (The Collins Press, 2017). In this work we pick up where *Killing at its Very Extreme* left off, continuing our account of the astonishing journey undertaken by so many of our ancestors during the War of Independence; many did not survive it, whilst others who did were left with indelible scars – both physical and mental.

In *Killing at its Very Extreme*, we divided our War of Independence work into two volumes; it would have been impossible to impart the level of vivid detail and information the story deserves into one. As in all our aforementioned works, we could not have done the participants justice if their stories were abridged simply for expediency.

The timeline featured here runs from November 1920 to July 1921, a far shorter timeline than *Killing at its Very Extreme*. This is because this pivotal period saw massively increased frequency of actions – military and political. Our previous work was not lacking in drama, intensity and brutality as the war escalated. However, November 1920 in Dublin unleashed unprecedented ferocity and political intrigue that continued right up to the Truce. The events of November and the subsequent eight months provided more than enough tumult to justify a similarly sized book of its own.

During early autumn 1920, the British military and police had taken the offensive in Ireland and gained a significant strategic advantage. Their grip was tightening, despite the Irish Republican Army's (IRA) tenacity. Round-ups and arrests were in full flow, facilitated by the recently enacted Restoration of Order in Ireland Act (ROIA). Their intelligence gathering grew in efficacy, while the looming Government of Ireland Act was expected – once and for all

– to unshackle the British government from the burdensome and frequently bloody Ulster question. This in turn would free up its agents to attack militant republicanism, paving the way for a settlement with moderate nationalists throughout the rest of Ireland that would be advantageous to the crown.

Attaining such strategic advantage had not come easily. Following a lengthy series of devastating blows to British intelligence, not to mention its very ability to govern, the world had watched in horror as the arrival of the Black and Tans and Auxiliaries led to atrocity after atrocity being inflicted upon the wider Irish population by the very forces whose official mandate was to restore law and order.[1] Their unrestrained brutality only served to undermine Britain's claims to Ireland, not only throughout Ireland itself, but also in the court of world opinion. Great Britain, perceiving itself as a beacon of enlightened democracy even beyond its empire, saw its international reputation plummet; a predicament worsened by global condemnation over Terence MacSwiney's death by hunger strike and Kevin Barry's execution. British politicians looked on in horror as their plans had backfired amid a worldwide and domestic wave of censure over the reprisals carried out by these new forces and their apparent disregard for life. Moderate nationalists became radicalised. Meanwhile, the military, repulsed by the lack of discipline displayed by the paramilitary units, accused the new forces of bringing their own sense of honour into disrepute. The army's commander, General Sir Cecil Frederick Nevil Macready, called instead for a transparent military strategy to fight the insurgency; effectively, to call it what it was and crush it by force underpinned by martial law. Westminster politicians were, however, loath to label as war what they considered the actions of IRA murder gangs. This lack of cohesion helped the IRA remain a step ahead.

The British had also faced an uphill military struggle. Resources were scattered across an empire struggling with a turbulent post-war world. Their initial successes of early 1920 in arresting huge numbers of IRA insurgents and suspects had foundered following the mass hunger strike in Mountjoy Prison, which saw many inmates released and hailed as heroes. Then, when much-needed logistical reinforcements finally arrived, the subsequent railway munitions and arms embargo forced the redeployment of military vehicles towards transportation rather than tactical roles. Macready's forces spent months hamstrung by frustrating organisational impediments.

Nevertheless, weight of numbers and huge advantages in material and money eventually saw the crown's composite forces closing in. Armoured cars bristling with machine guns patrolled Dublin's streets, as did Crossley Tender trucks packed with well-armed Auxiliaries. Police and military agents flooded the city. In November 1920, British Prime Minister David Lloyd George boasted of having 'murder by the throat'. However, he was about to be taught a harsh lesson.

IRA counter-intelligence, operating under a young and deadly triumvirate – Liam Tobin, Tom Cullen and Frank Thornton – directed by Michael Collins, was, alongside the Dublin Brigade, about to attack the very heart of Britain's counter-insurgency. The brigade commandant, Dick McKee, persuaded many comrades struggling with their own scruples that it was time to either strike hard at the British or accept inevitable defeat. Extreme ruthlessness was called for, the type employed by the squad of highly effective IRA assassins operating since summer 1919 in Dublin and mimicked by equally merciless enemy operatives.

November 1920 is where we pick up the story here. We deal with what became known as 'Bloody Sunday' – a day whose infamy still resonates – and its aftermath. As newspaper headlines brought Ireland's tribulations to the world, Dublin reeled from a well-orchestrated bloodbath followed by a massacre in Croke Park. Dublin Castle recoiled from the killings, as did the IRA, itself suffering a crushing blow afterwards. The aftermath saw incessant raids and mass arrests at the same time as tentative peace talks, set against a backdrop of state-sanctioned killings, further police atrocities and IRA attacks carried out by their newly created, full-time active service units (ASU) and by flying columns.

The end of the seven-month-long rail embargo – which itself had contributed to near starvation throughout Ireland, not to mention among the rail workers – freed up British Army logisticians to redirect their forces and attempt to get on the front foot once again. Meanwhile, as the Government of Ireland Act was passed, Éamon de Valera returned from the United States to reassume his position at the political helm of the nascent Irish Republic.

The year 1921 got off to a turbulent start for the IRA. Enemy intelligence was closing in. Open warfare began to take hold of Ireland's capital. IRA units and their enemies, both at times resembling murderous street-gangs, sought one another out. Military vehicles carried hostages, discouraging attackers. Curfews intensified, as did killings. Daring prison escapes emboldened the insurgents, while losses of agents within Dublin Castle dismayed them. Prisoner executions took place once again in the capital; accounts of poignant last-hour interactions of condemned men filled the newspapers, while, elsewhere, IRA flying columns held the media spellbound with audacious successes and bruising defeats.

Spring 1921 saw the departure of Lord Lieutenant John French, the survivor of countless assassination attempts, amid further escalations of violence and counter-measures. The IRA regrouped strategically with two additional battalions for Dublin, while also rejigging nationally. Casualties mounted on both sides. New elections took place, followed by clandestine meetings between adversaries.

Early summer saw an increased number of ambushes, raids and rescue attempts, followed by the burning of Dublin's Custom House – a monumental event in the city's history followed soon afterwards by further conflagrations. These later incidents preceded the threatened unleashing of full-scale warfare by the British. The IRA continued undeterred; attacks increased in frequency right up to the Truce, the point where this volume concludes.

It is an old maxim that victory, when unclear or disputed, can be attributed to those who hold the battlefield at the end of a battle or campaign. Therefore, the eventual transfer of power from a British to an Irish government in Ireland, largely derived from the events described in *Killing at its Very Extreme* and in this book, represented a victory for the nationalist and republican forces. Subsequent factors such as dominion rule, partition and civil war do of course present their own challenges to this. Unfortunately, the onset of the civil war brightly illuminates the danger of failing to recognise the value of even a partial, yet still substantial, victory.

Nevertheless, the principal aim of the majority of the Irish who fought between April 1916 and July 1921 was to remove British dominance from Ireland, and this was, by and large, achieved. In any event, history reveals that revolutions generally fail to deliver on aspirations, Ireland being no exception. But it is not our purpose to debate the rights, wrongs and flaws that tarnished the hopes of so many in not delivering fully on the objectives proclaimed in Dublin in 1916 and in 1919. What remains a fact is that the world's greatest empire was forced to concede that its protracted military and police campaign against the insurgents was unwinnable. This was a colossal achievement by the Irish Republican Brotherhood (IRB), the IRA, Cumann na mBan and others, particularly considering the close proximity between the proclaimed Republic and its historically dominant neighbour.

The republicans' steadfast methodology during these times was studied and mimicked afterwards throughout the world. Tactics and strategies employed by both sides were used in subsequent wars, including the Second World War; Winston Churchill sought to emulate the IRA with auxiliary forces planned to resist an anticipated German conquest of Britain. Sabotage and counter-mobility operations perfected in Ireland featured similarly throughout Axis-occupied territories. Soldiers and resistance fighters alike adopted tactics refined in Dublin for urban operations. Years later, in what is now Vietnam, a strategy of simply refusing to lose, despite massive enemy superiority, while draining the will of the enemy – be that military, politician or civilian – to continue fighting, was hugely effective for communist forces against the combined American and South Vietnamese armies, navies and air forces.

Our style here is as unflinching as the book's predecessors. We employ vivid accounts of violence, so often glossed over, while simultaneously warning the reader that parts of this work are not for the faint-hearted. To avoid repetition we have not added background to many characters featured already in *Killing at its Very Extreme*, while ensuring adequate elucidation for new characters and protagonists where applicable. Regarding the graphic depictions of violence and killing – as we stated in our previous books, it is only by striving to convey the brutal ferocity, agony, fear and suffering that we can do justice to those who lived through such tumultuous times. It has, once more, been a privilege to walk among them, to study their gripping accounts from one of our principal sources – Ireland's Military Archives – which, among other sources, has – yet again – left us amazed at their audacity and the heavy personal price paid by so many ordinary men, women and children. We hope to have done their actions and memories some justice.

DEREK MOLYNEUX AND DARREN KELLY

Abbreviations

ACRI	American Committee for Relief in Ireland
ASU	Active Service Unit
CIS	Central Intelligence Service
CRB	Central Raid Bureau
DDSB	Dublin District Special Branch
DMP	Dublin Metropolitan Police
GAA	Gaelic Athletic Association
GHQ	General Headquarters
GPO	General Post Office
HQ	Headquarters
ICA	Irish Citizen Army
IPP	Irish Parliamentary Party
IRA	Irish Republican Army
ITGWU	Irish Transport and General Workers' Union
MP	Member of Parliament
NCO	Non-commissioned Officer
O/C	Officer Commanding
OHMS	On His Majesty's Service
QMG	Quartermaster General
RAF	Royal Air Force
RASC	Royal Army Services Corps
RIC	Royal Irish Constabulary
ROIA	Restoration of Order in Ireland Act
TB	Tuberculosis
TUC	Trade Unions Congress
UCD	University College Dublin
USC	Ulster Special Constabulary

PROLOGUE

'I posed as a house-painter'

'I was still 1st Lieutenant of my Company ("B" Company, 2nd Battalion) and attending parades fairly regularly, taking out patrols or raiding houses for arms, shot guns etc. With other members of the Squad, I received instructions from G.H.Q. to keep away, and if necessary to resign, from the Volunteer Companies, which we did. This had a peculiar reaction in that many old members and new members of my Company, who were not aware of my permanent whole-time position with G.H.Q., believed that I had left the organisation and shortly after the Free State was founded I was openly accused of desertion on a few occasions.

'The usual method of allocating men to carry out an execution of an enemy agent was for the leader of the Squad, Paddy Daly or James Slattery, to nominate two men in turn.[1] This was adhered to very rigidly. This did not mean that two men went forth to carry out the execution as the Squad, at full strength, was always present at every execution and it worked in this fashion. The Intelligence Officer or Officers instructed to identify and point out the individual did so in a very direct fashion, usually by actually speaking to him and then pointing to him by a pre-arranged signal. The two members of the Squad detailed to carry out the actual shooting on receiving the signal usually waited apart from the remainder and walked towards the person and carried out the execution which, in the majority of cases, took place on main public streets. The remainder of the Squad, fully armed, were usually within fifty yards of the scene and at the time of the execution stepped on to the public streets, very often with guns drawn to protect and ensure the line of retreat for the two men who had been engaged on the shooting. In some cases it was usual to have a car in the next street to expedite the getaway but in very many cases the getaway was made on foot. Having temporary dumps on both sides of the city (there was one in a stable at the rere of a house in Fitzwilliam Place) it was usually possible to dispose of the guns and proceed across the city normally. I should mention that all of us carried fictitious papers of one sort or another not particularly organised by G.H.Q. although it was originally suggested by them. Each man was left to his own devices to have whatever paper or story

11

to suit himself and thus enable him to answer questions without hesitation if held up by the enemy and searched. It was no uncommon thing for the members of the Squad, having safely disposed of their guns, to be held up by the enemy advancing on the site of a recent execution. I was held up on several such occasions and I posed as a house-painter. I had a lot of house-painters' old Union cards and a few letters addressed to me as "T. Smith". I knew a lot of people in the house-building and painting line, as my father was a small building contractor, and I found it easy, if cross-examined, to discuss and explain my assumed trade in detail. Another member of the Squad was a cabinet maker, and Charlie Dalton, Intelligence Officer, who had been a clerk, posed as a law student.'[2]

The Lead-in to 'Bloody Sunday'

'The Particular Ones'

On Monday 1 November 1920, the day Kevin Barry's remains were interred in Mountjoy Prison's garden after his hanging, Dublin was in shock. An eerie atmosphere hung amid the smoke of the city's chimney tops. It was also 'All Saints' Day' – a religious holiday.

The IRA leadership had been desperate to spring Barry from the prison before his execution, with the suggested plan being to blow up the prison's outer wall, but the inevitability of civilian casualties had scuppered the prospect. Thousands of civilians had gathered in protest outside the prison's walls as his execution loomed, the low cadence of their prayers tapering away for hours afterwards.

Barry was the first republican executed in Dublin since the 1916 Rising, hanged for his part in an ambush that had killed three British soldiers; the first such killings in Dublin since the Rising. Coming hot on the heels of Cork Lord Mayor Terence MacSwiney's burial, following his death on hunger strike six days earlier, the public backlash from Barry's hanging echoed that of the 1916 executions. MacSwiney's seventy-four-day fast to the death in Brixton Prison had also aroused huge resentment and captured world attention.

That night, as pitch darkness descended, tension gripped the city. A curfew was in force between midnight and 5 a.m. Since February, Dublin Corporation's response in protest to curfews had been to extinguish street lamps. Heavily laden military and police vehicles ground their gears through Dublin's cobbled and tram-lined streets incessantly. Huge sixty-centimetre-diameter searchlights, operated by Royal Engineers, groped through the mist and hanging smog as raids were directed on countless homes and buildings, their operators seeking out IRA suspects or their political associates.

Tuesday 2 November saw another execution – an Irishman in British uniform, twenty-two-year-old Pte James Daly of the 1st Battalion Connaught

Rangers. Members of this unit mutinied in India in June over reports of atrocities carried out by crown forces at home in Ireland. Afterwards dozens of Rangers were detained in appalling conditions before their courts martial in August. Fourteen had been sentenced to death. Thirteen sentences were commuted. Daly, from Tyrrellspass in Co. Westmeath, was a ringleader. He was shot by firing squad in the subcontinent's Punjab region, 4,300 miles from home.[1]

Meanwhile, hunger prevailed throughout Ireland as winter drew in. In some areas the prospect of starvation loomed. Since May, the railway munitions embargo had seen train drivers refuse to operate locomotives carrying military personnel, supplies or armed police. Ireland's rail system became throttled. When, on many occasions, the frustrated military insisted on loading trains with personnel and supplies regardless – knowing they would not be moved as a result – accusations appeared in nationalist newspapers that British Minister for Transport Eric Geddes was exercising a spiteful stranglehold on Ireland's railways. This, combined with the rampant burnings of rural creameries – a valuable source of sustenance to local populations – as reprisals by crown forces for IRA attacks, led to allegations of deliberate starvation policies. These were underscored by the fallout from an unprecedented state of siege in the Kerry town of Tralee, cut off from the rest of the country for the first ten days of November by the RIC Special Reserve – the Black and Tans.[2]

North-east Ulster remained an exception to such interminable scourges as near-starvation, at least among the more trenchant unionist majority, who had asserted themselves in a wave of violent attacks against Catholics, suspected nationalists and republican sympathisers throughout summer and early autumn. Tens of thousands, including Great War veterans, were driven from work and rendered destitute, while many others were brutally killed. The impending Government of Ireland Act was set to isolate a six-county statelet, as sought by unionist leaders such as Sir James Craig and Sir Edward Carson, under the crown. On the same day that Kevin Barry was hanged, Ulster's special police, the blatantly sectarian Ulster Special Constabulary (USC), commenced recruitment to protect their impending territory.

The same day also saw IRA General Headquarters (GHQ) address its own hard-pressed police units. During June, Chief of Staff Richard Mulcahy had ordered the official creation of such units to supplant the beleaguered Royal Irish Constabulary (RIC) and Dublin Metropolitan Police (DMP). Simon

Donnelly had been appointed as national police chief. Serving Volunteers were to act as policemen.[3] Now, however, it was decided to separate the policing units from the IRA, at least nominally. Henceforth, IRA police – who had their work cut out with the escalating disorder – were relieved of army service and placed instead in a reserve.[4] Austin Stack, Dáil Éireann's minister for home affairs, was placed in overall charge.

The British military were relentlessly gearing up. Guerrilla warfare training took place in the Curragh in Kildare and was also attended by the RIC. Cycle patrol tactics were drilled, as were ambush responses and raiding from lorries.[5] In Dublin's numerous fortified military barracks, and in a similarly bulwarked Dublin Castle itself, units of troops and Auxiliaries rotated in a constant state of alertness for deployment. Vehicles were kept ready by Royal Army Service Corps (RASC) personnel and carried a multitude of spare parts and additional items, such as shovels, towing cables, searchlights, crowbars, wire-cutters, field-dressing kits and, frequently, several thousand rounds of ammunition – inadvertently marking them out as a tantalising prize to the insurgents. Tactical commanders regularly inspected convoy personnel or those to be used in raids to ensure they carried their standard combat equipment, including a .303 Short Magazine Lee Enfield rifle, seventeen-inch bayonet, helmet and grenades. Each man carried 100–120 rounds of ammunition. Barrels were left unchambered until units became engaged, before which all weapons' safety catches remained on. This was because they were not officially operating in enemy territory, a fact that – technically at least – left soldiers without the legal protections afforded by being 'in action' in the normal sense.[6] Officers carried powerful six-round .455 calibre Webley Army Service revolvers and seven-round Colt 1911 semi-automatics.

Beggar's Bush Barracks, in the city's south-east, housed the RIC Auxiliaries' Depot Company. They had drawn their first blood against the IRA's Dublin Brigade in September by killing Volunteer Seán Doyle in the Dublin Mountains. When not on duty, members generally converged on the city centre to drink in establishments frequented by similar units stationed in Dublin Castle, as well as IRA spies, such as Liam Tobin, Tom Cullen, Frank Thornton and William Beaumont, who each took colossal risks rubbing shoulders with such men. British spies and Irish touts also moved between the city's cafés, hotels, brothels, restaurants and pubs, as did their IRA enemies.

While this lethal cat-and-mouse game ebbed and flowed between drunken absurdity and bloody assassination, those overseeing Britain's attempts to subdue Ireland's revolt continued to vacillate and blunder between dilemma and disaster. The British Army commander, General Macready, an unwilling participant in a country he despised – his antipathy particularly rancorous when it came to hard-line unionists – found himself wedged between political subtleties that he did not see as the remit of a soldier. A *de facto* state of war existed that his government did not acknowledge, insisting instead that Ireland's troubles were a policing issue and would be contained by continued reinforcement of the RIC. Macready looked on in horror as those reinforcements ran amok, killing, looting and burning, unchecked by their commander, General Sir Henry Tudor, while, at the same time, political protagonists in Dublin Castle sought surreptitious dialogue with revolutionary leaders – their overall objective to marginalise and eventually isolate more radical republicans.

Macready saw things differently to those who had ostensibly advocated police rather than military action. He repeatedly protested that the uncontrolled reprisals plaguing the country were counter-productive. He advocated the imposition of martial law, an imperfect but at least transparent measure, which he felt would eventually bring moderate nationalists onside following the restoration of order. Prime Minister Lloyd George, on the other hand, feared that martial law would be perceived internationally as a forced reconquest of Ireland, while Field Marshal Sir Henry Wilson, chief of the Imperial General Staff, considered Macready naïve. He argued that, given requirements elsewhere and at home, the military manpower needed to take, and more importantly, hold the country in its current state was simply unavailable. Arguments abounded regarding the merits of regularised official military reprisals as an intermediate measure. All the while the IRA's Dublin Brigade, despite the crushing pressure it was under – worsening daily with the advent of Dublin Castle's Central Raid Bureau (CRB) toiling away relentlessly under Col Ormonde Winter to gather and collate 'hot' intelligence – geared itself towards upping the stakes in a manner the Castle establishment did not see coming.[7]

To date, one of the most constraining countermeasures to Macready in Ireland had not, in fact, been the IRA; it had been the rail embargo. This had curtailed and frustrated his attempts to launch a winter offensive against the IRA outside of Dublin.[8] In early November, as a redress, Chief Secretary Hamar Greenwood increased the burden on both the country's populace and the railway workers by warning that he would shut down the rail system completely.[9] To urgently forestall the consequent threat to the capital's lifeblood, a relief committee was formed under Richard Mulcahy, Brigadier Dick McKee and Labour leader William O'Brien, and included several others whose loyalties differed diametrically from these three. Thousands of census forms were printed to assess the needs of various city districts, although these forms were seized by the military in a raid before they could be distributed. Contingency transportation plans were formulated involving trucks, canal barges and even Dublin Corporation's Shamrock steamship, normally used for dumping sewage into Dublin Bay.[10] These would be employed to relieve the city by transporting food. It soon became clear, however, that any such efforts would be unable to prevent near-starvation should the entire rail system collapse. Meanwhile, despite tremendous pressure from the military, frequently at pistol point, railway staff stood firm and the embargo continued.

Harry Colley, twenty-nine-year-old 2nd Battalion adjutant, was one of several Volunteer officers who became concerned for Dick McKee's security because of his membership of the relief committee. Following a meeting one evening in Dublin Corporation's Rates Office in Lord Edward Street, Colley, having afterwards spoken to McKee outside, was surrounded by people asking who McKee was and what authority he had, disconcerting Colley. He then followed McKee to Dublin Brigade Headquarters (HQ), operating out of the Typographical Institute in No. 35 Lower Gardiner Street. There, Colley urged him to cease his committee work, deeming it too risky considering the differing loyalties of the members, and adding that, in any case, if the rail system collapsed the Volunteers would step in. However, his pleadings fell on deaf ears. McKee stated that someone needed to do it and that, if he were captured as a result, there would be others to take his place. Tragically for McKee, this soon came to pass.

Colley had recently been asked by McKee, as had all battalion adjutants, to compile lists of battalion members, including names, addresses and, in code, what weapons and ammunition each had at his disposal. To facilitate this, Colley then had four of the five Dublin Brigade rolls handed to him, a fact he considered most worrying in terms of security. Oscar Traynor, McKee's vice-brigadier, shared his concerns and suggested Colley burn them.

Nevertheless, McKee's idea was to employ the lists to facilitate rapid identification of Volunteer names from among the lists he was regularly receiving from IRA intelligence warning of imminent raids. These originated from informers. McKee was aware that many of the names on these lists were not actually Volunteers, having discovered this by paying endless visits with warnings to addresses due to be raided, only to discover that they were not connected to the IRA. Using Colley's collated list he created a cross-referencing card system using a clandestine office in the Mater Hospital. There, Volunteer names and addresses were entered on one set of well-concealed cards, linked by code to another set hidden elsewhere within the hospital that identified what weapons and equipment each man had. Each night, when McKee received the list of pending raids, he cycled to the hospital and cross-referenced this with the names on his initial list to see if they were Volunteers. Then, if applicable, he checked what weapons and equipment might be at risk and prioritised those who needed warning about imminent raids by dispatching a messenger or, if necessary, cycling to their address himself. [11]

Richard Mulcahy's equally frenetic and hazardous schedule was rudely interrupted during the night of 10 November, when the military raided a safe house he was employing that, unfortunately for him, had not made it to any such warning list – 49 Longwood Avenue in Portobello, home of Michael Hayes. Not for the first time, Mulcahy narrowly escaped at the last minute wearing nightclothes, by climbing through a skylight, traversing several rooftops and finally making his way to another safe house. Hayes was arrested and interned, and documents seized in two attaché cases provided an unexpected boost to British intelligence and their propaganda units. In addition to the rolls of over 200 Volunteers, papers were found that referred to plans to use bacteriological warfare against the military – firstly, by infecting their cavalry horses with glanders through oat feed stocks, and secondly, by poisoning the army's milk supply with typhus. Additionally, plans to blow up Liverpool docks and Manchester's Stuart Street power station, as well as the Clayton Vale water pumping plant, were uncovered. The latter operations were to be spearheaded by 5th Battalion engineer Garry Holohan, instructions having come from McKee and Peadar Clancy, in his former role as GHQ director of munitions. Holohan had recently returned to Dublin following extensive reconnaissance of both facilities.

Both sides quickly hurled accusations. From the British perspective these revelations of bacteriological warfare provided an opportunity to besmirch an enemy whose penchant for public relations far outmatched their own.

It was hoped that sympathy at home – a corrosive and chronic nuisance – would plummet for Irish republicanism. However, republican propagandists ensured the allegations were countered. Retaliatory claims were made of black propaganda, founded upon protestations that poisoning British Army horses would be pointless given that the army was heavily mechanised, and foolhardy because glanders was highly contagious. Moreover, it was asserted that to spread typhus among enemy soldiers would have placed the entire capital at risk of an epidemic.[12] Such assertions were bolstered by recent ridicule directed towards Dublin Castle propaganda over the supposed filming of a successful Auxiliary engagement against the IRA outside Tralee; this was exposed instead as a staged event in Dublin's Killiney. Nevertheless, despite this and other such effective counter-blows, the mere mention of bacteriological warfare underscored the threat posed by the IRA to ordinary British people, should such measures be planned for the British mainland, and added to their growing fatigue with Ireland.

The day after Mulcahy's narrow escape, Armistice Day, Dublin appeared to be returning to normality. Dame Street and Grafton Street were, for the third year running, decked out in Union Jacks, which sat at odds with the Irish Tricolour still flying above City Hall. Phoenix Park heaved with crowds marking the occasion. Mark Sturgis, one of two assistant under-secretaries for Ireland, along with Andy Cope, wrote in his diary that Dublin that day looked as British as London's Bond Street and added that Ireland was 'a queer country'.[13] In relation to the IRA he exulted: 'I think they're beat. We're on top and I'm sure they know it.'[14]

Recent successes in Dublin against the IRA were indeed noteworthy. On top of this, Kevin Barry's execution, despite vociferous protest, outwardly displayed that the British government stood fast, prepared to execute anyone whose swords crossed with theirs regardless of world opinion; police and military morale was up from this support. As if to prove Sturgis right, when a large nationalist crowd gathered outside the Bank of Ireland in College Green and mocked its hoisted Union Jack, they became silent when, at 11 a.m., a Crossley Tender truck full of triumphant-looking Auxiliaries pulled up adjacent to the nearby William of Orange statue. Its complement of fully armed cadets dismounted and stood to attention for the two-minute silence, to be cheered and applauded afterwards by other groups of bystanders.[15] The day itself was noticeably quieter than its previous two equivalents, which had seen considerable rioting in the capital, as well as raids on Sinn Féin buildings and audacious assassination plots against the viceroy, Lord French.

Even the American consul in Dublin, Frederick Dumont, observed what he considered to be a transformation in the state of Ireland. Strikingly, on the day after Armistice Day, Dáil Éireann's acting president, Arthur Griffith, called for the ending of the hunger strike in Cork Prison that had already claimed the lives of two IRA prisoners. It had run in conjunction with Terence MacSwiney's hunger strike, which had completely overshadowed the recent Cork deaths. That same day, a query was put to Patrick Moylett, a senior ranking IRB figure, businessman and gunrunner, who had been dispatched to London in October by Griffith to sound out peace feelers on behalf of Sinn Féin with the British Foreign Office. Moylett had been asked by the Foreign Office if the Dáil would stop attacking police and military in return for an end to British reprisals. When this was subsequently relayed to Griffith as a proposed prelude to a conference, Griffith responded favourably. Dumont subsequently wrote that the Dublin Castle administration was retaking the country. Moreover, he wrote that the IRA secret service was being matched by the Castle, which he even suggested may, by then, have been superior.[16] Dumont, however, was in for a surprise.

The fight was indeed being taken to IRA intelligence. Nonetheless, recent detentions and, astonishingly, the subsequent releases of none other than the two IRA agents closest to Michael Collins – Liam Tobin and Tom Cullen – suggested a gulf remained between the two sides. Moreover, Frank Thornton – the third man in this triumvirate – although held for ten gruelling days filled with interrogations following his recent arrest at Vaughan's Hotel in Rutland Square, was released without charge. Ominously, in just over a week, unprecedented events laid waste to suppositions such as Dumont's and almost resulted in Dumont being inadvertently killed.

It had become obvious to IRA GHQ that the British military had radically expanded its intelligence services and that the efforts of the Dublin District Special Branch (DDSB) were paying off. British intelligence officers, generally wearing mufti, were more frequently observed at raids. Although raid outcomes varied, every slip of paper found on a raid helped paint a picture of the key IRA players. The one thing British intelligence continued to lack was photographs, but GHQ realised this situation would inevitably change. Mulcahy's recent narrow escape was proof enough that the enemy were closing in on GHQ and that British intelligence intended to destroy the IRA from the top down.

Counteraction was required. Accordingly, the combined intelligence units of GHQ and Dublin Brigade had been put to work and began locating these new enemy agents and their touts.[17] In what was by now typical fashion, hotel receptionists, maids, porters, waiters, tailors, shop assistants and postal and office workers all continued to operate industriously as information sources. Incessant mail raids also revealed plenty. Additionally, the police had been thoroughly infiltrated. More than thirty DMP constables, controlled by Sergeants Patrick Mannix and Matt Byrne of Donnybrook and Rathmines respectively, watched and noted movements of individuals carrying passes during curfew hours, frequently noting their addresses when they questioned them, and helped the IRA detail a blueprint of British intelligence.[18] Added to this was the continuous flow of information from the men of DMP's G-Division working for Michael Collins: Ned Broy, David Neligan, the recently deceased Joe Cavanagh, and Cavanagh's protégé Jim McNamara. Added to this list was RIC Head Constable Peter Forlan, based in the RIC's Phoenix Park HQ and an invaluable source of intelligence. The IRA's pervasive intelligence tentacles had even penetrated the dreaded F Company of Auxiliaries at Dublin Castle, which was heavily compromised by twenty-two-year-old Sgt John Charles Reynolds, recently turned.

The toughest nut to crack for IRA intelligence, though, was the British Army. Individual soldiers passed on snippets of information while selling guns, but there was only one well-placed individual among its higher echelons: the typist at the adjutant's office at Ship Street Barracks, Lily Mernin. However, this deficiency was compensated for by Mernin's adeptness and audacity. One of her jobs was to type the names and addresses of British agents residing at private lodgings who posed as ordinary citizens.[19] This was done weekly as the agents changed addresses regularly.

Mernin had, since 1919, been passing information to the IRA. Her employment also provided her with access to army instructions and circulars, troop strength returns, information on military movements, and details concerning armoured cars and trains.[20] She made weekly visits to the home of Post Office Director Patrick Moynihan, at 118 Clonliffe Road in Drumcondra, to deliver notes and memos. These were written or typed from carbon copies from the Castle and left there for another agent whom she never met. More pressing messages, such as warnings of imminent raids, were delivered directly to Vaughan's Hotel or else to Mary O'Rahilly's bookshop in nearby Dorset Street. She also delivered such messages directly to her cousin, Piaras Béaslaí, editor of *An tÓglách*, the weekly IRA journal.

As well as such perilous duties, Mernin spent time socialising with Castle associates, usually accompanied by a date: her handler, Frank Saurin, posing as 'Mister Stanley'. Saurin, who also spent time as Mr Stanley drinking in the company of British agents and Auxiliaries alongside Tobin, Cullen, Thornton and Beaumont, was well known amongst his comrades for his debonair dress sense, the source of regular jibes, but this characteristic augmented his role. Mernin and he socialised amongst the IRA's most dangerous enemies, 'skilfully ingratiating themselves with people while simultaneously arranging their executions'.[21] Meanwhile, IRA intelligence officers stood ready to follow anyone singled out by them to their 'flats, boarding houses, and hotels'.[22] Similar work was carried out by twenty-one-year-old Molly O'Reilly at the United Services Club in St Stephen's Green, where she worked as a waitress and had endeared herself to its military clientele for equally duplicitous reasons.

Mernin had struck up a rapport with a fellow castle typist, Lil Dunne, daughter of a former Castle superintendent. Dunne's father's recent retirement had seen Lil and her brother move to 22 Lower Mount Street, home also to two British intelligence officers: twenty-nine-year-old Capt. Henry Angliss and thirty-five-year-old Lt Charles Peel. Angliss was operating under the pseudonym Patrick Mahon. Both were marked men, having participated in

killing unarmed Sinn Féin councillor John Lynch in his bed during the early hours of 23 September in the Royal Exchange Hotel in Parliament Street. Angliss had begun drinking heavily afterwards and developed a loose tongue.

Lil's brother spent time drinking with Angliss and frequently related to her afterwards the latter's information-laced disclosures. Lil,

Lily Mernin, seated here next to her cousin Piaras Béaslaí, was a pivotal and audacious IRA intelligence agent. Her position as a typist in the adjutant's office in Ship Street Barracks gave her access to information that proved fatal to several British agents on Bloody Sunday. *(Courtesy of the National Library of Ireland)* in turn, recounted many of these to Mernin at work. Any useful titbits of information were then relayed to IRA intelligence.[23] Mernin briefly came under suspicion one morning when, after Dunne's brother had gone missing and was feared abducted by the IRA, Lil insisted there must be an enemy spy in their midst who had revealed his associations with British intelligence officers. Mernin, maintaining her cool, had insisted this was ridiculous. Luckily, Lil's brother resurfaced.

Seán Hyde, a veterinary student and IRA intelligence operative living in 21 Lower Mount Street, next door to 22, had also disclosed the whereabouts of the two priority targets. He subsequently liaised with IRA intelligence officer Charlie Dalton, who set about organising their killings. Their movements were tracked between an ex-servicemen's club in Merrion Square and a billiard hall in Mount Street. Dalton and Joe Leonard, a seasoned IRA assassin, narrowly missed them one night, only to discover afterwards that the killings were to be postponed; they would be executed soon as part of a much grander operation, guided in no small part by Lily Mernin, and overseen tactically by Dick McKee and the recently promoted twenty-seven-year-old 2nd Battalion Commandant Seán Russell on the day that became known as Bloody Sunday.

Ironically, the type of horrific bludgeoning that was about to befall the Castle administration on that particular day had been anticipated. In September, with his forces gaining the upper hand, Macready had ominously forewarned of potentially desperate measures being employed by the enemy, writing: 'We may therefore expect to see a temporary increase in murder and outrage.'[24]

Macready's own forces were on the receiving end of a tidal wave of outrage and revulsion on Saturday 13 November, when soldiers from the Lancashire Regiment opened fire from an army truck on a small crowd of civilians on Charlemont Street, killing eight-year-old Annie O'Neill with a shot to the chest and wounding six-year-old Teresa Kavanagh in the arm. The soldiers assumed the crowd were IRA members because they had run on sight of the military. Annie died in the back of the truck minutes afterwards as its driver sped towards the nearby Meath Hospital. Her distraught mother had only recently lost her husband to tuberculosis (TB).[25]

Elsewhere in Ireland the killing continued. Two IRA members were shot dead by the RIC in Tralee on 12 November in a skirmish. The following day, three RIC constables and one Black and Tan were killed in an IRA ambush at Lisnagaul, Co. Tipperary, and four others wounded. One of the dead policemen had become trapped underneath the police truck after it had crashed. He was burned to death by ignited fuel.[26] Tipperary town suffered the Black and Tans' fury that night. On 14 November, twenty-eight-year-old Fr Michael Griffin of Galway was lured from his presbytery by crown forces. He was found buried outside the city almost a week later, shot in the head on the night of his abduction following a brutal interrogation. His death sparked further outrage.

Tensions rose. Tuesday 16 November saw Dublin Corporation call for the ending of the rail embargo at a meeting of the Labour Party and the Trades Union Congress (TUC) in Dublin's Mansion House. Tributes were paid to the sacrifices of rail workers, but it was emphatically asserted that the embargo was no longer sustainable given the living conditions prevalent among workers themselves and the beleaguered civilians dependent on the railways. Labour Party leader Thomas Johnson argued that maintaining the strike for much longer would set the country back a hundred years. However, not everyone agreed with such statements. A representative from Derry argued that sustaining the embargo was vital and that, if necessary, his constituents would rather carry food on their backs than give in.[27] No conclusive decision was reached.

McKee and Mulcahy received a full briefing of the meeting afterwards, their efforts continuing relentlessly to seek remedies for the never-ending crisis. However, more imminently calamitous events were careering headlong to their conclusion, and their attentions were diverted elsewhere.

On 17 November, McKee received a letter from Collins, which read: 'Dick – I have established the names of the particular ones. Arrangements should be made about the matter. Lt. G. is aware of things. He suggests the 21st. A most suitable day and date I think. M'.[28] The most suitable day and date referred to the most opportune time to kill the 'particular ones'. 'Lt. G', an abbreviation of 'Little Gentleman', was in fact Lily Mernin. The codename was deliberately obscure, suggesting the agent was a male military officer.

Mernin's information, as well as intelligence from various other sources, had been relayed for some time to Frank Thornton, toiling ceaselessly in a front office in Great Brunswick (now Pearse) Street's majestic Antient Concert rooms. IRA intelligence HQ in 3 Crow Street – still operating ceaselessly just 200 yards from Dublin Castle – was not large enough to accommodate Thornton's recently acquired workload. Assisted by Charlie Dalton, Thornton began constructing a detailed dossier on each suspected enemy agent.

Thornton had soon compiled an initial list of sixty 'particular ones'.[29] These were then watched and tracked. Subsequent incoming reports determined whether a name remained on the list. Eventually, Thornton trimmed his list to forty-five names. With McKee's help, he then submitted the dossiers to Cathal Brugha, the Dáil's minister for defence. Brugha combed over each one, subsequently dismissing a further fifteen names for lack of sufficient evidence. He was meticulous; he knew he was dealing with a kill list with no margin for error. If even a shred of doubt existed about a suspect's guilt, his name was removed. Nevertheless, as an extra layer of diligence, Brugha presented the full dossier list to the IRA Army Council for further review.

McKee and Thornton then had to present a detailed report proving that each suspect was either accredited to the Secret Service or had at least aided them. This took place before a joint meeting of the Dáil cabinet and Army Council.[30]

Frank Thornton, pictured here (standing to left) while imprisoned, was a veteran Irish Volunteer and served as IRA deputy assistant director of intelligence. Thornton was the third of a lethal triumvirate at the helm of IRA intelligence – along with Tom Cullen and Liam Tobin – whose efforts and actions sealed the fates of a large number of enemy agents. Thornton initially compiled the IRA's kill list for Bloody Sunday. *(Courtesy of Kilmainham Gaol Museum OPW, KMGLM 18PC–1P41–03)*

Ultimately, the cabinet and council accepted Brugha's recommendations, and the fifteen he had deemed doubtful were definitively struck off the list.[31]

It was then agreed that any operation to eliminate the remaining thirty would have to comprise a single swoop; to do otherwise would create a stampede of agents who, alerted, would scurry for the Castle walls, beyond which they would become untouchable but remain active. The council then insisted that McKee take charge of the operation. He had no objection and gained agreement for Seán Russell to assist him in the overall planning.

The two men wasted no time. Russell combed each brigade battalion for company commanders and men suitable for the planned operation. Soon 100 men were identified and divided into small units, each with an intelligence officer and, where possible, a Squad member. Tactically, each unit would split into two upon reaching its designated target building, be that a hotel or boarding house used by enemy agents. One group would enter the premises, the other would secure the exterior. Scouting sections would support units, and motor cars would facilitate quick getaways for assassins and accomplices, particularly the wounded. Cumann na mBan members would be deployed to collect and conceal weapons once the assassinations concluded. First-aid stations, operating from dozens of innocuous city residences, were placed on standby. Suitable escape routes were reconnoitred, a particularly important aspect considering that the 2nd Battalion would be heavily involved and would, in many cases, be operating outside its normal deployment area. Capt. Tom Kilcoyne of B Company was put in charge of commandeering a boat to have ready to ferry 2nd Battalion men across the River Liffey to its northern docks and safety.

McKee and Russell put details into place expeditiously, until all that was required to complete the deadly jigsaw was the operation's date. Collins' letter to McKee on 17 November provided the final piece.

Elsewhere the killing continued. On the night of 16–17 November, four IRA prisoners, having initially been captured by Auxiliaries, were marched by the regular RIC onto Killaloe Bridge between counties Clare and Tipperary and shot dead. In Cork, a civilian former British soldier and a sixteen-year-old Fianna scout were shot in a separate police reprisal.

Back in Dublin, during the evening of 20 November, the leaders of each unit detailed to carry out operations against the 'particular ones' the following

Seán Russell, 2nd Battalion commandant, who, alongside Dick McKee, oversaw the tactical organisation and planning of the Bloody Sunday assassinations. *(Courtesy of the National Library of Ireland)*

morning assembled in the Typographical Institute. The intensity of Dublin's war was about to escalate. In front of them stood McKee and Oscar Traynor, and next to them were Clancy, Russell, Mulcahy, Collins and Brugha. First to address those assembled was McKee. Aware that close-up killing was not for everyone, he nonetheless stressed the importance of the unpalatable job ahead, its dangers and, critically, the potentially catastrophic perils of failure. He asserted that it was a clear case of neutralising British intelligence before British intelligence neutralised them; any sentiment against such brutal killing had to be suppressed. Most accepted this readily enough, others less agreeably. Although no objections were raised, each officer had to grapple with another critical consideration: the fate of Kevin Barry, which illustrated what they could expect if captured.

As some shuffled uncomfortably at the glaring prospect of what loomed larger by the hour, each operational leader was taken aside individually and interrogated by McKee and Russell about their preparations and reconnaissance work. Afterwards, satisfied that all was in place, Collins addressed the gathered men. A few jibes and well-phrased encouragements galvanised them. Concluding, he emphasised one factor above all others: each job was to be carried out at precisely 9 a.m., declaring in his own unique style: 'These whores, the British, have got to learn that Irishmen can turn up on time.'[32]

The assembled officers were then dismissed to return to their battalion areas to issue final instructions. Some, having done this, sought distraction in the Gaiety Theatre, also attended by a few of the following morning's targets.

As the last few men were leaving the Typographical Institute, Paddy Daly, a seasoned Squad officer, approached McKee. Daly had been ordered by Russell not to participate directly in the following morning's operation, but to remain instead at its designated field HQ – 17 North Richmond Street, home of Peter and Catherine Byrne – and direct things from there along with

Squad leader Mick McDonnell. The house would also operate as a first-aid post, attended by the Byrnes' daughters, Catherine and Alice – both Cumann na mBan members – who would be under Daly and McDonnell's command. Daly was unhappy about not being actively involved and directed his concerns to McKee. The response was concise: 'Paddy, I'm not going either. Have you not full confidence in the men appointed?'[33] Daly recognised that McKee was always willing to lead from the front and, accordingly, realised that, by not going, he was demonstrating full trust in the men. Reassured by McKee's confidence, he quickly agreed that he shared it.

Matters accelerated. Minutes before 10 p.m., Traynor left brigade HQ, just as McKee was rolling up his paperwork, and cycled to his nearby home, 21 Clonmore Road, Ballybough, taking diversions to throw off pursuers – a regular IRA practice.[34] He assumed McKee would do likewise, but was wrong. The brigadier, accompanied by Clancy, had urgent business to attend to at Vaughan's Hotel, where a last-minute meeting between GHQ and some Dáil ministers had been convened.

Meanwhile, as the two men cycled to the hotel, an Auxiliary raid took place a mile away at 100 Seville Place. Officially the clubhouse for St Laurence O'Toole's GAA club, this was the mustering point for 2nd Battalion's operation the following day and it had also operated for some time as the Squad's HQ, as well as a marshalling and communication point for the battalion. As if to prove the accuracy of McKee's earlier warnings that evening of the growing threat of enemy intelligence, No. 100 was ransacked, while military lorries thronged with troops threw up a cordon outside. Luckily, those preparing for the morning's operation narrowly avoided the raid and Russell quickly implemented a contingency plan for just such an eventuality. Tara Hall, in nearby Gloucester (now Seán MacDermott) Street, became the alternative venue within which the units were given their final pre-mission briefings.

The meeting at Vaughan's had all but wound up by the time McKee and Clancy arrived. Mulcahy and Brugha, having left Gardiner Street earlier to attend it, had already departed when the inseparable pair joined Collins and Béaslaí upstairs in the hotel's smoking room. Seán O'Connell, a clerk at Kingsbridge railway station and messenger for Collins, was also there, as was twenty-seven-year-old Conor Clune, a plant manager at Raheen co-operative in Co. Clare and a Gaelic League member, who was in Dublin on business. The conversation within the room was relaxed, but McKee remained quietly focused on his work. He double-checked details for the following morning and sent out dispatches via couriers who stood by warily, close to the hotel. One, for Oscar Traynor, directed his attention to a military crest inscribed on a sheet of paper retrieved from a suspect's waste-paper basket and asked him to identify it.

Downstairs, with curfew imminent, the hotel porter, Christy Harte, became suspicious of a hotel guest named Edwards. Recently arrived, Edwards had just made a whispered telephone call and then quietly left the building.[35] Harte's instincts were well honed to potential threats to the hotel's most regular, and frequently troublesome, guests. He quickly made his way up to the smoking room to warn of a likely raid. Trusting him, the conspirators left. Clancy went first, followed by McKee, then Collins. However, Béaslaí, O'Connell and Clune, having just minutes earlier made their way downstairs to the pantry, did not receive the warning, so Harte sought them out.

Collins, making his way on foot to Devlin's pub nearby, had only made it as far as 39 Rutland Square when he saw several Auxiliary lorries screech to a halt outside Vaughan's. McKee and Clancy had by then reached Sackville Street on their way to their safe house – 36 Lower Gloucester Street. Collins concealed himself in the entrance to No. 39 and watched the raid unfold. Béaslaí, O'Connell and Clune, meanwhile, were still speaking in the pantry when thirty-six-year-old Dist Insp. William 'Tiny' King and Capt. Jocelyn Lee 'Hoppy' Hardy led their F Company men into the hotel, making straight for the smoking room, frothing at the prospect of seizing the prominent enemy officers they suspected were there. Béaslaí, hearing the raid, quickly slipped out the hotel's rear into Granby Place, followed soon by O'Connell. Clune, however, convinced he had nothing to fear as a civilian, hesitated. This proved fatal. He was wrenched from the pantry by a cadet and brought before Hardy. The captain – nicknamed 'Hoppy' because of his prosthetic leg – began questioning Clune, along with everyone else in the hotel. Clune was defiant. Hardy checked the hotel register for his name. It was not listed. He then searched his pockets and declared: 'This bloody fellow hasn't even got a toothbrush on him.'[36] All they found in his pockets was a notebook containing, among others, the names Collins and Treacy. Hardy suspected the latter referred to the late Seán Treacy, recently killed in Talbot Street. This was enough. Clune was arrested and placed in one of the trucks filling with other prisoners waiting to be driven to Dublin Castle.

CORK CITY LIBRARIES

McKee and Clancy, meanwhile, had split up on their way to their safe house. Clancy arrived first and was greeted by the house's owner, Seán Fitzpatrick. Soon McKee arrived, suspecting he had been followed. He warned Clancy and Fitzpatrick. His suspicions were well founded. He had been seen leaving Vaughan's by Edwards and then picked up by another pursuer in Gloucester Street. The latter individual, forty-eight-year-old John 'Shankers' Ryan, former military policeman and local resident, shadowed him to Fitzpatrick's front door. He left to telephone Dublin Castle and then returned to tie a piece of paper with some string to the house's doorknob – a marker for the Auxiliaries soon to follow. After this, he disappeared back into the darkness to lurk and watch. Time was running out for McKee and Clancy.

Despite McKee's suspicions, he and Clancy decided to remain where they were and risk a raid. The curfew was in effect and if they moved outside they risked being arrested or shot. They began burning paperwork, including the list for the following morning's assassinations.

Soon there was a knock on the front door. Fitzpatrick apprehensively went to answer. McKee and Clancy continued burning evidence. Then, suddenly, they heard Fitzpatrick shouting that they were being raided. Fitzpatrick slammed the door just in time to stall the intruders. He then held his weight against the door as they kicked and threw their shoulders against it. The frustrated Auxiliaries, led by Capts Hardy and King, shot at the lock. Cracks resounded, but the heavy door held. Other Auxiliaries covered the back of the house and shone torches at its windows. There was no way out. Eventually, Clancy, satisfied that any evidence was destroyed, shouted to Fitzpatrick to let the raiders in.[37]

Within seconds, Auxiliaries stormed through the house, kicking at doors and cursing profusely. Then, Hardy and King came face to face with McKee and Clancy. They were instantly recognised as senior IRA figures, particularly Clancy due to his leadership of the Mountjoy hunger strike the previous April. The pair, along with Fitzpatrick, were hustled onto a waiting truck. Neighbouring civilians woken from slumber stole cautious glances from windows as the trucks sped away to Dublin Castle.

Within ten minutes, McKee, Clancy, Clune, Fitzpatrick and twenty-two others arrested in round-ups during the night were shoved into the Castle guardroom in Exchange Court. The room was already packed with people sitting nervously. McKee quickly took stock, recognising faces among them, as they, too, recognised him but feigned otherwise. Some were due to participate in operations the following morning, others were IRA members who had not been selected. Clancy recognised Volunteer Ben Doyle, whom he knew well, but discreetly put his fingers to his lips in a signal not to address him or McKee.[38]

Throughout the night Hardy and King relentlessly interrogated the prisoners, each summoned in turn by F Company Auxiliaries at the guardroom door, then wrested and shoved on their way to the dark and dreary interrogation room lit by a single bulb. The room was situated to the left as one entered the lower Castle gate. Its floor had a drain in the centre. During more aggressive interrogations water from a nearby tap was regularly thrown over prisoners to revive them. Suspects were frequently tied to a wooden chair and beaten.[39] However, that night there were few such horrors. The atmosphere was unexpectedly tame given that the authorities felt relaxed, convinced they had the upper hand in the city. The prisoners were spared ordeals such as fingernails being pulled out with pliers, a common torture technique. Soldiers brought in rations and 'biscuit' mattresses – two-foot square and six-inches deep – for the prisoners to sleep on. A bucket acted as a latrine. McKee and Clancy, however, were called out repeatedly. Their night was sleepless, their captors anxious to unravel what their IRA roles were. The Auxiliaries were, unfortunately for them, completely oblivious to the terror that was about to be unleashed on their own ranks, largely at the instigation of this pair. An angel of death was about to swoop across the city, its path determined in no small part by McKee. Dublin's War of Independence was about to cross a bloody threshold.

2

Bloody Sunday: Assassinations

'There's a job on. Best clear out of this.'

No. 117 Morehampton Road in Donnybrook sat just yards from an important IRA safe house and operations hub in No. 131. It sat less than a minute's walk from Batt O'Connor's home in Brendan Road, still frequently employed as an IRA hideout. No. 117 itself was a picturesque red-brick two-storey dwelling on the wide suburban thoroughfare's western side.

At 9 a.m. on Sunday 21 November, ten-year-old Percival Smith answered the door to an unpleasant surprise – Capt. Laurence Nugent's twenty-strong IRA unit from K Company, 3rd Battalion. Half of them covered the deserted road outside, the other half pushed past the startled boy. Moments later his mother, hurrying to the front door from upstairs, was horrified by the sight of six armed men wearing flat caps and overcoats rushing up the stairs. Others remained downstairs. Their sudden command of 'Hands up!' was complied with. Just then, her startled husband, forty-six-year-old father of three Thomas Smith – householder, landlord and Dublin Castle informer – emerged from an adjacent bedroom. He was wrenched away from its door. Then, when a young child cried from the same room, Mrs Smith pleaded to be let into the room. The cries were from her three-year-old son. She was shoved inside. The crying stopped.[1]

Within seconds the Volunteers fanned out, two further upstairs to the converted loft and two more to a neighbouring bedroom, where they found Rifle Brigade senior intelligence officer Lt Donald MacLean in bed with his wife. Both had just woken. Four IRA men remained downstairs.

Thirty-one-year-old MacLean had recently been arrested as a spy by the IRA in Co. Clare, but was subsequently released on condition he return to Scotland, a pledge he reneged on. He recognised that the game was up. Nonetheless, collecting himself, he appealed not to be shot in front of his wife, Kate. She remained wide-eyed on the bed, paralysed with fear. MacLean was then dragged from the bedroom into a spare room at the front of the house to stand next to Thomas Smith.

MacLean's brother-in-law, twenty-two-year-old Scotsman John Caldow, formerly of the Royal Scots Fusiliers, only recently arrived in Ireland to join the Auxiliaries, was also surprised in his bedroom. He stood next to the other two petrified men. After several desperately tense seconds, eight shots resonated throughout the house, succeeded by screams. The men on guard outside the house braced themselves to escape as soon as they heard the muffled, coarse cracks, their eyes scanning for danger. Nugent and his men joined them and they made their getaway from the house, escaping on foot. Behind him, Nugent heard Caldow, badly wounded but still alive, call out desperately for his sister to summon a doctor.[2] Nugent cursed and kept going. MacLean and Smith lay next to Caldow, sprawled out on the carpeted floor soaked and spattered with blood, MacLean dead, Smith dying. Caldow lay helplessly on his back. His prospective career as an Auxiliary cadet was over.

Just over a mile away, at 8.55 a.m., IRA Capt. Francis Xavier Coughlan and a section from E Company, 4th Battalion, had met at Charlemont Bridge, straddling the Grand Canal close to Ranelagh. Coughlan had briefed each man present. James Kenny and four men took positions to the front, side and rear of nearby 7 Ranelagh Road, a two-storey, over-basement Georgian house, to block any escape route for those inside who were marked for death: Lt William Nobel, a twenty-eight-year-old intelligence officer with the Sherwood Forester Regiment, and his Irish mistress. Both had been adjudged to have passed information to the Auxiliaries resulting in the death of 4th Battalion Volunteer Seán Doyle and the arrests of forty others, mostly engineers, by the Auxiliaries' Depot Company on 19 September. This mission was personal.

Within minutes Coughlan stood at the house's front door with Todd Andrews and Herbert Earle, detailed as shooters. Kenny and a dozen others took up covering positions just as a taxi, in which sat Joe Dolan and Dan McDonnell of IRA intelligence, pulled up outside the house. Coughlan rapped on the front door using his walking stick. A teenage girl answered. Coughlan forced the walking stick between the door and its frame to prevent the suddenly unnerved girl closing it. The three men brushed past her. Seeing this, Dolan and McDonnell alighted from the taxi, stole along the short garden path and up the six steps to the house's front door, pausing there momentarily.

Once inside, Coughlan, Earle and Andrews cocked their revolvers and quietly climbed the staircase that led to a front parlour room, beyond which was a bedroom. There, their eyes fell upon Nobel's startled mistress, half-naked in bed, frozen at the sight of the three gunmen. She was wide-eyed in terror, but unaware that their orders were only to shoot her if she was with Nobel. He was nowhere to be seen. The search was on.

Andrews, jittery, burst into a bathroom to find a man shaving. He levelled his pistol to shoot. The man almost collapsed in fear. Luckily, Coughlan stepped up behind Andrews and told him to relax; the man shaving was a trusted man, who breathed a huge sigh of relief, as did Andrews as he de-cocked his pistol.

By now Dolan and McDonnell had entered the house and climbed the stairs. Moments later, when Andrews saw them, he asked who they were, to be told that they were with intelligence. With revolvers drawn, they quickly entered the front bedroom and scoured for papers. Dolan, frustrated and agitated at the target's absence, shouted at Nobel's mistress, still motionless on the bed: 'Where is Nobel?' She remained silent. Dolan, reminding himself that their orders were not to shoot her on her own, grabbed an ornamental sword scabbard from the bedroom wall and whipped her with it while she cried out. He demanded answers, which she soon provided: Nobel had left two hours earlier on a raid.

Dolan and McDonnell ransacked the bedroom, then, still frustrated, moved from room to room in the large house before descending downstairs, pushing gaping women and children out of their way in their quest for paperwork. Following this, Dolan returned upstairs to the bedroom and, as Nobel's mistress looked on, pocketed her rings and set fire to the bedroom. Coughlan, astonished and horrified, angrily ordered them out of the house, berating them for behaviour worthy of the Black and Tans. When they had left, Coughlan, himself a husband and father, ordered the women and children evacuated. He then ordered James Kenny to form men into a bucket chain to extinguish the spreading fire. The intelligence men re-entered the taxi, which sped away. Soon the fire was doused and the E Company men fled the scene on foot.[3]

At the same time as Capt. Coughlan's men had initially mustered, half a mile away his battalion comrade, Capt. Christopher Byrne of F Company, had stood anxiously on the pavement outside the Eastwood Hotel at 91/92 Lower Leeson Street. Lt Jimmy Donnelly stood at his side as they watched Lt Ned Bennett lead four other Volunteers up the steps to the hotel's front door.

Byrne had reconnoitred the area the previous night and noted the hotel's back entrance, which led to an alleyway onto Quinn's Lane. Consequently, two men had been detailed there to cover any escape by the man they intended to kill.

Within seconds of their knocking at the front door, it was opened by the hotel porter, who found a revolver pointed at his face. Speechless, he offered no resistance and let the five gunmen inside. Bennett rushed to the reception desk demanding the room number for Lt Col James Jennings. The nervous female registrar insisted that Jennings was no longer a hotel resident. When another porter arrived on scene, he was ordered at gunpoint to take Bennett to the manager's room. The dumbfounded manager then provided the room number but insisted that the colonel had left several days earlier. When a subsequent search confirmed his departure and revealed no useful intelligence, the IRA men departed the hotel, some frustrated, others relieved. The hotel, like 7 Ranelagh Road, was inadvertently spared a bloodbath.[4]

The same could not be said for two nearby addresses: 28 Earlsfort Terrace and 28/29 Upper Pembroke Street. As an unprecedented series of horrors was beginning to unfold throughout the city to the sound of early morning church bells, these particular buildings were about to witness their share of events that appalled and disgusted onlookers, victims and perpetrators, and, in the case of Pembroke Street, resembled a 'badly conducted abattoir'.[5]

At the Earlsfort Terrace address, situated between Upper Hatch Street and Adelaide Road, Lt Paddy Byrne of A Company, 3rd Battalion, knocked on the door at the stroke of 9 a.m. Servant Kathleen Haye, curious at the early call, opened the door. Byrne bid her good morning and, stepping forward, said he was there to see Mr Clement Fitzpatrick. She replied that there was no one named Fitzpatrick staying there. Byrne, preparing to pounce if necessary, elaborated; the man they sought was a lieutenant colonel. She responded, 'No, only Capt. Fitzgerald.'[6]

Her words sealed the fate of twenty-two-year-old RIC Acting Barrack Sgt John Fitzgerald, a former soldier from Tipperary convalescing inside. Like Donald MacLean, he had recently escaped the clutches of the Clare IRA. In his case, he had been wounded during a botched execution, played dead, and subsequently fled to receive local medical treatment before eventually travelling to recuperate in Dublin – an unfortunate move. He died simply because of his name's similarity to the IRA's intended target.

Byrne asked the girl to identify Fitzgerald's room. Nervously, she pointed upstairs. Byrne summoned five men to follow him inside the house and drew his revolver, ordering her to show him to the room, while reassuring her that she was in no danger. He and three others, with weapons readied, followed her upstairs. Another entered the ground-floor kitchen; the sixth guarded the front door.

Reaching the bedroom, the four Volunteers burst in. Fitzgerald cried out in alarm, raising his hands defensively. His subsequent cry was stifled by a shout of 'Come on!', which preceded four pistol shots. Fitzgerald's head was pulverised from point-blank range as he tried to scramble out of bed. Two bullets smashed into his forehead, splattering the bed and wall behind with brains, skull and blood as they exited explosively from his parietal bone. Another round struck his heart, then exited through his back, further bespattering the gruesome scene. The last shattered his wrist before gouging plaster and brick as it ricocheted from the wall.

Byrne and his men searched the room, seizing some papers before leaving the house, watched by the servant and the terrified landlady who had hidden downstairs. They looked on, half-frozen in shock as the IRA men strolled calmly into Lower Hatch Street to escape. Two medical students from nearby University College Dublin (UCD), residing in the house, then rushed to the bedroom with the landlady.[7] It stank of cordite and blood. Their eyes fell upon the hideous mess of Fitzgerald's sprawled body. He had died instantly.

The other address, 28/29 Upper Pembroke Street – two Georgian houses merged into one – also backed onto Quinn's Lane. Masquerading as a guesthouse by using the more official profiles of high-ranking regimental officers residing there to conceal its more clandestine purpose, this building housed a Secret Service HQ fed by two sub-headquarters.

Five minutes before the morning's killings had been scheduled, Charlie Dalton had arrived at a prearranged point on Pembroke Street to rendezvous with twenty-eight-year-old Capt. Paddy Flanagan of C Company, 3rd Battalion. C Company had a history of brutal engagements in Dublin. In 1916 its members had inflicted a bloodbath upon enemy soldiers at Mount Street Bridge. This standard was to be matched that morning, but in a less conventional manner. Dalton had been up all night with several other Volunteers, staying at the 'Dugout' hideout in Summerhill Dispensary, unable to sleep for fear of what lay ahead at this critical target.[8] Many others had suffered similarly restless nights. Some had been given no idea what to expect.

They had just been told by officers 'where to go, to be ready for a job in the morning'.[9]

As the twenty men selected to carry out the distasteful work gathered tensely on the street, having arrived on foot and by bicycle – among their number twenty-two year-old James Doyle, a veteran of Mount Street Bridge – Dalton nervously briefed Capt. Flanagan of an unexpected development. Two of their targets – Capt. George Bennett and Lt Peter Ames – had relocated to 38 Upper Mount Street. A maid in the house named Maddie, an old IRB man's daughter whom he had recently met several times, had only informed Dalton of this the previous evening. She had revealed to him the comings and goings of the house's occupants, as well the contents of their waste-paper baskets.

Two Volunteers, James Carrigan and Patrick Kelly, were driving towards the scene from Fitzwilliam Square in a Hudson touring car, detailed to transport wounded Volunteers to first-aid stations. They had driven from Volunteer Gerard Golden's house in Victoria Street, off the South Circular Road. As they drew closer, Flanagan, seeing them and satisfied that everything was ready, switched his attention back to the target building's front door. When he noticed the porter, James Green, shaking mats on the step outside the open front door, he seized the opportunity. Cigarettes were cast aside. He ordered his men in.[10]

Seconds later, with the porter subdued at gunpoint, Leo Duffy darted into Quinn's Lane beneath an archway to the house's left. There, he clambered over the eight-foot brick wall to his right and made his way silently to the house's back door to secure it. Ned Kelliher, acting with Dalton as intelligence officer, remained just inside the front door with a section of men as the remainder piled into the wide hallway. From there, two sections rushed for the two staircases that led to the upstairs bedrooms, detailing men to hold a maid and the house's proprietor, Mrs Gray, at pistol point when they got in the way.

In an upstairs flat at the back of No. 29, Caroline Woodcock, aristocratic wife of forty-two-year-old Col Wilfred Woodcock, stood at a bedroom window listening to church bells, slowly fixing the buttons on her blouse, quietly cursing their awkwardness. She noticed Leo Duffy climbing over the wall. Despite the sense of fear pervading the city, she initially dismissed this as a love-struck young man sneaking in to see a maid, until she noticed, to her alarm, the man pulling a revolver from his coat. She then turned and called for her husband. He promptly arrived and, seeing the gunman, ran downstairs to bolt the front door and warn the other residents, only to run into Doyle and a clutch of others just inside the front door. Doyle, rapidly advancing on him, pointing his pistol, ordered him to raise his hands. Woodcock, splendidly attired in full-dress uniform – he was due to command a regimental parade that day – complied.

Meanwhile, Flanagan, Dalton, George White and former medical student Andy Cooney, employing a plush carpet to soften their footsteps as they ascended the staircase of No. 28, reached their objective: the third-floor flat shared by Major Charles Dowling of the Grenadier Guards and Capt. Leonard Price of the Royal Engineers. The maid had briefed Dalton on their room location. Flanagan, announcing he had a letter for delivery, knocked on the door. Dowling, twenty-nine years old, answered in his pyjamas and was instantaneously overpowered before he had time to react to the sight of the four gunmen. Just then, thirty-five-year-old Price appeared in the doorway of the adjoining bathroom. Several dreadful seconds passed as the revelation of what was inevitable sank in with both officers. Dalton began rummaging through the room for documents as Flanagan fired his .45 calibre semi-automatic. Dowling was hit twice in the chest and died instantly when one round demolished his heart. The force of the shots cutting through him hurled his body backwards and blew blood, bone and tissue all over the walls and furniture behind him. One round ricocheted into the ceiling. Price was then hit once in the chest, with a similarly horrendous result. Both collapsed, the latter gurgling horrifically as his perforated lungs gasped for air while he choked on his own blood. Spent rounds rolled on the wooden floor. Within seconds Price's spasmodic jerks and twists ceased, his agony over. Dalton continued to search the room as Dowling and Price perished, until Flanagan, gathering himself, barked: 'Get out of here!'[11]

Back downstairs, in the ground-floor hallway, Woodcock, still under guard, heard the shots upstairs, as did forty-year-old Royal Marine Lt Col Hugh Montgomery, whose room was adjacent to the hallway. When its door opened suddenly, Woodcock shouted a warning: 'Look out Montgomery!' Doyle squeezed his revolver trigger, hitting Woodcock in the shoulder, forcing him to fall onto the staircase.[12] Woodcock, adrenalin pumping, quickly scrambled back up. Doyle fired again, hitting him in the back. Woodcock slumped.

Montgomery rushed from his room into the hallway. Doyle turned towards him. His gun's muzzle flashed again as he shot him twice through the torso. Montgomery's wife, standing behind the open door, was grazed in the knee by an exiting round that had punched through her husband. She screamed as he collapsed, semi-conscious, to the floor. Montgomery had been serving as an intelligence officer under Brig. Gen. Sir John Brind at Irish Command HQ. He died of his wounds within weeks.

More shooting followed. Up on the second floor, thirty-one-year-old Capt. Brian Keenlyside of the Lancashire Fusiliers, hearing the first shots, rushed to the door of his room with his wife, Rhona, to investigate what was happening. When three gunmen led by Mick O'Hanlon confronted them, Rhona, fearing for her husband, lunged at O'Hanlon, grappling with him to no avail; she was shoved back into her room as her husband was dragged downstairs. Just then, Flanagan's arrival on scene with his three accomplices brutally settled things. Flanagan fired four shots, hitting Keenlyside in the forehead with a grazing wound, in the jaw and in each arm. The British captain was left for dead on the floor, his wife's screams from her bedroom upstairs adding to the guesthouse's growing cacophony of gunshots and rushing footsteps.

On the top floor of No. 29, intelligence officer Lt Randolph Murray of the Royal Scots Regiment shared a room with fellow intelligence officer Capt. Robert Jeune. The latter had helped lead the disastrous Drumcondra Road raid the previous month in an attempt to capture Seán Treacy and Dan Breen, and this morning was four miles away in Richmond Barracks, having just raided Inchicore Railway Works for IRA arms with a unit of the King's Own Royal Lancaster Regiment under the command of Capt. John Rymer-Jones. As shouts and profanities resonated, Murray was dragged downstairs to the building's hallway and made to stand against a wall. Several IRA men faced him, panting. They levelled their revolvers, hands shaking. Men unaccustomed to close-up killing, where the expression on enemy faces as they died was so evident, suppressed their revulsion.[13] More shots followed. Murray was thrown against the wall next to the cellar staircase by the force of two rounds tearing through his chest before bursting out his back. He slumped to the floor leaving a trail of blood along the wall, from which chunks of plaster and clouds of dust had been sent flying by poorly aimed shots. He was badly wounded but lived. The air throughout both houses was rank with cordite and terror. Flanagan barked the order for his men to withdraw.

As the unit rushed out the front door and out the back into Quinn's

Lane, Woodcock began moving again. He crawled pitifully upstairs into his rooms, where his wife sat at the window, motionless, her stunned eyes fixated on the escapers in the laneway. Seeing her husband, she rushed to his aid. Soon her carefully buttoned blouse was soaked in his blood as she tried to stem its flow. The colonel passed out, his depleted strength sapped by his struggle up the stairs. Caroline sought help, further horrified as she observed splashes and smears of blood on the house's walls, floors, doors and stairs. Small clumps of plaster were strewn about.[14] Bullet holes perforated the walls next to where she came across Montgomery and his still screaming wife, then Murray, like Montgomery, barely alive. Both were lying in pools of blood in a guesthouse that resembled a battlefield.[15] Keenlyside was nearby, in a similar state. Caroline struggled to compose herself, focusing on getting help for her husband. Doctors were summoned from a nearby nursing home.

Less than 200 yards from this carnage, RASC Capt. John Crawford, thirty-one years old, lay in bed with his wife in their boarding house overlooking tranquil Fitzwilliam Square when, at 9.10 a.m., he heard a knock on his bedroom door. He invited the caller to enter, but no one did. Crawford indignantly arose to answer the door and found three revolvers pointing at him. He was pushed back into the room. Horrified, he demanded to know if this was a joke. The answer came: 'It's no joke – are you Major Callaghan?'[16]

'No I am not,' barked Crawford. He added that there was a Mr Callaghan upstairs but insisted he was not connected with the military. The three callers searched his room, keeping the captain and his wife under close guard. He was repeatedly accused of being a secret agent, which he denied. Old Great War photographs were found in his wardrobe, but this was not the type of evidence sought. Nonetheless, castigations flew that he should have stayed in his own country. He was ordered back into bed with his wife and kept covered while two of the callers stomped upstairs seeking Callaghan, but to no avail. Crawford was then ordered to stand. Fearing the worst, he drew breath and, composing himself, requested to be taken downstairs so his wife would not witness his killing. However, the gunmen backed out the door. Their leader shouted at Crawford that he had better leave the country. This warning was later heeded.

Nearby Lower Baggot Street, a Georgian arterial road between Ballsbridge and the city centre, was another setting for assassinations timed to coincide with the tolling of Dublin's 9 a.m. church bells. Two addresses had been marked out for operations: Numbers 92 and 119.

Capt. Thomas Burke of C Company, 2nd Battalion, stood at the front door to No. 119. Behind him stood Matty MacDonald, Jack Keating, Jack Foley and Seán Lemass. MacDonald nervously joked about the size of the hammer Keating had brought to smash the door in if required. There was, however, no need for it. As soon as they knocked the maid answered, to be told politely: 'We have a letter here for Capt. Baggallay from Dublin Castle', referring to him also as a one-legged man. Baggallay, a twenty-nine-year-old prosecuting court-martial officer, had, like Auxiliary Capt. 'Hoppy' Hardy, lost a leg in the Great War. He had also participated in the killing of Sinn Féin councillor Lynch in September, alongside Capt. Angliss and Lt Peel, themselves on this morning's target list. Baggallay's participation, brought to IRA attention by Lily Mernin and Detective Neligan, sealed his fate.

When the maid pointed the way to a first-floor bedroom, Burke, Lemass, MacDonald and Keating made their way up, drawing revolvers as they quietly approached the door. Finding it unlocked, having tested it carefully, they quickly swung it open and entered, surprising the man lying in bed, before posing the question: 'Captain Baggallay?'

'That is me,' came the reply.

MacDonald then asserted, 'I suppose you know what we came for.'

Baggallay, fearing the worst but clinging to hope, responded, 'I suppose you've come for my guns.'

MacDonald responded, 'We came for you'.[17] He then ordered Baggallay out of bed. When Baggallay stood up, four muzzles flashed, sending four five-ounce rounds at 500 miles per hour through his forehead, left eye and chest. The officer died instantly, his body hurled onto the bed, leaving a ghastly, twisted corpse mangled on the blood-soaked bedsheets. Fragments of his skull, brain and chest organs were spattered throughout the acrid-smelling room.

MacDonald rummaged through the dead man's belongings seeking whatever documentation he could find, before the four trembling assassins sped downstairs. Housemaids screamed. Foley stood guard downstairs, holding a 'balls naked' man at pistol point, his towel having fallen to his feet.[18] They assumed the man, who had been about to take a bath, was either a lodger or a British soldier; regardless, they had no orders to shoot him, so he was let go – a move that backfired within three months. As they escaped, led by Burke, they observed a military dispatch rider thump past on a Triumph motorcycle and sidecar combination in the direction of Baggot Street Bridge.

Baggot Street Bridge was where Joe Leonard, William Stapleton and seven others had themselves waited for the clock to strike 9 a.m. As they waited, Pat McCrea, another driver tasked with whisking away wounded Volunteers, pulled up opposite 92 Lower Baggot Street, just 300 yards north-west of the bridge and 500 yards south-east of No. 119. Two minutes later, Leonard led his handful of men from the bridge and ordered two to remain outside. He and the remaining six stepped up to the four-storey, over-basement house. Leonard knocked at the door. The landlady, Mrs Slack, answered. Leonard politely asked for Capt. William Newbury.

The landlady stood back, pointing to the hall flat just inside to the left. When Leonard and the others stormed in, it dawned on her what she had just facilitated. She ran upstairs, terrified, followed some of the way by three Volunteers who spread out to guard the staircase. Leonard and Stapleton, with two others guarding the hallway, knocked on the first door but received no answer. They tried the back-room door slightly further down the hallway and hammered on it with fists.

Newbury, a forty-five-year-old court-martial officer with The Queen's (Royal West Surrey) Regiment, was inside with his heavily pregnant Irish mistress. Curious about the audible fuss, and still wearing pyjamas, he opened the door slightly. When he saw those outside, he quickly tried to slam it, but Stapleton wedged his foot in it just in time to stop him. He and Leonard then fired their pistols through the door, wounding Newbury and forcing him and his mistress back from the door. They fled to the front parlour, pulling the folding doors between the rooms behind them to hinder their pursuers. Newbury, despite his wound, tried hopelessly to lock these doors, while his hysterical mistress stood to one side. Leonard and Stapleton, backed up by the two others from the hall, fired several more deafening shots through the folding doors, forcing Newbury to seek escape through the front room's sash window, unaware there were additional men outside.[19] He frantically unscrewed the window lock, wrenched the window upwards and began climbing out. He was shot six more times and died half in and half out of the window, where his shattered body was left hanging grotesquely.

Among the Volunteers in the cordite-filled room was Hugo MacNeill. He began searching for documents as Newbury's mistress sobbed in the corner and handed papers to Stapleton. Leonard then ordered everyone out. However, once back outside Leonard noticed they were missing a man. Having closed the front door behind them, they, bizarrely, knocked again. To their astonishment, the traumatised landlady answered the door. Leonard stomped inside, found the missing man upstairs and ordered him to get out.[20]

A minute later, Pat McCrea took some of the escaping IRA men in his car, while Slattery and Leonard walked to nearby Herbert Street en route to the city's north-side via the southern quays. The rest made their way elsewhere. Newbury's mistress, back in the house, covered her dead lover with a blanket.

Soon afterwards, the dispatch rider who had just passed No. 119, Pte Snelling, passed No. 92 and noticed Newbury's blood-soaked corpse hanging out the front window. He ignored the shocking sight, comprehending the city's dangers but having no urge to involve himself. Events, however, were spiralling beyond his control. He turned left into Herbert Street but ran straight into Leonard and Stapleton. Seeing their suddenly raised pistols, he stopped and was questioned about his errand. When the assassins realised he represented no danger, he was relieved of his motorcycle combo, which Leonard and Stapleton used to escape. However, Snelling's involvement in the morning's mayhem had just begun.

Just over an hour earlier, another dozen-strong squad of assassins from E Company, 2nd Battalion, commanded by Vinny Byrne, had assembled at St Andrew's church on Westland Row, their destination 38 Upper Mount Street. Byrne had no desire to be in command, but Capt. Tom Ennis, Byrne's senior

Joe Leonard, a seasoned IRA assassin, who led the raid on 92 Lower Baggot Street on Bloody Sunday during which Capt William Newbury was shot several times and killed as he tried desperately to escape through a window. *(Courtesy of the National Library of Ireland)*

officer, who was among the unit and no stranger to assassinations himself, had, nonetheless, far less experience in the craft than Byrne, a full-time Squad member. Accordingly, Byrne, like other Squad members taking part in the morning's grim work, assumed acting command.

This unit's initial orders had been revised the previous evening when Charlie Dalton had instructed Dick McKee of the relocation there of the two enemy agents, Lt Ames and Capt. Bennett, from 28/29 Upper Pembroke Street. No. 38 Upper Mount Street had initially been targeted for housing senior British intelligence officer Major Frank Carew. However, Frank Saurin, among the unit as intelligence officer, had just discovered that Carew would not be there. He had only moved the previous day and, frustratingly, had not yet been traced. Carew had been pivotal to the cornering of Seán Treacy in Talbot Street on 14 October, leading to Treacy's subsequent killing. Nevertheless, Bennett and Ames had entangled themselves in Frank Thornton's designs by inadvertently revealing to Thornton and Joe Dolan as they posed as touts that they knew the names Tom Cullen, Liam Tobin and Frank Thornton. Bennett and Ames slept soundly, their slumbers about to become permanent.

Minutes after the unit set off, Byrne detoured them to Jackie Dunne's arms dump in Denzille Lane to obtain first-aid supplies; the Volunteer detailed the previous evening to take care of first-aid items had brought none, much to Byrne's annoyance. However, with no such supplies available at the dump, Byrne was handed a revolver by Dunne instead. He then handed it to the surprised middle-aged first-aid man, saying abrasively that 'he might find use for it'.[21] Moments before 9 a.m., Byrne's team regrouped in Upper Mount Street, having made their way there through Stephen's Place, an adjacent laneway. No. 38 stood 150 yards to their left on the road's opposite side. Another hundred yards beyond stood St Stephen's church, nicknamed the 'Pepper Canister' due to its distinctive shape. Inside, its congregation prayed, as had many of the IRA members the previous evening, anticipating the dangers of their imminent work and comforting themselves that their souls should be prepared for the worst.

Byrne detailed Volunteer Michael Lawless to patrol outside No. 38 and watch for unexpected developments. He and Ennis knocked on the front door.[22] Catherine Farrell, the maid, opened it and was calmly told they were there to see Bennett and Ames. Obligingly, she stood aside. Byrne and Ennis stepped into the wide hallway, followed quickly by the rest of their men, except for Lawless. They shut the door behind them. Saurin then asked the maid where Bennett and Ames were.[23] She responded innocently: 'Lieutenant so-and-so [Bennett] sleeps in there' pointing towards the front room to the right, then: 'the other officer sleeps in the back room down there', pointing to the very rear.[24]

Byrne, Seán Doyle and Herbie Conroy, the last on his first such mission, moved towards Bennett's bedroom door. Ennis and Thomas Duffy crept quietly to the back room. Their remaining comrades braced themselves. Byrne tried the door handle. It was locked. The maid, looking on, provided a welcome contingency: they could gain access through an adjacent parlour via a folding door to the front bedroom. She assured Byrne that the folding door was unlocked.

Within seconds Byrne was in the parlour, followed immediately by Doyle. Byrne wrenched open the folding doors. Lying in front of him was twenty-eight-year-old Capt. Bennett of the RASC, at least ostensibly. Bennett grabbed for the pistol beneath his pillow. Byrne and Doyle were faster. They barked 'Hands up!', their pistol barrels pointing at his face. Bennett complied. Doyle then pulled Bennett's Colt .45 from under the pillow. Saurin stepped inside to search the room. Bennett gasped, wide-eyed, when he recognised Saurin as a 'friend' – 'Mr Stanley' – from Kidd's Buffet in Adam Court, off Grafton Street, and realised he had been duped by him.

Ennis and Duffy, meanwhile, had barged into Lt Ames' room, jolting him awake. Duffy's pistol covered Ames, who was serving with the Grenadier Guards. Ennis asked him his name. Ames replied in an American accent: 'I am a British officer.' Thirty-two years old, he had been born and raised in the USA and moved to England in 1912. Ennis asked if he was armed. Ames said, 'No.' Ennis, disbelieving, searched under his pillows and pulled out a Colt .45 and an ammunition pouch. Both were seized.[25]

Just afterwards, outside on the street, Lawless, still standing guard, heard shooting from the Lower Mount Street direction, 200 yards away, where another assassination was taking place. Suddenly, as he moved up and down Upper Mount Street, he heard the heavy footsteps of a man running behind him. He glanced behind and saw a khaki-clad soldier – Pte Snelling – approaching from the direction of the church. He pulled his pistol just as Snelling approached No. 38 and pointed it at him, shoving the cold steel of its barrel into his neck as he apprehended him.

Unfortunately for Lawless, his capture of Snelling was observed from a house opposite, No. 28, by a British Army private named Lawrence, the batman for Major Carew – the missing priority target on the original kill list for No. 38, residing there instead. Lawrence rushed to warn the major, who jumped out of bed and grabbed his pistol. Lawless, meanwhile, ordered Snelling up the five concrete steps that led to the front door of No. 38 and told him to knock. Then he heard a shout in a polished British accent from across the road: 'What's going on down there?' prompting him to glance across and see Major Carew brandishing his weapon. Lawless wrenched Snelling around to use as cover and fired at the man in the window, who withdrew.[26] Lawrence then joined the fight, firing from the front doorway of No. 28. The nearby church congregation heard the shots. Curious members peeked out of its massive timber doors, while others huddled fearfully in the pews.

Hearing the gunfire outside the house but remaining calm, Vinny Byrne ordered Bennett to the back of the house. Bennett asked anxiously what was going to happen. Byrne replied reassuringly, 'Ah, nothing.'[27] Then, as soon as they entered the hallway, the doorbell rang. The Volunteer covering the door looked to Byrne. Byrne shouted abruptly: 'Open the door!' Pte Snelling was then shoved and pulled inside, followed swiftly by Lawless, just as Byrne led Bennett into Ames' room. Ames was standing on his bed facing the wall. Bennett was told to do likewise. Byrne, with no idea what was going on outside the house, muttered: 'The Lord have mercy on your souls', as he aimed at them with his Mauser C96 semi-automatic 'Peter the Painter' pistol. Then, the firing began.[28]

Ames was hit three times in the back by rapid fire. All three shots exited through his chest, splattering his bodily tissue and blood over the wall to his front as he was hurled against it under continuous deafening fire. Two more rounds hit his right armpit, one hit his right arm and, finally, another his right leg. Bennett was shot twice through the back of the head, four times through the back and chest, and twice in the right arm. Both bodies collapsed, mangled, in a bloody heap on the bed. The entire room was spattered with blood, bone, tissue and brain.

Byrne ordered the unit out. They made their escape through the house, past the sobbing maid, and past the petrified Snelling, listlessly resigned to his own imminent demise, then out onto the street, where they came under fire again from Carew and Lawrence, both firing from the doorway of No.

28 opposite. Shots struck the brickwork and door arch of No. 38. Meanwhile, Frank Saurin, in his frantic efforts to get his hands on as much intelligence material as he could, had not heard Byrne's evacuation order. He eventually heard Ennis shouting at him as the latter bolted for the front door, passing Snelling on the way, who rushed for safety towards the house's rear. Saurin, seeing him and with no idea who he was other than an enemy soldier, fired several rounds but missed. Snelling dived for cover in an alcove as the maid crouched helplessly in a corner. Byrne had spared Snelling's life as he passed him on the way out, reasoning that he was just a soldier. The decision proved costly – the IRA was leaving witnesses.

Ennis waited for Saurin just inside the front door, watching Carew firing at his fleeing comrades. Ennis and Saurin then dashed after them, under further fire from Carew, until their return fire sent him reeling back into the house. Ricochets flew from its Georgian archway and brickwork. The two caught up with their comrades in Stephen's Place.

Just as Byrne had initially led his unit into Upper Mount Street, Tom Keogh and James Slattery had led six men from the same 2nd Battalion company to the front door of 22 Lower Mount Street, the boarding house in which resided Lts Angliss and Peel, as well as Lily Mernin's colleague, Lil Dunne, and her brother. They did this to the backdrop of the same church bells punctuating the still morning air. A young housemaid, Nellie Stapleton, opened the door. Here there was no subtlety getting in. Keogh, Slattery and the others barged into the hallway, leaving two men, Billy McLean and Jim Dempsey, guarding the front door. Keogh asked the alarmed maid to point out 'Mahon's' room – referring to Angliss' assumed name. She complied, led them upstairs, but called out to the resident in question that there were men there who wished to see him.[29] Keogh and Volunteers Denis Begley and Andy Monaghan soon stopped outside the room identified to them. Slattery, Frank Teeling and a Volunteer named Bennett continued to the second floor; Slattery already knew which room Peel slept in there. The maid, meanwhile, fled downstairs.

Angliss' door was unlocked. Keogh, Begley and Monaghan burst in and found him sharing a bed with an unknown man, Lt Connolly, an intelligence officer not on their list. Keogh ordered his two accomplices to cover both with their pistols while he searched the room. Picking up a nearby coat he asked 'Mahon' if it was his. Angliss replied, 'No.' Keogh then found a fictitious identity card in one of its pockets which suggested otherwise. Examining it, he shouted at him, 'You are a liar. Where are your guns?'[30] Angliss, an officer of the Royal Inniskilling Fusiliers, responded, 'Look here we are two R[oman] C[atholic]s but the guns are in that bag', pointing to a leather portmanteau within which Keogh discovered three semi-automatic pistols.[31]

Meanwhile, outside on Mount Street, sixteen off-duty Auxiliaries were being driven by truck to Kingsbridge railway station from Beggar's Bush. Temporary Cadet Thomas Mitchell, in command, suddenly heard a shout: 'They are killing officers upstairs!' from a ground-floor window of No. 22, on their left as they passed slowly down the road. He was the first to jump from the truck and rush to the building's front door.

Billy McLean, suddenly seeing the onrushers, used the barely ajar front door to shield himself, stuck his gun out and fired a single shot. Fire was returned. Ricochets flew from the surrounding doorway sending blinding splinters flying through the hallway. Tufts of plaster fell from the inner walls. Back outside, Mitchell reacted quickly, ordering two cadets, Frank Garniss and Cecil Morris, back to Beggar's Bush to summon reinforcements. It was a one-way trip.

Two floors up, meanwhile, Slattery, frustratingly, could not open Lt Peel's locked door. The maid's earlier warning call had alerted Peel in time for him to lock and barricade it. Seventeen shots were then fired through it. Peel cowered as a deluge of red-hot bullets tore through the door and embedded themselves in his hastily constructed fortifications. Slattery's men then desperately kicked at the door to try to break it down. The house was a battle zone.

Back downstairs McLean had by now slammed and bolted the front door. Suddenly a pistol barrel appeared through its waist-high letter box. The weapon was fired. McLean was struck in the hand, the bullet burying itself in an adjacent door frame. He felt little pain initially. Adrenalin-fuelled but bleeding, his mind was focused purely on keeping the Auxiliaries out. They attacked relentlessly, hammering at the front door, seemingly indifferent to the sporadic return fire through the door from Dempsey. Then Mitchell split his men into two groups: one to maintain fire on the front door from outside, another to enter No. 21 – situated to the right as they faced the house – and attempt entry into No. 22 via its back garden. This bought precious seconds for McLean to bandage his hand, while Dempsey called out alarmingly to those upstairs: 'Are you fellows all right? They are surrounding the house!'[32] Slattery, still trying to batter down Peel's door, cursed; there was no chance of getting him. He ordered his men back downstairs. Next door, Seán Hyde, the IRA intelligence operative who lived there, listened warily as the Auxiliaries tore through No. 21 – the results of his recent intelligence work playing out.

Angliss was not as fortunate as Peel. Keogh, a seasoned killer, raised his revolver to execute him. Connolly, still in bed next to Angliss, rolled away suddenly as Angliss tried pitifully to shield himself with his hand and forearm. Five shots rang out. One missed, but three struck Angliss in the chest, another tore into his buttock. His body danced grotesquely under the savage impacts of the .45 calibre bullets.

The IRA men quickly regrouped in the hallway and made for the house's rear, desperate to escape. Slattery led, followed by Dempsey, Teeling and Begley. But as soon as they entered the garden they came under withering pistol fire from next door. Slattery and Dempsey initially scrambled for cover against the wall to their right, between the two houses, then, crouching, made for the back wall. Begley was forced back inside by intense fire. Teeling bolted for the rear wall just as Slattery and Dempsey scaled it and then landed beyond in Verschoyle Place. As Teeling climbed the wall he slumped, shot through the stomach. His comrades beyond, fearing the worst, called to him but got no reply. Teeling, stupefied, slowly gathered himself to stop the blood oozing from his stomach. Gunshots continued to fill the air as Slattery and Dempsey escaped.

Keogh, still inside No. 22, regrouped the remaining men, telling them the only way out was through the front. The four with him, including Begley, drew breath, reloaded weapons and then yanked the door open. The five burst onto the street, shooting. Shots reverberated along the wide street. The half-dozen plain-clothed Auxiliaries still on the street were surprised and sought cover behind their truck, allowing precious seconds for the five to sprint into Grattan Street, diagonally across the road to their left, its hundred-yard incline leading towards Grand Canal Street. Keogh dropped his pistol accidentally as he rushed into the street. He stooped, picked it up from the cobblestones and fired a final salvo at the regrouping Auxiliaries.

Vinny Byrne's men, at this point making their own escape from Upper Mount Street, stopped at the junction of Stephen's Place and Lower Mount Street in time to witness their comrades' frantic escape to their right, before sprinting across Lower Mount Street themselves into Grant's Row, a narrow laneway leading in the same direction as Grattan Street, while also drawing the Auxiliaries' fire and inadvertently assisting their comrades. Soon, both fleeing groups, having reached Grand Canal Street, walked the rest of the way towards the southern quays unpursued, weapons ready.

As soon as No. 22 was secured by the Auxiliaries, Cadet Mitchell, wondering where his reinforcements were, telephoned Beggar's Bush Barracks to enquire. Worryingly, he was told that neither Garniss nor Morris had arrived at the barracks from Mount Street. He then requested reinforcements himself.

Meanwhile, in the back garden, Frank Teeling, despite his gushing stomach wound, loaded fresh ammunition into the handle of his semi-automatic, struggling with his bloody hands, seeing no option other than to fight to the end. When called upon to surrender he refused, until, eventually, he realised his situation was hopeless. He cast the reloaded pistol aside and was taken prisoner.

By now the missing Auxiliaries, Garniss and Morris, were under armed guard in the back garden of 16 Northumberland Road. They had been observed by IRA men from D Company, 3rd Battalion, as they quick-stepped along that street towards nearby Beggar's Bush. The enemy, who had set up a temporary command post under Capt. Francis Casey in No. 16 to provide scouting support for the morning's operations, having told complaining residents that they had no choice in

Frank Teeling, E Company, 2nd Battalion, Dublin Brigade IRA, wounded during intense fighting at 22 Lower Mount Street on Bloody Sunday. (*Courtesy of Kilmainham Gaol Museum OPW, KMGLM 19PC–1K44–25*)

the matter, suddenly surrounded the two Auxiliaries. Disarmed and with their hands up, the cadets were searched at the front gate of No. 14 before being taken to Capt. Casey next door in No. 16. Questioning quickly revealed that they were Auxiliaries. They were then taken into the back garden just as another IRA scout rushed inside, warning that he could hear motor horns from Beggar's Bush. Casey was unhesitant and ruthless. He ordered both prisoners up against the garden wall. Seven shots rang out. Garniss, thirty-four years old, was hit in the head and chest. Morris, twenty-four, was hit three times in the head. Both collapsed to the ground, their heads a pulverised mess. Garniss and Morris became the first Auxiliaries in Dublin to die at the IRA's hands, and the repercussions from their deaths were quick.

The IRA men rapidly evacuated the house. Moments later, a lodger stepped into the back garden to investigate. Horrified, he made his way out to the front just in time to intercept the same truck of passing Auxiliaries that had alerted the IRA men moments earlier. Half stuttering, he informed them of the two bodies out the back. He was told that the truck's passengers were on urgent business but would return.

Less than a minute later, the same truck screeched to a stop next to the other outside 22 Lower Mount Street. Brig. Gen. Frank Crozier, their overall commander, stepped down from it with his men and entered the house. Crozier remarked that it looked like a bad billet from France during the Great War, 'shot up by French mutineers'.[33] Crozier had a personal interest in this particular dwelling; his daughter and fiancée had both recently rented rooms on its upper floors.

Crozier assessed the situation and was informed by Mitchell that they had a wounded enemy prisoner in the back garden. He then stepped out to see one of Mitchell's comrades with his revolver pressed against Teeling's head, counting backwards from ten. Teeling's eyes were closed as he braced himself for death at the imminent zero count. Crozier, however, barked at the cadet to 'Stand down!' The enraged cadet held the gun in place momentarily, wrestling the compulsion to disregard the command and blow the prisoner's brains out, before pulling it away and clicking its safety catch on. Crozier ordered Teeling to be taken to the heavily guarded King George V Hospital, satisfied that legal channels following his treatment there would see him court-martialled and executed. Crozier was then led back into the house and upstairs, where he was shown Angliss' blood-soaked remains. Lt Connolly stood nearby recounting Angliss' killing to a nearby cadet. Meanwhile, upstairs on the next floor, Lt Peel, traumatised, was still locked in his room and refusing to come out. Crozier soon managed to reassure and convince him that it was safe to remove his improvised fortifications. Moments afterwards the door slowly opened.[34] Peel stepped out, trembling, his face chalky white.

Just over a mile from Mount Street, on the city's opposite side, moments before 9 a.m., Capt. Paddy Moran, veteran Volunteer and O/C of D Company, 2nd Battalion, had met with Volunteer James Cahill and IRA intelligence officer Patrick Kennedy on Sackville Street directly opposite the fashionable Gresham Hotel. They were about to execute the only successful assassinations on the city's north-side that morning.

Moran, thirty-two years old, from Roscommon, glanced at his watch as the nearby pro-cathedral's bells chimed. The three men then crossed the wide boulevard and stepped up to the hotel entrance beneath its metal and glass portico. One of two newspaper boys there called out to Cahill in a thick Dublin accent, addressing him by name and asking him if he wanted a paper. Cahill glanced over, frowning as if disturbed by the recognition. The streetwise youngster quickly sensed that something far removed from a newspaper sale was about to happen and muttered to his young colleague: 'There's a job on. Best clear out of this.'[35] Cahill knew these youths would keep their mouths shut. They were left undisturbed as they stepped away.

Suddenly, as if out of nowhere, an additional dozen D Company men stepped quickly inside from the street, having assembled discreetly nearby in small clusters. They joined Moran, Cahill and Kennedy and entered the hotel lobby, then sprang into action.

Moran ordered one man to disconnect the telephone. Another Volunteer pulled a pistol and pointed it at the doorman, Hugh Callaghan, demanding the hotel register. Several guests in the lobby, gasping in shock, were placed under guard. Three names were quickly identified in the register. Moran asked Callaghan if the three were all there. Callaghan paused, but when Moran indicated that he had neither the time nor the inclination to tolerate hesitation, Callaghan nervously replied that one of them had recently departed for mass, but the other two – Capt. Patrick McCormack, formerly of the Royal Army Veterinary Corps, a forty-three-year-old veterinary surgeon from Castlebar, and twenty-eight-year-old Lt Leonard Wilde, formerly of the Sherwood Foresters Regiment, currently in the employ of the Foreign Office – were in their rooms. Capt. Moran, taking no chances in any case, detailed three units to seek out the targets.

Cahill, with a small section of men next to him, ordered Callaghan to

A selection of pistols used during the War of Independence. (*Courtesy of Mercier Archive*)

show him to Capt. McCormack's room, No. 22 on the second floor. Volunteer Michael Kilkelly, with another section, followed just behind. Kilkelly's target, Lt Wilde's room, was No. 12 on the first floor. The third unit also followed – their destination another room. Moran and Kennedy stayed put on the ground floor with a handful of others, who spread out quietly, pistols primed. Breakfast was being served in the hotel's adjacent dining room. It hummed quietly as guests ate and spoke, some rustling newspapers, blissfully unaware of the horrors unfolding in the city and about to be visited upstairs.

All three assassination parties passed along the first-floor corridor when, unexpectedly, the door to room No. 12 opened from the inside. A tanned man stood in the doorway – Lt Wilde. Cahill, reacting instantly, pointed his pistol in his face and demanded his name. The reply was unexpectedly cavalier: 'Alan Wilde, British Intelligence Officer, just back from Spain.'[36] Wilde, mistaking the gunmen for an undercover British military unit, had just sealed his own fate.

Cahill kept Wilde covered until Kilkelly and two others took the lieutenant inside his room and shut the door quietly behind them. Cahill's unit continued to the next floor, while the third unit sought its own designated room. Less than a minute later, to the sound of three muffled pistol cracks from below, Cahill's men stopped outside Room 22. Its door was unlocked. Cahill turned the doorknob slowly and entered, revealing their target sitting up in bed, absorbed in reading *The Irish Field* newspaper while munching on his breakfast until disturbed by the sudden noise below. McCormack was a cousin of Land League founder Michael Davitt. He had arrived in Dublin the previous August to purchase horses for the Alexandria Turf Club in Egypt, where he was also planning on moving with his Irish wife and daughter.

Cahill and Nick Leonard's guns blazed as soon as they rushed in. McCormack was shot through the head, wrist, neck and groin, and died instantly, his head blown to pieces by the .45 calibre round that struck it. The bed and his newspaper became saturated with blood.[37] On the floor below, Lt Wilde's body lay sprawled on the floor of Room 12, face down with clumps of brain next to his head, which had been shattered by two rounds; the third had struck his thigh as his body collapsed under the force of the shots.

Within minutes the three groups rejoined their comrades in the lobby. The leader of the third party shook his head, indicating that their intended victim was indeed elsewhere. Moran ordered his men out. They strolled calmly out of the hotel and dispersed through the streets. Back inside the hotel, Hugh

Callaghan rushed to find the manager, James Doyle. Doyle asked him what the muffled cracks had been. Callaghan informed him. Soon afterwards their sickened eyes fell upon the horrific scenes upstairs.

The morning's killings had concluded, but Sunday 21 November 1920 was about to get much bloodier.

3

BLOODY SUNDAY: REPRISALS

'If you get through, Fitz, give my love to my mother'

Another 2nd Battalion unit had been detailed to Church Road in East Wall on the morning of 21 November to hunt down an enemy intelligence officer residing in one of the road's red-brick townhouses. On arrival, the unit had discovered that the officer had recently left the country. Nevertheless, they seized a sizeable number of papers.

A more daring raid was initiated in Exchequer Street's Central Hotel, not 200 yards from Dublin Castle. Twelve Volunteers waited just outside as the hotel register was demanded by an IRA officer inside. When this was refused, he reacted angrily. Some Volunteers standing by suggested shooting the registrar on the spot, as well as everyone else in the hotel – it was known to be a regular military haunt. Such radical action was, however, dismissed. The job was abandoned.

Two more assassinations had been planned in Phibsboro. Patrick Lawson had rendezvoused with five comrades from F Company, 1st Battalion, at Rutland Square, only to be instructed by Company Commander Patrick Holohan, brother of Garry, to go home as both had been cancelled.[1]

Back on the south-side, Patrick Mullen of C Company, 4th Battalion, had, with several others, approached the Standard Hotel at 80 Harcourt Street, only to be told on scene by a breathless intelligence officer that their target no longer resided there. Two more assassinations were attempted on the same street: Capt. Hardy – a priority target – and his notorious company commander, Capt. 'Tiny' King – his nickname a paradox, he was well over six feet tall. King, an Englishman, had been a policeman in South Africa and fought with distinction throughout the Great War with a South African regiment. Hardy, a Connaught Ranger whose wartime exploits as an escaped prisoner of war became legendary, had been a priority target since the killing of Peter O'Carroll in Manor Street the previous month. Hardy and his wife shared a Harcourt Street flat. She had previously been provided with a code word to deliver by telephone to Dublin Castle if she suspected her flat was under IRA observation. Her employment of it had already seen intelligence officers Patrick Caldwell and Joe Guilfoyle arrested, but, astonishingly, released soon afterwards when both their cover stories held. Guilfoyle had been lucky to survive. Hardy would have shot him but for the intervention of a policeman sympathetic to the IRA. Hardy and King were equally lucky. By 9 a.m. on the day of the assassinations, both were in Dublin Castle and remained there all morning.

Elsewhere throughout the city that morning, other hit squads turned up at boarding houses and hotels to find their targets either absent or no longer residing there. In one case, the targets had a lucky escape when a jumpy IRA man shot at his own mirror reflection in the Shelbourne Hotel, scuppering the element of surprise and the mission there. A previous operation in the Shelbourne – a hive of British spies and Dublin Castle officials – had only recently been cancelled in favour of that morning's coordinated assault on British intelligence.

An air of tension enveloped the city. As Volunteers escaped from their target areas, telephones at Dublin Castle rang incessantly. Panicked voices relayed horrific stories of the morning's slaughter. Place names were scribbled down – Leeson Street … Ranelagh … Mount Street … the Gresham … Pembroke Street … Baggot Street – which were then relayed throughout the Castle, layered with increasingly dramatic embellishments. One was communicated to General Crozier, after he had reported to Dublin Castle from Mount Street, suggesting more than fifty officers had been shot.

Panic ensued. Michael Collins' name resonated with trepidation; his prowess considered practically supernatural amongst those who never suspected that the far more surreptitious men who, along with Seán Russell, had actually directed the morning's killings – McKee and Clancy – were already in custody. When a call came into Richmond Barracks detailing the killings, Capt. Jeune, shocked at the news, nonetheless breathed a huge sigh in relief that he had been out all night. Capt. Rymer-Jones, on the other hand, had to restrain his men from driving to the city to lash out in revenge when they heard about the shootings.[2]

The IRA units, meanwhile, beat their retreats and went to ground. Paddy

Daly and Seán Russell waited anxiously for reports in North Richmond Street. First to arrive there were Joe Dolan, Dan McDonnell, Tom Keogh and Billy McLean. The former pair had happened across Keogh and McLean in their taxi as they and the others escaped towards the south docks, and provided both Keogh and the wounded McLean with a lift to North Richmond Street – also functioning as a first-aid station. As the Byrnes' daughters, Catherine and Alice, tended to McLean's hand, Keogh detailed to Daly that the Lower Mount Street operation had been a success – at least partially – but that he was uncertain of the fates of Frank Teeling, James Slattery and Jim Dempsey. He then spoke of wounding several Auxiliaries during the escape. He also joked about having asked the maid there for a date as they were initially let in. Slattery and Dempsey, meanwhile, had made their escape from Verschoyle Place on foot to Gerard Golden's safe house in Victoria Street. There they cleaned themselves up. Later that day, word came in from them that Teeling had been captured.

Reporting in soon afterwards were Vinny Byrne, Charlie Dalton, Joe Leonard and William Stapleton. Byrne and his remaining men, including Frank Saurin, had reached Sir John Rogerson's Quay and met with Charlie Dalton, only to find that the boat due to ferry them across the Liffey was not where they expected it to be – a precarious situation given that they expected enemy patrols to quickly seal the city's bridges. Luckily for them, Capt. Kilcoyne, who had concealed the boat among dozens on the quayside, came to their rescue. They descended the quayside's concrete steps and escaped to safety across the 200-yard-wide, serenely calm river. By the time they arrived in North Richmond Street, Herbie Conroy had already reported the Upper Mount Street mission's success to Russell; he had been picked up by Pat McCrea on his way from Lower Baggot Street, as Conroy was making his way alongside Byrne and the others from Upper Mount Street to the quays. Dalton briefed Daly about the Pembroke Street operation. Joe Leonard and William Stapleton had already reported in by then, having stashed Pte Snelling's Triumph in a nearby dump. Paddy Moran had also reported with details about the Gresham attack. While the other IRA men had breakfast and washed, Daly trawled through papers handed to him by Dalton, Stapleton, Saurin and Matty MacDonald, after he too arrived. Saurin's haul of papers was particularly revealing: the overall British intelligence structure appeared to mirror that of the IRA.

James Carrigan, from the Pembroke Street operation, returned the car he had driven afterwards to Golden's safe house on Victoria Street. Other IRA operatives from the 3rd and 4th Battalions remained on the city's south-side, their reports soon reaching senior officers via their intelligence network and couriers such as Cumann na mBan member Annie Cooney and Michael Collins' aide-de-camp and confidential courier Joe O'Reilly. Cooney and her sister, Lily, had been in position that morning since 7 a.m. at Stephen's Green's University church, attending two separate services to blend in as they waited tensely. Annie had heard distant gunshots from the Leeson Street/Pembroke Street area soon after 9 a.m. Minutes later she and Lily saw three men from F Company, 4th Battalion, walking smartly towards them, having expected them to be there. Passing, the men handed them their pistols – in this case unused – and kept walking. Both sisters then made their way to safe houses via back streets and relayed the weapons to couriers in tenement dwellings.

Michael Collins was in Liam Devlin's pub, 68 Great Britain Street, all morning, anxiously awaiting news. He had not slept. Nor had Joe O'Reilly, further exhausted from having cycled all over the city gathering the news. He arrived in Devlin's mid-morning with his initial report, erroneously reassuring Collins that the IRA had suffered no casualties, then setting off again to warn officials from the Gaelic Athletic Association (GAA) – feverishly preparing for a challenge football match between Dublin and Tipperary due to commence at 2.45 p.m. in Croke Park – of the morning's events and the danger of reprisals. Collins appeared satisfied with O'Reilly's reports of a predominantly successful morning but was wary of a backlash. He was, as yet, unaware of the losses of McKee and Clancy. However, their silence after the mammoth operation was disconcerting. O'Reilly was sent back out to find them.[3]

O'Reilly cycled to 36 Lower Gloucester Street but could neither locate nor find word of either man, or of Seán Fitzpatrick, until a local youngster informed him that they had been captured the previous night – the raid now the talk of the area. O'Reilly's heart sank. His stomach churned as he absorbed the bombshell. He sped back to Devlin's. When he relayed his shocking news, Collins fell apart, entering into a stunned silence, mirrored by his surrounding close associates. He then sighed loudly, saying, 'We're finished now. It's all up.'[4]

Pat McCrea drove to his Dollymount home having left North Richmond Street. Over breakfast, when his wife asked where he had been, he answered: 'out with the boys, fishing'.[5] His wife then asked why he had no fish. McCrea made himself scarce, taking a tram into Marlboro Street to attend midday mass at the pro-cathedral. When he left the church shortly before 1 p.m., he noticed 'military and Tans all over the city', as the authorities slowly began to take stock and react in a way that saw the day's thus far gruesome events assume a far more malevolent course.[6]

For several hours, the same authorities had been paralysed in disbelief at the incessant reports coming in. Such destructive coordination had been evident before in barrack burnings. However, the precision of the assault, despite its setbacks, momentarily overwhelmed Dublin Castle.

The authorities desperately regrouped. Agents, touts and others deemed at imminent risk were summoned to the sanctuary of the Castle, soon to resemble a fortified ghetto. Others were rushed to the Central and Royal Exchange Hotels to be garrisoned. Hastily packed baggage was strewn everywhere. The surrounding streets became clogged with hackney cabs, motor cars and military lorries.[7] Ormonde Winter, meanwhile, was nervous and agitated. British officers living outside barracks were recalled. Winter had recently, along with General Tudor, been compelled to move to the Castle from the heavily guarded Park Lodge in Phoenix Park, adjacent to Irish Command HQ.[8]

Officers and Auxiliaries, fearing for the safety of wives and mistresses, summoned hard-pressed drivers for them after word was circulated that Dublin's roads were to be sealed for twenty-four hours and that trains and trams would stop running for that time. Dublin's imminently departing mail boat was to be searched.[9] City Hall and the neighbouring rates office, both filling with British troops, were occupied by the Castle authorities – the former's Tricolour would no longer fly. This development greatly appeased Mark Sturgis, who wrote about City Hall's occupation that: 'It's too near the Castle to be in enemy hands.'[10] With General Macready holidaying in France, his deputy, Major Gen. Hugh Jeudwine, commander of the British Army 5th (Curragh) Division, ordered the widespread escalation of security measures. The midnight to 5 a.m. curfew would commence at 10 p.m. Round-ups rapidly increased in number. The recently proposed establishment of an internment camp at Ballykinlar in County Down – a former training camp for Ulster's 36th Infantry Division – was expedited. Winter quartering of troops for training was cancelled in favour of maintaining operational readiness.

Meanwhile, the city's telephone exchange buzzed with calls being transferred between residents in the city's affluent districts, swapping news and rumours of scores of dead being transported to the city's morgues. Prominent among such voices was that of diplomat Frederick Dumont, who had only just finished playing cards with some of the Pembroke Street victims and, luckily, had declined an offer to stay the night there. His recent expressions of the crown's impending victory seemed hollow.

The Castle's F Company Auxiliaries drank heavily that morning, furious at their corps' first fatalities in the city. Unfortunately for McKee, Clancy and the rest of the Castle guardhouse's prisoners, this fury was vented on them. Prisoners were wrenched out viciously for interrogation with kicks, blows and abuse. Elsewhere shots were fired at imaginary enemies as cadets became paralytic.

At one point three drunken cadets entered the guardroom, their leader swaying, his squinting eyes darting malevolently from prisoner to prisoner. Spotting Seán Fitzpatrick, he roared: 'I know you!'[11] He then beat Fitzpatrick around the head with a revolver as his comrades pointed their cocked sidearms at the rest of the prisoners. Luckily for Fitzpatrick, a passing British officer, hearing his screams, rushed in and berated his assailants. He ordered the Auxiliaries out and took Fitzpatrick to the medical officer.

For the remaining twenty-five guardhouse prisoners, however, this respite was brief. Col Winter soon joined Hardy and King in interrogating them, his agitation escalated to fury. The lack of forewarning of the morning's attack incensed him. He concluded that it must have involved hundreds of

Members of F Company, Auxiliaries. *(Courtesy of Mercier Archive)*

operatives, given its scale, yet not a single branch of British intelligence had come across a snippet of information about it. Winter knew his Central Raid Bureau was obtaining results as it relentlessly scrutinised captured documents, but it dawned on him that his intelligence was fundamentally ineffectual. He reasoned that some of the twenty-six prisoners must have some information on the attacks. In an effort to uncover this, the ensuing beatings became incessant and were soon accompanied by false executions: revolver barrels were forced against prisoners' skulls, the prisoners unaware that they were not loaded before their triggers were pulled. For McKee, Clancy and the hardened IRA men accompanying them, this was endurable, despite their growing exhaustion; for the civilian prisoners it was harrowing. McKee, Clancy and Fitzpatrick stuck to their stories: they were Fitzpatrick's lodgers, that was all – they knew 'nothing' of IRA activity.

Despite Winter's incandescence, all was not lost for British intelligence. Significant numbers of Secret Service remained at large in the city. The morale of the IRA's enemies had been momentarily shattered, but Scotland Yard's web of agents remained fundamentally intact and soon regrouped. More immediately, however, Dublin Castle's more visible subordinates – the RIC and its paramilitary reserves and cadets – were about to cross a brutal Rubicon to repay some of the destruction wrought by their enemies. The day's killings had just begun.

The Dublin versus Tipperary match in Croke Park was expected to draw thousands of spectators. High-profile GAA features were rare because of the recent troubles. This game was a fundraising event to assist the family of an injured 2nd Battalion Volunteer badly beaten in a fracas with betting touts. The Tipperary team had travelled to Dublin by train early the previous evening, engaging in a huge fistfight themselves with British soldiers en route. The soldiers had come off worse and alighted from the train to await a later one. A cordon of khaki had then greeted the team as they stepped off the steam train at Kingsbridge station, but no trouble ensued. The players then spent the night in Barry's Hotel – a republican haunt in Great Denmark Street. Several made their way to Phil Shanahan's pub in Montgomery Street with IRA dispatches from Tipperary for GHQ and had picked up murmurings there of a big job the following morning.

At 1.30 p.m. on Sunday, Lt Col Robert Bray, commanding the 2nd Battalion, Duke of Wellington's Regiment (West Riding), nicknamed 'The

Dukes', at Collinstown Aerodrome, six miles north of the city, received orders from Irish Command HQ to surround Croke Park during the match and picket each exit with units consisting of one officer and fifteen men.[12] Armoured cars were deployed. Fifteen minutes before the match was scheduled to end, intelligence officers were to employ megaphones to warn the crowds to leave only by the stadium's official exits under instruction that searches on all males would be conducted. Anyone seen trying to escape would be shot.

Simultaneously, Gen. Crozier, having since left Dublin Castle and lunched at the far more relaxed Shelbourne Hotel – despite the morning's botched shooting there – received his own orders to assist military operations in Croke Park. Accordingly, an Auxiliary company of fifty men awaiting transport to County Meath, under the command of Crozier's adjutant, forty-year-old Major Edward Mills, was hastily assembled at Beggar's Bush. Six Crossley Tenders were lined up for transport.

A meeting had taken place in Croke Park at noon to discuss a proposed ban on GAA players playing soccer or rugby.[13] Attending was IRA Dublin Brigade former adjutant and republican judge Jack Shouldice – a thirty-eight-year-old 1916 veteran – that day in charge of managing gate takings. Luke O'Toole, the GAA's secretary general attended, as did its president, James Nowlan. Joe O'Reilly's warnings of the potential repercussions of the morning's shootings sidelined their original agenda. There was an imminent danger of a backlash. As crowds congregated, in spite of road and rail closures, to the raucous shouts of street-traders, hawkers and fruit sellers, an argument raged – whether or not to cancel the game. Ultimately, it was decided to proceed. The GAA did not wish to be seen associating with 'a violent, political act'.[14] Crucially, they misread the danger, reasoning that raids were nothing new and wary of the reaction of the huge crowds already converging on the area.

Among the gathering crowds were IRA men from the morning's killings and many other members not directly involved, including former Comdt Seán McLoughlin. His recent ill health, from repeated imprisonments, incessant police raids at his home and lingering Spanish Flu complications, had subsided enough to enable him to travel soon to England as a labour agitator, masking a surreptitious mission of weapons procurement, particularly in Liverpool. But he had decided to take time to enjoy the game first.

Tom Keogh, Dan McDonnell and Joe Dolan, meanwhile, made their way to Hill 60 – a huge mound named after an infamous war-torn hill in Gallipoli

– situated to the pitch's north-east.[15] They figured Croke Park was safer than staying at home, given the likelihood of raids. Paddy Moran had arrived in time to watch Dunleary, the club of which he was chairman, take on Erin's Hope in a warm-up game.[16] William Stapleton made his way to the game, as did Tom Ennis. Vinny Byrne stayed away, suspecting trouble. IRA men played on both teams. Cumann na mBan members were out in force for the game, including both Byrne sisters from North Richmond Street.

The previous evening, Harry Colley had been nervously anticipating the following morning's operation, having witnessed the Auxiliary raid at Seville Place. For weeks beforehand, he and his 2nd Battalion comrades had baulked at the upper hand apparently held by the enemy. Auxiliaries patrolled arrogantly in his battalion area, while the IRA were conspicuously absent. Armed touts were also on the streets. A plan was formulated by 2nd Battalion to redress this by aggressively patrolling on a particular night and arresting any touts, who, if armed, would be shot on sight. These plans had been cast aside in favour of the far more ambitious 21 November operation.

Colley had been among other battalion officers issuing instructions for Volunteers to act as stewards for the upcoming match. Croke Park, being in 2nd Battalion's area, rendered this standard procedure. The plan had been to rescind these orders, but not until after the morning's assassinations – everything was to appear normal until then. It was anticipated that the match would then be called off for fear of reprisals, but whether or not it went ahead, their men would not be sent out to steward it.

At 2.30 p.m., Colley met Seán Russell and Tom Kilcoyne in North Strand. They walked through Spring Garden Street towards Croke Park a half-mile away. Russell looked fearful and repeated to Colley what Kilcoyne had just told him before he had joined them: a DMP sergeant had warned that Auxiliaries and police were mobilising to Croke Park, where they intended to 'mow down the people'.[17] The sergeant, although unsympathetic to the republicans, was appalled at the prospect of a massacre and felt duty-bound to report it. He had approached Kilcoyne, suspecting him rightly of IRA involvement.

With urgency paramount, the three sped on foot to Croke Park's main entrance on Jones's Road where they met Luke O'Toole and Jack Shouldice. They relayed the DMP sergeant's warning and appealed for the game to be cancelled and for the gates to be closed immediately, painting a grim picture of what enemy machine guns could do to such a crowd – numbering almost 15,000.

Throw-in was in fifteen minutes. O'Toole and Shouldice, momentarily veering between disbelief and alarm, vacillated, then warned that any announcement calling off the game in such threatening circumstances could lead to 'panic and death in another form' from a dangerous stampede, a situation aggravated by the lack of available stewards.[18] It was argued that people stopping to demand refunds would add further danger. When it was pointed out that the refund issue would have detrimental impact on the family of the wounded Volunteer due to receive the game's proceeds, Russell, Kilcoyne and Colley retorted that this was unavoidable, but, given the circumstances it was imperative to prevent further admissions and to attempt to get the people out safely.

The three then stepped away. Colley suggested that with so few stewards they themselves should assist. They went to the stadium's St Joseph's Avenue entrance to its east and instructed the turnstile operator there that no one else was to be let in. Despite complying at first, the operator then sought confirmation from his superiors. However, the moment he stepped away, the thickening and agitated crowd, knowing the game was about to start, began pressing against the turnstiles, shouting in protest. The operator returned and, swearing at Colley and the others, relented. The crowd flooded in. The three, now powerless, walked away and dispersed, rightly fearful.[19] The afternoon, like the morning, remained mild and bright. Meanwhile, throw-in was postponed until 3.15 due to crowd control problems.

Over 400 RIC were stationed at their Phoenix Park depot three miles away, plus 270 Black and Tans. While Colley and the two others had been hastily striding to Croke Park, over 100 Tans and RIC had been driven from the depot to Beggar's Bush in a convoy of twelve Tenders. They were commanded by Major George Vernon Dudley – an Auxiliary. They then linked up with Major Mills' Auxiliaries at Beggar's Bush to drive to Croke Park; their function: to carry out searches at the game's conclusion.

At 3.15 p.m., just after both teams posed for photographs, the ball was thrown in and the game started. Players jostled and tackled, marking their men, throwing shoves, jibes and taunts. The surrounding thousands roared in a collective cacophony, almost drowning out the buzz from the radial engine of a military biplane circling slowly overhead at low altitude. Ominously, its pilot fired a red signal flare.

At this point Col Bray mobilised his 'Dukes'. Twelve trucks full of soldiers had by now rendezvoused with three Peerless armoured cars at the junction of

Fitzroy Avenue and Lower Drumcondra Road. Now, two of these armoured cars trundled into Clonliffe Road, one in front, one behind the trucks. When, minutes later, the column reached the junction of St Joseph's Avenue 800 yards away, 150 British infantrymen quickly debussed accompanied by officers and non-commissioned officers (NCOs), each raucously detailing men to stadium exits. Residents in Clonliffe Road's red-brick terraces looked on in trepidation from behind their window blinds as squads ran past in hobnailed boots. Ironically, 118 Clonliffe Road, employed by Lily Mernin to type and deliver the dispatches so instrumental to the morning's bloodbath, was the very house outside which the lead vehicle stopped, its crew oblivious to the connection. Meanwhile, Col Bray had entered the third armoured car just as the convoy had set off. He ordered its driver to Jones's Road, within effective view of the canal bridge at Croke Park's south-western side, anticipating the imminent arrival of the police there with whom he would liaise. The unsuspecting crowd inside the stadium was captivated by the game.

Dublin played out from the canal end, attacking north as the cheering crowds relished the spirited contest. Tipperary played to the south. A packed grandstand and pavilion was positioned to the west of the pitch adjacent to Jones's Road. Just inside its entrance stood a large earth mound to the north. To its east stood the much larger Hill 60, also thronged. The entire pitch was surrounded by a cinder athletic track, with walls, corrugated iron and barbed-wire fencing to protect the stadium when unattended. To the east was St Joseph's Avenue. Entrants there were funnelled between the wall of Belvedere rugby grounds to their south – a former stomping ground of the late, recently hanged, Kevin Barry – and a corrugated iron palisade to their north. A high wall running south to north, then east, separated the rugby grounds from Croke Park itself. Opposite, to the stadium's south-west, was the manager's office, which sat beside another set of turnstiles at the canal entrance. Entrants there were funnelled through to the park between an adjacent wall and another railway line. Railways sandwiched the park from south and north, behind an embankment in the latter case.

The revised timing of the throw-in was soon succeeded by the departure of the combined RIC forces from Beggar's Bush. Their eighteen heavily laden vehicles sped through the city, along the southern quays and Sackville Street observed by wary civilians, then through Mountjoy Square and, finally, up Russell Street and Jones's Road, Major Dudley in the lead car, Major Mills in the thirteenth, at the head of the Auxiliaries. Mills was in overall command.

At 3.35 p.m., Col Bray, in Jones's Road, saw the convoy of Tenders approach at the brow of the canal bridge to his south. Its first sighting prompted ticket sellers outside the stadium to run away, shouting in alarm: 'The Tans are coming!'[20] The lead Tender crossed the bridge and pulled up on Jones's Road. Major Dudley then stepped out and directed six vehicles into the road beyond.

Suddenly, within seconds, without warning or orders, dozens of RIC and Tans leapt from the Tenders positioned behind those just ordered forward and rushed for the turnstiles at the stadium's canal end, weapons primed. Then the shooting started.

Their first volley hit eleven-year-old William Robinson, a schoolboy from Little Britain Street. He was struck in the right side of his chest and knocked from a tree. He lay half-conscious, gasping desperately as panic ensued. He was attended to by a ticket seller but died the following day. Then, ten-year-old Jerome O'Leary from Blessington Street was shot through the head and killed instantly. Horrified shouts and screams filled the air as rifle rounds whizzed. More RIC and Tans rushed into the stadium. Auxiliaries wearing mufti joined them, firing revolvers. The crowd's initial confusion at the unprovoked onset gave way to a rapidly growing stampede from the canal end. Other policemen shot rifles from outside the canal end; the adjacent elevated bridge on Jones's Road providing enough clearance to aim, fire, work rifle bolts and aim again over their comrades' heads into the mass of running and collapsing humanity. To the staccato of rifle cracks, crowds fled to the Jones's Road and St Joseph's Avenue exits, only to find them barred by soldiers and recently arrived police. Crowds surged again and again under a hail of fire, creating stampedes. Hundreds rushed for perimeter walls, some becoming tangled in barbed wire like trapped soldiers in no man's land. Men who had already seen such horrors as British Army soldiers in trenches instinctively threw themselves to the ground, as did Volunteers.

Thomas Ryan, vice-comdt of 5th and 6th Battalions, 3rd Tipperary Brigade, was Tipperary team captain. He was lining up a penalty when the shooting started. He and six other players wearing both Dublin and Tipperary jerseys, also Volunteers, threw themselves down as trained when they heard the first volleys. Ryan saw sparks cascade from the railway embankment wall to his front as bullets ricocheted. Two players close by, initially prone, then dashed towards Hill 60, seeking the railway wall beyond, sprinting for all they were worth, prompting the remaining Volunteer players to prepare to follow their lead one by one, among them twenty-four-year-old Tipperary player Michael Hogan. Ryan saw Hogan creep forward but fall suddenly as a bullet tore into his back and out his chest. Ryan and nearby teammate Josie Synott rushed to Hogan's aid, as did a nearby civilian, also named Thomas Ryan, from Wexford. The three tried to lift Hogan. Blood spurted from his back and chest drenching their hands and garments. Hogan exclaimed in agony: 'Jesus, Mary and Joseph! I am done!'[21] His mouth filled with blood. He gulped, gagged and choked. His eyes became lifeless as he bled out. Thomas Ryan, the civilian, recited the Act of Contrition in his ear. Then a bullet tore into his stomach, mortally wounding him.

Pulsating with adrenalin, Vice-Comdt Ryan took flight. Then, glancing behind, he saw through the onrushing crowds an Auxiliary looking hatefully towards him, reloading his rifle. The Auxiliary raised it to shoot. Ryan threw himself back down, risking being crushed in the stampede. The round struck a youngster running close to him; the youth cried out and fell. Others tumbled around him. To the seemingly endless whisps of bullets piercing the air, Ryan eventually escaped over the embankment wall and the railway, but his ordeal was far from over.

One spectator, Michael Feery – a recently demobbed Royal Marine – impaled his leg on a cast-iron railing as he sought escape from the whining, spinning bullets that thudded into bone and flesh throughout the stadium. Others fleeing in frenzy used him to cushion themselves as they escaped over the same railing.[22] Feery screamed in agony. He eventually freed himself, only to bleed to death on the road having dragged himself from the stadium, leaving a ghastly blood trail; his body was not identified for days.

Spectators fell as they ran left, then right. Others stumbled and tripped avoiding them, creating a terror-stricken, writhing mass. People trapped on the ground by others toppling and careering into them grappled to free themselves. Petrified children screamed. As the crowds surged relentlessly at the Joseph's Avenue exit, some escaped. However, by now the lead armoured car had deployed there. Its machine gunner opened fire with its Hotchkiss machine gun. He fired a fifty-two-round metal ammunition belt into the air in warning, the hissing weapon echoing, creating even more terror and causing the crowd at the gate to turn and reel hysterically back inside, crashing headlong into hundreds of others. The screams and shouts were deafening.

Intense firing from the canal end continued. People were swept from each other as the crowds convulsed, whirled and surged. There was no way out.

Hordes more invaded the dressing rooms, which quickly became packed. Droves of others rushed for the wall of the adjacent rugby grounds to scale it, some stepping on the prone bodies of the fallen, who cried for help until unable to continue, their empty lungs immobilised by the weight of those around or above them. Mercifully, for some the crush abated; others were not so lucky. Some who had scaled the wall hurled themselves headlong over the far side, a long unceremonious drop. Some remained in full view of the police while reaching back to help others with the difficult climb, compelled by the desperation and panic on the faces of friends, relatives and strangers. Some fell, shot as they wrestled themselves and others over. Pistol and rifle bullets pinged off the blood-stained wall, ricochets inflicting further horrific wounds. Escapers, many wounded, scrambled along the railway line next to the canal, fleeing eastward. But Auxiliaries sealed off the nearby streets, subsequently barring ambulances from tending the wounded, one of whom, Joseph Traynor, a 4th Battalion Volunteer, died in nearby 5 Sackville Gardens, home to Christopher and Caroline Ring. This house was itself soon raided.

William Stapleton was splattered with blood from a man next to him, who slumped to the ground, badly wounded. He fled from his perch on top of a newly constructed stand and scrambled over a wall into the garden of a house in Jones's Road, as did numerous others, despite the fifteen-foot drop. Once in the garden, they stood or knelt to seek comfort from rosary beads clasped with shaking hands as they panted, murmuring stuttering prayers. From there Stapleton escaped into Jones's Road and fled.[23] The same red-brick house quickly became thronged with the fleeing and wounded, as did neighbouring houses. Stapleton was lucky; just beyond Jones's Road sat Russell Street. There, Daniel Carroll, an unarmed civilian, was less fortunate. He was shot and mortally wounded while limping away from Croke Park, having just escaped the carnage inside.

Tom Keogh, on Hill 60, had his cap shot off and suffered a flesh wound to his arm. As he picked the cap up, a rifle round tore into the man to his front, narrowly missing Keogh . Like Vice-Comdt Ryan, he escaped over the railway and barbed-wire-strewn wall between Hill 60 and Clonliffe Road. Luckily, Harry Colley saw him. Colley had gone to his mother's house for dinner but rushed to the front door upon hearing the shooting, only to see soldiers everywhere. He remained where he was, sickened by what was unravelling, until several minutes passed and he saw Keogh holding his arm. He saw other wounded people escaping into nearby houses as he took Keogh inside to be treated by his twenty-six-year-old sister, Gertie, a Cumann na mBan member. Before the afternoon was out, houses along the entire road and in the surrounding streets were treating wounded on kitchen tables and chairs.

Ryan had escaped into another house on Clonliffe Road. Moments later its door was kicked in. An old man living there cursed the Black and Tans storming in and was struck on the head with a pistol butt, knocking him out. Ryan was wrenched out to the words: 'There is one of the … Tipperary assassins! Take him out and shoot him![24] He was kicked and punched to the ground before having all his clothes torn off with bayonets. An officer then ordered Ryan to be taken, stark naked, back to Croke Park. Ryan feared he was to be shot with his teammates. As he was marched back, he saw people still escaping over walls and railings. A man under armed guard on the road with his girlfriend, seeing Ryan's embarrassing predicament, threw him his coat and was struck in the back of the head by an Auxiliary's rifle butt for his kindness.

Entering the stadium Ryan saw a priest ministering to the dead and wounded, amid agonising groans. Soldiers tended to the wounded here and there, some looking in disgust at the perpetrators. Thousands of spectators still stood under guard. Ryan saw that the shooting had stopped. Major Mills had rushed into the stadium from his Tender in Russell Street, beyond the canal bridge, then repeatedly shouted at the top of his voice the command to cease fire, as had Major Dudley. Now rows and columns of people stood, crying, shaking and struggling to keep their hands in the air as they endured vicious abuse from the police accompanied by commands to keep them raised.[25] Children sobbed.

Coats, hats, walking sticks, umbrellas and hundreds of bicycles were strewn all over the pitch among prone bodies, some struggling, others motionless. The match ball lay on the field, punctured by a bullet aimed by a Black and Tan. He had shot it from 100 yards to display his marksmanship to a colleague who had mocked his previous shot, which had felled a victim, as a fluke.[26]

Vice-Comdt Ryan, still naked, stood among the Tipperary team, who had been marshalled by a cordon of bayonets at Hill 60 and told that two of them would be shot for every captive within the park who gave trouble. The Dublin players, meanwhile, were being relieved of their possessions in their dressing rooms. In the Tipperary rooms the RIC were searching players' clothing and similarly helping themselves to cash, watches, tobacco and cigarettes. Then, the civilian searches began.

Fourteen people had been killed or mortally wounded during the onslaught, and hundreds wounded, scores seriously.[27] Nearly 300 live rounds had been fired.

The shooting from Croke Park could be heard in the city centre, as if a battle were taking place. Word quickly filtered in from escaped city dwellers rushing home from the stadium of the horrific massacre. Civilians fled indoors. Others did the opposite; parts of the city became thronged with people seeking news.

Meanwhile, Michael Collins, having by now recovered from his earlier momentary stupefaction triggered by news of McKee's and Clancy's arrests, was preoccupied with rescuing them. Everything else took second place. Intelligence operatives left no stone unturned in frantic trawls for their whereabouts. Finally, Jim McNamara, inside the Castle, heard they were being transported to the Bridewell DMP station behind the Four Courts. He rushed this information to Collins.

Collins sprang into action. Ignoring all risks, he sped to Vice-Brig. Traynor's home, close to Croke Park. There, he asked Traynor to urgently muster six of 2nd Battalion's best men to be used in a rescue of McKee and Clancy. They were to report to him at the Gaelic League's Keating Branch HQ in 46 Rutland Square. Soon afterwards, Traynor and Seán Russell made their way on foot to Rutland Square with the requisite number. En route they stepped cautiously along Great Britain Street on either side of the road, pistols in pockets, ready to open fire on any interfering enemy. Soon they saw Black and Tans and policemen 'unmercifully beating a few unfortunate people who had the temerity to be out'.[28] One man, on his knees, was bashed about the head with a revolver near the Parnell Monument. There was no time to intervene, however, given the urgency of their orders.

Within moments they were at the junction of Great Britain Street and Rutland Square, yards from Devlin's pub, when they saw a military lorry approach suddenly and screech to a halt outside their destination. With no choice, Traynor and the others remained separated and waited along the street. Twenty agonising minutes passed as No. 46 was ransacked. Then the soldiers came out with several prisoners, loaded them into the lorry and drove off. The late autumnal evening's darkness had closed in and it was difficult to identify those arrested. When the lorry sped off, Traynor, Russell and the others rushed in to find a solitary boy crying because the soldiers had arrested his father. The boy said that other men had fled out the back as the British stormed in. Traynor hoped he was referring to Collins. They waited for ninety minutes, hoping Collins would return. He never did. The streets were crawling with police, army, Auxiliaries and Black and Tans, and Collins had discovered by now the true whereabouts of McKee and Clancy.

Neligan had, at this point, contacted Collins with details. The policeman had been instructed earlier, via Frank Thornton, to blow his cover if necessary to get information on the indispensable pair. Thornton assured Neligan that he would be whisked away to the USA if unmasked, but that it was imperative to locate both men 'at all costs'.[29] Neligan had then made his way to the Bridewell, suspecting they would be there, but found no one matching their descriptions. He then crossed the Liffey to St Michael and John's church on Lower Exchange Street, where a dozen IRA men waited impatiently with Thornton to rush to the Bridewell once given the word. He told them regretfully that the pair were not there. To Neligan the revelation meant one thing: McKee and Clancy were still in the Castle and therefore 'as good as dead'.[30]

Pat McCrea had, like Vinny Byrne, purposely avoided Croke Park that day, sensing trouble. Returning home after mass, his family were surprised to see him; he normally attended games, especially those such as this. He had simply told them he was tired and fell asleep. He was woken at 4 p.m. by his angry wife holding a 'stop press' newspaper edition detailing the morning's shootings. She furiously scolded him, demanding to know if this was what he meant when he said he was out fishing. McCrea's response was equally spirited: 'Yes, and don't you see we had a good catch.'[31] He insisted that he had no problem with the shootings, but left the house soon afterwards, the row unreconciled.

Back in Croke Park, Vice-Comdt Ryan was forced to stand naked for two hours, shivering alongside his teammates. They expected to be shot when the searches concluded. With the stadium almost cleared of spectators – and a mere handful arrested – that eventuality appeared imminent. Those under arrest shared their apprehension. The pitch resembled 'a battlefield that had been abandoned by the combatants'.[32] Then, unexpectedly, Major Mills took charge of their custody and assured them they would be safe. Surrounding Black and Tans became enraged. Mills escorted the team to their dressing room, where they and their clothing were searched and pilfered a second time. He came across Jack Shouldice there. Mills personally searched him and his documents but, unexpectedly, left him with the day's gate takings. Then, finding nothing incriminating, he discreetly said to Shouldice, 'There has been enough shooting and bloodshed here to-day.'[33] He advised him to leave quickly. Shouldice and the players did so, hearts heavy, minds exhausted and confused. Some made for Barry's Hotel. Whatever money they had, apart from the gate takings, was gone.

Ryan made for Seville Place, where many of the Dublin players resided and, released earlier, they had rallied there to support him and his teammates. Ryan was eventually introduced to Jack Kavanagh, a local former British Army officer, who gave him £50 to divide amongst them. This took place in 100 Seville Place, operational again following the previous night's raid.

Back towards Croke Park, many Black and Tan and Auxiliary vehicles remained on Jones's Road and Russell Street. The military had departed after the last civilians had been let go. Many Tans were drunk and laughing at the day's horrific reprisal, as ambulances and priests came to collect the dead and wounded, many of whom still lay unattended. Finally, after the last of their Tenders had fired up and departed, civilians arrived to reclaim belongings in the darkness. In the eerie silence, broken only by Fire Brigade ambulance engines and carriages coming and going, looters also began combing the grounds.

The same ghostly silence hung over the city for a time, punctuated by sporadic gunshots, which increased intermittently to a crescendo. One of many military raids took place close to where Ryan was staying in Seville Place, during which shots were fired. Less than a mile away, an eighty-year-old man, William Barnett, was shot through the heart in Mountjoy Square.[34] Across the city in Lincoln Place, RIC and Auxiliaries ordered a party of civilians to run along the street, then opened fire on them, wounding seven, one mortally.[35] In Capel Street, a seventy-one-year-old man and a fourteen-year-old boy were killed.[36] A British agent working for Col Winter shot himself in Dublin Castle. A huge fire, started accidentally, blazed on the city's southern quays, illuminating the night sky, and was mistakenly associated with the day's events.

For the rest of the night, military and police vehicles 'rattled through the streets; at their approach men and women threw up their hands and ran distractedly about, like frightened hens, or fell on their knees on the pavement'.[37] In one such vehicle, Caroline Woodcock, on her way to visit her wounded husband in King George V Hospital, seething with anger, gaped at the crowds filling Dublin's streets. She felt contempt and hatred that night for those falling to their knees and would happily have seen them shot or worse. As her truck sped and jolted at speed, its driver shouted obscenities at the crowds breaching the revised curfew – most because they were unaware of it – frequently threatening to run people over. The troops accompanying her were itching to fire their weapons. Rounds were chambered; legal protocols and regulations received scant consideration that night. In anticipation of such sentiments, troops not detailed to specific duties had been confined to barracks by an earlier order, their commanders fearing a bloodbath if they were let loose.

Nevertheless, shots and small explosions could be heard all over town. A police car collecting luggage to bring to Dublin Castle from some of the addresses visited that morning by the IRA was fired upon by the military. There were no casualties. Richard Mulcahy had been staying in 36 Ailesbury Road, the imposing home of Anna O'Rahilly, sister of Michael O'Rahilly, gunned down in Moore Street in 1916 during the frenetic GPO evacuation. Despite the availability of a secret room built into the house by Batt O'Connor, Mulcahy feared an imminent raid and consequent capture. He spent the night shivering in a hay loft in a monastery in nearby Donnybrook, walking there innocently linking arms with twenty-one-year-old Sighle Humphreys, Anna O'Rahilly's niece and fellow Cumann na mBan member. Mulcahy soon moved to one of the twenty-two different hideouts afforded to him during the war.[38]

Back in Dublin Castle, at 10 p.m., an Auxiliary entered the guardroom and called out a list of prisoner names. Those called then lined up in a dark narrow corridor leading to the lower yard. Among them was Volunteer Patrick Young. When his name was called he looked around for his cap but could not find it. Dick McKee, nearby, took his own and handed it to him. Young looked at him curiously, to be told, 'I don't think I will want this any more.'[39] Young took the cap and lined up with the others, stunned by what McKee had said. When the Auxiliary was finished, three names remained uncalled: McKee, Clune and Fitzpatrick. The officer then barked the command to move. The twenty-three worn-out prisoners lined up and shuffled along the corridor, Clancy among them. Just then, a shout was heard: 'Stop, hold on a minute.'[40] Capt. Hardy stepped forward from the shadows, limping slowly along the line of prisoners shining a torch into each man's face, asking his name. When Clancy's turn came Hardy recognised him immediately. He wrenched him out of the line, shouted, 'Get over there, you bastard!', and then pushed him back into the guardroom.[41] Hardy then called out Fitzpatrick and told him to take Clancy's place in the line. As Fitzpatrick stood, McKee grabbed him by the arm and muttered, 'If you get through, Fitz, give my love to my mother, sisters and brother.'[42] The words shocked Fitzpatrick. He suspected he would never set eyes on McKee or Clancy again. Nevertheless, he quickly assured McKee that he would pass the message on. He then joined the lined-up men and was marched outside to a truck waiting to transport them to Beggar's Bush.

For the rest of the night McKee, Clancy and Clune suffered continuous beatings. They were interrogated incessantly and at one point confronted by a line of drunken cadets holding rifles and revolvers, who gloated about what was in store for them. McKee, at one point, gave them a cold hard stare and responded contemptuously, saying, 'Go on, and do your worst!'[43]

Towards sunrise, McKee, Clancy and Clune, having not slept for forty-eight hours, stupefied from exhaustion and continued beatings, were ordered to stand. They were then marched to a narrow courtyard leading from F Company's quarters to the military guardroom and told to stand against a wall.[44] They were then shot; McKee by two bullets, Clancy by five, Clune by seven. No precautions had been made to prepare the scene with sandbags beforehand and rounds ricocheted wildly from the wall behind the collapsing three, who died instantly. The blood-drenched bodies were then carried back into the guardroom and placed around its fireplace. The wall against which they had been stood for their final moments was then hosed clean of their spattered blood. Officially, their deaths were recorded as a result of being 'shot while trying to escape' from the guardroom. The IRA Dublin Brigade had lost its commander, Dick McKee, and his most trusted accomplice, Peadar Clancy.

Left to right: Dick McKee, Conor Clune and Peadar Clancy – killed in Dublin Castle during the early morning of 22 November 1920. *(Courtesy of the National Library)*

4

Bloody Sunday: Aftermath

'If you fire sooner there will be no ten seconds'

Early on Monday 22 November, Dan McDonnell walked from his home on Infirmary Road to Crow Street, where IRA intelligence operations resumed. There, a dismal atmosphere hung in the air with the knowledge of McKee's and Clancy's capture, later to drastically worsen with news of their deaths. Meanwhile, the previous day's results against the enemy were discussed with disappointment given that so many agents had slipped through their fingers. Nevertheless, this was tempered with the knowledge that many more had now gone to ground.

Charlie Dalton was exhausted following two sleepless nights. He had woken tortuously time and again the previous night, convinced he could still hear Lt Price's horrific gurgling after he was shot – in reality a tap had been left running.[1] Kevin O'Higgins, the Dáil's deputy local government minister, wrote: 'These times will have more than a passing effect on those who are in close touch with the crude horrors that occur from time to time.'[2]

For some IRA men, the previous day marked their last on active service as they were unable to cope with witnessing further such up-close action. Mick McDonnell and Liam Tobin were also suffering terribly with nerves, Tobin recently having suffered a breakdown. Dan Breen, currently being shifted from place to place following his slow recovery from grievous wounds, admired Tobin's composure under his workload. Nonetheless, his resilience was frayed, as was McDonnell's. Others, conversely, were more enthusiastic about the work, some relishing the notoriety it brought.

Gen. Crozier, viewing the previous day through his contrasting prism, was surprisingly cavalier, as were some of his fellow officers. They had scoffed over Sunday lunch in the Shelbourne about arrogant and pompous intelligence officers thinking they were superior. In any case, Crozier blamed the situation on Sir Henry Wilson's introduction of undercover murder gangs at the beginning of the year and hinted that such gangs were merely being repaid in their own currency. Piaras Béaslaí, as if to concur, wrote justifying the Sunday morning killings in *An tÓglách*, saying: 'We were satisfied that there was a conspiracy to murder Irish citizens, deliberately carried out by the Intelligence Department of the English forces in Ireland.'[3]

Wildly differing accounts of the previous day's events filled newspapers on both sides of the Irish Sea on 22 November. Damning comparisons were made by *The Freeman's Journal* between events in Croke Park and the previous year's Amritsar massacre in India. That day's *Journal* coined the term 'Bloody Sunday'. *The Irish Times*, referring initially to the morning's killings, wrote: 'A country whose capital can be the scene of fourteen callous and cowardly murders on one Sunday morning, has reached a nadir of moral and political degradation.'[4] The newspaper then suggested that those responsible had stolen into the capital posing as football supporters, providing vindication for the military and RIC to converge later upon Croke Park in their pursuit. *The Journal* was later raided and vandalised by Black and Tans, as was the *Irish Independent*; *The Irish Times* was not. This did not stop the *Independent* from going on to claim that: 'Dublin has just passed through a week-end the like of which it has not experienced since 1916.'[5] Liberal British newspapers called for British troops to be brought home and for Ireland to be left to itself but were generally counterbalanced by conservative papers. Noteworthy, however, was the outraged *London Times*, which castigated the forces of the crown, writing: 'An army already perilously undisciplined and a police force avowedly beyond control have defiled by heinous acts the reputation of England.'[6] Dublin Castle's version of events at Croke Park suggested that the military and police had simply deployed to conduct crowd searches following the match and had responded to being fired upon from both inside and outside the stadium, including from the ticket sellers on Jones's Road when they first arrived. Claims were also made that thirty pistols had been found at the stadium. Two inquiries were set up: one a military court of inquiry, held in camera in the Mater Hospital with predominantly police and military witnesses; the other in Jervis Street Hospital under the ROIA, where the witnesses were civilians, medical personnel and victims' relatives.

Similar claims by the authorities of blamelessness were soon applied to the deaths of McKee, Clancy and Clune. Pictures of the Castle guardroom later appeared in *The Graphic* newspaper, betraying an attempt by Dublin Castle's

Public Information Department to depict the brief captivities of the trio as a far more placid affair than that attested to by their fellow prisoners, at least until the three men had, as claimed, brought about their own deaths. Staged photographs appeared: one portraying the three sitting quietly amongst their captors; another, the wreckage strewn from their alleged escape attempt during which, it was claimed, they had thrown hand grenades which failed to explode and seized rifles, resulting in their being killed by return fire.

The Castle was slow to release news of their deaths. Their bodies were due to be transported to King George V Hospital that evening. Before the truck departed, Capt. Hardy, rested and preparing for another night of raids and interrogations, held a lantern over the three corpses' bruised and lacerated faces and 'battered the dead bodies in a maniacal fury' as they lay in the back of the truck.[7] He took one last gloating look and covered them in a canvas sheet.

Michael Collins attended a wedding in Terenure that day. It was subdued. Julia O'Donovan, IRA Adjutant General Gearóid O'Sullivan's aunt, hosted the subsequent reception at her home in 16 Airfield Road, Rathgar. No. 16 was a regular safe house and had been the setting for a conclave of senior IRA personnel the previous month following Seán Treacy's death. That incident's impact had accelerated the audacious plans just executed against British intelligence.

During the reception a group photograph was taken outside the house. Three rows of guests posed; Collins stood second from left at the back, next to O'Donovan herself. Smiles were modest. Collins,

Above: **A staged photo taken of McKee, Clune and Clancy in Dublin Castle.** *(Courtesy of Mercier Archive)*

Right: **Another staged photo depicting the wreckage strewn from their alleged escape attempt.** *(Courtesy of Mercier Archive)*

unsmiling, bowed his head away from the camera. When, afterwards, he received word of McKee's and Clancy's deaths, he was inconsolable, repeating again and again that 'it was over'.

Among the countless venues raided that day and night was Irish Transport and General Workers' Union (ITGWU) headquarters in Liberty Hall. Heavily armed Auxiliaries stormed in and spent hours destroying the premises. Inside they discovered documents, papers, weapons and ammunition belonging to the Irish Citizen Army (ICA), still headquartered there. The Auxiliaries piled a load of the union's papers, banners and flags onto a bonfire outside on Beresford Place. Among those arrested were Thomas Johnson, TUC leader Thomas Farren, and ITGWU General Secretary William O'Brien. These three and others were then taken to the Castle guardroom. The ITGWU was forced to move its HQ to 35 Rutland Square. The ICA shifted its HQ to the Trades Hall on Capel Street.

On Tuesday morning, Pat McCrea walked to Moreland's Cabinet Makers, 10 Upper Abbey Street. Moreland's was being set up as a new IRA Squad HQ. It stood behind large double gates and high walls. Strewn about were 'buckets, fresh shavings, pieces of furniture and tools. Inside, the Squad posed as carpenters, though always carrying concealed weapons under their white aprons.'[8] McCrea passed through a city still in shock. Hospitals were at bursting point, particularly Jervis Street. Many civilians still did not venture out unless necessary. People walked and cycled warily to work, from checkpoint to checkpoint. Officers eyed them up and questioned them. Trams were stopped and searched. Soldiers looked out from transports lumbering from raid to raid, some with remorseful faces, others seething with hate. Some of their former comrades – Irish Great War veterans – cursed the British crown. Service medals were destroyed or burned in anger over the Croke Park killings.[9]

News had arrived at Moreland's the previous evening of McKee's, Clancy's and Clune's deaths. McCrea spoke with Oscar Traynor, acting as brigadier in McKee's place, grappling with grief and anger. Collins, also simmering, had written a dispatch to Traynor instructing that McKee's and Clancy's remains were not to be handled by Black and Tans. Traynor was asked to prepare a small team of less prominent Volunteers to travel to King George V Hospital's mortuary to arrange collection of the bodies, the risk deemed justifiable. McCrea was detailed by Traynor to see to this, but to ensure he did not participate, given his importance to operations.

Since October, Patrick Moylett had been acting as a secret envoy to London on behalf of Arthur Griffith. He had shuttled back and forth from Dublin engaging with the Foreign Office, as well as others acting in a consultational role for the Westminster government, such as novelist H. G. Wells. Recently, a dispatch Moylett had brought from London appeared to tacitly recognise Dáil Éireann. Lloyd George, its author, had introduced the idea of Sinn Féin nominating representatives to speak on the Dáil's behalf if a conference to settle matters could be held. This revelation had reduced Griffith to tears of joy.

Moylett received news of Sunday's killings in Dublin with trepidation, fearing it would unravel his work. He received an urgent dispatch from C. J. Phillips, chief assistant on Irish affairs to Foreign Secretary Lord Curzon, summoning him to the Foreign Office in Downing Street the next morning. On arrival, he had no idea what to expect and anticipated at best a brusque dismissal of further talks. However, Phillips relayed to Moylett an unexpected message from the prime minister 'to keep his head and not to break off the slender link that had been established'.[10]

Meanwhile, panic set in in Westminster. Barricades had stood in Moylett's way in Downing Street. Armed guards were drafted into the House of Commons. Speaking in the House that day, Hamar Greenwood – who had, since Sunday, armed his own private staff – listed the names of officers shot on Sunday morning and graphically detailed their killings. Angry heckles flew from the surrounding benches amid cries for martial law; Lloyd George and Secretary of State for War Churchill looked on. When, afterwards, Irish Parliamentary Party (IPP) Member of Parliament (MP) Joe Devlin angrily asked Greenwood why he had neglected to mention the Croke Park killings, the chamber became a vocal battleground. Greenwood retorted that he had no problem addressing the matter, insisting the police and army had merely sought to conduct searches in Croke Park and were fired on from the crowds, forcing the police to return fire. Greenwood already carried a reputation for misrepresenting events in Ireland. This was pounced upon when it was asked why no one had been arrested, despite the official report into the tragedy stating that thirty pistols had been found at the stadium and the fact that no one knew their current whereabouts. Even the British press picked up on this.[11]

Curiously, the overall attitude betrayed by cabinet ministers towards Sunday morning's assassination victims mirrored General Crozier's serene detachment. Churchill spoke in a more private forum of the officers' apparent recklessness. Lloyd George's attitude was even more striking: asserting that those killed and wounded had been soldiers and such risks simply went with the job, and that it 'served them right to allow themselves to be beaten by a crowd of "Dublin counter-jumpers".'[12] This infuriated Henry Wilson, who baulked at the government's apparent refusal to govern in Ireland. He urged Churchill to declare martial law there for the sake of the Union. Greenwood echoed Churchill's lack of sympathy for Sunday's victims of the IRA, chastising them for carelessness. Greenwood nevertheless reassured Under-Secretary for Ireland John Anderson that he would leave no stone unturned in obtaining adequate resources to reclaim Ireland from the abyss into which they feared the country was descending, just when victory had appeared so close.

Back in Dublin, during Tuesday's late afternoon, Pat McCrea saw the evidence of the treatment of McKee, Clancy and Clune in Dublin Castle when, contrary to orders, he entered King George V Hospital, situated just behind Arbour Hill, to arrange recovery of their bodies. He had only managed to get hold of two others, including intelligence officer Thomas Gay. He drove them close to the hospital, before they parked and walked. On their way in, Black and Tans lurking in the grounds, hearing why they were there, turned their backs in what McCrea considered a 'spirit of decency' and stepped slowly away from the red-brick hospital.[13] Inside the mortuary, McKee's fifty-four-year-old mother, Bridget, his sister, Máire, and his twenty-seven-year-old fiancée, Cumann na mBan member May Gibney, identified his and Clancy's bodies.

The three corpses lay in open coffins and their beaten bodies were examined. McCrea saw a large hole in Clancy's temple and a wound to his throat, both plugged with cotton wool. He observed that Clancy's badly bruised face still bore his particular smile, even in death. McKee's face and head were badly marked. A bullet wound was visible in his neck as well as slash marks on his hands. Clune's torso had taken the multitude of shots that had killed him. Meanwhile, Frank Teeling remained in military custody there, while his stomach wound was treated. In separate wards those wounded by his accomplices were tended to; in the mortuary lay some of their victims.

May Gibney helped McCrea and his two comrades carry McKee's and Clancy's coffins to waiting hearses. Clune's remains, meanwhile, were taken to Quin in County Clare by his employer. A small cortège followed McKee and Clancy to the pro-cathedral. The evening was cold, misty and gloomy, as if 'a sadness' hung over the city.[14]

Collins cycled to the pro-cathedral through a cordon of spies and detectives in the surrounding streets. He had rallied several men around him for the trip, against the emphatic advice of others who saw such a venture as suicide. Collins and his accomplices were, however, determined to see that McKee and Clancy were buried in Volunteer uniforms and carried to their graves in Tricolour-draped coffins. Sympathetic doctors had also been summoned to examine the two bodies.

Two-dozen mourners had gathered in the church, speaking in murmurs. Neatly pressed uniforms bearing McKee's and Clancy's rank insignia had already arrived. Candles flickered in the vault as the two coffin lids were slowly removed. The doctors then examined the bodies. Helpers reverently turned them to facilitate this. Gaping holes revealed they had been shot at point-blank range.[15] Both bodies were then dressed in their uniforms before their coffins were nailed shut. The clergy did not want their lacerated and bruised faces visible during the funeral mass. Collins appeared listless with grief, as did others.

McKee's and Clancy's funeral took place on Thursday 25 November, following requiem mass at the cathedral. Collins brought a wreath to the ceremony, which read: 'In memory of two good friends – Dick and Peadar – two of Ireland's best soldiers. Mícéal Ó Coileáin'.[16] Afterwards, Collins, assisted by Frank Thornton, Tom Cullen and Gearóid O'Sullivan, carried the Tricolour-draped coffins to their waiting hearses outside on Marlboro Street.[17] An *Evening Herald* photographer photographed Collins; its offices were later visited and its presses smashed up, copies were recalled and distributing newsagents visited by IRA teams to ensure his picture did not fall into enemy hands.

Massive crowds lined Sackville Street as the hearses, covered in flowers and each drawn by four jet-black horses, made their way northbound towards Glasnevin Cemetery. There, McKee and Clancy were buried side by side in the growing Republican Plot. Hundreds of Volunteers marched behind, formed into companies, each comprising four single columns. Officers marched at their front as they stepped together somberly behind their beloved brigadier and his indispensable comrade.

The huge turnout of IRA members, despite a decree from Dublin Castle stipulating that there were to be 'no flags, banners or public displays' that day, was facilitated by the absence of enemy forces owing to a slew of other funerals in Dublin resulting from Sunday's killings.[18] Thursday 25 November was the day that ten of Sunday morning's victims were carried in Union Jack-draped coffins – each covered in floral tributes and mounted on gun carriages – along Dublin's quays, to be ferried across the Irish Sea for funerals in Britain. Their passage was marked with grandeur and formality, and attended by officials of all grades and statures, journalists, the military and tens of thousands of civilians.

The Dublin ceremonies were conspicuously grandiose. Each carriage was pulled by six horses, with each lead animal flanked on its left by a mounted cavalryman and three cavalrymen driving each team. Crossley Tenders driven behind gun carriages transported the bodies of three Black and Tans recently killed elsewhere in the country. A huge turnout of military and police lined the route of the first of two processions, which travelled from King George V Hospital to North Wall Quay. As the cortège left the hospital, commands sounded out from military subalterns and NCOs – 'Rest on Arms Reversed' – directed at reverent single lines of British troops flanking the cortège on either side, heads in steel helmets bowed, rifle barrels resting on their impeccably polished right boots and held firmly vertically by overlaid hands at chest height. Officers, uniforms similarly starched and polished, wearing black armbands, stood fast nearby, saluting.

The second procession made its way from the city's south side, passing Stephen's Green, travelling through a cordon of Union Jacks at half-mast along Grafton Street, eventually joining the first procession at the Custom House. Civilians lining its route removed caps and hats to the sound of horse hooves and carriage wheels on cobblestones as carriages passed followed by mourners, females among them wearing black veils.

The procession along the quays was meticulous, with military drummers and pipers. Cavalry squadrons paraded. Hundreds of additional soldiers joined them, marching with arms reversed between right arms and ribcages, others with hands rigidly at their sides, along with Royal Air Force (RAF) and naval personnel. RIC members took their places in formations, arms reversed, but with rifles wedged underneath left arms, distinguishing them from the military. The DMP provided cordons, with each man spread eight feet apart to control the crowds. Other DMP units marched in the procession.

Bridges were blocked and tram services cancelled. Prominent Protestant clergymen stood along the procession's length with senior members of the judiciary, barristers, civil servants and Dublin Castle staff. Senior Catholic clergymen were, however, notably absent. RAF Airco DH.9A light bombers and Bristol F.2 Fighters flew overhead, engines humming, as John Anderson and Andy Cope, themselves flanked by senior administrators, looked on from an O'Connell Bridge thronged with thousands, the hum from their subdued exchanges tapering away as the lengthy procession slowly passed them towards North Wall Quay and the awaiting S Class Destroyer HMS *Sea Wolf*. There, each coffin was lifted slowly from its carriage and carried by six military pall-bearers, flanked once again by infantrymen resting on arms reversed, police and military officers again saluting. Twelve-man sections stood in the background, arms presented. An officer directed pall-bearers to a ramp to board ship. A band on the destroyer played the Last Post.[19] Its naval complement lined up on deck, caps removed.

Thousands of civilians watched from the quays between Kingsbridge and the Custom House, a great many harassed, harried and beaten by Auxiliaries forcefully removing caps and hats from those refusing to do so and hurling them into the Liffey. Eventually an armada of hats flowed seaward on the outbound tide, as if mocking HMS *Sea Wolf* as she lurched from the quayside.

Sgt Fitzgerald – killed in 28 Earlsfort Terrace – was buried in Glasnevin Cemetery the previous day, as was Capt. McCormack, killed in the Gresham. Fitzgerald's coffin was also draped in a Union Jack and carried on a gun carriage. Auxiliaries acted as pall-bearers and carried wreaths. A small procession including Fitzgerald's relatives followed. Shots were fired over his grave following a playing of the Last Post. Within days the man he had been mistaken for by Lt Byrne's IRA unit, Lt Col Fitzpatrick, resigned his military commission in fear of his life and left the city.

Businesses across the city were told to close on Thursday 25 out of respect. Those that did not received unwelcome visits from Auxiliaries.

Many of those killed in Croke Park were buried in Glasnevin and elsewhere that day, as well as on preceding and subsequent days. Masses took place throughout the city, as did more modest funeral processions. IRA Volunteers fired shots over Joseph Traynor's grave in Bluebell. A volley was fired over Michael Hogan's grave in Grangemockler in Tipperary. British soldiers drafted in to maintain order had presented arms and saluted Hogan's coffin as it passed through Clonmel's streets the previous day; a gesture of respect to a fallen enemy mirroring other similarly poignant displays.[20]

Police and military raids ratcheted up in Dublin and elsewhere. The palpable sense of tension, escalating for months, hung oppressively in the capital's air like a fog. Dublin County Council's offices, situated in 10–11 Rutland Square, were among dozens of buildings raided on the day of the vast funerals. Kevin O'Higgins, who was lucky to have been filtered through several recent police cordons, had only just moved his office and staff onto the council building's top floor following a raid on his ministry's offices in 29 Wicklow Street. When all the building's staff was lined up on the ground floor, council workers instinctively shuffled away from O'Higgins and his colleagues, sensing they were the reason for the raid; their trepidation at being associated magnified by the sound of furniture and glass being smashed throughout the building, followed by assaults on anyone the Auxiliaries deemed suspicious. Council staff were hit in the face with pistol butts and kicked. O'Higgins had a pistol barrel shoved into his face by an officer demanding his name. O'Higgins replied 'Wilson' – his pseudonym. He was then asked how he would like the contents of the officer's pistol emptied into his ribcage. O'Higgins' response: 'Well I would hardly feel the last half-dozen of them', referring to bullets, got him punched in the face.[21] O'Higgins' bravado masked his fears that the seizure of his department's files and his own arrest could see the effective collapse of the Dáil's Local Government department, which he had been running since William Cosgrave had recently gone into hiding among the clergy in the Wicklow Mountains. The files lay strewn and gathered between desks on the top floor, but luck favoured O'Higgins. The raiders instead sought council finance books, which had not been submitted for a Castle audit. They seized these and departed, blissfully unaware of what they had overlooked. Ironically, the IRA later returned the favour by stealing the finance records necessary for future Castle audits. The Rutland Square raid followed another across the road the previous day on the General Post Office (GPO), still operating in the Rotunda grounds. A huge amount of mail was seized and brought to Dublin Castle for examination.

Soon it was Paddy Daly's turn to be arrested. He had been on a tram heading to Clontarf on Thursday evening when the conductor warned everyone that Fairview was blocked off by Tans conducting searches. A similar search had even seen William Wylie, Dublin

Kevin O'Higgins, the Dáil's indefatigable deputy local government minister. *(Courtesy of the National Library of Ireland)*

Castle Law Adviser, ordered off a tram at pistol point with the words: 'Come down yer bloody Irish Barsterd.'[22] Daly made his way on foot to 10 Bessborough Avenue in North Strand, home of Michael Love, where Daly's son was also staying. Love was married to Daly's late wife's sister. At midnight he heard people jumping into the small backyard, their jingle of equipment betraying that they were military. Daly had a gun safely stashed in the bungalow, but asked Love if he too had any arms. Love said no. Daly then answered the door to face a cordon of bayonets. An officer asked for Mick Love. Love identified himself. The officer asked: 'F Company, 2nd Battalion?' Love sarcastically replied that he had been in 2nd Company years earlier when the late John Redmond commanded the Volunteers, most of whom had joined the British Army during the Great War. The officer apologetically told Love he had orders to arrest him, regardless.

Then came Daly's turn. He insisted he was a widower, staying there with his son because the curfew prevented him from going home. Dick McCarthy, a policeman accompanying the raiders, reassured the officer, when asked about Daly: 'Is he a Shinner?', that he was simply a widower with no political connections. A house search revealed nothing. Const. McCarthy took the time to discreetly inform Daly that his Clontarf address, 5 Cecil Avenue, was still a safe one; Clontarf DMP station, under C Division, had no knowledge of Daly.[23]

Daly's luck did not last, however. Another raid at 2 a.m. the following morning saw him nabbed by a cranky but diminutive army officer, who explained to Daly that he too was looking for Michael Love. The house was again searched, revealing nothing. Daly protested that Love had already been arrested. The officer simply replied that he could not trust him, so he was placed in a truck with other arrested Volunteers.[24]

Minutes later, as their small convoy passed the nearby Five Lamps, a Tender of Black and Tans pulled up alongside. Its commander demanded the prisoners be handed over. The army officer's foul-mouthed reaction surprised the prisoners, as well as the Tans. He referred to the latter as 'jail-birds' and 'dirt'. When the response was indignant, the army officer commanded his Lewis gunner to train his weapon on the Tans' vehicle. As the distinctive drainpipe-like weapon with its circular forty-seven round horizontal ammunition pan was swivelled and cocked, the officer, gaining Daly's respect, pulled out his pocket watch and, following another salvo of expletives, commanded them to: 'Move, or I fire in ten seconds. If you fire sooner there will be no ten seconds.' The Tender drove away. To Daly's surprise, the officer then turned to him, his rancour expended, and suggested humorously that he assumed Daly and the others would sooner be under the custody of the military than the Tans. He replaced his pocket watch and took out a cigarette case, snapped it open and handed Daly and the others a cigarette each. Daly, a non-smoker, handed the cigarette to an infantryman guarding him. The prisoners were then brought to Portobello Barracks where, fifteen minutes later, the officer jokingly informed the sergeant in charge that he had another four 'Michael Loves' for him, laughingly adding: 'You had better keep all the Love you can get.' He ordered the sergeant to prepare tea for the prisoners given that it was so cold.[25] Daly spent three nights in Portobello before being transferred to Arbour Hill Prison.

Arthur Griffith was arrested at his home, 122 St Lawrence Road in Clontarf, at 3 a.m. on Friday 26 November – one hour after Daly – in one of 500 raids across Dublin that week which also netted Dáil members Eoin MacNeill and Éamonn Duggan. Griffith's arrest, by order of Gen. Boyd of Dublin District Command, despite explicit orders not to arrest him having been issued the previous month, provoked a backlash from Sir John Anderson and Lloyd George, who saw it as 'an intrusion of the military arm into the area of political prerogative'.[26] Gen. Macready, still on holiday, weighed in, justifying the arrest as providing leverage against the IRA threatening his own military subordinates. Macready painted a grim picture of what might happen to the city should such an action materialise. Further justification was forwarded that Griffith, clearly a moderate, could be protected from reprisals in prison and – prophetically – that his confinement provided a means of isolating him until he might be wheeled out should negotiations begin – an increasingly attractive option to the British since the previous Sunday.

Meanwhile, Patrick Moylett had been in continuous daily contact with the Foreign Office. When word got out in London of Griffith's arrest, Moylett and C. J. Phillips were inching towards the tentative prospect of a peace conference. This had all but foundered when the British insisted that there would be no amnesty for either Dan Breen or Michael Collins in such an event. Moylett, however, protested that the alternative was no peace at all. He highlighted the hurdles facing both camps hindering a truce, insisting that the British would have to act first in standing down their forces, and that even this might not be enough to assuage the hatred felt by the victims of crown atrocities to get them to consider a ceasefire. Matters progressed nevertheless, with assurances – quickly to be proven empty – that Griffith and MacNeill would soon be released.

On the same date as Daly's and Griffith's arrests, Galway was the setting for an episode underscoring Moylett's reference to widespread hatred. Following the killing of a local policeman, two brothers – twenty-two-year-old Harry and twenty-nine-year-old Patrick Loughnane – both Sinn Féin activists and IRA members, were arrested by Auxiliaries from D Company while working on their family farm. Their bodies were discovered days later in a bog. Both had been beaten, then tied together and forced to run behind a lorry until they collapsed from exhaustion, then dragged until almost dead. They were then beaten again by Black and Tans before being shot. Their bodies were burned and dumped in muddy water to which oil was added to further obscure any possibility of discovery. When their bodies were eventually found despite this, a local doctor discovered the letters 'IV' carved into their flesh and assumed it stood for Irish Volunteers. Both of Patrick's legs, arms and wrists were broken, and his skull fractured. Deep diamond-shaped wounds resembling Auxiliary cap badges were found on his torso. Harry's right arm was broken and almost severed. Two fingers were missing. The doctor suggested that hand grenades had exploded in both men's mouths, such was the extent of their facial mutilations.

On the day after the Loughnane brothers' arrests, 27 November, long-standing IRA designs on Liverpool docks were realised when more than £500,000 worth of damage was inflicted in arson attacks. Fifteen cotton warehouses and timber yards were gutted in conflagrations visible for miles. Further incendiary raids took place throughout the city and a civilian was shot dead during a gun battle with Merseyside police.[27] IRA engineer John Plunkett had crossed the Irish Sea weeks earlier and expended considerable effort alongside local IRA officer Tom Kerr in studying the docks area and planning such an attack. This was done in conjunction with Rory O'Connor, IRA Officer Commanding (O/C) Britain, during the weeks preceding the raid on Richard Mulcahy's safe house in Longwood Avenue, during which the plans were subsequently discovered. Nevertheless, despite this setback, Kerr, a member of a Liverpool family with strong ties to Irish republicanism, along with his brother, Patrick, and father, Neill senior, oversaw the attacks with revised plans. The family, based in Liverpool's Scotland Road, were behind almost every arms and ammunition transaction that passed through the city's docklands en route to Ireland, as well as assisting in smuggling fugitives. Neill Kerr junior had been killed in September during a firearms accident. The attack was not without drawbacks for the IRA, however; Neill senior and Tom were arrested and incarcerated afterwards. Nonetheless, the assault's propaganda impact was colossal. Even better news was to follow.

Shortly after 4 p.m., Sunday 28 November, thirty-six IRA Volunteers of the recently formed 3rd West Cork flying column ambushed and killed sixteen Auxiliaries from C Company on a narrow, winding, remote roadway in Kilmichael, six miles south-west of Macroom, from where the Auxiliaries had driven in two Crossley Tenders. Tom Barry, the twenty-three-year-old column commandant and former British Army NCO, planned and oversaw this daring and well-executed ambush. He had deployed the column the previous Sunday and had been scouting suitable ambush locations ever since. This particular location left no margin for error. It afforded no line of retreat; the fight was to the finish.

Since August that year Auxiliaries had arrogantly patrolled in Cork wherever they saw fit, such was the fear they instilled. This changed after Kilmichael, when it became clear that they could be beaten. The ambush was a brutal, close-quarter affair. Barry deployed three sections, using his tactical experience, in mutually supporting positions and only lost a single man to enemy gunfire while subduing the Auxiliaries. Two more were then lost when Auxiliaries shot them after initially surrendering. Barry, enraged, immediately ordered his men to kill the entire enemy. However, one escaped and fled to a house several miles away. He was later tracked, shot dead and buried in a bog. One wounded Auxiliary survived, having been left for dead with several bullet wounds, one to the head.

The tremors from Kilmichael quickly shook Dublin Castle. This was the first time an entire British patrol was wiped out by the IRA. The fact that the Auxiliary unit was part of their own elite vanguard increased the trepidation that rapidly spread to Westminster. Typically, reprisals followed throughout Cork. In Fermoy, drunken Auxiliaries accosted forty-four-year-old hotelier and former British Army captain Nicholas Prendergast in the Royal Hotel, beat him severely about the head and threw him into the nearby Blackwater River, where he died. The Auxiliaries kept drinking after this incident, before burning several of the town's buildings. When the Fire Brigade arrived they slashed their hoses. The following night, a local shopkeeper was thrown into the same river and shot at but escaped. Soon afterwards, a statement was issued from Auxiliary HQ in Macroom Castle warning local civilians not to be seen with hands in their pockets; such apparently suspicious behaviour would see them shot on sight.

Back in Dublin, the end of November saw a subdued meeting of the IRA Army Council. Such conclaves were convened weekly and this one was held at 4 Upper Ely Place. The anguish over McKee's and Clancy's deaths was palpable. Cathal Brugha instructed Oscar Traynor that he was to replace McKee as brigadier. Traynor replied that he would prefer election by his fellow officers to simple assignment to the post, which he would then accept without hesitation. This was agreed. A vote was scheduled for the following week.[28]

December kicked off with the activation of countrywide motor restrictions. Motorists could only operate motor vehicles within very specific times and areas.[29] Meanwhile, the same day saw an attack by F Company, 2nd Battalion IRA, on a military truck making its way from Dollymount to the city centre, the after-effects of which could have proved disastrous to their own leadership.

Shortly before 8 p.m., Lt Daniel Ryan deployed several three-man sections along North Strand Road close to Newcomen Bridge to attack the truck that passed there each evening at roughly the same time. They concealed themselves in the darkness behind a granite wall between the road and the lower pavement on the road's eastern side, adjacent to the bridge. Their wait for the truck was a nervous one, fearing local informants. Nevertheless, the truck arrived on schedule. Each attacker carried a pistol, Ryan had a semi-automatic and a Mills grenade. As the truck lumbered slowly up the hill from Fairview towards the bridge, the attackers pounced. Several shots rang out. Ryan hurled his bomb, which exploded, wounding several soldiers. The attackers made their escape, under ragged return fire, onto Ossory Road.

However, approaching Newcomen Bridge soon after the attack was a car containing Michael Collins, David Neligan, Ned Broy and Jim McNamara, en route to the city from a meeting in Thomas Gay's home in 8 Haddon Road, Clontarf. Approaching, they were halted by a patrol on North Strand. Collins, typically, stepped out, primed to approach and bluff the nervous-looking officer in charge. Broy saved him the trouble. Displaying his identification he called to Collins: 'Step in Sergeant!'[30] Fortunately for them, the officer then advised them not to proceed, warning of enemy in the area. They turned and drove off.

Paddy Daly was still incarcerated in Arbour Hill, where he shared a tiny cell with two others, including twenty-two-year-old Thomas Whelan, a Connemara man living in Dublin's Barrow Street. Whelan was with the 3rd Battalion. Whelan revealed to Daly that he had been identified as a participant in the killing of Capt. Baggallay in Baggot Street on Bloody Sunday, one of his accusers the naked man momentarily held under guard by Jack Foley on that day, who was, indeed, a soldier. Whelan had actually been at mass in Ringsend during the killings. Daly, initially suspecting that he had been planted in his cell as a spy to glean information from him, a common ruse, innocently asked Whelan why he had become mixed up in a thing like that. Whelan shrugged, asserting that he could hardly call himself mixed up when he had never even fired a shot.

Daly played his next card, asking: 'Don't you think these shootings are terrible?', adding: 'I don't belong to any of these things.'[31]

Whelan's response impressed Daly. He suggested that, as an Irishman, despite having never fired a weapon, he might be able to save a good soldier's life by taking his place on the scaffold. Daly responded, saying: 'God bless the mother that reared you.'[32] Daly felt guilty for having deceived him but could not risk giving his IRA involvement away for fear of putting Const. McCarthy at risk. Notably, a hangman's noose indeed awaited Whelan.

December had also commenced with discussions between Gen. Jeudwine and Hamar Greenwood regarding the proposed implementation of martial law throughout Ireland. Preparations accelerated. The conclusion of recent US presidential elections removed a significant propaganda hurdle, where the huge Irish-American lobby could have been used as leverage against Britain. The bombshell of Kilmichael furthered its case dramatically as far as the military and Westminster cabinet were concerned. Nonetheless, reservations lingered.

The advantages of martial law to the military were clearly spelled out by Jeudwine, a proven tactician with an impressive record. They included: unity of command, swiftness of action and administration, lengthy sentencing for arms possession or for harbouring rebels, restriction of movement, easier identification of individuals, control of the press/censorship, internment and, finally, moral effect.[33] Jeudwine further advocated greater naval assistance for the army, combined with preparations for interning over 5,000 IRA suspects, a seductive proposition for the chief secretary. Proclamations were soon drawn up declaring that a 'state of armed insurrection' existed, which placed the Irish military garrison officially on active service, thus unshackling it from inconvenient civil legal restraints.[34] The British Army's judge advocate general, however, did not view things so simply, portraying demarcation lines between civil and military authority as unclear and laced with legal pitfalls, a situation worsened by the advent of police and paramilitary reinforcements running amok.

The British government still feared a public backlash to martial law. Therefore, vacillation persisted, reinforced by fears of an unconstrained military – or at least elements of it – unleashing brutality in Ireland more commonplace in distant colonies. It was feared that this would render it impossible to restore civil order afterwards on an island with such close proximity to the very land that saw itself as a beacon of civil order – Great Britain. Consequently, the situation was steered instead towards a reduced measure of martial law restricted to certain Munster counties. Moreover, it was felt that not putting Dublin under martial law would enable communication channels for Sir John Anderson, Mark Sturgis and Andy Cope to be maintained, as the three awaited opportunities to negotiate surreptitiously with Sinn Féin's moderates.

Such negotiations had attained greater urgency since Bloody Sunday. In the last week of November, Patrick Moylett appeared to have been making further progress with the Foreign Office towards a truce. C. J. Phillips had even suggested publicly announcing a proposed arrangement on the night of Saturday 27 November. He also conceded that any amnesty would more than likely apply to Collins and Breen. Burdened with terrific responsibility, Moylett, following a sleepless night, spent Saturday with Phillips ironing out the details of the proposed truce. Moylett was eventually instructed to return to Downing Street on Monday morning to collect a safe conduct to see him to Dublin carrying its details. However, he arrived in Downing Street to be told by Phillips that 'Lloyd George had led off on a new set of cards'; in other words – all bets were off.[35] Phillips clarified the situation to a dumbstruck Moylett in strict confidence: word had just arrived from Dublin Castle that the entire executive there would resign if arrangements with Moylett were effected. Instead, they themselves were planning contact through a different intermediary: the archbishop of Perth, Australia: Dr Patrick Clune. Clune was to be asked to mediate between Sinn Féin and the British government. They sensed that he would procure Dublin Castle a more favourable deal.

Clune, currently in England, had acted as Catholic chaplain general to the Australian forces during the Great War. Coincidentally, he was also the late Conor Clune's uncle. He had been staying in Ennis, Co. Clare, with the bishop of Killaloe, Dr Michael Fogarty, in September, when Black and Tans had killed six people and sacked Lahinch and nearby Miltown Malbay. When Joe Devlin, MP, proposed arranging a meeting with Clune and Lloyd George to convey the brutality being visited upon Ireland, Clune accepted, as did the prime minister. The timing was opportune for the latter: Friday 26 November had seen the publication of an appeal by Archbishop Gilmartin of Tuam for a 'truce of god'.[36] This had followed an earlier appeal from the same archbishop for a truce in conjunction with Home Rule. The archbishop also wrote similarly to Winston Churchill. When his appeals were then endorsed by Cardinal Logue, archbishop of Armagh and primate of all Ireland, as well as Archbishop Walsh of Dublin, the prospect of mediation via the Catholic hierarchy seemed attractive both to Dublin Castle and Westminster. Both centres of British rule were then further tantalised by a letter to *The Times* proposing peace from, of all people, a prominent Sinn Féin supporter – former IPP MP John Sweetman. Disconcertingly for those at the revolution's helm, many more of these unwelcome overtures were to follow.

5

Divisions, Peace Talks, Raids and Continued Killings

'I will put a bullet through you'

On Saturday 4 December, former commanding officer of the IRA's Mid-Galway Brigade, Joseph Howley, took a train to Dublin from Galway, where the authorities were pursuing him. He planned to meet up with Thomas 'Baby' Duggan, Galway Brigade quartermaster, and Jack Comer, on his arrival in Dublin, and lodge with the pair. Once established, Duggan would introduce Howley to GHQ. Paddy Mullins, East Mayo brigade commander, accompanied Howley on the four-hour journey.

The pair were spotted entering Galway station by plain-clothed RIC men monitoring arrivals and departures, as they did constantly. A sergeant named Healy was ordered to board the train, observe them and identify them to detectives carrying out surveillance at Dublin Broadstone. However, when the train stopped at Athlone, a streetwise ticket inspector, Joe Henigan, boarded. Henigan, an IRA sympathiser, quickly suspected that Howley and Mullins were not on their way to the capital on civilian business.

As the train neared Broadstone, Henigan approached Howley and Mullins and discreetly suggested they get off early. He had just arranged for the train to slow down on its approach to enable this.[1] However, Howley refused, suspecting it was a trap. His decision was about to cost him his life.

When the train rolled slowly into Broadstone, Mullins sensed something was wrong. As it stopped, he quietly appealed to Howley to at least alight onto the opposite platform. Howley remained dismissive. Mullins took his own advice and alighted onto the track side. Then, quickly scanning around, he strode unobserved to the platform opposite. Howley alighted with the other passengers, observed by Sgt Healy.

Healy then quietly approached four silent, onlooking men, assuming correctly they were also police. Detectives watching train stations were operating in groups of four since the killing of Const. Laurence Dalton by the Squad the previous April near Broadstone. Healy introduced himself and pointed Howley out. The four sprang into action, flicking cigarettes away, reaching into their coat pockets as Howley stepped from the terminus, oblivious. Mullins remained in the station. He then heard four shots and momentarily stood powerless among startled passengers before they were directed by staff and police to either board the return train or exit the station. On his way out, Mullins saw Howley slumped in a pool of blood, his eyes open and lifeless, four bullet holes in his back. The detectives' cover story was a familiar one: the suspect was 'shot while attempting to escape from arrest'.[2] Elsewhere that night, guided by the RIC, Black and Tans shot forty-two-year-old Thomas Hand several times in the head and chest. Hiding out at his family home in Baltrasna, Skerries, IRA member Hand was shot having escaped through his bedroom window into the house's back garden as it was being raided. Hand was also a republican judge and the second IRA man, the first being twenty-two-year-old John Sherlock, to be killed by Black and Tans in the surrounding area since the killing of William 'Jack' Straw. Straw, a British spy, was shot by the IRA following the infamous sacking of Balbriggan in September.

Joseph Howley had been at Comdt Liam Mellows' side during the 1916 Rising in Galway. Mellows, twenty-eight-years-old and the son of an avowedly unionist father, had recently returned from the USA, having fled there in autumn 1916 and worked to procure arms ever since. Mellows resided in 131 Morehampton Road, a guest of Mary (Molly) Woods, a close associate of Michael Collins. Mellows was IRA director of purchases, his office situated in 11 Westland Row, a role that saw him come into conflict with Collins.[3]

The seeds of this clash had been germinating for some time. Cathal Brugha had developed a dislike for Collins' penchant for sticking his nose into areas where others held responsibility, whilst Collins' own station remained impenetrable. Brugha also mistrusted the IRB. A great deal of arms procurement was carried out by the IRB, under Collins. Brugha decided to call Collins out over what he perceived as obscurities within arms purchases accounts. These had materialised after a raid on a house where Tom Cullen had concealed account ledgers detailing arms purchases from Glasgow, subsequently found by the enemy. Mellows, as director of purchases, took Brugha's side. The result saw a practical halt to arms and ammunition procurement to review the books at a moment the IRA could ill afford it, particularly given the recent arrests of the Kerrs in Liverpool and the death of Peadar Clancy. Clancy had, for some time, overseen an arms-smuggling operation from Manchester, Chester and Liverpool.

Meanwhile, further divisions surfaced. From his Dublin Castle office, Gen. Boyd that same week submitted a memorandum to the War Office of a meeting between himself, Frederick Dumont and a senior, but anonymous, IRA source who had, apparently, claimed the IRA had lost faith in both their own political leaders and in Lloyd George, and were seeking direct peace discussions with the military. When Sir Henry Wilson saw the report he called yet again for immediate martial law, eager to exploit such apparent discord.

In addition, on 3 December, six members of Galway County Council issued a statement repudiating the Dáil's authority and offering their own services to mediate for peace. The statement read: 'We view with sorrow and grief the shootings, burnings, reprisals and counter-reprisals taking place all over England and Ireland by armed forces of the Irish Republic.'[4] The fact that Sinn Féin held a majority of council seats and that the meeting from which the statement had emanated did not have a quorum meant nothing; its release meant the damage was done. Unionists in the city and elsewhere were delighted, more so when Galway Urban District Council followed suit, justifying a similar resolution as a cry for action given that Dáil members were either locked up or on the run.[5] Then, Westmeath County Council announced a meeting to discuss the prospect of resubmitting its accounts to Dublin Castle. However, the meeting was cancelled, presumably, some suspected, under IRA duress. These setbacks rode on the back of another letter published in newspapers recently from John Sweetman's son, Roger, Teachta Dála (TD) for Wexford North. He wrote that he was 'absolutely convinced that the methods of warfare being employed are deplorable in their results to our country, both from a material as well as a moral standpoint'.[6]

Then, on 6 December, a telegram from Fr Michael O'Flanagan, Sinn Féin vice-president – albeit in a marginalised capacity – to Lloyd George was widely published. It addressed recent peace overtures and read: 'You state that you are willing to make peace at once without waiting for Christmas. Ireland is also waiting. What first step do you propose?'[7] That day, desperate to parry the prospect of further such setbacks, Arthur Griffith wrote from prison to Dáil Cabinet Secretary and IRA Director of Organisation Diarmuid O'Hegarty, asking him to contact Collins and Brugha and get them to instruct local authorities not to put their 'foot in it' by following Galway's example.[8] It was into this maelstrom that fifty-eight-year-old Archbishop Clune ventured upon arrival in Dublin on the mail boat, disguised as Revd Doctor Walsh; mediators, even acting on behalf of the prime minister, risked incurring the wrath of gunmen from both sides in this war. Clune was taken initially to All Hallows College in Drumcondra. From there he was driven to the Gresham Hotel to meet Archbishop Fogarty, who would be at his side during meetings soon to be convened with, among others, Collins. Fogarty had been telegraphed about Clune's imminent arrival by Archbishop Daniel Mannix, still in England, having been dramatically refused entry to Ireland during August. Mannix's telegram inadvertently saved Bishop Fogarty's life; while Fogarty was in Dublin to meet Clune, his home in Clare was raided by Auxiliaries with blackened faces. The bishop was a known Sinn Féin sympathiser as well as a Dáil Loan trustee. When told by servants that the bishop was not there, they had torn through the house, even searching under beds for him, before making off with some papers and the archbishop's whiskey.[9] The flagrant attempt on Fogarty's life horrified Gen. Crozier when he heard of it. He was told by a confidant that the bishop's potential killers had planned to drown him in the River Shannon in a sack.

On the evening of Monday 6 December, Joe O'Reilly called to the Gresham to inform Clune that a driver would collect him at All Hallows the following day and drive him to meet Collins. O'Reilly warned the archbishop that he would be driven circuitously to the meeting to throw off any unwanted pursuers.

The next day Clune finally met Collins, having remarked as his car pulled up outside Dr Robert Farnan's gynaecological practice in 5 Merrion Square that respectable Georgian Dublin was the last place he expected to be meeting revolutionaries. Collins travelled there by bicycle. The meeting was a nervous one. As they spoke upstairs in the consultation room, the premises was visited by Auxiliaries. Dr Farnan, forty-seven-years-old, was warned they were at the door. Terrified, he answered, only to be handed a letter from a cadet written by the latter's wife, whom Farnan had been treating. When Clune met Collins again for a subsequent discussion, they had been walking down the building's staircase to its wide-open hallway together when the huge front door opened to reveal a truckload of Auxiliaries patrolling slowly outside. Collins, anticipating a raid, hid behind the door, pistol cocked, before escaping out the house's rear garden. Clune was impressed.

Clune moved between Dublin city and Killiney, twelve miles away, where he stayed at 'Ard Einin', the luxurious home of solicitor Sir John O'Connell. O'Reilly cycled there with dispatches. Andy Cope arranged meetings in Mountjoy Prison for the archbishop, again accompanied by Archbishop Fogarty. Clune carried messages to Griffith from both Archbishop Mannix and Art O'Brien, Dáil envoy to Britain. He met with Eoin MacNeill, as well as Alderman and IRA Director of Supply Michael Staines, the latter having just been arrested by 'Tiny' King during an Auxiliary raid on City Hall during which the entire surrounding area was fenced in by dense barbed-wire entanglements resembling a battlefield. Griffith consulted Staines to assess the potential IRA reaction to a truce. Staines assured him that as long as the IRA could keep its arms its members should be agreeable.

Clune was stirred by Andy Cope's desire for a truce and felt it marked him out from other hawkish Castle players. He also detected that Griffith was the most amenable within Sinn Féin to a truce, the terms of which Clune then drafted for Dublin Castle, before returning to London to meet Lloyd George. His departure left behind an exasperated Mark Sturgis; baffled that Clune had managed so effortlessly to meet the very man the entire combined Dublin Castle and military intelligence apparatus could not detect – Collins. On his voyage, Clune received unexpected feedback for his truce proposals from an unlikely source – Cope. He was unwillingly travelling among a party of Castle officials who appeared eager to convey to Lloyd George that the timing for a truce was wrong because they had the IRA all but beaten. Cope expected Lloyd George to dig his heels in having heard them, which disheartened him, a fact he divulged to Clune after they accidentally met on the ship's deck.[10]

Cope's instincts were correct. Clune's proposals foundered, principally over two key sticking points: that the Dáil was to be permitted to meet freely and that the IRA would keep its arms. The impression that Sinn Féin and the IRA were disjointed saw Lloyd George demand otherwise, given his perceived stronger hand. On 9 December, with Gen. Macready and John Anderson sat among his cabinet, Lloyd George professed his determination to 'break up these terrorists'. Martial law was finally to be announced for the counties of Cork, Tipperary, Kerry and Limerick. Macready suggested waiting two weeks before implementing this to allow further appeals to the Irish clergy to urge the IRA to surrender its arms once and for all. He also persuaded the cabinet to concede in principle that if he thought it necessary to widen the martial law area, he could do so without further cabinet sanction. Field Marshal Wilson was effervescent with the news and wrote: 'It is the beginning of the Government governing.'[11] Nevertheless, Lloyd George discreetly approached Archbishop Clune again and asked him to return to Dublin to continue secret negotiations. Clune agreed.

Meanwhile, back in Dublin on the same day, rebel leaders were retaliating. Griffith compared this crucial moment for Ireland's destiny with pivotal points in the American Revolution when victory was snatched from the jaws of defeat, quoting George Washington with the words: 'Patriots, stand fast.' Collins wrote several letters to the *Irish Independent* warning of the Irish people being railroaded by 'false promises' and stressing the need to avoid 'foolish and ill-timed actions'. He also wrote of 'a lot of foolish people here talking peace', before paraphrasing Griffith with the words 'stand fast'. Their publication saw yet another raid on the newspaper by the police.[12] Collins and Diarmuid O'Hegarty also met with Patrick Moylett at Phil Shanahan's pub in Dublin's notorious 'Monto' red-light district, Moylett considering it the filthiest pub he had ever set foot in. Collins urged Moylett to get word to Fr O'Flanagan to reign himself in, while angrily castigating the cleric.[13] Collins later relayed criticism of Moylett to Griffith, having only recently expressed satisfaction at his work; the frustration and pressure on Collins was telling.

The same week saw the verdict of the military court of inquiry into the Croke Park massacre. The proceedings' records were, however, to be kept secret.[14] The inquiry concluded that firing had come initially from civilians within and around the stadium, apparently to warn of a raid and create a panic to facilitate escaping IRA members. Gunshot wounds, it was claimed, had been inflicted by small arms fire from the canal end by the RIC firing excessively and without orders, mostly over the crowd's heads, but in some cases at suspected IRA fugitives. No firing was attributed to the military other than warning shots from the armoured car.[15] The subsequent judgement of the Jervis Street inquiry was similar.

Dublin District Special Branch (DDSB) had, meanwhile, quickly regained momentum following its recent bloody nose. Many of those who slipped through the IRA net on Bloody Sunday, or who remained unknown to them, were back on the streets recruiting new touts to replace those gone to ground.

A fresh influx of tougher and better-trained agents from Hounslow spy school, operating since May, had also arrived. Additionally, security had tightened, one example being the reassignment of civilian staff away from army intelligence, leaving only military staffing such roles.

Ormonde Winter, codenamed 'O', knew that when provincial IRA Volunteers became suspects in their own districts, they moved further afield, and in the cases of prominent members, such as the late Joe Howley, fled to Dublin.[16] In the capital they moved through the city with impunity, unrecognised by police or military. To address this, Winter consulted with Gen. Tudor. By now Tudor was official police chief, since his nominal predecessor, Insp. Gen. Smith – having conspired cynically with Lord French the previous year to attain the position, only to regret the fact – had resigned the previous month. Smith's December 1919 appointment had paved the way for the Black and Tans. Winter sought Tudor's permission to create an identification branch of the police intelligence service, composed of RIC from similar provincial villages and towns to the fugitives, who had themselves been driven out because of their visible hostility towards Sinn Féin. Tudor quickly sanctioned this branch to identify and arrest IRA fugitives. He also informed Winter of plans to bring Army intelligence under the control of the police's Central Intelligence Service (CIS). Meanwhile, Winter, anticipating Tudor's approval, had spent December's first week trawling through Dublin Castle files for suitable candidates for the new identification branch. Soon the man he hoped would lead his proposed new unit stood before him – Const. Eugene Igoe.

Igoe, thirty-one years old, was over six feet tall, with dark hair combed back from a receding hairline and a moustache typical of his profession. Originally from Ballina, Co. Mayo, he had served most of his career in Galway. He had witnessed the killing of Const. Patrick Whelan during a skirmish with Irish Volunteers in 1916. In early 1920 he had transferred to Limerick. He was known for his determination to fight the IRA.

Igoe bore a confident but suspicious expression. He and Winter sized each other up, the latter's eye monocled, a cigarette hanging from his lips. Winter briefed Igoe of his idea, stressing the ruthlessness it required. Igoe agreed to take the post. Winter got straight to specifics, telling Igoe he had a twenty-man squad awaiting him at the Phoenix Park's RIC depot, equally determined to fight 'Shinners'. He also detailed dispatches sent to the country's various district inspectors to supply additional men with sufficient credentials to the unit.

Eugene Igoe, the ruthless and formidable RIC constable brought to Dublin to lead the police intelligence service's Identification Branch. *(Courtesy of Kilmainham Gaol Museum OPW, KMGLM 19PO–1A32–03)*

Igoe quickly started studying police and newspaper reports, and any available eyewitness testimonies about IRA assassinations in Dublin. He then adapted enemy tactics involving sections of armed men, each divided into several pairs, spread out lengthways along city footpaths in close enough proximity to provide sufficient mutual support to either fend off attackers or rapidly envelope and isolate suspects. Individual suspects would be accosted with minimal fuss in order not to alarm passers-by or alert enemy comrades. Mobile military or police units were deployed to operational areas. The shrill blasts of police whistles called upon these to provide backup. Soon, Igoe's unit was patrolling Dublin's streets.

This tactical departure was launched to the background of incessant police and military raids throughout Dublin and Ireland, yielding valuable intelligence dividends, leading, in turn, to even more effective raids – a vicious circle for the IRA. Gen. Boyd applauded. There was no let-up. On 9 December, William Cosgrave's home in 174 James's Street was raided. Cosgrave was, however, safely in hiding. Charlie Dalton's home in 8 Upper St Columba's Road, Drumcondra, was raided on the same day by a unit from the 'Dukes' based at Collinstown aerodrome. Charlie was not there at the time, but his older brother, Emmet, was arrested, along with his father. Both were taken to Collinstown, also doubling as a temporary internment camp.[17] Emmet Dalton's arrest backfired on the British establishment. The twenty-two-year-old was an experienced and decorated former British Army officer, with both combat and staff experience, both of which soon served the IRA well.

Ballykinlar internment camp in Co. Down was, meanwhile, becoming operational. Each night British military lorries carried a 100 or so suspects to North Wall Quay where two destroyers: HMS *Sea Wolf* – recently employed to transport flag-draped coffins – and HMS *Valorous*, waited to ship them to Belfast en route to Ballykinlar, regardless of sea conditions. The transport convoys, escorted by armoured cars, operated after curfew to prevent civilian interference.[18] Internees arriving in Belfast, many suffering from cold and seasickness, were often met with the same barrages of heavy bolts, jagged rivets – nicknamed 'Belfast confetti' – and venomous taunts that had been used against Catholic workers when they were driven from the city's shipyards the previous summer.

Meanwhile, Collinstown itself was rapidly filling with prisoners; 120 in its first week of operation. Joe Lawless, former proprietor of an IRA bomb factory and subsequent owner of a car rental company used to provide cars for operations, was arrested by a British intelligence officer in Swords on 8 December for not having a car permit. His subsequent arrival in Collinstown was coincidental, as he had participated in the arms raid there in March 1919, Dublin Brigade's first high-level offensive operation of the war. It also revealed a disconcerting fact: almost all the IRA Fingal Brigade's senior officers were interned there, alongside rank and file Volunteers, sympathisers and ordinary civilians caught up in round-ups. The camp itself consisted of 'four or five wooden sixty foot huts of the standard British Army pattern'.[19] Many Volunteers detained there recognised the hut type from their post-Rising internments at Frongoch camp in North Wales. The huts occupied half an acre of ground surrounded by a double-apron barbed-wire fence 'guarded night and day on all sides by armed sentries – the entire area being floodlit at night by electric lamps set upon poles around it'.[20] Huts were frigidly cold, the entire surrounding area flat and windswept, ideal for the aerodrome. Family members of internees called most mornings with food parcels and cigarettes, not all of which were forwarded to the prisoners. In most cases personal visits were not allowed. Occasionally, when camp authorities became confident that certain internees were innocent, family visits were permitted while enquiries were made to establish their innocence. Camp guards were, in the main, affable towards internees, particularly in the case of a British major whose cordiality led to suspicions that he was an intelligence officer trying to build rapport with prisoners whose names and faces he memorised. Fresh consignments of prisoners arrived each night, among them thirty-seven-year-old Peadar Kearney, who had composed 'The Soldier's Song' (*Amhrán na bhFiann*).[21]

Back in the city, his fellow officers had by now elected Oscar Traynor as Dublin Brigade O/C. For security reasons Traynor quickly moved HQ from the Typographical Institute in Gardiner Street to the Irish Engineering, Shipbuilding and Foundry Trades Union building in nearby 6 Gardiner Row.

Comdt Oscar Traynor, who took command of Dublin Brigade IRA after Dick McKee's death. *(Courtesy of the National Library of Ireland)*

The next IRA Army Council meeting saw him gain agreement to a proposition of the late Dick McKee's – to form a permanent IRA ASU to be available for action at short notice. Like the Squad, this necessitated members leaving their employment. It was proposed to pay each member the same weekly wage as the Squad – £4.10. Funds would be ring-fenced for this. Traynor insisted that only the best Volunteers from each of Dublin's four original city battalions would be chosen.[22] The 5th Engineer Battalion would not be affected at present; each of its companies worked in conjunction with the other Dublin battalions. However, it was agreed that this decision could be revisited if necessary. By now the Dublin Brigade had also established a 6th Battalion to operate in South Dublin and Bray. McKee had ordered its establishment before his death, under the command of Andrew McDonnell, a veteran of both the 1916 Rising and the 1920 Mountjoy hunger strikes. However, 6th Battalion still had to find its feet at this point.

Traynor had one man in mind for ASU commander: the decisive and ruthless Capt. Paddy Flanagan of C Company, 3rd Battalion, who readily agreed. Soon afterwards, at the next brigade council, each battalion commandant was informed of the development and that each of them was to order their own company captains to present lists of the best men from their individual companies to be put forward as ASU members. At least two from each company would be chosen. Later, when the companies were informed of this, the idea of losing their finest Volunteers was not well received. Nevertheless, orders were orders. Over the ensuing days, Flanagan worked with each captain to procure the requisite number, eventually whittled down to fifty. The IRA would, it was hoped, have its own answer to the Auxiliaries in Dublin city, albeit on a smaller scale.

Michael Collins' intelligence staff was, meanwhile, desperately trying to glean intelligence regarding Const. Igoe's new unit, Igoe's name quickly having been forwarded by police contacts. Frustratingly, however, they could not procure his photograph. Regardless, orders went out to the Squad to find 'Igoe Gang' members and eliminate them. Collins also sent word to Galway

Auxiliaries in Crossley Tenders outside Amiens Street station. The IRA ASU would now take the fight to these cadets and their comrades on a full-time basis. Dublin's war was about to radically escalate. *(Courtesy of the National Library of Ireland)*

that he needed a man who recognised Igoe. Thomas 'Sweeney' Newell, a blacksmith, was selected. Newell was a 1916 veteran who had served under Liam Mellows and could identify Igoe on sight. Newell travelled to Dublin with 'Baby' Duggan, who introduced him to Collins.[23] Soon, Newell began scouring Dublin's streets accompanied by an intelligence officer. He spotted Igoe twice shortly after arriving, but quickly lost track of him. Igoe was clearly a wily adversary. Newell soon learned this to his own detriment.

Meanwhile, Collins' endless myriad of tasks was added to on 11 December when he was nominated to succeed Arthur Griffith as acting Dáil president. Two recent Dáil cabinet meetings before Griffith's arrest had seen the Ceann Comhairle (chairperson), J. J. O'Kelly, implore Griffith to nominate a successor to cover such an eventuality. Griffith's first and second choices were Austin Stack and Cathal Brugha respectively. Both, however, refused when asked to assume the role by Griffith's solicitor, citing prohibitive ministerial workloads; Stack with Home Affairs – his control of which Collins, and several others, considered a joke – and Brugha with Defence. Collins was nominated next and reluctantly accepted. His tenure was short; word had reached Dublin that Éamon de Valera would soon return from the USA to reassume the role of president.

The day before Collins' acceptance of the acting presidency had seen Lloyd George announce in the Commons that there would be no accommodation with Sinn Féin or the IRA. He cited the recent messages from Fr O'Flanagan and both Galway councils as a signal that Irish people were desperate for peace, whilst their revolutionary compatriots, by refusing to surrender arms, were clearly not. He also heralded that there would no longer be safe conduct for anyone 'guilty of crimes of violence, of murder, of very brutal murder'.[24] The skewed interpretation of his uncompromising message in Ireland, within thirty-six hours, contributed to another reprisal the magnitude of which drew further international condemnation and drove most of those on the Irish side who had publicly exhorted the merits of moderation firmly back into the ranks of those who urged otherwise.

Following an ambush at Dillon's Cross in Cork by a small IRA unit determined to either kill or capture a senior enemy intelligence officer, during which one Auxiliary from K Company was mortally wounded and more than a dozen others seriously wounded, several Auxiliary and military lorries left Victoria Barracks in the city and drove to the nearby ambush scene. They set fire to local houses and a passing tram. Afterwards, Auxiliaries, soldiers, Black and Tans and RIC, some out of uniform, descended upon the city, firing into the air as they entered Patrick Street, the city's main shopping street. Trams were halted and civilians brutally assaulted. Shop windows were smashed and shops themselves torched as the marauders fanned out. Grant's department store was set ablaze, as was the Carnegie Library. Soldiers poured cans of petrol,

Scenes of utter destruction in Cork city centre. *(Courtesy of Mercier Archive)*

transported by truck, into burning buildings. Hand grenades were hurled into others. Many other buildings were added to the conflagration. Looting was widespread. At 3 a.m. on Sunday 12 December, firefighters, whose fire hoses were cut by the arsonists, came under rifle fire from Black and Tans at City Hall. An ambulance transporting a wounded fireman was shot at. At 4 a.m., following a terrific explosion, City Hall itself was ablaze.[25]

The damage to the city was later estimated at over three million pounds. Between 10 p.m. on 11 December and 8 a.m. the following morning, forty business premises were destroyed, along with 300 residential properties. Twenty-four other shops suffered partial damage. More than 2,000 civilians lost their jobs. Many more became homeless.[26] One Auxiliary wrote afterwards, in a letter intercepted by the IRA, of how he had relished the occasion and added that nothing he had experienced in the Great War had come close to what he witnessed that night in Cork. This was soon published in the *Irish Bulletin* – the hugely effective republican gazette published several times a week and circulated widely. Just outside the city, two IRA Volunteer siblings, Cornelius and Jeremiah Delany, whose home had provided a line of retreat to the IRA party behind the Dillon's Cross ambush, were shot dead by eight intruders with English accents as they stood next to their beds at 2 a.m.

The ruins of Cork City Hall. *(Courtesy of Mercier Archive)*

Writing up their own versions of what had taken place in Cork soon afterwards were members of the British Labour Party Commission. The commission had arrived in Ireland two weeks earlier to allow members to assess recent events for themselves. Their version of what transpired in Cork conflicted radically with Hamar Greenwood's assertions in the Commons that the police and military had nothing to do with the fires other than having helped put them out. Greenwood added, evocatively, that no business owned by Sinn Féin members had been destroyed, and invited house members from both sides to draw their own conclusions from that. However, the fact that Auxiliaries had held Labour Commission members at gunpoint and threatened to shoot them as they entered the city afterwards did not lend weight to Greenwood's well-practised verbal contortions. A telegram from the commission to Lloyd George stated that it was 'convinced that the fires were the work of the Crown Forces'. It also offered to produce damning evidence to back this up.[27] Notably, when K Company members were subsequently redeployed to Dublin, they provocatively wore burnt cork tied to the backs of their caps.

Meanwhile, the acute arms supply issue for the IRA saw a meeting convened at Barry's Hotel in Great Denmark Street on 13 December, attended by several prominent IRA figures recently arrived from Cork with horrific descriptions of the destruction wrought upon the city. An ambitious plan was

Sir Hamar Greenwood inspecting Auxiliaries at Beggar's Bush Barracks. *(Courtesy of Mercier Archive)*

hatched to procure surplus war arms and ammunition from Italy. Donal Hales, Irish consular and commercial agent for Italy, and brother of prominent IRA commanders from Cork, Seán and Tom Hales, acted as a go-between in the Italian port city of Genoa. Attending the meeting alongside his fellow Cork men – who included Florrie O'Donoghue, intelligence officer for Cork No. 1 Brigade – was Michael Collins. At his side were Brugha and Mellows, the three, despite appearances, still embittered from their ongoing spat. Cork was decided upon as the destination for the proposed shipment. The potential haul was tantalising: 20,000 rifles, 500 machine guns and five million rounds of ammunition. A recent conference held secretly at the Italian War Ministry in Rome on 21 November had seen, among others, Benito Mussolini pledge to support and finance the venture. Ultimately, however, the arms and ammunition never materialised. Mussolini's promise of financial assistance proved hollow and British naval intelligence's Mediterranean prowess rendered the operation too risky given the cost.

A critical event highlighting the arms issue was a successful raid on the IRA's principal bomb and munitions factory in the basement of 198 Great Britain Street. The raid took place two days before the Barry's Hotel meeting. The factory had been discovered during a raid on a neighbouring premises. By now it had been operating for over two years, despite a raid there in May 1919 led by the late G-Division detective Daniel Hoey. Any pretence of a simple foundry was long gone. Grenades of various sizes, but most commonly the pineapple-sized GHQ 'Number Nine' grenade, as well as casings, brass and aluminium caps, detonators, springs, levers, pins and an assortment of other munitions were placed on shelves throughout the basement. The shop counter was reinforced with steel plating. If raided, the plan was for the basement's occupants to take cover behind this, bomb and shoot their way out, or die trying. Luckily for them, on the morning of 11 December the raid by Auxiliaries and RIC occurred too early for Mick Keogh, Thomas Young – a 1916 veteran who had acted as Peadar Clancy's arms procurer in England – and Patrick McHugh, a Volunteer from Dundalk, to have been there. Keogh had stopped for 'an early morning pint' en route and was alerted by a local civilian. Young, meanwhile, had stopped at a nearby newsagent and was similarly warned.[28] When a young boy arrived by bicycle at the shop to borrow a bicycle pump he cycled away at speed when he saw what was underway. The raiders opened fire on him but missed. Their shots alerted the entire neighbourhood. Press reporters converged. A huge haul was emptied from the basement and seized for examination.

McHugh, twenty-five years old, had been elsewhere that morning. Recent weeks had seen him establishing an additional munitions factory in Nos 1–2 Luke Street. This had been at the behest of the late Peadar Clancy, who had, through his web of contacts, come across blueprints for German MP-18 sub-machine guns and, having consulted with IRA engineers, decided that a stand-alone unit would be required to manufacture the IRA's equivalent. The premises procured by McHugh was leased from a retired RIC constable – ideal cover for such an ambitious enterprise operating just around the corner from Great Brunswick Street police station. Its operation was expedited following the Great Britain Street raid.

Tuesday 14 December saw 3rd Battalion carry out 'the first direct attack on the Auxiliary Division by a Unit of the Dublin Brigade'.[29] This had been planned several weeks earlier but postponed following the deaths of McKee and Clancy. Auxiliaries collecting mail from Ballsbridge post office on Shelbourne Road came under attack from a unit of B Company Volunteers under William O'Brien and Leo Fitzgerald, the latter a veteran of recent notable raids and from a family of prominent IRA members. A successful ambush would provide IRA intelligence with the home addresses of Auxiliaries. This, it was deemed, would provide a means for the IRA to hit them where it hurt by targeting their homes in revenge for their own reprisals.

A Ford touring car was driven every Tuesday from Beggar's Bush to the post office, less than a mile away. The original plan was to launch the ambush from a house adjacent to the post office as soon as the mail was collected. However, fearing retaliation against the house owner, the plan was revised so that, on the morning itself, Volunteers armed with pistols and grenades took up concealed positions around the post office. Lt Fitzgerald and several others stood ready to provide supporting fire from within and around a brigade car parked discreetly nearby. They waited nervously, aware that GHQ had given the job top priority.

The Ford car pulled up outside the post office on the road's eastern side at 9.10 a.m. Some distance away IRA support units quickly sprang into action, stopping any further traffic entering Shelbourne Road from Lansdowne Road to the north. Others stopped a tram approaching from Ballsbridge to the south. A single uniformed Auxiliary and several others in mufti entered the post office. Two stood guard at its door. They returned soon afterwards with several mailbags, which were thrown onto the front passenger seat and the floor. Just then, as the car was restarted, the attackers pounced. A hail of shots flew at the car. A grenade was hurled at it but bounced off before exploding. The Auxiliaries, overpowered, retreated into the post office. Shots followed them, one smashing a post office window, another lodging in its wooden door. Terrified civilians huddled inside as glass splinters flew and ricochets resounded. Screams and curses rang out. Amid the chaos a call was placed to Beggar's Bush for support.

Just up the road Fitzgerald and the brigade car's occupants, anticipating this, had alighted onto Shelbourne Road. Passing pedestrians there looked on fearfully as Volunteers with rifles slung across shoulders and carrying pistols ordered them to remain still with their hands up. Other Volunteers lay prone on the pavements, weapons trained north to fire at enemy reinforcements.

Finally, a Volunteer driver rushed towards the Auxiliaries' car under covering fire and jumped into its driver's seat. A postman crouching nearby shouted angrily at him to throw out the mailbags. The response 'I will put a bullet through you' put an end to any further such demands.[30] This was followed by the echoing thud of a detonating smoke grenade outside the post office, signalling to the surrounding support units to beat a retreat. The car was then driven at speed across Pembroke Road and rendezvoused with another in Herbert Park. Both vehicles then sped towards Morehampton Road. The mission, without casualties, was a success, and left the Auxiliaries red-faced and deeply concerned for their family homes. Several mailbags soon arrived at Crow Street.

Notably, on the same day, Gen. Tudor ordered Auxiliaries and Black and Tans to cease reprisals.[31] Meanwhile, Archbishop Clune conveyed a *quid pro quo* message to the IRA from Downing Street to: 'Ask your fellows to lie low for a month or so. Then the atmosphere and temper over there will be different.'[32] It appeared to Clune, and to Griffith, that the backlash from the recent Cork burnings had bolstered the position of the Westminster moderates in favour of a deal potentially more digestible to the republicans, one that could possibly be steered through if the IRA called a momentary halt to operations. Collins was unconvinced. He had written earlier to Art O'Brien that negotiations were merely a cynical attempt to 'put us in the wrong with the world and particularly with our own people', while also criticising those whom, he felt, expected to get a good deal from England from any means other than acts of self-defence.[33] Unfortunately for the republicans, the morale-boosting effect of the Shelbourne Road ambush was tempered the same day with the official ending of the rail embargo. That day the National Executive of the Irish TUC and the Labour Party advised railwaymen and dockworkers 'to offer to carry everything that the British authorities are prepared to risk on the trains'.[34] It was simply no longer feasible to expect members to endure the near destitution wrought among so many of them by this point. Disenchantment was felt towards the lack of support offered by the National Union of Railwaymen in England to the embargo. Despite expressing sympathy for its underlying cause, union leaders there refused to commit to supporting it for fear of losing support among northern Irish unionist members and in Britain itself.

Gen. Macready, his position reinforced by the embargo's lifting, justified Collins' misgivings concerning the British government's intentions by asserting that he could have the IRA defeated within three months. When, soon afterwards, the surrender of IRA arms was officially insisted upon as a prerequisite for a truce, any prospect of peace in 1920 withered. Meanwhile, back in Cork, on 15 December, an Auxiliary section leader shot dead twenty-four-year-old Tadhg Crowley and seventy-three-year-old Canon Thomas Magner as they assisted a local resident magistrate whose car had broken down, causing further uproar. The Auxiliary, thirty-six-year-old Vernon Hart, was later court-martialled and declared insane. It was claimed he had been suffering from *delirium tremens*, having remained intoxicated for days following the death of a close comrade after the Dillon's Cross ambush. The reaction to the canon's shooting was typically critical of the Auxiliaries. Mark Sturgis wrote that those who had allowed such a man to carry arms were the insane ones. John Anderson, weary of their indiscipline, called for their disbandment. Macready, however, backtracking, disagreed. He cited the blame for such acts on a small minority within the force and warned that this was not the time to deplete the crown's security forces. However, Macready assured Anderson that when sharing barracks, the police reinforcements would be subject to stringent military discipline in order to prevent a collapse in morale of his own forces.

Meanwhile, following Paddy Daly's arrest and incarceration, the Squad had undergone a change. Mick McDonnell remained in charge, but by this time he had suffered several breakdowns under the role's crushing strain. Tom

Keogh had stepped into Daly's shoes as McDonnell's *de facto* deputy in time for McDonnell, notwithstanding his worsening health, to order the execution of a new target – Dist Insp. Philip O'Sullivan. Keogh was ordered to mobilise four Squad members to carry out this assassination.

O'Sullivan was a twenty-three-year-old ex-Royal Navy subaltern. His primary duty in Dublin Castle was code-breaking, making him a priority target. Frank Thornton had given Ned Kelliher a description of O'Sullivan. Kelliher soon located him and, having trailed him for a week, knew all his movements and, more importantly, the most suitable location for his execution.[35]

At 6 p.m. on Tuesday 17 December, Kelliher met the four Squad members under the lit street lamps of Henry Street, bustling with workers and shoppers making their way home. They had initially assembled at Moreland's, minutes away, to collect weapons. Among them was twenty-eight-year-old Joseph Byrne, recently recruited from C Company, 1st Battalion, as a Squad member by Joe Guilfoyle. Kelliher explained to the four that O'Sullivan was scheduled to meet his fiancée, Ms Moore, when she finished work at Arnott's department store. When the briefing concluded, two Squad members detailed to carry out the shooting took position in the doorway of McDowell's shop on Henry Street's southern side, facing Moore Street; this was the direction O'Sullivan was expected to take. One of them inconspicuously took out a newspaper while the other kept watch for a signal from Kelliher.[36] Byrne, Kelliher and the other member took up positions on the street's opposite side providing cover.

Soon afterwards, Ms Moore stepped out of Arnott's, but, seeing no sign of O'Sullivan, turned right and began walking towards Nelson's Pillar on Sackville Street. She noticed one of the two men at McDowell's looking at her as she passed but ignored the pair when her eyes fell upon her smiling fiancé pacing towards her through the crowds from the direction of the still ruined GPO. Unfortunately for O'Sullivan, Kelliher also spotted him. He signalled the pair at McDowell's. One stepped away from the doorway in pursuit, then, realising his comrade was still absorbed in his newspaper, he stepped back and tugged his arm. The paper was folded. Both men walked briskly towards their target, who was apologising to his fiancée for being late. The couple turned and began ambling towards Nelson's Pillar, passing a shop named Fancy Fair to their left, the GPO to their right. Suddenly, from behind they heard a voice ask loudly, 'Hello, are you ready?'[37] O'Sullivan quickly turned to find a revolver pointed at his face. Before he could react, a blinding flash and deafening crack followed.

He was sent spinning off his feet as a .45 calibre round tore through his left eye and exited his temple, narrowly missing Ms Moore before ricocheting from a nearby shop. Ms Moore recoiled in shock momentarily as the gunman prepared to fire again. She then launched herself at him, grabbing the pistol muzzle, screaming and grappling desperately with the assassin. Surrounding crowds, startled, scrambled for cover as the other gunman quickly aimed his pistol at the collapsed victim and shot him in the back of the neck. Just then Ms Moore lost her grip on the first shooter's pistol and it fired again, hitting O'Sullivan in the back. His body jerked under the point-blank impact.[38]

Several more shots echoed along the enclosed street to subdue the crowds as the five IRA men made their getaway, causing a near stampede. They escaped into side streets before returning on foot to Moreland's. Minutes afterwards, a passing army truck was flagged down in the street. O'Sullivan was rushed from the blood-soaked scene to nearby Jervis Street Hospital, just 100 yards from Moreland's, with his sobbing fiancée. He was pronounced dead soon after his arrival. His death sent a resounding signal to Dublin Castle, and to Westminster: the Dublin IRA still possessed the means and the willingness to ruthlessly prosecute the war.

6

Government of Ireland Act, Active Service Unit

'Things are being done in the name of Britain'

The Government of Ireland Act received Royal Assent on 23 December 1920. Two parliaments – one for six predominantly unionist counties from Ulster, another for the country's mostly nationalist twenty-six-county remainder – were planned for spring 1921. British strategy, given the recent failure to advance a settlement, was to eradicate the war, thus creating favourable conditions for parliamentary elections within each territory. The act was painted by the British as stretching their boundaries for compromise to the limits. In Westminster, its enactment was expected to convince moderate nationalists to accept Home Rule – albeit with partition – once and for all, and reject rebellion, thereby depriving the IRA of its bedrock of popular support. In most of Ireland, however, it was greeted less than enthusiastically.

Also on 23 December, the Labour Party Commission was back in London to deliver its recent findings in Ireland to a packed party conference. The commission portrayed a horrific image of crown forces rampaging and terrorising throughout the country. One paragraph stated: 'Things are being done in the name of Britain which must make her name stink in the nostrils of the whole world'.[1] Reports of the brutal rape and murder of forty-five-year-old Kate Maher in Tipperary on 21 December at the hands of the Lincolnshire Regiment did nothing to bolster arguments for the report's critics.[2] But the report was countered by claims that its authors had been misled. The commission's itinerary in Ireland was ridiculed, its members accused of having been taken for a ride on the 'Republican Scenic Railway' to the country's most troublesome parts, whilst ignoring the numerous areas with little disturbance.[3]

Meanwhile, ensuring Britain's international reputation remained odious were Kathleen McKenna, Frank Gallagher and Robert Brennan, the three

Propaganda was a pivotal element of the separatists' campaign against Britain. At the campaign's helm was Sinn Féin Director of Propaganda Desmond Fitzgerald. *(Courtesy of the National Library of Ireland)*

overseen by Desmond Fitzgerald, Sinn Féin director of propaganda. They were conducting their business in 11 Molesworth Street, in a fashionable second-floor flat above a firm of solicitors, several doors down from the Grand Lodge of Freemasons. They worked in two large rooms. One contained desks upon which sat piles of newspaper cuttings and files detailing seemingly endless lists of British atrocities. On the other sat a cast-iron Gestetner printing press. Two elderly ladies lived above the offices, oblivious to their activities, as were the solicitors below. Fitzgerald established links with reporters from a host of countries who were based in London and, aided by *The Freeman's Journal* – which allowed the *Bulletin* to transmit 300 words daily on its telegraph wire to the English capital – ensured such reporters had plenty to relay to their respective national broadsheets.[4]

Each evening, on her way to her Berkeley Road flat, McKenna went to a republican communications centre known as 'The Dump', above Mansfield's

Kathleen McKenna, on the right, one of the *Irish Bulletin*'s authors. The *Bulletin* was a hugely successful means of highlighting Ireland's struggle to the international press. Given its constrained working conditions, its influence was astonishing. Second from left in the picture is Michael Collins' finance secretary, Alice Lyons. Between Lyons and McKenna stands Arthur Griffith. *(Courtesy of the National Library of Ireland)*

Boot Shop at Sackville Street's junction with Middle Abbey Street, and to Devlin's pub to receive documents for publication. Concealing them as she walked, she prepared them for the next day when she got home.

Secrecy in Molesworth Street dictated that they could not allow caretakers in whom they did not know to clean the flat. Therefore, fires could not be lit. Winter 1920 was particularly cold. Consequently, the huge flat was freezing. Duplicating ink froze in its tubes but was thawed by burning newspapers, which at times also helped thaw out numbed fingers. Fitzgerald coughed all day long as Christmas approached. Brennan and Gallagher 'huddled writing all day in their often rain-soaked overcoats'.[5] Blotting paper was rolled into stockings as insulation. Their only relief came in the evening when the daily rush to catch the post office drew their minds from the cold and damp.

The *Bulletin*'s stream of 'damning but irrefutable accusations' prioritised the discovery of its offices among the enemy. Streets were cordoned off during house-to-house searches, providing its writers with further material.[6] Meanwhile, also on Dublin Castle's target list, as well as becoming a keynote *Bulletin* feature itself on 22 December, was City Hall. Temporarily occupied by the military on Bloody Sunday, it was raided two weeks later by Auxiliaries, and taken over permanently alongside the adjacent rates building. At 7.30 a.m. on 5 December, under Gen. Boyd's orders, troops seized both buildings, rolling out additional barbed-wire cordons in the streets around City Hall and Dublin Castle.[7] Extra metal plates were bolted to the Castle's gates while onlookers gaped, wide-eyed.

Thursday 23 December saw the long-awaited return to Ireland of Éamon de Valera, referred to by many as 'Chief' or 'The Long Fellow'. He was greeted as he stepped off the Liverpool ferry at Custom House quay by Batt O'Connor and Tom Cullen.

Barbed-wire defences and sentry post at Dublin Castle. (*Courtesy of Mercier Archive*)

De Valera had spent his time in America speaking before state legislatures and conferring with governors. He attained the freedom of several cities, received two honorary doctorates, spoke to massive crowds and heightened awareness of Ireland's struggle.[8] His time there, during which he challenged long-standing Irish-American power monopolies, had also contributed to deep divisions in Irish-America – observed with gratification by Westminster – and highlighted 'the capacity of the republican movement to split into bitter factions'.[9] He also raised over five million US dollars to support the war, much of which became trapped in American banks owing to legal disputes just when it was badly needed.

De Valera's return voyage from the USA to Liverpool was as arduous as his initial crossing. He was forced to hide in a disused water tank on board the liner SS *Celtic* and nearly drowned at one point when the tank was accidentally filled with water. He became very ill. In Liverpool, waiting to cross the Irish Sea for home, he was almost arrested. His early morning arrival in Dublin was celebrated by his fellow revolutionaries and his large family. In particular, Collins was looking forward to his 'Chief' helping to heal the divisions between himself and Brugha, which had escalated to include Austin Stack. However, he would be disappointed.

Notably, when De Valera asked Cullen and O'Connor how things were going in the country, Cullen replied, 'Great! The Big Fellow is leading us and everything is going marvellous.' De Valera, frustrated, struck the quayside's guard rail and proclaimed: 'Big Fellow! We'll see who's The Big Fellow ...'[10] The unfiltered response betrayed a fundamental aspect to De Valera's overall strategy – to reassert his position. John Devoy, renowned exiled Irish leader and De Valera's bitter opponent in the USA, had – based largely on reports from a ground-breaking interview by American journalist Carl Ackerman with Collins the previous August – irked De Valera by recently branding Collins 'Ireland's Fighting Chief'. This also aggravated the animosity felt towards Collins by Brugha, who had greeted Devoy's words with indignation for undermining his Dáil position as commander of the Republic's armed forces. Notably, Ackerman had not only been reporting to his news editor following his Collins interview – he also provided a profile of Collins to Basil Thompson of Scotland Yard, whom he admired.

Events were, nonetheless, conspiring to see Collins' reputation soar at home, abroad and among both friend and foe. Devoy's homage reinforced perceptions that Collins was the Republic's singular driving force. On Christmas Eve, the day after De Valera stepped off the boat, this was effectively conveyed to Lloyd George by Archbishop Clune, when he suggested Collins was the only man he could expect to do serious business with. The late John Charles Byrnes – operating under Basil Thompson as a spy using the name 'Jameson' until his own eventual discovery and bloody execution – had singled Collins out a year earlier. 'Jameson' had relayed to Scotland Yard that Collins was the IRA's lynchpin. Since then, capturing Collins had become a priority. The fact that Collins' intelligence staff had repeatedly outmanoeuvred British intelligence with lethal consequences only served to further his growing mystique. Moreover, now that Dick McKee's towering influence had been removed from the tiller of Dublin Brigade, Collins' prodigious persona filled the chasm in the minds of brigade members aware of the formidable mutual respect between both men. Collins, accepting the additional role of acting Dáil president, then magnified the impression.

De Valera rapidly proved to be a more conspicuous president than Griffith as he sought to restore vitality to the position, having reassumed it upon his return. He set up a President's Office, wanting to be apprised quickly about events throughout the revolution's numerous spheres.[11]

De Valera was equally quick to express misgivings about how the IRA campaign was being perceived in the USA, telling Richard Mulcahy on Christmas Eve that the shooting of policemen was drawing negative publicity there. He elucidated, suggesting that more conventional military engagements would be more digestible to the wider public, particularly as they would be less likely to trigger civilian reprisals. Tactically, such engagements were unpalatable to Mulcahy and Collins, the latter of whom had spoken to De Valera earlier that morning, after Brugha had talked with him first at Dr Farnan's in Merrion Square. De Valera resided there until Collins secured him a house in Sandymount. De Valera quickly detected the animosity between Brugha and Collins, further reinforced by Brugha's continuing mistrust of the IRB, a sentiment De Valera shared, despite that fact that Harry Boland, whom De Valera had selected to act as his envoy and aide for his USA mission, was a member of its Supreme Council, and that it had been Collins' secretive IRB contacts who had spirited him to and from the USA, and would soon do so to his pending Sandymount hideout.

Unfortunately for Collins, however, his own and the IRB's secretive prowess could not prevent the crown's composite forces closing in. Christmas Eve 1920 started badly; his photograph appeared on the cover of *The Police Gazette*, also known as *Hue-and-Cry*, alongside Mulcahy and Piaras Béaslaí. Despite this, Collins maintained the strategy of 'hiding in plain sight', a method articulated by the novelist G. K. Chesterton in *The Man Who Was Thursday*, a book about revolutionary anarchists who extolled the idea that if one did not appear to be hiding then, with luck, one could walk casually among one's pursuers. Executed Easter Rising leader Joseph Plunkett had given the book to Collins. Notably, its author was a member of the London based Anti-Reprisals Association formed the previous month in reaction to the horrific reports from Ireland.[12]

Collins behaved as if it was a normal Christmas, savouring the atmosphere the capital struggled to harness. David Neligan's emphatic advice to lie low was ignored. Collins dispatched the long-suffering Joe O'Reilly on a whirlwind of errands bearing gifts. He made a host of seasonal house calls to friends and associates. O'Reilly was sent out with small parcels for almost everyone who had assisted the IRA during the year in the capital, bearing packages and cards to sailors, pub, café and hotel workers, cinema ushers, pawnbrokers, policemen, hotel workers, brothelkeepers, shopkeepers, nurses, doctors and hard-pressed railway workers. Heartfelt messages accompanying gifts conveyed appreciation and were cherished, a fact Collins understood. One of his conspicuous strengths was the ability to relate to and remember people from all backgrounds. When this mountain of errands was accomplished, Collins made for the Gresham, where his staggering luck was tested to its limits.

He sat down at 4 p.m. in the Gresham's dining room with Rory O'Connor, Liam Tobin, Gearóid O'Sullivan and Tom Cullen for a brief interlude in his recently self-imposed alcohol hiatus. Collins was recognised by James Doyle, the hotel manager, as he and his associates strolled through reception. Doyle feared a repeat of Bloody Sunday as he also noticed an RIC district inspector in the hotel. When they sat down to eat, however, Doyle sighed in relief, sensing there would be no such repetition. Notably, the RIC officer then departed.

Ten minutes later a waiter appeared at Collins' side and whispered: 'You might like to know sir; the Auxiliaries are in the hall.'[13] Each man at the table, momentarily perplexed, looked towards one another before their well-rehearsed charades kicked in. They laughed and joked. Whiskey was poured into five glasses. Toasts were raised. When approached by the enemy officer in charge, Collins greeted him ebulliently but soon found himself being questioned by the officer in the adjacent hallway. Collins identified himself as 'John Grace', producing identification to match.[14] Doyle looked on, suspecting the departed RIC officer had alerted Dublin Castle. A hip flask and notebook were found in Collins' jacket pockets, the former, asserted Collins, a gift for his landlady.[15] The notebook, however, intrigued the officer, particularly when he saw the word 'rifles' in it.

Collins thought fast, insisting the word he was reading was instead 'refills', stating that he used a lot of notebooks as an accountant, for which he needed refills. The ruse worked. Then, as the Auxiliaries fanned out to check the hotel's other diners and guests, Collins made for the lavatory under the watch of another Auxiliary, who followed him. This cadet grabbed hold of Collins and rough-handled him under a bright light above the sink mirror. He pulled a photograph of Collins from his pocket for comparison. Just then Tobin walked in and saw the cadet tussling Collins' hair to make it resemble that in the photo. Collins prepared to grab the cadet's pistol, but, suddenly, the cadet let him go. The sound of merriment from the dining room jolted him from his inspection. Moments later, Collins returned with Tobin and the cadet to the dining room to find O'Connor ordering a second bottle of whiskey for the Auxiliaries, having already poured them several glasses from the first. Warmed with whiskey, the cadets soon departed for Dublin Castle to launch their own festive celebrations alongside Capts King and Hardy, both of whom had been busy that day torturing a prisoner, Ernie O'Malley. Collins and his companions departed the Gresham later and reconvened celebrations in nearby Vaughan's, before Collins and O'Sullivan made for Julia O'Donovan's in Rathgar, waking on Christmas Day nursing crucifying hangovers.

Ernie O'Malley was a prominent IRA organiser. He had been arrested in Kilkenny posing as Bernard Stewart on 9 December and suffered repeated torture following his arrest, before being transported to Dublin Castle where King and Hardy spent days working him over. They rightly suspected he was a prominent IRA figure. A hot poker was repeatedly held just millimetres from his eyes, singeing his eyelashes and brows. O'Malley's recent exploits setting fire to barracks in Tipperary meant singed eyebrows were not a novel experience. He was beaten with fists, throttled and suffered a mock-execution similar to those recently experienced by Dick McKee and Peadar Clancy; however, in O'Malley's case a blank round was fired, causing severe bruising and burns. McKee's sister, Máire, passed his holding cell one day with fellow

Cumann na mBan member Áine Malone, while collecting her late brother's belongings. The cell was tiny, dungeon-like and contained a small iron bed, mattress, two blankets, a table and chair, and a slop bucket. Its thick wooden door contained a small peephole beyond which was a narrow, dimly lit corridor; it was impossible to tell night from day.[16] Malone returned later with some fresh clothes and sweets for O'Malley.[17] Now, on Christmas Day, as the Castle's Auxiliaries guzzled whiskey, Dist Insp. King offered a tumbler glass to O'Malley to toast the king. O'Malley refused. Christmas was bleak, but he soon had the last laugh.

Also in custody that Christmas Day was Garry Holohan. He was arrested after ammunition was discovered in the Clontarf water pumping station while he repaired the pump's engine at midday. Driven through the city centre, Holohan feared he was en route to Dublin Castle and a similar fate to McKee and Clancy, until his transport turned towards Capel Street, eventually reaching the North Dublin Union. There, Holohan was placed against a wall and instructed to pray. A revolver was pointed at his face. Holohan braced himself, relieved that his death would at least be instantaneous. He was then beaten about the head, suggesting otherwise. However, onlooking soldiers baulked at this. One winked at Holohan – a signal that the death threats were a bluff. The beating ceased and Holohan was taken inside a mess room where soldiers were tucking in to Christmas dinners. His own consisted of leftovers.[18] Holohan joined the interned, their number approaching 1,500.

Ironically, British military operations were wound down towards Christmas 1920 because prisoner congestion had become critical. Arbour Hill, Mountjoy and Kilmainham were packed far beyond capacity and there were no longer enough barrack cages for prisoners. The pace of evacuating internees to Ballykinlar and other camps operating around the country could not keep abreast of arrests. This was aggravated by the fact that persons arrested under civilian law were entitled to legal representation, creating colossal administrative hurdles. Among those arrested were the owner and the editor of *The Freeman's Journal*. The public relations ramifications quickly saw the Castle government backtracking to save face. Both were soon released 'on medical grounds'.[19]

Christmas 1920 was subdued in Dublin. Nevertheless, on St Stephen's Night, 26 December, city-dwellers who could went out, flocking to picture-houses and pubs; queues were lengthy. Plays took place. 'Old gentlemen, who had prolonged their dinners at their clubs beyond the curfew hour, glanced apprehensively up and down the street, and made a run for home as though they were criminals.'[20] The IRA stood guard around Oriel Hall near Seville Place that night. Volunteers from throughout the Dublin Brigade arrived singly and in pairs, nodding at one other as they arrived, each summoned following selection for a special task, the significance of which was revealed. Oscar Traynor and Seán Russell – promoted to vice-brigadier – sat at a table at the top of the hall, both known to most Volunteers. Lesser known was Capt. Paddy Flanagan, who sat with them.

When Traynor stood up, everyone else followed, saluting their new brigadier. He then addressed them, saying that those present had been selected by their company officers to join a new unit which would be known as the Active Service Unit of the Dublin Brigade.[21] The unit's job would be to take the fight to the police on the streets of Dublin. Traynor expanded: the ASU was to be a full-time outfit called to action at any moment. Therefore, each member needed to leave his employment. He reassured them of payment for their service but warned the likelihood of long-term survival in the ASU was minimal. Consequently, it would not reflect badly on any man who did not wish to transfer to it. A small number stood up, citing reasons why they could not, and departed. Traynor continued, pledging that should Ireland's independence struggle succeed, then the surviving ASU members would become the first officers in the Irish Regular Army.[22]

Those remaining were introduced to the unit's O/C, Capt. Flanagan. He explained that the unit would be divided into four sections, each given its own battalion number. Sections one and two would operate north of the Liffey under nineteen-year-old medical student Lt Frank Flood from Summerhill. Sections three and four would operate to its south under Lt John Dunne. Each section would have its own commander. The ASU's quartermaster would issue each member with a .45 calibre semi-automatic pistol and twelve rounds of ammunition. Grenades would be provided for city ambushes.[23] The ASU would also have its own intelligence officer and medical orderly.

Flanagan explained that each section would be responsible for selecting the best ambush locations in its own operational area. Reconnaissance of laneways, streets, back alleys, roads and escape routes was pivotal. Each section member was to have detailed knowledge of these. Every attack would be launched with surprise and last no more than five minutes. No attack was to become drawn out, otherwise superior enemy numbers would quickly overwhelm the unit. When appropriate, two sections would merge for larger ambushes.

Finally, those gathered were segregated into their sections. Lts Flood and Dunne selected section commanders. The ASU HQ was to be located in Flanagan's office in 17 Eustace Street. The men were told to prepare for imminent action before being dismissed.

On the opposing side, the following day, control of the DDSB was transferred to the police from Army Intelligence, as previously foretold by Gen. Tudor to Col Winter. This strategy shift prompted the resignation of Lt Col Walter Wilson – appointed the previous summer – along with several others, as a result of unwillingness to operate under the remit of a civil power. Wilson was replaced as head of Special Branch by thirty-seven-year-old David Boyle, a veteran intelligence officer who had worked with MI1c.[24] Boyle had served throughout the world, including in New York, where his office had closely monitored De Valera's movements. Since Boyle's arrival in Ireland, he had operated as Tudor's advisor and assistant. Special Branch was renamed 'D Branch' of Col Winter's CIS.

CIS consisted of five branches, A to D and a separate raids branch, with specific duties such as administrative, legal and raiding assigned to A–C and the raids branch, intelligence gathering and collating falling under D Branch.[25] Plans were also prepared for a new Auxiliary company, Z Company, consisting of men from other companies with proven aptitudes for intelligence work. Dispatches were issued to company commanders seeking suitable candidates. Z Company would be built around the core of cadets already assigned to the police advisor's office.

Senior army commanders resented the transfer of Special Branch. With over 500 enemy suspects and prisoners in custody awaiting interrogation, they felt they were making impressive inroads. Nevertheless, the die was cast. GHQ Military Intelligence would remain under the military command of Gen. Brind and Col Hill-Dillon. Henceforth, the police and army would cooperate fully on intelligence.

Two days later, the impetus to reset the overall balance in intelligence terms in favour of Britain was reinforced by Gens Macready, Boyd, Tudor and Strickland – commander of 6th Division headquartered in Cork's Victoria Barracks – when they asserted, at the commencement of a two-day cabinet conference in Downing Street to discuss the military situation, that any kind of truce would 'give Sinn Féin a chance to regroup – particularly in the intelligence field'.[26] Macready repeated his earlier assertions that his forces would defeat the IRA within three to four months, paving the way for civil elections. Strickland was equally optimistic. Macready also called for the expansion of martial law beyond the four existing Munster counties to deny the enemy breathing space, initially to Counties Clare, Waterford, Wexford and Kilkenny. Sir John Anderson also rejected any further truce suggestions.

The conference's conclusion was that elections could be set for May 1921, but that an expansion of martial law was unnecessary. Macready was livid, given assurances he had received about his powers to extend martial law on 9 December. He had written almost a year earlier in trepidation of being sent to Ireland, a task he had instinctively felt 'would be affected by every variation of the political weathercock'.[27] In this regard he had been correct, but that weathercock turned again within days. On 4 January 1921, martial law was declared by Lord French in the additional four counties. Frustratingly for Macready, subsequent attempts to introduce martial law in the capital were overruled.

However, Macready remained hamstrung for additional reasons. Despite audacious plans to 'sweep from one end of the country to the other with infantry on foot and in vehicles', backed up by cavalry, aircraft, shallow-draft boats for river patrols, a naval blockade of ports, and all backed up by incessant police raids acting on improved intelligence, the empire simply could not spare him the resources to secure, and more importantly, contain Ireland, given its wider commitments.[28] Rigid conservative imperialists in England baulked at compromise, citing: 'To give way in Ireland would be to give way everywhere', and applauded the hard-line stance.[29] But something had to give somewhere; military theorists had understood for centuries the maxim applicable to overstretched forces that: 'He who defends everything, defends nothing.'[30]

On the first night of the cabinet conference, the Cork IRA shot dead three RIC members in the small town of Midleton, triggering the war's first official military reprisals. Seven houses were set alight after leaflets were distributed throughout the town warning of house burnings. The press was typically hostile, suggesting that innocent civilians who could not possibly have forewarned authorities of the attack were being persecuted. These castigations were followed by widespread street protests. Ironically, some of the properties destroyed belonged to the unionist 1st Earl of Midleton, William St John Brodrick, soon to become a pivotal player on Ireland's tumultuous stage.

Back in Dublin, as 1920 ended, civilians grappled with the war's side effects. Eking out an existence was almost impossible for a great many. Unemployment was rampant, law and order invisible. Bank robberies were rife, some carried out with a precision that spawned accusations that the Auxiliaries were behind them. Suspicion was initially directed towards the IRA for many such robberies, until customers at the Dublin Savings Bank on Lower Abbey Street had their pocket contents and handbags stolen during a raid. This bank's clientele were generally less well off than that of other banks, so suspicion fell away from the IRA, given that such behaviour would have constituted propaganda suicide, which the Auxiliaries clearly cared little about.

Disease was rampant. More than 10,000 city dwellers suffered from TB. Hospital funding was sparse and their precarious existences relied heavily upon philanthropy and fundraising. Unfortunately, this was not always enough. Infant mortality remained staggeringly high compared with other European cities, caused primarily by poor sanitation, cold and poor ventilation in the city's sprawling slums. St Ultan's Hospital for infants in Charlemont Place, founded by Dr Kathleen Lynn and Madeleine fFrench-Mullen, struggled to cope.

Dubliners looked forward to 1921 with apprehension and cynicism, but also with hopes of peace and change. Sinn Féin, meanwhile, had managed to maintain its core support. Its military wing had proved adaptable, tenacious and ruthless, despite setbacks; none more critical than the loss of McKee and Clancy. Its nemesis, the RIC, was unrecognisable compared to its former image of respectable propriety. More than 1,600 of its members had resigned in 1920 alone, to add to the 178 killed throughout the country. Further pay rises for its rank and file had drawn some, but not nearly enough, recruits. To compensate, enlistment to their paramilitary reinforcements had been ramped up, particularly in the year's second half. In October alone, more than 1,100 had joined up. Notably, one-fifth of the overall number were of Irish birth. The coming months saw the number of men who had passed through recruiting stations for the Tans and Auxiliaries, since recruiting for the Tans began in January 1920, reach 14,000.[31] The IRA had its work cut out, and for those at its forefront, 1921 was about to get off to a bad start.

On New Year's Eve, Tom Cullen visited the top-floor flat of thirty-four-year-old Eileen McGrane. A university lecturer, McGrane was captain of

Cumann na mBan's University Branch, which was affiliated to 3rd Battalion IRA. Joe O'Connor acted as liaison between the two.[32] McGrane shared the upscale flat just yards from the Mansion House with Mary McCarthy and Margaret Trench.

Cullen was a regular visitor, as was Collins. A centre room of the flat acted as a small office, where Collins and Griffith had met regularly until Griffith's recent arrest. Rory O'Connor also visited often. Collins stored documents there; frequently those no longer of use to the IRA, but which, if discovered by the enemy, would provide detrimental intelligence. Collins, however, seemed loath to dispose of files, a habit that proved costly.

Cullen warned McGrane on arrival that he had observed a suspicious-looking woman who had appeared very interested in him as he entered. So he told her that he would have to stop visiting and then left. Later that night, fifteen F Company Auxiliaries, under Dist Insp. Kenneth Crang and Platoon Commander Robert Simpson, stormed the flat looking for Cullen. McGrane was arrested when piles of unsecured documents were discovered in a large wooden box in the office. Personal details of Volunteers were found, as well as copies of Ned Broy's police notes and several secret reports from G-Division; many were over a year old and included documents taken by Collins during his daring overnight visit to the central police station facilitated by Broy back in April 1919.[33] McGrane was taken to Dublin Castle. While city dwellers rang in the new year, she was interrogated rigorously by Winter, a process alternating with more subtle interrogations from equally cunning Castle lawyers. She divulged nothing, but the damage was done, and this marked the beginning of a long and arduous incarceration for her. Critically, the discovered documents implicated Broy and, by association, his fellow IRA mole Jim McNamara.

Within twenty-four hours, the seized documents were handed to DMP Chief Commissioner Col Walter Edgeworth-Johnstone. They became the subject of tense speculation amongst individual detectives. So many sensitive documents having been found in enemy possession led them to fear that their own ranks were riddled with informers.

Castle authorities immediately investigated. Luckily for Broy, however, Supt. Owen Brien, a bitter enemy of the IRA, had recently retired and been replaced by the less antagonistic Supt. Purcell, who liked Broy. Purcell warned Broy he could be implicated as an enemy collaborator given his oversight of the political office when the documents had originally been typed up. 'Every vestige of political duty' was immediately removed from Brunswick Street to Dublin Castle. Broy had to be particularly careful when meeting Collins and feared arrest at any moment.[34]

Less likely to be arrested was De Valera. Sir John Anderson had instructed Gen. Macready not to arrest him when they heard he was back in Dublin, hoping his return might eventually pave the way for more fruitful negotiations than the recent failures. Indeed, Fr Michael O'Flanagan was again about to attempt to intervene to talk peace with, among others, Lloyd George and Andy Cope. Macready was aghast at Anderson's instruction, protesting: 'It is impossible to carry out a repressive policy if we have one hand tied behind our back.'[35] He later complained that IRA men were using De Valera as cover to avoid their own arrests by being in his proximity, while also warning of the dangers of De Valera getting killed in a crossfire in such a situation.

Tom Cullen's New Year's Eve escape was fortuitous; he was to be married on 3 January. Devlin's was the venue for his stag night celebrations the night before. Mick Leahy, vice-commandant of Cork No. 1 Brigade, arrived in Dublin that day to progress plans for the proposed Italian arms shipment and was astonished at the blowout involving most of IRA GHQ, although Mulcahy departed into the streets just before curfew. Leahy's choice of lemonade, when whiskey was flowing, was mocked by Collins, who 'seemed to be master of the revels'.[36] Leahy's plans were discussed among men with very sore heads over breakfast the next morning.

The party was in full swing when military and auxiliary patrols passed Devlin's, oblivious to the tantalising haul of senior enemy staff proceeding to the pub's upper floors, after its doors were locked, for a long night of drunken shenanigans, much of it at the expense of Devlin's furniture. Devlin's was occasionally visited by Auxiliaries, as was Kirwan's pub, another sympathetic establishment in nearby 49 Great Britain Street.

Meanwhile, by early January, Col Winter had promoted Eugene Igoe to sergeant owing to his unit's rapidly proven proficiency. Additional provincial officers transferred to it. Dublin Castle's holding rooms were filling with captured Volunteers from outside Dublin. Their growing success was not lost on IRA intelligence. The hunt for unit members intensified.

On several occasions, intelligence officers had picked up the unit's trail, only for Igoe's men to double back on their tracks, causing their pursuers to lose contact before the Squad could be mobilised against them.[37] One intelligence officer, James Hughes, came face to face with 'Igoe's Identification Squad' in College Green late one afternoon as he walked from Crow Street to the Antient Concert Rooms with a parcel of documents, hoping to look innocuous among the crowds. Two of Igoe's men eyed him suspiciously but stood aside. Then, as he carried on, several more did likewise. Hughes quickly realised who they were. He pressed on. Hughes was lucky; Igoe's men left him alone.[38] When he eventually returned to Crow Street he reported this, and the threat they presented.

Thomas Newell, meanwhile, was operating full-time for IRA intelligence. Early each morning he and another officer combed the city streets hoping to spot Igoe's men in a daunting game of cat and mouse. They paid particular attention to train stations, knowing the policemen were monitoring arrivals.

Early on Tuesday 7 January, Newell left his North Circular Road flat. By 9.30 a.m. he was outside McBirney's department store on Aston Quay, awaiting his comrade. He suddenly noticed Igoe, accompanied by eighteen of his men spread out in twos and threes, approaching from O'Connell Bridge. Newell darted into McBirney's doorway hoping they would pass.[39] His action paid off; Igoe and his men strode past heading westward, then turned left into Bedford Row.

Newell stepped back out into the street looking for his comrade while maintaining observation on the enemy, then followed them alone. He trailed them onto Dame Street, Trinity Street and, eventually, Wicklow Street.[40] There, he bumped into Charlie Dalton, whose father ran a decorating business on that street. Newell told Dalton who he was following and that they had just turned into Grafton Street. Both then made for Crow Street. A runner was dispatched from there to Moreland's to fetch Tom Keogh, who soon arrived. Keogh was then told to assemble the Squad at Stephen's Green West; they would ambush the policemen on their return journey from Harcourt Street railway station, their suspected destination as an inbound train was due.[41]

Newell and Dalton left Crow Street and strode towards the station, but just as they turned right from Wicklow Street into Grafton Street at Switzer's department store, Newell came face to face with Igoe who, unexpectedly, was already making his return journey. A look of suspicious recognition appeared on Igoe's face. Newell and Dalton, seeing the rest of Igoe's men, realised they were in a hornet's nest. They kept walking until Newell suddenly felt a hand grip his coat collar. He turned to find Igoe's face inches from his as

Igoe declared menacingly: 'Come on Newell, I want you.' Newell feigned innocence, claiming that was not his name. Igoe smirked and replied, 'I know you anyhow.'[42] Dalton was also surrounded and warned not to move.

Both were ordered to walk into Wicklow Street under close guard by a number of policemen. The rest spread out in pairs laughing and chatting among the city's pedestrians.

Tom Keogh, James Slattery and Vinny Byrne arrived at Crow Street, where Liam Tobin, agitated, asked if they were armed. They replied, 'No.' Unaware that by now Igoe had already been and gone, Tobin demanded: 'For God's sake, get them quick. Igoe is on his way to Harcourt St. railway station.'[43] Keogh ordered Byrne to get to Moreland's fast, grab three pistols and meet them at the Green.

Minutes later, Byrne collected Slattery's long-barrelled Webley, Keogh's 'Peter the Painter', as well as his short-barrelled Webley, and his own 'Peter'. He slung all four holstered guns onto his belt and threw on his long overcoat to conceal the small arsenal, then hurried towards Stephen's Green, crossing the Ha'penny Bridge, the carrying on into Dame Street. His planned route to the Green was via Exchequer Street, Drury Street and South King Street.[44]

Igoe halted his unit outside the Wicklow Hotel on Wicklow Street, tactically positioned to fend off attackers. Between the bodies of his surrounding captors, Newell saw Keogh and Slattery fifty yards away on Grafton Street stomping towards the Green, oblivious to his predicament. Igoe ordered a small number of his unit to Dublin Castle to secure transport and meet him in Dame Street, and then ordered the rest to move out. Soon afterwards, Newell and Dalton were shoved against a wall of 38 Dame Street, a narrow five-storey building on the wide street's southern side, and questioned separately. Igoe demanded to know why Newell was in Dublin and who Dalton was. Newell insisted he did not know Dalton, claiming to have just met him. Dalton responded similarly, protesting that Newell had simply asked him for directions.

Across Dame Street Vinny Byrne observed Dalton among the group at No. 38. Dalton quickly noticed Byrne but feigned otherwise. Byrne mistakenly assumed Dalton was speaking with ASU members. He pressed on, nodding as he passed. Dalton knew better than to respond.

Igoe then switched back to Newell and continued interrogating. Newell, sensing the game was up, retorted: 'I know you, Igoe, and you know me.'[45] Igoe smiled, assured now of why Newell was in Dublin. He then turned his attention back to Dalton and, apparently satisfied with his explanation, told him to 'walk on and not look back'.[46] Dalton stepped away, but as he walked he suspected he was being followed. Every corner he turned saw him increase pace, fearing being shot any second. His father's business was based in an upper floor of 15 Wicklow Street, just yards from where he had been held earlier. He made his way there, rushed up its narrow staircase, stopped, heart palpitating, listening for the sounds of footsteps that never came. With no time to waste he turned and made for Stephen's Green, where he found the Squad members and told them to hurry back to Dame Street.

However, on Dame Street, Igoe had enough of waiting for his transport so Newell was marched off with two men to his front, one on either side and two behind. The remainder spread out in tactical formation. Newell was then led across the Liffey. Fifteen minutes later they halted at the junction of Greek Street and Chancery Street, behind the Four Courts. Igoe's unit spread out at the junction, while Igoe interrogated Newell again. Newell remained silent, but Igoe knew why he was there – to identify him for assassination. He decided, therefore, to send the IRA a warning. He pointed into Greek Street and told Newell to 'run into that street'.[47] Newell refused, fearing the worst. His heart raced as he braced himself. Then, defiantly, he told Igoe to shoot him where he stood. Igoe punched him hard in the face. Newell reeled into the street. Then, suddenly, four shots rang out.

Pedestrians in the surrounding market area scattered. Newell was hit in the right calf, the stomach and twice in the right hip. He collapsed, haemorrhaging, writhing in agony. Igoe blew a whistle and a police van soon arrived from the adjacent Bridewell station. Newell was lifted and manhandled into the back. From there he was driven to the Bridewell where his tribulations worsened. He was taken to a basement cell and beaten around the head with revolver butts. Answers were demanded. He divulged nothing. Luckily for Newell, his stomach wound was not imminently life-threatening, and, despite losing four teeth, his interrogation was short-lived. He was eventually taken to King George V Hospital.[48] Newell survived, but was under continuous surgical care for a year.

Collins quickly heard about Newell. His shooting increased the impetus to eliminate Igoe. Meanwhile, Ned Broy was, astonishingly, still risking his life for IRA intelligence. When bringing information to Collins, fearing he was being followed continuously, he travelled by tram throughout the city, but, instead of boarding along with other passengers, he waited until trams had passed, then sprinted to catch them, knowing he would not be followed – Broy was a competitive athlete and could outrun almost any pursuer.

At one point, Broy discovered that an Army and Navy store in D'Olier Street – one of many in the post-war city – was expecting a consignment of Webley revolvers and 'some thousands of rounds of ammunition' for a British quartermaster. When he relayed this to Collins, Tobin was placed in charge of seizing them, which he did. Dublin Castle wrote the incident off given what was happening daily in the city.[49]

During mid-January, Broy noticed Collins was perturbed about recent overtures from De Valera indicating that Collins should be transferred to the USA; a move which, if successful, would happen in conjunction with a gradual easing off of the war. De Valera had emphasised to Collins the staggering influence he could have in the USA. Collins sounded out Broy's opinion, which he greatly respected; it was Broy who originally suggested to Collins the well-proven strategic benefits of targeting rural RIC barracks in April 1919. Broy told Collins, typically attentive, that any such easing off would be seen as weakness and, consequently, would be a huge morale boost for the enemy. Broy elaborated, saying that the relationships Collins had built up over time involving matters of life and death would render it impossible, 'psychologically, to establish the same microscopic understanding with any other person who might replace him as had been laboriously built up over a critical period of years with him'.[50] He added that resentment would result from those regularly risking their lives in the event of such an arbitrary move.

Collins seemed anxious and worn out to Broy, which concerned him. He viewed Collins, as did the IRA and its enemies, as the face of the national struggle. Some feared that De Valera was undermining Collins. Austin Stack had by now been appointed by De Valera as president designate rather than Collins, despite the latter having so recently accepted the acting role when Stack had refused it along with Brugha. Some who questioned Stack's ability to cope with even his own ministerial brief noted this move apprehensively. The separation of Volunteer police units from active IRA units as decreed on 1 November had so far not been successful. Active Volunteers were still being called upon for policing, and Stack appeared devoid of workable solutions. Republican courts were also under relentless pressure, caused by widespread arrests of judges and registrars, and a reluctance of others to step into the breach.

Stack was not the only minister grappling with an underground government department under relentless pressure. By now 'nervous breakdowns were an occupational hazard in the Dáil administration'.[51] William Cosgrave's Local Government department was under crushing financial strain and Cosgrave was drawing ire from his colleagues, including Collins. Kevin O'Higgins continued to take up the slack from Cosgrave's repeated lengthy absences. To compensate for his department's financial dilemma, O'Higgins had recently issued a warning to vacillating rate collectors who appeared unconvinced of their obligations to Dáil Éireann as decreed by its TDs. O'Higgins had adopted a coercive stance employing the IRA, which was moderately successful, and funds began to flow again. Now, in January, De Valera ordered Cosgrave to come out of self-imposed exile in Glencree and take visible control of his department.

Meanwhile, the ASU was determined to ensure there was no let-up in hostilities. During January's second week, Capt. Flanagan met with Lts Flood and Dunne, as well as Section Commanders Mick Dunne and Tom McGrath at HQ. Flanagan instructed them that an action was to be launched against the Auxiliaries, primarily to observe how they reacted. He also wanted to trial their ambush tactics. Accordingly, he decreed that sections one and two would merge to ambush a Crossley Tender full of Auxiliaries that drove westbound daily along Bachelors Walk. A small number from sections three and four would also participate, including Lt Dunne.[52]

Flanagan detailed his plan. Bachelors Walk was a busy thoroughfare full of auctioneering rooms, cabinet makers and antique dealers – excellent cover for unit members waiting to attack. Additionally, these premises offered good escape routes into North Lotts Lane running parallel behind. The Tender normally travelled across O'Connell Bridge and turned left; therefore the chosen attack zone was the 250-yard stretch of Bachelors Walk between Litton Lane and Lower Liffey Street. The attackers would be divided into three groups: group one – armed mostly with grenades – would deploy along the length of the attack zone; group two – armed with handguns – would spread out along North Lotts to guard the escape route; group three – carrying handguns and grenades – would deploy on Liffey Street at the junction of Great Strand Street and North Lotts. This was in case the enemy turned right into Liffey Street in pursuit. Flood would lead the operation with Dunne deputising. Flanagan would observe from across the river. The ambush was scheduled for Wednesday 12 January.

During Wednesday's early afternoon, Flood relayed Flanagan's orders to sections one and two in the Oxford Billiard Rooms in Upper Sackville Street, next door to the Granville Hotel.[53] Ten men of group one would deploy as planned between Litton Lane and Liffey Street, but dividing into three smaller sections: with two men detailed to Litton Lane, two more to the halfway point along the ambush route, and six close to the junction of Liffey Street. Four more from group two would guard their escape route on North Lotts, while the remainder of the combined sections – group three – would deploy as initially planned. Spotters would be positioned on O'Connell Bridge and at Mansfield's boot shop to warn of the Tender's approach, the precise time of its anticipated arrival uncertain; it normally travelled during late afternoon. Before they left the billiard hall, the men were warned not to draw unwanted attention.

On Sackville Street the ASU dispersed and walked nervously to the ambush area in twos and threes. Dunne took position with another Volunteer at Litton Lane. Christopher Fitzsimons and James Carrigan took position outside Wren's auction rooms, 9 Bachelors Walk. Tom McGrath, Christopher 'Kit' O'Malley, Joseph Gilhooly, Patrick 'Ninepence' O'Connor, James Harpur and one other Volunteer positioned themselves outside Scannell's auction house, No. 4, close to Liffey Street.[54] Scannell's was full of women and children attending an auction. This was worrying as their line of retreat was through this building. To keep it open a man would have to run inside and clear a path to the back door while another held the front door open. The remainder – group three – deployed with Flood around Liffey Street.

The unit members waited tensely, smoking and trying to blend in as trams chimed slowly past, adorned with advertisements. They chatted, read newspapers, nodded at passers-by and browsed shop windows until 4.30 p.m., when the Tender was suddenly spotted on O'Connell Bridge. On Aston Quay opposite, Flanagan, observing, folded his newspaper and stood at the quay wall.[55] He saw the lookouts administer signals just as the Tender turned onto Bachelors Walk. The signals were relayed as far as Liffey Street. There, Flood quickly looked at each man mustered around him. They drew breath. It was time to strike.

The Tender lumbered along Bachelors Walk. Next to the driver sat a cadet, in the rear six more. All wore the distinctive dark green 'Balmoral' caps that marked them out, except the driver, who wore a standard RIC cap.

All hell broke loose as soon as the Tender drew abreast of Litton Lane. Dunne stepped out and lobbed a grenade, which landed among the six cadets in the back and detonated. Its impact, however, was minimal, injuries slight. The sudden whining of the Tender's engine, as the driver increased speed, followed the blast. Civilians scattered, while on the opposite quayside people's eyes were drawn to the spectacle. Flanagan observed Dunne and his comrade disappear into Litton Lane as the rallying Auxiliaries shot in their direction.

As soon as the explosion was heard, a Volunteer at Scannell's ran into the building brandishing his revolver and shouting at the terrified women and children to clear a passage.[56] They quickly did. Women shielded their children. Desperate cries rang out amid appeals for divine protection. The Volunteer then held the back door open, while shouting repeatedly to keep the passage clear.

The Tender approached Wren's as its adrenalised passengers stood shooting their pistols, wedging legs for support and clasping side boards. Christopher Fitzsimons stepped out onto the tram-lined cobblestones and hurled two more grenades.[57] One exploded close to the Tender. The other landed on the pavement next to the quay wall. A nearby off-duty soldier reacted with lightning speed, picking it up and casting it over the wall where it plopped harmlessly into the river. Fitzsimons and James Carrigan, meanwhile, raced into Wren's and, in seconds, escaped out the back into North Lotts.

Return fire from the Tender was wild. Shots flew everywhere, ricocheting from brick façades and breaking windows.[58] The terrified driver maintained speed. One Auxiliary, up for the fight, shouted at him to 'pull up' as he approached Liffey Street, but to no avail.[59] Then, to his horror, the driver suddenly noticed two more IRA men, 'Ninepence' O'Connor and Tom McGrath, step off the pavement swinging arms and threw two more grenades, which curved through the air and exploded next to the Tender. As his comrades ducked, a single cadet shot rapidly at the pair, quickly escaping alongside comrades through Scannell's, bullets peppering the shop front. Women and children inside screamed in fright, bolting for cover, knocking furniture over in the pandemonium.

Frank Flood readied his few men, expecting the Tender to turn into Liffey Street. However, its driver instead made for Capel Street Bridge beyond. The operation was over and within a minute the ASU had vanished, the only evidence of their attack the shocked civilians gathering on the streets outside Scannell's.

Flanagan was satisfied; the enemy had been taken completely by surprise, with no idea where the attack had come from. Indeed several bullets had glanced off buildings on Aston Quay, across the river.[60] Unit members had carried out orders as planned and the engagement had not become drawn out. He was unaware of the extent of enemy casualties, but confident that the ASU had proven its worth.

Early the following morning, Thursday 13 January, hot on the heels of this attack, it was the turn of the ASU's sections three and four to make their mark on the south-side. Lt Dunne was briefed by Flanagan at ASU HQ, acting on intelligence that a Ford touring car transporting four Auxiliary intelligence officers travelled from Dublin Castle to Beggar's Bush daily between 11 a.m. and midday.[61] Dunne's mission was to ambush the car in Merrion Square.

Dunne mustered the unit. They were briefed about the target and its typical route: Nassau Street, Clare Street, Merrion Square North and onto Lower Mount Street. Unit members were detailed to attack positions. Philip 'Onion' Quinn was to lurk on Merrion Square, 150 yards from Holles Street. From there he would signal the car's approach to his comrades further east. George Nolan, James Harpur and Paddy Rigney would then attack first, from Merrion Square's junction with Holles Street, outside the National Maternity Hospital. Next up, Jim Dolan and William Philips would attack from Gough's sales yard if the car made it past the first ambush point into Lower Mount Street.[62] Then, a 100 yards further, twenty-eight-year-old Section Leader Augustine 'Gus' Murphy, Paddy Collins and Patrick Brunton would launch the final attack, if necessary, from Grant's Row, a narrow laneway to the left as the car approached. Lookouts would be posted in the surrounding area. Dunne would guard the ambushers' escape route from Holles Row, running between Holles Street and Grant's Row, parallel to the car's direction of travel.

At 11 a.m., the men took position. At 11.20, the touring car approached leisurely from Clare Street onto Merrion Square as anticipated, containing five Auxiliaries in mufti. When 'Onion' observed the car he waited to ensure it was the target vehicle, crossing the road and glancing inside as it passed. He then quickly whipped out a white handkerchief and waved it, signalling his comrades to attack. However, the car's occupants saw the indiscreet signal and drew revolvers as the driver depressed the accelerator.[63]

Within seconds the car reached the junction of Holles Street. Rigney, Nolan and Harpur darted out. Two grenades flew at the car, followed by a succession of pistol shots. One grenade smashed a window and landed inside.

The other bounced off onto the road and failed to detonate. The car sped on, passing the hospital to its left as the three attackers retreated into Holles Street. Bullets chipped the cobblestones as they ran from return fire.

The grenade in the car exploded, causing it to swerve violently as windows shattered with the blast. It then zigzagged towards Gough's yard before halting, its engine still running.[64] Its wounded occupants, lacerated and half-blind from shrapnel and broken glass, were dazed. Dolan and Philips joined the fray, emerging and firing. Their assault jolted the driver. As the car pinged with ricochets, it took off again with the three men firing raggedly through the smashed back window. Dolan and Philips vanished from sight as the car passed Grant's Row, where it came under fire again. Paddy Collins raced out beneath the pedestrian archway where it joined Mount Street and threw his grenade. Seeing this, the disoriented Auxiliaries braced themselves again, but the bomb bounced off the car and rolled harmlessly onto the street, also without exploding.

The car then sped away along Lower Mount Street with the three cadets still firing from the back seat. Within minutes its badly wounded occupants made it to Beggar's Bush. The Volunteers on Grant's Row made their escape.

Miraculously, both ASU attacks had resulted in no casualties to its members or to civilians. This trend would not continue as operations escalated. However, at 4.30 p.m. that day on Aston Quay, at a British Army checkpoint, the growing tension in the city saw two civilians, twenty-two-year-old Martha Nowlan and sixteen-year-old James Brennan, killed and seven others wounded. Trigger-happy soldiers had fired on a nearby crowd after a rifleman accidentally dropped his loaded rifle from a passing military truck. The rifle discharged, causing the soldiers to fear they were under attack.[65] Meanwhile, throughout the country the daily killings and maimings continued.

In Dublin it was not only the ASU escalating their campaign. In early January, an IRA Army Council meeting convened at 40 Herbert Park, home of the O'Rahilly family, during which De Valera's expression of preference for conventional military style attacks led to the selection of two potential targets for such an operation: Beggar's Bush, and the Custom House. Attending the meeting were Traynor, Brugha, Stack, Mulcahy, Collins, Diarmuid O'Hegarty, Gearóid O'Sullivan, Liam Mellows, Seán Russell, Director of Training J. J. 'Ginger' O'Connell, Quartermaster Gen. Seán McMahon, Piaras Béaslaí and De Valera. De Valera had come close to arrest en route, having been detained at a cordon.[66] When asked to raise his hands he had, by force of habit from previous imprisonments, assumed the appropriate convict stance for such a command, arms outstretched sideways, an involuntary move likely to arouse suspicion.[67] Luckily for him, the gesture went unnoticed.

Outlining his rationale for larger-scale attacks, De Valera asserted that a really spectacular coup should be attempted which would 'reverberate around the world'.[68] He declared that it would need to take place in Dublin; the city was, he argued, as well-known abroad as London or Paris.[69] Then, referring again to negative international perceptions of current IRA tactics, he insisted that such a large action would send a clear message to the world and to England that 'they had not cowed the citizen soldiers of Ireland'.[70] He then introduced Beggar's Bush and the Custom House as potential targets, the former due to its position as Auxiliary HQ, the latter because of its pivotal importance to the British Civil Service in Ireland. Located within its walls were Inland Revenue, Local Government headquarters, Estate Duty control register, Customs and Excise, the Stamp Duty office, the Income Tax office and Joint Stock Company register.[71] The Custom House had already been pinpointed under the late Dick McKee's extensive plans to resist conscription in 1918, along with detailed plans to contain the enemy in barracks during any such large-scale operations. McKee had also advocated attacking it the previous Easter, but the plan was bypassed in favour of hugely successful widespread operations against other Revenue offices.

Following further detailed discussions, Collins looked smilingly at Traynor and, referring to the feasibility of such a plan, said, 'That'll be up to you Traynor', to which Traynor told the council that, in his opinion, Beggar's Bush was virtually impregnable. Nevertheless, he said he would take the required time to explore both possibilities.[72] To assist, the council pledged that GHQ intelligence would be placed at his disposal whenever necessary, emphasising that, whichever target was selected, any attack would become a brigade operation, and GHQ's full cooperation would be afforded.[73]

Traynor then spent two weeks, assisted by Frank Saurin, Liam Tobin and Tom Cullen, studying the feasibility of an attack on Beggar's Bush, eventually concluding that it would indeed be impossible. It was surrounded by fifteen-foot-high walls and contained a large number of highly trained, well-armed and motivated enemy forces. Traynor then focused on the Custom House.[74]

Meanwhile, the British military were themselves gearing up and about to turn large areas of Dublin city into fully fledged war zones.

7

Attacks Intensify, IRA Setbacks and Successes

'We'll give you fucking bubbles'

On Saturday 15 January, a ring of steel enveloped North King Street, Lower Church Street, Capel Street and the north quays, within which more than 600 British soldiers were deployed, half forming a cordon, the other half conducting house-to-house searches. Barbed-wire entanglements stretched across perimeter street junctions, each guarded by between twelve and twenty infantrymen. Sandbagged machine-gun emplacements were set up overlooking adjacent River Liffey bridges. Raids and searches within the densely packed streets lasted two days. Operation Optimist, its code name, was directed towards capturing Michael Collins. Five detachments from the King's Own Regiment, Prince of Wales Volunteers, Welch Regiment, Rifle Brigade and Royal Berkshire Regiment, each with sixty men, commenced searches after dark, starting in North King Street, inching into Beresford Street, North Anne Street, Halston Street and Green Street, before clawing their way to the quays.

North King Street was the scene of vicious fighting and a massacre during the Easter Rising. Officers and NCOs warned deploying troops that the area was dangerous. However, this time there was no repetition of the bloodbath, and the volleys of well-directed fire that had five years earlier resounded throughout the warren of cobbled alleyways were replaced by taunts and jibes in thick Dublin accents. Provisions to allow food into the area were poorly planned. Consequently, 'the soldiers displayed an obvious willingness to let friendly people pass in and out', to the disgruntlement of senior officers.[1] The operation yielded little for the military, its failure contradicting its code name. Security was subsequently deemed ineffective and it was conceded that IRA warning systems were too agile for such unwieldy operations. It was castigated by nationalist newspapers and the *Irish Bulletin* as an unwarranted siege.

Auxiliaries searching a group of civilians. *(Courtesy of Mercier Archive)*

The *Bulletin* also highlighted a noteworthy development from England that week, when the Labour Commission to Ireland's report dismissed as a fallacy Dublin Castle's claim that police had come under fire first at Croke Park during Bloody Sunday.

Meanwhile, the IRA's E Company, 3rd Battalion, were in action on 18 January. Six Volunteers ambushed a military lorry at the junction of Bird Avenue and Clonskeagh Road. Two direct grenade hits accounted for several casualties. The lorry was disabled and its driver wounded; drivers were a useful target given their general scarcity. However, just as the attackers, among them Patrick Brennan, were preparing to collect enemy weapons, one of their own men went berserk and had to be restrained. The approach of further military vehicles saw the E Company men take flight.[2]

Despite such casualties, Dublin District Command wrote that day that a long-anticipated surge in attacks on vehicles in the capital had finally materialised but with little impact. Conversely, it was asserted that more damage had been inflicted on IRA morale as a result of their ineffectiveness. The writer also mocked the potency of IRA grenades. These points would soon be driven home dispiritingly to the IRA.

The lack of killing power was glaringly illustrated on the night of Wednesday 19 January, during three separate grenade attacks. Wednesday was a busy day for the Dublin Brigade, as many employees enjoyed a half-day from

A British officer searching a civilian in Dublin. *(Courtesy of Mercier Archive)*

work on that day, allowing time for members to participate in operations; the same applied also to Saturdays. Despite Oscar Traynor's original instructions, some ASU members had yet to leave their jobs to become full-time activists.

The first of two ASU attacks on that date took place on Parliament Street and involved seventeen men, a composite of sections one, two and three, who had mustered earlier at nearby HQ with Capt. Flanagan. It was one of Volunteer Joseph O'Carroll's first actions with the unit.[3] The plan was to attack a Crossley Tender after its Auxiliary cargo departed Dublin Castle.

Flanagan positioned six pairs of men along East Essex Street, plus a spotter at its Parliament Street junction, the vehicle's anticipated route. He and four others, including O'Carroll, took position at its Crane Lane junction, twenty yards from Parliament Street. They would attack first, with the six pairs acting as backup in case the Tender stopped or turned right into East Essex Street. Unit members shivered in the frigidly cold darkness.

Then, at 7.15 p.m., a Tender carrying eight cadets from I Company left Dublin Castle and turned into Parliament Street, their caps emblazoned with the typically distinctive red diamond with RIC harp and, in this case, the letter 'T'. As soon as the ASU spotter saw the Tender, he signalled Flanagan, who quickly readied his men. Hearts pulsated. Adrenal glands went into overdrive. Moments later, the Tender reached the junction of East Essex Street and Parliament Street. Flanagan and the four men with him ran out onto the junction, Flanagan throwing a grenade among the Auxiliaries. The others fired pistols. Civilians scattered. The ASU disappeared into the darkness as the Tender stopped. The eight Auxiliaries brought their guns to bear, just as the grenade exploded with a resonating blast. The cadets were blown off their feet, momentarily disoriented, and came around to find two of their unit, Cadets Barrett and Strassman, badly wounded in their lower bodies and legs, the remainder less seriously wounded. Within seconds the Tender's wheels were rolling again. It detoured to King George V Hospital where treatment would be sought for the casualties.

Section four of the south-side ASU was also out that night – in Rathmines. A Tender was being driven towards Portobello Bridge from the nearby barracks, when Volunteers in Grove Park ambushed it. Four grenades were thrown at the Tender, three of which missed but showered the truck and area with shrapnel. This was accompanied by a lightning-fast fusillade of pistol fire. Then the attackers, like ghosts, were gone. Two cadets were wounded.

E Company, 3rd Battalion, attacked a lorry full of Auxiliaries later that night on Mespil Road.[4] Again, four grenades were flung at the lorry en route to Beggar's Bush. Following their explosions a brief firefight ensued before the IRA men withdrew. The truck sped away carrying several wounded cadets.

Two days later, on the morning of Friday 21 January, ASU section one was detailed to Binn's Bridge at the junction of Lower Drumcondra Road and Dorset Street, taking position at 8 a.m. Its mission was to ambush a party of Black and Tans driving to the Phoenix Park RIC HQ from Gormanston, crossing Binn's Bridge at roughly 8.20 a.m. each morning.[5] Section two, meanwhile, was detailed to Summerhill to ambush an anticipated Auxiliary convoy.[6]

Section one, eight strong, waited at Binn's Bridge until 9.30 a.m., but with no sign of the enemy and the area becoming busy with pedestrians and commuters, Lt Frank Flood decided to relocate his unit half a mile further up Drumcondra Road, where it intersected with Richmond Road and Millmount Avenue. There, civilian casualties would be less likely.[7] Arriving ten minutes later, Flood took stock of his surroundings. To his left, looking north, was St Patrick's Boys' School. Beyond stood St Patrick's College. Opposite the school to his right was Clonturk Park, a field containing allotments for local residents, widely used in the city. Facing the road beyond Clonturk Park was a petty sessions courthouse. Further up sat red-brick dwellings. A chest-high wall ran from the courthouse back to Richmond Road, offering concealed cover for their ambush.

Flood divided the unit into four pairs, initially positioning Thomas Bryan and Dermot O'Sullivan on the corner of Richmond Road, which ran to their east. Furthest away from Richmond Road, along the wall towards the courthouse, he positioned twenty-four-year-old Mick Magee – a seasoned Easter Rising veteran – and Seán Burke. He then placed Mick Dunne and Bernard Ryan slightly back from the courthouse towards himself and Patrick Doyle, who were closest to Bryan and O'Sullivan back at Richmond Road; 150 yards separated the four pairs. The plan was to attack when the enemy transport passed the entrance to St Patrick's College. Magee and Burke would fire first, followed by Dunne and Ryan, then Burke and Flood, and finally Bryan and O'Sullivan.

As soon as they had taken positions, Sgt Thomas Singleton of Clontarf DMP station was observed walking from Drumcondra Bridge, straddling the River Tolka. O'Sullivan, closest to the bridge, briefly approached Flood, suggesting that they detain the sergeant until after the ambush.[8] However, Flood had a standing order not to interfere with the DMP unless absolutely necessary. Singleton carried on. He noticed the IRA men and returned to the area soon afterwards with Constables Patrick Kennedy and Martin Hegarty.[9] Robert Pike, a thirty-eight-year-old former soldier living at 20 Tolka Cottages, just to the south, had also spotted the IRA men while walking. He alerted Dublin Castle. It was 10.15 a.m.

Dist Insp. King was hastily dispatched from the Castle to intercept the unit with a detachment of F Company Auxiliaries in two Tenders, supported by a Peerless armoured car. They would approach from Lower Drumcondra. Simultaneously, two Tenders from I Company, keen to strike back after their recent bloody nose at Parliament Street, set out with similar orders, but to approach Drumcondra from Ballybough, along Richmond Road.

Shortly before 10.45 a.m., at Clonturk Park there was still no sign of a target vehicle and the ASU members were drawing unwanted attention. Flood decided to abandon the ambush, signalling them to assemble at the corner of Richmond Road. Then, unexpectedly, the lorry they were awaiting approached downhill from Whitehall, passing Magee and Burke, then Dunne and Ryan before they could react. Dermot O'Sullivan, suddenly seeing it, shouted to Flood: 'We might as well have a go at this.' Flood quickly nodded.[10] O'Sullivan hurled a grenade. It exploded seconds later, just above the Tender, sending its cadets reeling from a shower of red-hot shrapnel. The driver swerved, then increased speed across the Tolka Bridge. Beyond this, seconds later, its driver saw F Company's Tenders and armoured car approaching along the Drumcondra Road at the junction with Hollybank Road. He slowed down to allow his own passengers to warn 'Tiny' King about what was ahead. King ordered his column on. Robert Pike, seeing them from Tolka Cottages, signalled the direction of the ambushers.

Magee, Burke, Dunne and Ryan had stopped in their tracks as soon as O'Sullivan attacked, awaiting revised orders. Flood, fatally, hesitated. He now stood on the corner of Richmond Road with Doyle, O'Sullivan and Bryan, just as the column from F Company came into full view, their distinctive yellow diamond cap insignia marking them out. The armoured car followed slowly and ominously behind. Flood barked repeated orders to 'Run!' O'Sullivan glanced north, only to see two more enemy vehicles bearing down. They had one option for escape – Richmond Road. The four men already on the corner of Richmond Road were now joined by Ryan, and dashed eastwards into Richmond Road, just as both pairs of Tenders screeched to a halt at the wall next to the courthouse, the armoured car just behind. Their three comrades, having hesitated, were still further up along the wall. They sprinted into the field containing the allotments in an attempt to catch up with the others via a laneway that led to Richmond Road, weaving between plots after Dunne fired a few pistol rounds to delay the Auxiliaries.

King, with lightning speed, grabbed a Winchester pump-action shotgun and fired at Magee, running next to Burke towards the rear of the Richmond Road houses. Magee was wounded in the thigh and collapsed. Burke dragged him back to his feet. Seeing this, Dunne returned fire, inviting a deluge of whizzing bullets in response, which drove him away from his two comrades. Magee was hit again, twice, the rounds making dull thuds. He fell into an allotment. Burke wrenched him up again, only for another bullet to hit him. Burke persevered, dragging Magee, who was groaning, covered in blood and mud, to a wall at the rear of a house that provided cover.[11] Magee lost consciousness. Burke, presuming he was dead, left him and sprinted after his fleeing comrades. Suddenly, he spotted an open back gate to a house and, seizing the opportunity, rushed through and entered the building. There he faced a startled elderly man and a housemaid. Panting, Burke spotted a pair of glasses. He put them on and asked the man his name, while concealing his pistol in a fireplace. When the name was provided, Burke, anticipating a raid, asked the man to tell the authorities he was his son. The elderly man nodded, terrified. The maid appeared sympathetic. Burke cleaned himself up. Meanwhile, Dunne diverted to Church Avenue, just to the north, scaled the seven-foot wall of St Joseph's blind asylum and ran to safety.

When Flood and the four others, concealed from King's view by the terraces on Richmond Road, reached its junction with Grace Park Road, they saw several escape routes, the nearest behind a row of cottages. Suddenly, however, the two I Company Tenders bore down from Richmond Road's easternmost side. The escapers wheeled north into Grace Park Road, sprinting up the steep hill for 200 yards, until, gasping, they turned right into Grace Park Gardens, a short cul de sac with a three-storey, red-brick terrace of houses to their left.[12] As they passed No. 5, Flood, hearing the Tenders' engines whine in pursuit up the hill just behind, rushed with his men for the front door. It was locked. Flood drew his revolver and shot the lock, only to find the door jammed.

The game was up. Two Tenders screeched to a halt just outside, followed by sharp commands to drop their weapons as a dozen enemy revolvers were aimed at them. Flood raised his hands, as did the others. Pistols slung in their lanyards, their pockets bulging with grenades, they were disarmed and arrested.

King ordered the area around Clonturk Park and the houses on Richmond Road searched. Magee was discovered. Regaining consciousness, but in agony, he was carried to a Tender by Auxiliary Reynolds – the IRA's recently turned double agent – and another cadet. Magee's lower body and legs were badly wounded. The Tender was quickly smeared with his blood. Soon the house Seán Burke was in was searched. Luckily for him, its occupants assisted his charade. Burke, cleaned up and wearing the elderly man's spectacles, was made to show the Auxiliaries around the house. Along with his unexpected accomplices, he was questioned for an hour until, convinced he was innocent, the cadets departed.

Less fortunate were Magee and four of the five men captured in Grace Park Gardens. Magee, from Arbour Hill, died following surgery the next morning in King George V Hospital. The others soon faced the hangman's rope; only Dermot O'Sullivan's youth – he was seventeen years old – saved him from the gallows. However, it did not save him from the clutches of Sgt Igoe and his men, soon to viciously interrogate O'Sullivan and his comrades. Robert Pike also eventually pad the ultimate price for his action as an informer on that day.

Section two, which had deployed to Summerhill that morning, did not see action. They heard the distant blast and shots from Drumcondra, and waited for some time afterwards, only to eventually disperse. I Company had approached Ballybough from Fairview en route to Drumcondra, and had, luckily for them and unfortunately for Flood's section, bypassed Summerhill.

Section one ASU was decimated. Section two learned of their comrades' fate later that day. Their families were alerted, rightly expecting imminent raids. Brig. Traynor's perilous warning in Oriel Hall the previous 26 December regarding their life expectancies as ASU members loomed large in their minds.

After the Drumcondra attack, crown forces were reminded to alternate travel routes and timetables; a tactic Lord French had employed effectively in 1919 to thwart multiple assassination attempts. However, by now both the military and the paramilitary police had other tactics in mind. As well as armouring their vehicles, in many cases with chicken wire to stop grenades landing in their midst, they would use hostages on their vehicles to ward off attacks. Five days after the ambush, loitering was outlawed under the ROIA.

Tuesday 25 January saw the Dáil's first meeting since October take place, in Fleming's Hotel, Gardiner Place. Armed lookouts patrolled nearby. The meeting had been postponed previously over security concerns, but it was deemed that discussions on the state of the country were now imperative, regardless of risk.

De Valera, speaking first, expressed regret at his lengthy absence in the USA, but added that it had enabled him to see Ireland's situation from the outside, until the prospect of the Irish people breaking under the strain of war compelled his return. He proposed a strategy that provoked rigorous debate: tapering down military operations, while maintaining the illusion that the fight was still being prosecuted with full rigour. He did not reveal his earlier petition to the Army Council for higher profile engagements. Tapering down, he argued, would ease the burden on civilians. He emphasised the importance of not letting it be seen externally that there was any such let-up, citing Lloyd George's recent hawkish reaction to the appearance of weakness within the Dáil and its military and civil administration.

Following this, De Valera read a summary of the recent peace feelers and criticised diehard British cabinet members, whom he claimed had gone for the kill once they had perceived weakness. He asserted that time and public opinion were on the republican side; therefore, they could afford to slacken off militarily and bide their time, as long as they themselves remained solid and unified.

The responses were far from unified. Liam de Róiste, TD for Cork city – scene of such huge civic burdens since December – asserted that with no effective acquaintance with Dáil policies recently, regional TDs were compelled to rely on their own judgement. He raised the issue of censure being unjustifiably directed towards Roger Sweetman over his recent newspaper letter condemning IRA methods at such a critical time, arguing that Sweetman had no other means of effectively articulating his opinions and, like most others, had no knowledge of truce negotiations. De Róiste agreed with De Valera's proposed 'easing off' strategy, stating that whilst people's resolve was robust, such fortitude would not stop fire, bullets and bayonets from killing, wounding and rendering intolerable numbers destitute. He advocated a strategy shift – an economic campaign against Britain.[13]

Piaras Béaslaí spoke up, firstly stating that 'easing off' was 'a vague and indefinite phrase'. He claimed that the current military campaign was already economic by its very nature, given the massive financial cost to Britain of maintaining a huge military presence and having to house, guard and feed so many prisoners and internees. He warned that easing off militarily would invite disaster and presented an alternative to ease civilian burdens: transferring active operations away from troublesome areas and going on the offensive in areas that had thus far escaped the worst enemy reprisals.

Roger Sweetman countered this, protesting that the IRA tactics horrifically illustrated on 21 November were merely bringing destruction upon the Irish cause, both from a reactionary standpoint resulting in endless civilian suffering, and from a propaganda perspective, particularly in America. Sweetman said he 'could understand the general argument of not showing weakness, but he considered the highest form of weakness was the weakness of being afraid to show weakness'. He proposed a conference of public bodies, most of which were sympathetic, to discuss a preliminary truce. He then contended that his controversial letter had no effect on British cabinet attitudes to peace talks, which had already been made evident with the arrest of Arthur Griffith, which had preceded his letter.

Seán Etchingham, Dáil director of fisheries, from Wexford, asked that the Dáil be given some assurances by Sweetman of his future actions. Pulling no punches, Etchingham claimed to have heard from a third party that Sweetman had publicly alleged that Collins, as minister for finance, could not produce records of expenditure of the huge sums passing through his department. The speaker asked if this had a bearing on the day's agenda. Etchingham countered, claiming that this was just one of many examples of Sweetman's questionable behaviour. He then accused Sweetman of aligning with the British in referring to IRA actions as far back as the Soloheadbeg ambush two years earlier as murders, whereas the military actions of the British instead were described with far less indictment – as killing during warfare.

Joseph MacDonagh, TD for Tipperary North and brother of the late Thomas – executed in 1916 – then spoke, initially voicing his disagreement with Sweetman's 'defeatist' views but, equally, recoiling from Etchingham's recriminations. His opinion was that any slackening off by republicans would see immediate enemy escalation. On the contrary, he proposed ratcheting up the military campaign, asserting that whatever the British dished out, the Irish could take. MacDonagh also suggested diverting resources to a propaganda campaign on the British mainland, as well as conducting a boycott of English goods, citing the fact that Ireland was the world's biggest consumer of its exports and that such a boycott would, therefore, have an immediate strategic effect. MacDonagh had been made chairman of the Belfast Boycott when it came into effect the previous August.

Kevin O'Higgins agreed, while challenging another disconcerting assertion made by Sweetman – that local government funds would be expended by March – by affirming that recent measures in ensuring better rates compliance were bearing fruit. A cash injection of £100,000 was also advanced from the Dáil; there was, therefore, no such danger. He underscored Béaslaí's economic appraisal of the war to the British: estimates suggested it cost Britain 100 million pounds annually to govern Ireland, while its revenue from the country amounted to only half that. O'Higgins highlighted industrial pressures within

Britain, which, combined with wider empire concerns, rendered her Irish position brittle, and it could be weakened further with an economic boycott. He would soon launch an additional offensive against local government officials who continued to recognise the authority of the Custom House, accusing them of treason and citing detrimental consequences for them.[14]

Seán MacEntee, representing Monaghan South, vented his spleen at the recent peace feelers, and recommended no further lengthy hibernations of the Dáil regardless of risks, claiming the position of so many TDs being divorced from the assembly had been the root cause of the near disaster. He backed the boycott idea and proposed expanding the Belfast Boycott to unionist areas throughout Ulster. In terms of the Dáil's military strategy, MacEntee argued it would be a huge mistake to ease off.

When Michael Collins spoke, he first agreed with MacEntee about the need for more regular Dáil meetings. He then praised those who possessed the courage to express views but asked that TDs consult the ministry henceforth before putting its members into such a fix, adding that 'no deputy should step into the net of the enemy at a critical time'.[15] He stated that Archbishop Clune was the only intermediary they could trust and that, having travelled to Ireland at the behest of Lloyd George and expecting to meet 'frightful ruffians', Clune had instead faced surprisingly reasonable people. Yet the productive work that had been advanced with Clune amounted to nothing due to the mistimed and ill-conceived actions of men claiming to have acted because they were divorced from the Dáil, when, in fact, they had experienced no problems hitherto accessing the ministry with more mundane issues such as land cases. He sardonically suggested that members with such access handicaps might take a train to Dublin periodically, as those who did make the occasional journey professed no such misunderstanding of policies or the positions of men and women and their commanders risking their lives daily to protect the Republic.

Regarding the war's prosecution, Collins spoke of Irish history, arguing forcefully that in previous freedom struggles acquiescence was met with even greater terrorism, and that this was presently visible in the country's quieter regions. With the exception of Cork city, Collins claimed that in places where there was significant resistance, there was comparatively little repression. This inadvertently contradicted Béaslaí's suggestion of taking the fight to quieter areas to draw reprisals from more active regions. Afterwards Collins referred to Sweetman's comments regarding ministry accounts. Collins claimed he would produce copies for any deputy on the understanding that the deputy would ensure their subsequent destruction to prevent them from falling into enemy hands, before finally digressing to financial estimates.[16]

Austin Stack backed the policy of full-scale war. He referred to the lack of emigration during the Great War, suggesting Ireland could 'well afford to lose some of the 180,000 young men saved in the last few years'.[17] He then added that even if the war cost Ireland another fifty million pounds, that would only equate to one year's revenue to England.

Richard Mulcahy, speaking as TD for Dublin Clontarf, was more restrained. He simply insisted that whatever the decision made on military strategy, it was to be administered to the IRA through the proper army authorities and not from the mouth of a Dáil member.

Liam Mellows, speaking as TD for both East Galway and North Meath, echoed De Valera, also referring to his recent years in America affording him a different perspective. He praised the resistance in the country since 1916 and ridiculed Britain in only being able to hold Ireland with the actions of the Black and Tans, a fact that spoke volumes to the world. He urged maintaining the fight. He strongly disagreed with Sweetman's claims regarding American public opinion and asserted that once America knew how hard Ireland was fighting for her freedom, it would embrace such actions.

Collins was accurate in his judgement of Archbishop Clune. Clune was in Rome, and – whilst ensuring to detail how, 'amongst other atrocities, his own nephew had been murdered by Crown forces' – was effectively neutering British efforts to have the Vatican issue a public condemnation of the IRA, a move that, if successful, would have wounded the republican cause at a sensitive time, given a recent controversial proclamation by Bishop of Cork Daniel Cohalan that IRA members involved in ambushes and assassinations should be excommunicated.[18] This statement illuminated divisions within the Catholic Church as well as Sinn Féin over the war's prosecution methods. Clune had arrived in Rome having passed through Paris, where Seán T. O'Kelly, a member of the Dáil's blossoming Department of Foreign Affairs and its representative in Paris, dined with him. Clune told journalists there that he admired Sinn Féin's courage, adding that he never saw a man among them flinch or tremble, despite their meetings with him having placed each of them at grave risk. He referred to having countered Lloyd George's description of them as assassins with: 'No sir, not assassins but the cream of their race.'[19]

Further comments flowed throughout the Dáil meeting, some dismissive of an English goods boycott as impossible to administer and police, particularly given conflicting loyalties, and the huge bulk of English goods already in the country that would complicate the situation. Nonetheless, such a boycott was implemented within two months, a noteworthy side effect being a resultant rise in the prices of many staple goods – an effect already visible in the wake of the Belfast Boycott. The forthcoming census was also boycotted, a strategy of De Valera's which Stack's Home Affairs department successfully enforced.

Ned Broy, meanwhile, along with Collins, had been at pains to figure out what Dublin Castle knew of his true loyalties. Luckily for both, Super. Purcell was an associate of Phil Shanahan's. Therefore, Collins was able to glean updates on the investigation extracted discreetly from the superintendent. Collins then relayed these to Broy.

Towards the end of January, Collins confided to Broy his relief that De Valera's suggestion of his travelling to America had been abandoned. De Valera had laid out several reasons for the initial suggestion, namely: to secure further finances and munitions, lay the groundwork for a much larger boycott of British produce, and hopefully to 'restore unity in the Irish American forces'.[20] However, the obvious widespread resentment that would follow the removal of the man who symbolised IRA resistance to both friend and foe, spoken of recently by Broy, had led to the idea's abandonment.

Disconcertingly for Broy, a suspicious DMP detective sergeant had identified him as having typed up two reports captured in the New Year's Eve Dawson Street raid. However, by coincidence, 'the copies of these two reports had been typed by a machine which typed twelve letters to the inch instead of the usual ten'.[21] When Broy illustrated this, it perplexed the investigating police commissioners, as all the machines in the detective offices were of the ten-inch variety. Luckily for him, Broy had taken carbon copies of his original reports and given the copies to Collins, who then had a secretary type fresh versions on a smaller typewriter from the carbon sheets before destroying the sheets themselves. When Broy was later summoned before Chief Commissioner Edgeworth-Johnstone and several other senior police figures, however, he could provide no explanation of the other reports found in Dawson Street.

Broy sensed that he was living on borrowed time as a policeman, although the reports with the smaller type left just enough doubt to sustain him. Nevertheless, he was no longer of use as an IRA mole; he was under too much suspicion. Astonishingly, despite the risks, he maintained clandestine contact with Jim McNamara and, knowing they would not be followed after dark, the two met with Collins regularly at Thomas Gay's Clontarf home to brief him about how the investigation was going. Broy painted an optimistic picture, sensing the unendurable strain Collins was under. Nevertheless, he justifiably feared his own imminent arrest, or worse, an untimely and violent demise.

Meanwhile, thirty-eight-year-old Dubliner William Doran, the Wicklow Hotel's chief night porter and former British Army veteran – having been observed conferring with since executed British agent Frederick McNulty, alias Brian Fergus Molloy the previous year, and monitored since – was next in the Squad's crosshairs. Doran had been warned repeatedly by the IRA to cease reporting the movements of senior republican figures and sympathetic guests at the hotel to the enemy under threat of his own untimely and violent demise.[22] He chose to ignore the warnings and paid the price.

The hotel, on Wicklow Street's northern side, yards from Grafton Street, was a regular stopping point for Collins, Tobin, Cullen, Thornton, Gearóid O'Sullivan and Diarmuid O'Hegarty. Collins dined there frequently and had recently been warned by waiter Paddy O'Shea that Doran, having complied with his warnings for a period, was once again supplying the police with information.[23] Doran suspected he was now being followed and had reported this to his wife, Emily. He had also instructed her to tell house callers that he was out. To disguise himself, he shaved off his moustache.

Dan McDonnell was indeed stalking him, collecting new evidence of his collaborations to add to existing proof. This was eventually brought before Brugha and the Army Council, who concluded that Doran was indeed an informer and, consequently, could be killed. Tobin instructed Joe Dolan to oversee the execution. McDonnell would play his part by identifying Doran.[24]

On the night of Friday 28 January, four men were noticed lurking outside the Wicklow Hotel by its manager, Thomas Mahon; two with backs turned to its entrance and two opposite, outside Switzer's, who maintained a watch on the hotel. Mahon, anticipating trouble, busied himself away from the hotel's front. The watchers dispersed shortly before curfew.

The following morning, at 8.30 a.m., they were back with an additional two men. McDonnell and Doran stood outside with their backs to the hotel entrance. Facing them across the street stood Charlie Dalton and Vinny Byrne. To their right, fifty yards away on the corner of Clarendon Street, stood

William Stapleton and one other Squad member. The latter two pairs were acting as covering parties. McDonnell and Dolan waited for Doran to enter the hotel foyer when his shift ended.[25] Paddy O'Shea, inside the hotel, would signal when this happened.

Fifteen minutes later O'Shea raised the hotel's dining-room blind – the signal.[26] Dalton took a handkerchief from his pocket and waved it discreetly, relaying the signal to Dolan and McDonnell, who then turned in an instant and entered the hotel lobby just as Doran also entered from the adjacent billiard room.[27] McDonnell, seeing him, muttered to Dolan: 'That's Doran.'[28] Doran heard this and turned suddenly, with terror in his tired eyes, but before he could react, Dolan, his pistol already loaded and cocked, 'shot him through the head and the heart'.[29] Doran collapsed backwards as his blood, brains, tissue and skull fragments splattered the foyer and reception. The shots shattered the hotel's morning tranquillity. McDonnell pulled out his pistol and shot him again, twice in the stomach, after he fell. His body jerked violently as if trying to crawl into the nearby coffee room where hotel guests gaped, petrified. Dolan and McDonnell turned casually away from Doran's lifeless body and left the foyer stinking of cordite, turning right as they exited into Wicklow Street. Screams followed from the hotel. Doran's contorted body lay in a growing pool of blood, his shattered head resting against the coffee-room door.[30] Horrified guests looked away. When Stapleton and his nearby accomplice saw Dolan and McDonnell exit the hotel they led the way for their escape on foot towards Exchequer Street; Byrne and Dalton followed behind the assassins.[31]

News of Doran's killing was received in GHQ alongside word filtering in of a severe defeat the previous night involving the 6th Battalion, 1st Cork Brigade. A sixty-man flying column had lain in wait for an enemy convoy in Dripsey, when they themselves were surrounded by seventy enemy infantrymen from the 1st Manchesters, backed up by armoured cars. The column fought its way through a gap in the enemy cordon in a protracted skirmish, but lost eight men captured and five wounded.

Back in Dublin that Saturday night, shortly after 8 p.m., a military raiding party consisting of a driver, ten privates and an NCO, under Lt Newton of the 2nd Battalion, Royal Berkshire Regiment, pulled up outside Terenure police station. They had just raided Cullenswood House in Ranelagh, a building used by senior republicans and targeted regularly. The police station was positioned on the eastern side of Terenure Road North, 100 yards from Terenure crossroads.

Newton, eager to get his men to Portobello Barracks, entered the station to check if they would be required for further raids that night. In his haste he neglected to issue standing orders for stationary armed parties: leave engines running, roll up canvas covers to afford visibility to infantrymen and post lookouts.[32] It would prove costly; none of his men noticed an IRA scout cycle past the truck.

The scout was with the 4th Battalion. Elements from E and G Companies, two officers and twenty-six men under Capt. Francis Xavier Coughlan, were patrolling the surrounding area, having initially rendezvoused at an arms dump in nearby Harold's Cross. The scout quickly reported the lorry's position to Coughlan.

Unfortunately for Newton, he was delayed in the station long enough for the IRA to place half-a-dozen four-man sections between Eaton Road and Kenilworth Road in Harold's Cross, primed to ambush. When Newton was eventually told his unit would not be needed later, he stepped back outside the station and ordered his driver to return to Portobello Barracks a mile away.

The truck lurched away slowly, but before it had travelled fifty yards it passed Eaton Road. There, a Volunteer ran out and hurled a grenade into the back of it. His supporting G Company comrades, under Lt Hugh O'Byrne, opened fire with pistols. This was followed by a muffled blast as the grenade exploded amid coarse pistol cracks. Razor-sharp shards of metal cut into the faces and flesh of the infantrymen. Bullets tore through the surrounding canvas, wounding several more. Luckily for the soldiers, two attackers' pistols jammed. The driver, having stopped momentarily under the shock of the explosion, accelerated away to the groans and cries of his human cargo. The NCO and two privates returned fire as best they could with limited visibility, the remaining eight too badly wounded to engage. Moments later, the truck came under fire again, 300 yards north at St Enda's Road. Newton was hit in the face by a pistol round, knocking him unconscious.[33] Another grenade explosion next to the truck sent it swerving violently, throwing wounded soldiers around in the back. The driver straightened the vehicle and sped towards Rathmines and the barrack hospital, passing the IRA section on Kenilworth Road, where the truck ran a further gauntlet of fire.

Moments later, another military truck approached Kenilworth Road from Harold's Cross. Todd Andrews from Terenure and his comrade Larry Kane, positioned there with two others, prepared to open fire again, when, to their amusement, they heard its cargo of soldiers singing 'I'm Forever Blowing Bubbles' in full voice. Kane shouted: 'We'll give you fucking bubbles!' as he appeared from the shadows firing his pistol.[34] Their two comrades lobbed grenades, one of which hit home. Two further explosions, followed by loud cries, echoed along the fashionable terraces as the truck sped away, also to Portobello, some on board returning fire. The attackers sped away on foot into Rathgar Avenue, where they stumbled across mortally wounded forty-year-old local civilian John Doody, struck by the troops' return fire.

Descriptions of the wounds suffered by both trucks' occupants were relayed to a warder in Arbour Hill, who, in turn, described their condition to Joe Lawless, transferred there from Collinstown. '[H]is description of the state of blood and gore of the lorries left little to the imagination.'[35] The military and Auxiliaries later ran amok in Harold's Cross and Terenure, shooting wildly, raiding homes and terrorising civilians in their search for IRA suspects.

Auxiliaries also struck that night at the home of sixty-six-year-old retired Brig. Col Maurice Moore at 5 Seaview Terrace in Donnybrook. Moore had a distinguished British Army career as 1st Battalion commander with the Connaught Rangers for many years in Africa. He was highly decorated but had, nevertheless, exposed a range of human rights abuses by the British during the Second Boer War. Moore joined Sinn Féin in 1917. In September 1920 he was appointed chairman of the Dáil's Resources and Industries Commission, set up in June 1919.

Moore had penned a letter to the *Irish Independent* earlier in January, criticising the recent tactic employed by the crown forces, on foot of an order from Gen. Strickland on 19 December, of carrying hostages on transports to ensure safe conduct. On some occasions this was done while dragging Tricolour flags tied to axles. Moore was arrested during the raid for possessing seditious literature including the *Irish Bulletin*. He subsequently found himself enduring the indignity of a tour of Dublin for the entire following day as a hostage. He was released, exhausted, on 31 January because of his position and age but warned about his future conduct. Moore quickly wrote to Gen. Macready, stating indignantly that 'the seditious material was in fact his post', and protested that every paper dealing with either politics or the authorities' actions at this point could be deemed 'seditious'.[36] The Dáil responded to this new tactic by proclaiming that British cabinet members would be held personally responsible for hostage deaths. The practice was soon largely

Maurice Moore, former brigadier colonel with the
British Army's Connaught Rangers, was the chairman
of the Dáil's Industries and Resources Commission. He
was arrested by Auxiliaries and, controversially, driven
as a hostage throughout Dublin for a day as a 'human
shield' to ward off IRA ambushers. *(Courtesy of the
National Library of Ireland)*

discontinued, with a few exceptions. Military and police transports employed
wire netting around the cargo areas of open lorries to protect from grenades.
A commentator mockingly noted: 'It has been said that it took the Boers to
put the British Army in khaki, the Germans to put them in tanks, and the
IRA to put them in hen-coops.'[37] Moore later joined the Dáil's Department
of Foreign Affairs as envoy to South Africa.

On the same day as Col Moore's abduction, Lloyd George told Conservative
Party leader Andrew Bonar Law that Éamon de Valera wished to secretly
meet him.[38] Bonar Law, a stringent advocate of coercion in Ireland, attempted
to deflect the idea. Lloyd George pressed him. Former director of national
service and current ambassador to Washington, Sir Auckland Geddes, brother
of transport minister Eric, had suggested that a settlement at this point would
be advantageous to Anglo-American relations, particularly with strategic
post-war reshaping of the world shifting into gear. Lloyd George recognised
the proposition's merit.

The following day, 1 February, Deputy Cabinet Secretary Tom Jones urged
Bonar Law to consider the meeting, emphasising his own distaste at 'ghastly'
events in Ireland. Bonar Law dismissed Jones, asserting that rebellions were
a common occurrence there and, once crushed, were succeeded by longer
periods of peace. He currently saw no reason to suspect a different outcome
this time, despite the insurrection's longevity and virulence. He added 'that the
Irish were an inferior race'.[39] However, Bonar Law was preparing to step down
as party leader for health reasons. So too was fellow diehard Walter Long.

Meanwhile, Sir Edward Carson, epitomising unyielding unionism, was
also preparing to settle down in London with a lordship, while imploring the
government to 'hold the fort'. Carson was simultaneously exploring peace
proposals with Fr Michael O'Flanagan and assuring Catholics in Northern
Ireland that they had nothing to fear from their governing Protestant majority.

This was taken with a sizeable pinch of salt after the previous summer's pogroms, stirred up by Carson; the man Macready considered responsible for much of Ireland's troubles. Carson and James Craig – the latter soon to be appointed as Northern Ireland's inaugural prime minister – had conspired with Imperial Germany in 1914, as Germany geared up for war with Britain, to smuggle arms to be used against British soldiers if Home Rule in Ireland had been implemented by their own Westminster parliament. The ripple effects had destabilised the British Army while Germany looked west and primed her armies. Long's secretary, William Bull, had been actively involved in the gunrunning. Bonar Law had pledged to those resisting by such methods: 'I can imagine no length of resistance to which Ulster can go in which I should not be prepared to support them.'[40] This was after the parliamentary party leader had asserted, tellingly, that there were more powerful things than parliamentary majorities.

De Valera would wait, but his sights were becoming trained on precisely such parliamentary majorities. With elections looming, strategies were being formulated between him, Collins and Griffith to undermine the unionist grip in six-county Northern Ireland and to cement Sinn Féin's hold on the rest of the country. Forthcoming elections were seen as an opportunity to create a new Dáil for, eventually, the entire island. Meanwhile, the diminution of the staunch triumvirate of Bonar Law, Carson and Long would help lay a frail foundation for the possibility of compromise and peace under its remit. However, first there was a lot more backroom dealing, and killing, to be done.

8

Vengeance, Shoot-outs, Escapes

'They'll hang you for certain if we get through'

On Tuesday 1 February, at 8.01 a.m. in Victoria Barracks, Cork, Capt. Allan Clarke, Royal Army Medical Corps, stood over the bloodied remains of thirty-year-old Cornelius (Con) Murphy of E Company, 7th Battalion, IRA Cork No. 2 Brigade. Capt. Clarke noted that Murphy's life was extinct from shock and haemorrhage due to rifle fire. Murphy was the first person to be executed for carrying arms under the recent martial law legislation. He was arrested by Auxiliaries while carrying a loaded revolver during a raid at Rathmore in Cork on 4 January. Murphy, who had been operating with a local flying column, was the first republican prisoner in Ireland to die by firing squad since James Connolly five years earlier.[1] His was also the first execution carried out before his sentence was made public.

The following day, three gunmen in Fagan's public house in George's Square, Balbriggan, shot twenty-one-year-old RIC Const. Samuel Green. Wounded, he staggered to the local RIC barracks, from where he was driven to Dr Steevens' Hospital in Dublin. He died in agony the following day. By this time a flying column was operating around Balbriggan, based near Oldtown, under Paddy Mooney. Balbriggan remained in ruins following its sacking by Black and Tans the previous September. Comdt Michael Rock, O/C of the IRA's Naul Battalion, had recently overseen an audacious and successful raid to capture mail from the Black and Tan HQ in Gormanston as it was delivered to Balbriggan post office. A car chase throughout north Dublin ensued as the Tans tried unsuccessfully to retrieve it. The mail was sought for the same reason as the recent Shelbourne Road post office raid: the IRA wanted to issue the Tans a taste of their own medicine, bringing the fight to their own homes. During February, the IRA in Britain used this information in shootings and arson attacks.

Also that day, in Clonfin, Co. Longford, two Auxiliary Tenders transporting seventeen men were ambushed by the twenty-one-man North Longford flying column under twenty-seven-year-old Comdt Seán Mac Eoin of the 1st Battalion, Longford Brigade. A mine was detonated under the lead vehicle, disabling it. During the ensuing skirmish, four Auxiliaries were mortally wounded. Notably, despite discovering concealed weapons on them, Mac Eoin dispatched eight additional wounded Auxiliaries in the undamaged Tender to receive medical treatment after they surrendered. He then withdrew his men under fire from enemy reinforcements with a haul of captured weapons, including a Lewis machine gun. Mac Eoin became a priority target for the authorities. Towns and villages in the area suffered reprisals that night; an elderly civilian, Michael Farrell, was shot dead.

That same night, in Dublin's Trinity Street, thirty-four-year-old Const. Patrick Mullany was shot as he cycled with a colleague to the Phoenix Park RIC depot. Four gunmen had ordered the two policemen to halt. When they refused, Mullany was shot several times through the back and died within minutes. His fleeing colleague escaped injury.

On 3 February, at 3 p.m., two flying columns of the East and Mid Limerick Brigades, under Comdt Donnacha O'Hannigan, combined forces to achieve the IRA's most significant victory since Kilmichael, when forty-five of their members ambushed a party of eight Black and Tans and five regular RIC at Dromkeen in Limerick. The police were travelling in two Tenders, which were shot to pieces having driven into a well-laid kill zone. Eleven were killed, including three Black and Tans after their surrender, one because he was still carrying a rifle, the remaining pair after a hastily convened IRA court martial.[2] Section Commander Maurice Meade, formerly a British Army prisoner of war who had joined Roger Casement's Irish Brigade while captive in Germany, shot all three. Two policemen escaped, a driver and a district inspector.

The ASU was back in action in Dublin on 4 February. Lt Tom Flood, the twenty-one-year-old O/C of 2nd Battalion, A Company, and one of seven brothers of the recently apprehended Frank, had stepped into his brother's shoes as commander of sections one and two since Frank's arrest.[3] Tom received orders from Capt. Flanagan during the morning to ambush an Auxiliary Tender that patrolled daily at around 3 p.m. along Eden Quay/Beresford Place/Lower Abbey Street. He relayed the orders to the section. The Tender would be attacked having turned left into Beresford Place. It would be travelling slowly at that point with an additional left turn ahead into Lower Abbey Street.

At 3 p.m., four unit members – James Cahill, Paddy Evers, Christopher Fitzsimons and George Gray – took position on the Abbey Street side of Brooks Thomas builders' yard at the corner of Abbey Street/Gardiner Street. A covering section was deployed in Gardiner Street. Four others – Tom McGrath, John Muldowney, Joseph Gilhooly and Jim Heery – stood concealed behind the massive Loop Line railway pillars opposite Beresford Place/Eden Quay junction.[4] Their planned escape route was across Butt Bridge, upon which Lt Flood and a small group stood primed.

Fifteen minutes later the enemy vehicle, carrying six occupants and a driver, drove along Eden Quay, its cadets eyeing up buildings and pedestrians to their left. As it turned left at Liberty Hall, the scene erupted. McGrath and the three others at the railway bridge hurled two grenades and fired several shots. One bomb detonated beneath the truck, the other just behind. Civilians rushed for cover; some fell, wounded. The Tender shook and lurched. The Auxiliaries responded with a torrent of fire. Sparks flew as bullets ricocheted from the bridge pillars. The four ASU men raced for Butt Bridge, darting between pedestrians and carriages, with rounds whizzing through the air as they ducked and weaved.[5] Flood's section provided supporting fire.

Oil and coolant spewed from beneath the Tender, leaving a slick trail behind as the driver nursed it onto Abbey Street. Cahill, Evers, Fitzsimons and Gray then pounced. Another grenade flew at the truck and clashed with its panelling but failed to detonate. Pistols cracked as the truck's engine seized outside the Dunlop building, 100 yards up the street, but the ASU's fire was ineffective and quickly suppressed by return fire. The four IRA men scattered. The cadets, blood boiling, raced in pursuit, sprinting towards Beresford Place but, to their frustration, were confronted there by civilians converging from Eden Quay and Old Abbey Street and tending to a small boy who, along with five men, was wounded in the fracas.

Cahill and his group escaped into Gardiner Street. Across the river, Gilhooly and McGrath commandeered a horse-drawn dray cart to escape along City Quay. McGrath was shot in the leg but did not notice initially, until Gilhooly saw the blood.[6] Gilhooly signalled Flood and the others to press on without them while he and McGrath persuaded the dray-cart's elderly driver to help them.[7] Gilhooly and the old man covered McGrath's wounded leg with a blanket and as the cart took off, Gilhooly made his own escape on foot.

The following morning, 5 February, set the scene for a retribution that brought immeasurable satisfaction to the Dublin Brigade: John 'Shankers' Ryan's bloody and violent punishment for alerting Dublin Castle to Dick McKee and Peadar Clancy's whereabouts on the night before Bloody Sunday. Ryan left his home at 16 Railway Street with his brother-in-law, making for Hynes' public house at 12 Lower Gloucester Place for a morning pint. It was Ryan's last such journey.

Since McKee's and Clancy's deaths, the hunt to track the informer had been given top priority. Eventually, enough information filtered from Dublin Castle to Michael Collins implicating Ryan. Ironically, Ryan had fallen into IRA crosshairs as a suspected informer the previous autumn, only for his execution to be vetoed by McKee for lack of sufficient evidence.[8] Frank Thornton was detailed with collating the necessary evidence against him. Thornton then assigned Patrick Kennedy to shadow Ryan. Ryan's sister, Becky Cooper, a well-known brothel keeper in the Monto area, also passed information gleaned from loose-tongued clients to the British. Kennedy soon established Ryan's routine, his route to work in Dublin Castle with the Military Foot Police, and crucially, where and when he took a drink. When Hynes' pub, situated on a corner at the junction of Old Gloucester Place and Corporation Street, was identified as his establishment of choice, Kennedy became a regular there and got to know Ryan's traits. He also discovered that Ryan was, tellingly, free to travel during curfew hours.[9]

When enough evidence was compiled and brought before the IRA Army Council, the order was given 'that the informer, John Ryan, was to be shot'.[10] There was no shortage of volunteers given the desire among Squad members to avenge McKee and Clancy. Speculation as to who would be given the honour reached fever pitch.[11] This was personal: McKee had been the one to inform Squad members in July 1919 that they were to form the 'Special Duties Unit'. Additionally, he and Clancy were long-standing friends with most of its members.

William Stapleton, Squad member and close friend of McKee's, was given the task of shooting Ryan. Eddie Byrne, twenty years old and recruited by McKee for the Squad, was selected as the second shooter, while Kennedy would identify Ryan for them. Jimmy Conroy, a recent recruit, would guard the pub's door from outside, James Slattery and four others providing cover. Slattery had been the first man to step forward as a Special Duties Unit member when McKee and Mick McDonnell had first sought volunteers.

On Saturday morning, Ryan left his home with his brother-in-law for their short stroll to the pub. Kennedy followed, then rushed away to alert the nearby Squad. They quickly arrived outside the pub. Ryan stood at the bar with his back to the door reading a newspaper, pint glass in hand.[12] His brother-in-law chatted nearby. Stapleton, Byrne and Kennedy entered the pub at 10.30 a.m., Kennedy's face concealed with a handkerchief. Conroy stepped to the door and waited just outside. The remainder took covering positions, eyes scanning the chattering crowds of city dwellers going about their morning business. Some quietened, sensing trouble.

Inside, Kennedy pointed to Ryan, saying: 'That's him.'[13] The barman, seeing what was about to happen, discreetly stepped away. The three assassins pulled their semi-automatic pistols, quietly clicking off safety catches. Within the blink of an eye Stapleton stood three feet from Ryan and attested: 'You are Ryan.' Ryan replied haughtily with his back to him, 'Yes, and what about it?', as he lowered his newspaper and turned towards Stapleton.[14] Stapleton fired just as Ryan's head instinctively jerked away the moment he made out the pistol barrel less than a foot from his face.

Ryan was thrown sideways by the .45 calibre round that smashed his left temple and blew his left eye to pieces as it exited and shot through a wooden drawer, rupturing a gas pipe before embedding in a wall. Blood, tissue and bone were splattered all over the bar and its furnishings. The deafening crack was met by the pub's few punters ducking behind tables and rushing for cover. Three more bullets were pumped into Ryan, still alive and twitching spasmodically on the wooden floor with a bloody gaping hole where his left eye had been. Two bullets smashed into his chest, the third into his abdomen. Onlookers, including Ryan's brother-in-law, were horrified as the shooters then turned and exited, leaving Ryan in a pool of blood, spilt beer and broken glass, his clothing smouldering from powder burns. Their comrades outside covered their escape to North Great Charles Street to dump their pistols in Mick McDonnell's converted stable. Ryan's brother-in-law rushed to his aid as an ambulance was summoned. Astonishingly, Ryan was still alive when it arrived to take him to Jervis Street hospital but died en route.[15]

Auxiliaries arrested three local men over the shooting. They were brought back to the pub to be identified by Ryan's brother-in-law. When he told the cadets that the three were not the assassins, they were, nevertheless, detained as IRA suspects.

An Auxiliary stands guard outside Hynes' pub following John 'Shankers' Ryan's shooting, 5 February 1921. *(Courtesy of the National Library of Ireland)*

That night, as the Squad members revelled in the news of Ryan's killing, 4th Battalion was in action. Capt. Andrew Walsh and twenty-two A Company members prepared an ambush at Rathmines church, situated on Lower Rathmines Road's eastern side, 300 yards from Portobello Bridge. The church, a landmark with a conspicuous copper dome and portico, as well as a Greek façade of four pillars and a huge pediment, was set back from the tram-lined road and its grounds were entered between two pillars, on each side of which were cast-iron railings. The church, the vault of which served as an IRA arms dump, had been severely damaged the previous year by fire.

Walsh had heard from battalion intelligence that a lorry of British troops passed Lower Rathmines Road en route to Portobello Barracks each evening between 8 and 9 p.m.[16] He planned to attack it. By now the route between Dublin Castle and Portobello Barracks was a perilous gauntlet for the military and police to run. It soon became referred to as 'The Dardanelles', a reference to the stretch of Turkish water where the Royal Navy had come under fire during the Great War's Gallipoli campaign. It was also lethal for civilians. That day, three-year-old William Fitzgerald was killed in Camden Street by a grenade fragment.[17] Shortly before this, the ASU under Lt Dunne shot up a car travelling between Aungier Street and Bishop Street containing British intelligence officers. Two occupants were wounded by Patrick Mullen's pistol fire.

Capt. Walsh's unit included four bombers, fifteen men with pistols, two cycle scouts and one first aid man.[18] The scouts had been sent out to locate the enemy, one to the north, the other south. At 8.45 p.m., the former returned from Portobello Bridge and told Walsh the truck was fast approaching.

Walsh quickly split his men into two sections, one left of the church gate, one right. Two bombers took position between the gate pillars, the remaining two posted one in each section.[19] Positions were taken seconds before the truck drew abreast of the church with the ambushers to its left. Walsh shouted, 'Open fire!'

Chaos ensued. The fifteen gunmen fired with a coarse salvo of cracks and muzzle flashes. Four grenades arced upwards in the darkness towards the truck. Two detonated next to it in seconds with blinding, deafening bursts. Two more landed in the back among the troops, one exploding, the other a dud. Over a dozen bullets, shattering window glass, wounding the officer in charge and ripping through its wooden side boards, hit the truck. Some soldiers fell wounded, others shot back. The Volunteers maintained fire, cursing profusely as pistols jammed. Bullets flew everywhere, ricocheting and sending sparks from bricks and roof slates. The truck slowed momentarily, swerving, almost stalling, then sped on again until, tyres screeching, it turned a sharp right into Ardee Road making for the barracks.

Walsh ordered his men to retire. One IRA man was wounded.[20] All escaped.

By now, another 4th Battalion intelligence officer, twenty-year-old Vincent Fovargue from Dunville Avenue in Ranelagh, had been broken and turned by Col Winter into an informer. Suspicion about him became compelling on 1 February, when Fovargue had escaped from a military transport in Dolphin's Barn en route to Dublin Castle from Kilmainham Gaol – none of his escort opened fire as he fled. David Neligan had quickly conveyed his suspicions to Collins after he read the escape report relayed to him by Jim McNamara, which dictated, tellingly, that the British Army were to be notified in the event of the escapee's recapture by the DMP. Neligan did not yet have the escapee's name. He did, however, have a description.

Fovargue had been supplying information for some time. Joe Kinsella, whose shoes Fovargue had stepped into as intelligence officer when Kinsella was transferred to munitions late in 1920, became initially suspicious as soon as raids began to take place at addresses supplied by Kinsella to Fovargue. Peter Ennis, commander of Dublin's republican police, and brother of Tom, had been captured in such a raid at Seville Place and subsequently lost most of his teeth to Capts King and Hardy under repeated beatings in Dublin Castle. Fovargue's successes had led to him fearing for his own safety. He subsequently staged his own arrest. Then, while held at Kilmainham Gaol, he aroused suspicion in a fellow inmate, intelligence officer Seán Kavanagh – who had also experienced the brutal interrogation methods of King and Hardy – owing to the nature of Fovargue's questions masked as innocent conversation between cellmates. Kavanagh, like Paddy Daly, was attuned to such tactics. Fovargue was soon dispatched by British intelligence to England to penetrate the IRA there under the name Richard Staunton. He suffered a lonely death on a Kent golf course, shot several times in the head with the message 'Spies and traitors beware' pinned to his body.[21]

Meanwhile, it had come to Frank Thornton's attention, from one of his own operatives, that another enemy agent was monitoring 100 Seville Place. Thornton ordered his operative to watch this man but not to take countermeasures.[22] He then relayed the information to Tom Cullen, who told Collins. Collins quickly saw an opportunity, which he detailed to GHQ. His subsequent proposition was agreed to: the Squad, the ASU and all 2nd Battalion companies would combine and lure a large enemy force into Seville Place to be ambushed. For now they would increase visible activity around the building and use the enemy spy's information as bait.

The plan was outlined to the various IRA units. O'Toole's GAA Club agreed to co-operate. Activity increased. The spy was observed making calls from a telephone kiosk at the nearby Seville Place/Amiens Street junction.[23] Then, early on 7 February, the incessant activity absorbed the spy so much that he failed to notice himself being surrounded. He was then whisked away in a car at gunpoint to a safe house and, under interrogation by Thornton and Cullen, disclosed his name, his code number, his Castle contact and the contact's telephone number.[24] Cullen began practising impersonating his voice, planning to make a bogus call to the Castle. Cullen had experience with such a ruse; he had, in late 1919, drawn Supt Brien out from Dublin Castle by impersonating since-executed spy Timothy Quinlisk.

Early that evening, 2nd Battalion prepared their ambush under overall direction from Seán Russell – recently promoted again, to GHQ as director of munitions – and Tom Ennis, now 2nd Battalion commandant and referred to affectionately throughout Dublin Brigade as 'The Manager'. Ennis' deputy, Vice-Comdt Patrick Sweeney, apprised officers of the plan and its significance; they expected a large enemy force to converge upon the building that night. When some officers protested that their men had pitifully few weapons, a simple but foreboding solution was forwarded: take weapons from wounded comrades.[25]

At 7.30 p.m. twenty-two officers and men from C Company under Capt. Tom Burke accessed the railway overlooking Seville Place via Coburg Place, an L-shaped cul-de-sac on its south-eastern side. Several rail lines intersected at this point and the bridge itself was 100 yards wide. They occupied sheds and signal boxes, dismantling telephone lines to prevent local informers alerting the enemy. A section was dispatched 500 yards south to Amiens Street station to lock its Talbot Street gates.[26] Cullen then made the phone call to Dublin Castle mimicking the agent, employing his codes. He emphasised that a big meeting was under way in Seville Place, stating that many suspicious individuals had recently entered.[27] His call was a success; the responder assured Cullen that a large force would be there promptly.[28]

Ten minutes later, thirty-seven members of B Company under Capt. Kilcoyne deployed around Coburg Place, one unit taking cover behind a wall, the remainder moving up to the railway line overlooking Seville Place's southern side. Simultaneously, Capt. William Byrne and an additional forty-one B Company men, thirteen from D Company and eight from A Company, accessed the railway line at Guildford Place just north-east of Seville Place.[29] These then manoeuvred along the line until a single section took position above Seville Lane overlooking the rear of 100 Seville Place, while the larger force deployed overlooking the direction of Amiens Street, from where the enemy was expected to approach; Vinny Byrne, Charlie Dalton and Dan McDonnell were among the latter.

Taking positions, Byrne and Dalton became wide-eyed in sudden amazement at a huge 'super-bomb' a nearby Volunteer was carrying, and his medieval-looking sheet-metal face mask with holes for his eyes and nose.[30] Both laughed discreetly, carefully positioning themselves away from him. Dan McDonnell remained next to him. McDonnell asked the bomber about the contents of his deadly contraption, to be told in a strong Dublin accent: 'gunpowder, slugs and gelignite'.[31] He planned to drop it on a military lorry, adding: 'When I do drop it, it should blow the whole outfit out.'[32] McDonnell moved towards Byrne and Dalton, sniggering nervously as he made sure there were several men between himself and the bomber. Such 'creativity' in explosive devices would flourish under Russell's direction.

An additional forty-three F Company Volunteers under Capt. John Walsh, William Stapleton and three other Squad members among them, took concealed positions across the wide 'Five Lamps' junction of Portland Row/North Strand Road. Armed with Lee Enfields, this detachment would engage any enemy retreat from Seville Place, as well as dealing with reinforcements.

The lethal trap, involving approximately 170 Volunteers – set to become the largest single engagement in the capital since 1916 – was primed to be sprung as Cullen and Thornton, walking along Talbot Street en route to Seville Place, were passed by a military and Auxiliary convoy of ten lorries and two armoured cars, one in front, one behind.[33] Pedestrians rushed for doorways and side streets expecting trouble. The convoy then snaked left at Amiens Street and sped towards Seville Place, engines whining, suspensions creaking, until halting unexpectedly as it approached the wide junction. There, both the officer in command and the intelligence officer's instincts kicked in; something appeared wrong. The area was ominously still and there was no sign of their own informer whom they assumed had made the recent call to the Castle from the nearby kiosk.

Both armoured cars, each carrying searchlights, were ordered into Seville Place, where they halted again. 200 yards to their front sat the railway bridge. No. 100 was the last house on the left before it. Searchlights clicked on. The IRA men on the bridge crouched and ducked, terrified but electrified in the silence broken only by the barking of dogs, as the beams dispelled the surrounding darkness. Hearts raced as the searchlights probed and lit up the bridge's huge steel and brick façade.[34] Local civilians recoiled from windows. Then, the cars withdrew.

Although their subsequent report indicated no enemy presence, the convoy's commanding officer remained wary. Trusting his instincts, he ordered the lead armoured car into North Strand Road; the rest of the convoy followed. Soldiers and Auxiliaries held weapons ready, with no inkling of the brutal mauling they just eluded. Machine-gunners scanned surrounding terraces and laneways for the enemy. The IRA men looked on, exasperated, some with heads held low, others relieved as, minutes later, they were ordered to stand down.[35]

While this was happening on Dublin's north-side, there was more action in the 'Dardanelles' area, where another young boy was injured. An army lorry was ambushed from Lennox Street while being driven along South Richmond Street at 7.50 p.m. This attack was the last straw for Gen. Boyd, who extended curfew hours in Dublin to commence at 9 p.m. instead of 10 p.m., exception being made for the Dún Laoghaire area policed by the DMP's F Division, as it had been the previous year. The time would soon be brought back further, to 8 p.m. Even unionists were appalled at these measures, seeing the extended curfew as a further nail in the coffin of a commercially dying city. Trams became packed as they left the city before curfew, as if fleeing 'from an infected area'.[36]

On 9 February, at 8.30 p.m., two civilians – eighteen-year-old Patrick Kennedy and twenty-seven-year-old James Murphy – were arrested in Talbot Street by patrolling F Company Auxiliaries under Dist Insp. King.[37] Taken initially to Dublin Castle under suspicion of being republicans, they were beaten in the Castle's lower yard by drunken cadets, despite having no weapons or documents on them.[38] Lt Commander Fry, a clerk in the office of chief of police, watched from his office window, repelled.[39]

Soon afterwards, King emerged from the intelligence office and ordered the assailing cadets to back off. However, any relief Kennedy and Murphy may have felt was misguided. King reassuringly told them he would transport them home given that it was after curfew. Lt Herbert Hinchcliffe was ordered to guard them while King procured a Ford touring car. On his return both battered prisoners were placed in the back. Hinchcliffe sat next to them, his service revolver trained on them. Then, as the car slowly approached the lower Castle gate King stopped and collected Capt. James Welsh. A sentry called out to them: 'Are you coming out?' King replied buoyantly: 'We are going out to shoot.'[40] Laughter erupted from his two colleagues. Their silent passengers, trembling, prayed. Fry watched the car speed out the gate.

Fifteen minutes later it pulled up at Clonturk Park in Drumcondra. Kennedy and Murphy, protesting and pleading desperately, were shoved and pulled from the car and told to hop over the wall next to the courthouse. The three Auxiliaries followed. Two tin buckets lay nearby. One was placed on each of the prisoners' heads as both, petrified, were ordered to stand with their backs to the wall.[41] They stood momentarily, shaking, until several shots echoed in the surrounding silence. Kennedy was killed instantaneously by a shot to the head. His body crumpled like a sack, the blood- and brain-splattered bucket still over his head. The cadets also aimed for Murphy's head. A round punched through the bucket and tore through his left cheek, then his right. Another shot smashed into his chest, nicking his heart but not killing him instantly. He wheezed, thrown back against the wall, collapsing in a bloody, mangled heap.[42] The three shooters calmly returned to their car and made for the city, believing both men dead. Their reports stated they were 'shot trying to escape'. However, Murphy still lived.

Two patrolling constables heard the volleys and sped to the source. On the way they observed the Ford car being driven towards the city centre. They arrived at the gruesome scene to find Kennedy dead and Murphy groaning in agony but clinging to life, the wall behind them blood-spattered. The policemen recoiled at the bloody sight, worsened by the perverse absurdity of the buckets. An ambulance was summoned. Murphy was rushed to the Mater Hospital where, before perishing on 11 February, he detailed what had happened. King was suspended from duty within days, then arrested for murder.

That same night saw the business and residential premises of Mr and Mrs Richard Chandler, a unionist couple in Trim, Co. Meath, looted by Auxiliaries. Ammunition had been planted at the address by a disgruntled policeman, who then ensured his colleagues were alerted. When the premises was subsequently raided and the ammunition discovered, several dozen N Company cadets ransacked the premises, stealing hundreds of pounds worth of liquor and produce, and then set the place on fire. Mr Chandler was arrested but later released. Despite this incident representing a fraction of the damage inflicted on the same town the previous September during a vicious reprisal, the consequences for the perpetrators radically differed.

Gen. Crozier investigated the looting and within days placed five ringleader cadets under arrest in Beggar's Bush, dismissing nineteen others. However, those dismissed took up their case in London, travelling, coincidentally, with Gen. Tudor en route there to receive censure from Lloyd George over his force's indiscipline. In London they argued that their instantaneous dismissal was unfair, given that their arrested colleagues could defend themselves in a court martial, while they could not. Crozier's patience with his Auxiliaries was wearing thin, a fact aggravated the night after Trim, when their antics saw them steal two cases of Lord French's champagne from Neary's pub in Chatham Street, next to Grafton Street.[43] French had left six cases of a brand he disliked to be sold on his account there. The lord lieutenant was incandescent. The cadets also helped themselves to boxes of cigars and several whiskey bottles while terrorising staff and customers. Mark Sturgis saw the amusing side and recorded the irony in his diary – given the respectability of the establishment itself. Gens Macready and Tudor insisted the perpetrators be sanctioned discreetly. The prospect of enemy propaganda getting hold of this story horrified them.

The propagandists behind the *Irish Bulletin* capitalised with typical expertise to bring the events at Trim to its pages alongside the rest of the material provided daily by rampaging Auxiliaries and Tans. A temporary setback was dealt to the *Bulletin* with Desmond Fitzgerald's arrest on 11 February, an arrest claimed by Dublin Castle to match Arthur Griffith's in significance. Luckily for the republican publicity machine, Erskine Childers, a zealous recent convert to republicanism, bestselling author, former Westminster civil servant and one-time member of British naval intelligence, was selected by De Valera to fill Fitzgerald's shoes after Michael Collins had introduced the pair. Childers, since his conversion, had been a director of the Dáil's successful Land Bank, a republican judge and the author of several effective recent publications. In July 1920 he penned a booklet titled 'Military Rule in Ireland', a damning indictment of crown reprisals, atrocities and pogroms, set against an impassioned vindication of the Dáil as having effectively supplanted the outmoded British government. Childers was, however, not trusted by all his Sinn Féin contemporaries. Griffith baulked at an Englishman attaining such a prominent position, particularly given his family lineage, which included Hugh Childers, former war secretary, chancellor to the exchequer and home secretary. Cathal Brugha mistrusted him owing to his former intelligence role. Others protested the fact that Childers was the first Dáil director who was not an elected TD.

Nevertheless, Childers proved a hugely effective asset in the critical coming months, due to his innate knowledge of British government and the machinations of its players, a key one of whom was about to step aside as secretary for war – the forceful Winston Churchill. Sir Laming Worthington-Evans replaced him on 13 February, the same day that Walter Long stood aside. Churchill became secretary for the colonies. Crucially, in conjunction with the bowing out of Long, Carson and Bonar Law, Gen. Tudor no longer had the ear – and crucially, the blind eye – of his close friend the former war secretary. Churchill's friendship with Tudor and the *laissez faire* attitude towards the unruly forces under his command had insulated Tudor from repercussions.

While Worthington-Evans was no friend of Sinn Féin, Tudor was unsure if he could count on a similar stance from the new minister.

When Lloyd George reproached Hamar Greenwood over the relentless indiscipline and insubordination of the forces he had so often advocated, at the same time as Sir John Anderson weighed in with vociferous criticism of the police, Gen. Macready used this to further his own case for complete military control, commencing in existing martial law areas. As a compromise, he suggested attaching a senior RIC liaison between the two arms, but nonetheless, castigated the lack of control exercised over the police by existing leaders, painting a picture of police and paramilitary reinforcements treating martial law areas as a 'special game reserve for their own amusement'.[44] Macready had been selected as military commander in April 1920, partly because he had previous experience of combined military and police command. However, Macready refused joint command upon arrival the previous year, rightly fearful of lack of discipline among military RIC recruits. The lack of such unified command was a source of endless frustration to Dublin Castle.

Tudor took note of the criticism, but nonetheless reinstated the nineteen dismissed Auxiliaries pending a full inquiry, which would take months to conclude. The move saw Gen. Crozier finally lose his patience and resign on 19 February, a propaganda windfall for the republicans. It was subsequently asserted that Crozier had been forced to resign over threats that the dismissed Auxiliaries would, if not reinstated, sell the stories of 'the black deeds' committed in Ireland under their watch.[45]

Five days before Crozier's controversial departure, republican propaganda had been handed another huge boost. This resulted from an audacious escape from Kilmainham Gaol, practically next door to Macready's own HQ in the Royal Hospital, Kilmainham.

The gaol – Ireland's 'Bastille' – constructed in 1796 but ceased operations as a prison in 1910, had, since the Great War's outbreak, served as a military detention centre.[46] Fourteen Easter Rising leaders were shot by firing squads in its Stonebreakers' Yard during May 1916; constituting a colossal British propaganda own goal. On 14 February 1921, the gaol's infamy presented a further boost to IRA publicity.

Frank Teeling, from Oriel Street, wounded and captured in 22 Lower Mount Street on Bloody Sunday, was court-martialled in City Hall and sentenced to death for murder. City Hall was chosen for its close proximity to Dublin Castle, from where prisoners were brought through a side entrance and up the stone steps to its echoing Council Chamber.[47] Barrister Charles Bewley – relative of the famous Dublin coffee family and convert to radical Irish nationalism – had defended Teeling and two others charged with the same offence. Two were acquitted, but Teeling, caught red-handed, had no such hope. Nonetheless, British court-martial officers remarked to Michael Noyk, the republican solicitor who had hired Bewley, about how well Teeling had composed himself since his capture and court martial – a trait that would gradually disintegrate; like many others, the war's ruthlessness and brutality was corroding the twenty-year-old's mind. Less cordial than the court-martial officers were Castle Auxiliaries, who threatened defence solicitors representing two others, Frank Potter and William Conway, warning them ominously of the dangers of sleeping at home if their clients were acquitted.[48] Attorney General Denis Henry had released an additional prisoner following a *nolle prosequi*.[49] Potter and Conway were convicted, but their sentences commuted to life imprisonment. Their solicitors received no unwelcome nocturnal visits.

Plans had been in place to spring Teeling from Mountjoy Prison in January while held in its infirmary. This would have required explosives to blow a hole in the prison's canal-facing wall. However, there were not enough available. Paddy Daly, also in Mountjoy, had angrily upbraided the Dublin Brigade for its 'dilatoriness' in not procuring enough in time to prevent Teeling's transfer to Kilmainham.[50] Daly had since been interned in Ballykinlar.

GHQ immediately expedited a revised escape plan. Patrick Kennedy, while shadowing 'Shankers' Ryan, was forwarded the names of two soldiers stationed at Kilmainham – Ptes Ernest Roper and Paddy Holland, the latter from Belfast – who were willing to help. When Kennedy initially sounded them out, he was suspicious of their notably high intelligence. They detailed a daring means of assisting Teeling and several others escape. Kennedy sent word to IRA intelligence, where again, their acumen was deemed dubiously high for ordinary soldiers. They claimed to have keys to several cell doors and a master key, and offered to drug the sergeant on duty to facilitate an escape. Eventually, Kennedy was instructed by his superiors to introduce both men to Oscar Traynor. A meeting was convened in Kirwan's. Seán Russell also attended, alongside Traynor's deputy, Vice-Brig. Seán Mooney.[51]

Finally, trust was placed in the pair. Plans were then made to smuggle bolt cutters into the gaol to cut through a lock on an outer wall gate on the fortress-like prison's western side. Backup would be provided with a rope ladder. Foremost on the escape list alongside Teeling was Bernard Stewart, alias Ernie O'Malley. Given O'Malley's overall importance to the IRA, Richard Mulcahy demanded he be the first out; a strategic overhaul of the IRA was to be undertaken and O'Malley's input would be pivotal. O'Malley was aware of what would befall him should his captors discover his true identity. He had pledged that he would escape or die trying rather than hang. Nevertheless, Traynor insisted Teeling would be first; he was a Dublin Brigade member sentenced to death. Mulcahy yielded, O'Malley would be second. Third would be Capt. Paddy Moran. He had been arrested at the Blackrock greengrocer's shop where he worked on 26 November and subsequently identified, wrongly, in Arbour Hill Prison by Pte Snelling as the man who had kidnapped him at pistol point outside 38 Upper Mount Street on Bloody Sunday.

Moran was one of eleven prisoners charged for murder and sent for courts martial from eighteen initially selected in identification parades.[52] Among those brought in to identify prisoners, in her own case unsuccessfully, had been Caroline Woodcock, witness to Bloody Sunday's Upper Pembroke Street bloodbath. She had been escorted from prison to prison where suspects' dispositions varied. Some were terror-stricken, others defiant. She knew some of the latter had the blood of her husband and his officer comrades on their hands.[53] She also suspected ordinary criminals were being deliberately fed into the parades to help IRA suspects slip through the identification net. However, the opposite also applied. Captured Volunteers, despite being innocent of the charges they actually faced, were regularly put in front of dubious witnesses in order for them to be wrongfully identified.

Moran's court martial was imminent. Originally scheduled for 5 February, it was postponed when a critical witness, Major Carew, who had been staying in 28 Upper Mount Street, was shot in a café in Dame Street; an incident rumoured to be personal rather than political.[54] Moran was confident of acquittal. He had a false alibi; claiming to have been in church in Blackrock at the time of the shootings, when he had actually led the Gresham Hotel operation. He had several witnesses backing the alibi. It was Moran who contacted Patrick Kennedy about Ptes Roper and Holland.

Twenty-five to thirty-foot-high granite walls surrounded the gaol. Lewis guns and searchlights were positioned to provide interlocking visibility and fire if necessary. Additional observation was provided from the Royal Hospital's

Richmond Tower, underneath which, through an archway and a thick cordon of sentries, stood the avenue leading to the huge seventeenth-century HQ building, itself surrounded by barbed wire, searchlights and guard dogs. Despite this, the prisoners had one advantage; they had won over many of the gaol's Welch Regiment guards. Moreover, those they had not yet won over were slack and disinterested in guarding this, or any, prison.

Michael Smyth, of E Company, 2nd Battalion, was ordered to procure bolt cutters from his workplace – Breen's garage in Donnybrook.[55] To solve the problem of their lengthy handles rendering them impossible to smuggle, Smyth cut them so that they became operable by tubular extension bars attached by sockets to the cut handles, which he also provided. Twenty-year-old Pádraig O'Connor, soon to attain prominence in the ASU, from nearby Inchicore, was charged with making the rope ladder. Both were temporarily stashed in Devlin's along with a .38 revolver.

Each cell in Kilmainham's upper corridor, known as 'The Murder Wing', where the proposed escapees were kept, was secured by an iron bolt and padlock. Above each bolt was a small hole wide enough to shine a torch into each cell. The plan was for the two soldiers to leave the appropriate cells unlocked but appear secured. O'Malley, who had the smallest hands, would squeeze his hand through his door's spyhole and slide back the bolt, then open his comrades' cell doors. Moran's cell was next to his; however, Teeling's was beyond the guard station. Despite this, O'Malley stealthily rehearsed the process several times without alerting the guard, who was known to drink on duty. O'Malley also made a practice run along his planned escape route, via the nearby corridor that had housed 1916 leaders awaiting execution, down a metal staircase and, finally, out into the gravel-strewn exercise yard. Beyond a nearby wall in another yard stood the escape gate. Past this, in turn, was a laneway.

Lt Flood and the four ASU members captured with him in Drumcondra on 21 January were also in Kilmainham. Flood, knowing their cell doors were frequently left open, had considered making a similar breakout attempt along this route, but feared it was an enemy trap given its blatant simplicity. His cautious rationale would soon prove costly.

On Sunday 13 February, everything fell into place. The bolt cutters and revolver, retrieved from Devlin's and smuggled into the gaol, were concealed in a filthy disused cell close to the escapers. Lt Jimmy Donnelly, at the Eastwood

Hotel on Bloody Sunday under 4th Battalion, F Company Capt. Christopher Byrne, collected the rope ladder from Devlin's. He later rendezvoused with Byrne and Volunteer John Dowling. After dark, the three, armed with revolvers, walked to Kilmainham Gaol, followed by a support unit. Outside the gaol they saw three enemy soldiers with girlfriends using the darkness of the laneway where the gate sat to facilitate pre-Valentine's Day embraces. These were rudely disturbed and held in the laneway at gunpoint. The support unit was summoned and dispatched to procure a car to transport the unexpected prisoners to a nearby safe house for detention, pending developments. The three rescuers then stood by outside the wooden gate, nervously awaiting their comrades. The rest of the support unit lurked on Inchicore Road.

At 7 p.m., O'Malley made his well-rehearsed move, sliding back the bolt on his door with quiet ease. Moran and Teeling quickly joined him. The three, pulsating at the imminent prospect of escape, crept silently along the gaol's dimly lit flagstoned passages, down the staircase and out the door to the exercise yard. O'Malley took stock of the formidable walls in the darkness. Moments later they were at the gate, their freedom a simple matter of assembling the bolt cutters and cutting the lock. However, this they could not do.

They were unable to operate the bolt cutters to provide sufficient leverage to break the lock, trying several times, almost breaking the bolt cutters, until, finally, they opted for their backup plan. Having whispered details of their predicament through the gate, Byrne's men then threw a lead weight attached to a rope which itself was attached to the rope ladder. The three escapees held their breath as they then heard the weight strike the inner wall just within reach after its rope snagged on the high wall above. This at first suggested a simple problem; however, it was stuck fast. They took turns trying to free it, at one point all three pulling simultaneously on the rope. Their audacious plan was unravelling. Finally, to their horror, the rope snapped. They gave up, detailing their situation to Byrne outside, who cursed profusely. Teeling, O'Malley and Moran, crestfallen, made their way stealthily back to their cells, hiding the bolt cutters and revolver back in the disused cell.

The following morning brought additional bad news. Repeated prisoner complaints about filth having built up in the same disused cell had eventually persuaded the military to clean it. This risked both assets being discovered. Thinking quickly, the prisoners volunteered to clean the cell, claiming they needed the exercise. Their ruse worked.

Their luck increased just after tea that evening, when Teeling entered O'Malley's cell with the staggering news that he and one of the friendly soldiers had just succeeded in cutting the lock with the bolt cutters. O'Malley was stunned. Teeling's excitement was intense. He snapped his teeth to illustrate how easily the lock had broken. O'Malley stood, momentarily wide-eyed as Teeling, grabbing his arms, eyes darting, explained that one of the assisting soldiers had feared being perceived as purposely orchestrating their previous failure. To pre-empt this he had contacted Oscar Traynor again. Traynor had arranged further instruction on the use of the bolt cutters' tubular handles, which the soldier had smuggled out. Following this the soldier had smuggled them back into the gaol and personally cut the gate lock.

O'Malley's heart pounded as he and Teeling pounced on the opportunity. They approached Moran. However, Moran, to their surprise, had changed his mind about escaping. Writing a letter as O'Malley and Teeling entered his candle-lit cell, he said he was convinced he would be acquitted at his court martial; it therefore made more sense to let another prisoner escape. O'Malley and Teeling were having none of it. They argued with him in hushed tones but could not convince Moran. O'Malley, perplexed, left Teeling to convince him, while he made for the cells of Flood's ASU members to get them to join the escape. However, fortune was against them; they had been moved earlier that day to punishment cells. O'Malley quickly sought the friendly soldier, knowing he had a key to these, but he could not be found. Abandoning this idea, he then approached Simon Donnelly in a nearby cell and told him to get up – they were escaping. Donnelly joked in disbelief. He had recently been arrested over the Bloody Sunday killings and was still badly bruised from his mauling in Dublin Castle, its interrogation room referred to as 'the knocking shop'.[56] O'Malley convinced him he was serious and needed him as he knew the surrounding area. Donnelly did not need to be asked again.

Moran, however, would still not budge, reasoning that if he escaped he would have to go on the run, whereas if acquitted at his court martial – as others already had been – he would be of better value to the Dublin Brigade as a free man. He also feared for the safety of those who had provided his alibi if he escaped. Teeling was aghast. O'Malley, back in Moran's cell with Donnelly at his side, in a final attempt to change Moran's mind, implored: 'Someone has to die for this Paddy.' He paused, then added: 'Maybe Teeling or myself, but they'll hang you for certain if we get through.'[57] It was to no avail. Moran reassuringly placed his hands on their shoulders and told them he would get his fellow prisoners to sing in concert to distract the police and guards as they escaped.

O'Malley, Teeling and Donnelly then entered Desmond Fitzgerald's cell. Fitzgerald was not facing a death sentence, so his escape was not a priority, nor did he wish to jeopardise theirs. He reassured O'Malley that he was not being held for 'atrocities' and gave him sixpence for tram fares.

Moments later, O'Malley and Teeling stood again at the gate, with Donnelly. They then tried to force the corroded bolt back, only to find it stuck fast, a contingency they had, however, anticipated. They quickly smeared the bolt with fat, butter and grease, and eventually it shifted. They opened one side of the gate and were out. O'Malley held the revolver at the ready as he saw the silhouettes of what he thought was a military patrol, only to discover another soldier embracing a girlfriend. They slipped past undetected.

Fifteen minutes later, the three dishevelled fugitives sat upstairs on an open-topped tram making for the city, savouring the cold breeze on their faces, the colours and the smells, prodding and pinching each other jokingly, until they alighted in Camden Street. Donnelly then set off on his own, thanking O'Malley and bidding both men good luck. O'Malley and Teeling made for nearby 13 Grantham Street, home to Brigid and Áine Malone. Brigid, a Cumann na mBan member, was Dan Breen's fiancée, as well as Michael Noyk's typist. Their late brother, Michael, was a republican legend, killed in 1916. Brigid knew of Teeling, having typed up documents relating to his court martial. O'Malley introduced him in person after they were pulled inside the house by the delighted sisters and brought to the kitchen, where Áine, having last seen O'Malley following his series of beatings in Dublin Castle, ran her hands over his face, laughing and crying in turns, saying: 'If only poor Peadar Clancy and Seán Treacy were here to see this day.'[58] Soon afterwards Áine set off to find a safe house close to Mount Street Bridge for the pair, suspecting her own was being watched.

Gen. Macready was livid when he heard of the escape. Teeling was the one man they had thus far successfully convicted and sentenced to death over Bloody Sunday. He strongly suspected his own men had assisted the escapers, whom he knew were prominent enemy officers, a fact symptomatic of disillusionment and indiscipline. The entire prison guard was changed. Macready promised to 'move the regiment to the most God forsaken part of the country' he could find.[59] An inquiry quickly took place in Kilmainham courthouse. Simon Donnelly was suspected, with hindsight, to have purposely allowed himself to be arrested to orchestrate the escape.

Less angry than Macready were the three apprehended British soldiers and their girlfriends, who were let go from the safe house by being blindfolded and driven from it in turns. Warnings of what awaited them if they spoke of their captors were fully understood. Nevertheless, each professed to being otherwise well treated, their families even notified of their unexpected detention and their safety otherwise. Ptes Roper and Holland were less fortunate; both received eight years' imprisonment for assisting the escape.

On 15 February, most Kilmainham inmates were transferred to Mountjoy. Within weeks, six more prisoners were buried there beside Kevin Barry, four in no small part because they had by simple happenstance been moved to punishment cells on the day of the escape. Before his departure for Mountjoy, Dermot O'Sullivan etched his name into his cell wall. He wrote: 'Diarmuid O Súilleabháin (Poundey) I left here on 15 Febr. 1921 For where I don't know'.[60] However, he would soon be back.

9

Pandemonium, Intelligence Blunders,

Courts Martial

'The war would have to be won outside'

On Tuesday 15 February, as Gen. Macready fumed over the escapes conducted under his own nose, the news was mitigated by reports of two IRA setbacks in Cork. The first was at Upton train station in West Cork and was costly to the IRA in terms of men and propaganda.

Trains transporting military were regular targets. At Upton, a thirteen-man IRA unit from the 3rd West Cork Brigade fired on a train carrying fifty Essex Regiment infantrymen at 9.30 a.m. However, the attackers had been incorrectly informed that most of the troops were positioned in a single carriage, which instead carried both soldiers and civilians. This proved disastrous.

The IRA subjected this carriage to a storm of bullets. When, however, fire was returned from the entire train, a ten-minute engagement ensued before the IRA withdrew, losing two men dead, another mortally wounded and three seriously wounded, including Brigade O/C Charlie Hurley. Six British were wounded. Crucially, however, six civilians were killed, two more died later and eight were wounded. Unionist propaganda had a field day.

Also, at 11 a.m. that morning, the 2nd Cork Brigade lost four men dead and eight captured at Mourne Abbey in another failed ambush. In this case the hunters became the hunted due to an informer.

Back in Dublin's City Hall that day, Paddy Moran stood trial alongside another prisoner, Paddy Rochford. Pte Snelling wrongly testified that Moran, who referred to him afterwards as 'Private Black Eyes', had abducted him outside 38 Upper Mount Street.[1] Major Carew, his wounded arm in a sling, also identified Moran as one of the same house's attackers, albeit cautioning that he could not swear to this definitively.[2] Carew's batman, Pte Lawrence, identified Rochford from the same episode and swore he had seen Moran loitering in Upper Mount Street the evening before Bloody Sunday.[3] A photograph of Moran in his Volunteer uniform brandishing a pistol, found at his home, was also produced in evidence.[4]

Rochford was acquitted of murder, there being only a single witness.[5] Moran, however, was less fortunate. Despite several witnesses testifying that he had been elsewhere on Bloody Sunday, he was convicted. His death sentence resounded throughout City Hall. Ernie O'Malley had been correct the previous evening; he would hang.

Also to hang was Thomas Whelan. He had been tried alongside three others for the murder of Capt. Baggallay on Lower Baggot Street on Bloody Sunday. Whelan was convicted on the false evidence of the naked British soldier there, despite five witnesses testifying that he had been in church. The three others were acquitted. Whelan would, indeed, as he had professed to Paddy Daly in Arbour Hill in November, assume another soldier's place on the scaffold.

The following Friday, a similar ring of steel to that deployed during Operation Optimist enveloped the Mountjoy Square area, extending from Summerhill into Great Britain Street/Hill Street/Dorset Street and back, sealing the area. Once again soldiers combed through houses, sheds and alleyways to colloquial taunts and protestations. Some acted with restraint and empathy towards the population; in other instances a twenty-nine ton Mark V Tank was used as a battering ram to break down doors. The results were similarly fruitless to the preceding operation. A thirty-six-hour search revealed little, despite Mick McDonnell's Charles Street arms dump being just one of several within the search zone.

The military's conclusion from this and other similar operations was that, in future, cordoned areas should be smaller and search periods should last no more than twelve hours. This was to enhance the element of surprise and concentrate the search of Dublin's honeycombed cellars and underground passages to find the enemy's hidden weaponry. Smaller searches would be reduced to maximum three-hours duration, such as those in Nassau Street and Molesworth Street on 19 February and in Kildare Street six days later.[6] The former raid uncovered an office frequently used by Richard Mulcahy in South Frederick Street, alongside valuable documentation. It also provided unexpected merriment at Col Winter's expense. Winter, an avid foxhunter, had imported bloodhounds to pursue suspects. Their prowess in a built-up city was,

British intelligence officers examining captured materials. *(Courtesy of Mercier Archive)*

however, limited. Two kilts found at the scene, which the raiders assumed were Mulcahy's, were used to set the scent. The kilts actually belonged to an actor living there who spent time on the building's open rooftop, precisely where the hounds led Mulcahy's pursuers, while their target smirked among the chuckling gathered crowds watching the unfolding farce as they led their handlers from rooftop to rooftop.[7] However, the last laugh was not Mulcahy's. A British colonel later gloated to Michael Noyk that Mulcahy 'ought to be scrapped; he is always losing his papers'.[8] This was the third such occasion involving Mulcahy that inadvertently increased the British trawl of suspects for Noyk to defend.

At 10.45 a.m. on Sunday 20 February, the ASU was in action again. A Ford car was expected to pass St Peter's church, situated at the junction of Cabra and North Circular Road in Phibsboro, containing four I Company Auxiliaries travelling from the RIC Phoenix Park depot. This was a regular Sunday morning movement, as Auxiliaries often stopped to search church congregation members as they left.[9] On this occasion, a welcoming committee of six insurgents led by Tom Flood awaited them.

Next to the apex of the church railings, shaped like a ship's bow, furthest from the car's expected direction of travel, stood James Carrigan and Christopher Fitzsimons, both carrying grenades.[10] Section Commander Mick Dunne and another Volunteer skulked across the road in a laneway leading to Dalymount Park, home of Bohemian Football Club, armed with pistols. Lt Flood and 'Ninepence' O'Connor positioned themselves nearby in Cabra Road, at its junction with St Peter's Road.

St Peter's church, Phibsboro, scene of an IRA ASU ambush on Sunday 20 February 1921. *(Courtesy of the National Library of Ireland)*

Flood and 'Ninepence' were discussing the morning newspaper to appear inconspicuous, awaiting the imminent end of mass, the customary arrival time of their targets. Unexpectedly, however, the Ford car was spotted approaching early from the opposite direction – the city.[11] It pulled over to its right between the nearby laneway where Mick Dunne and his comrade were positioned and the church itself. The Auxiliary in charge, Platoon Commander William Waitt, alighted and approached two passing policemen. The ASU men looked on tensely from their vantage points as Waitt then turned to re-enter the car. Then, they pounced.

Carrigan and Fitzsimons hurled their grenades at the car.[12] Both exploded within seconds, sending shrapnel flying all over the street and into the car itself along with shattered glass. Cadet Oliver Utting, in the car, suffered a burst eardrum. Carrigan and Fitzsimons, with no side arms, withdrew to the North Circular Road. Church attendees gasped in fright and blessed themselves, while the priest instructed lay helpers to lock the church doors as the sound of pistol cracks resounded from the laneway and St Peter's Road.

The four Auxiliaries scrambled out of the car, pistols drawn. One rushed for the Gothic-styled church and got in just before the main door could be bolted. Congregation members looked on, terrified, as he then stomped along the packed pews brandishing his weapon, seeking the attackers he was convinced had fled there. Another dashed towards St Peter's Road, only to find Flood and 'Ninepence' gone. Commander Waitt and the remaining cadet sprinted to the laneway leading to the football club, pistols ready. Stealing a glance into the lane, Waitt saw Dunne, twenty-five-yards away, turn and shoot, narrowly missing. Waitt fired in response, but his shots missed and ricocheted through the lane. Sparks flew from its walls. Dunne and his unseen comrade quickly disappeared around a left turn. Waitt, blood boiling, gave chase, but reaching the same turn saw no sign of the pair. Like ghosts, they had vanished. Waitt cursed as the scene quietened. Moments later the church congregation gathered curiously in clusters, wary of the Auxiliaries assessing the car's damage. A passing civilian, wounded, was taken to hospital. Within two weeks, touring cars used by Auxiliaries and the military were fitted with armoured seats.

Later that same day, Cork was back in the headlines again. In Clonmult, twenty miles east of Cork city, a twenty-two-man unit from Cork No. 1 Brigade under Capt. Jack O'Connell, preparing to attack a train due two days later, was surrounded by infantrymen from the Hampshire Regiment. A bloodbath ensued. Initially, two IRA members were shot dead, having themselves fired to alert their comrades to the approaching enemy. In the ensuing gunfight, during which the Cork men holed up in a farmhouse, three were shot dead as they fled to summon reinforcements. O'Connell, however, escaped. Reinforcements did quickly arrive, but in the form of RIC and Auxiliaries. After the farmhouse's roof was set alight with petrol by a British officer, himself under fire, the besieged men inside unsuccessfully tried to escape by burrowing through a gable wall. Their subsequent surrender an hour later, after further fighting, saw another seven IRA men shot dead by Auxiliaries before the British officer in charge, Lt A. R. Koe, commanded them to stop the killing. Twelve IRA men died at the scene, eight were captured, four of whom were wounded. Patrick Higgins was shot by a pistol shoved into his mouth and subsequently left for dead. Miraculously, he survived. Clonmult marked the biggest single loss of IRA lives during a single operation. Enemy spies were suspected of alerting the military of the IRA presence at the farmhouse. Consequently, counter-intelligence operations were ratcheted up, leading to numerous executions of civilian suspects in the area.

Meanwhile, British counter-intelligence had closed in on Ned Broy, his fears of arrest finally justified during February's third week. Broy was hauled before Supt Purcell and Commissioner Edgeworth-Johnstone, where Purcell, quivering at the prospect of being singled out as his accuser, told Broy he was under arrest. Although unsurprised, Broy nevertheless resisted a compulsion to reach for his .32 Webley and Scott automatic pistol, 'socking the two officers' and shooting his way out of Dublin Castle, 'running the gauntlet of the steel-armoured gate, past the Auxiliaries' guarding it.[13] He knew it would constitute an admission of guilt, as well as implicate Jim McNamara considering they were known associates. Broy also liked and respected Purcell. His backup strategy kicked in; he feigned indignation at the mere suggestion of disloyalty. Broy was searched and his pistol taken before being moved to

Arbour Hill Prison. Ironically, without the need to maintain constant alertness, he slept better than he had for weeks.

McNamara had been in Glasgow when Broy was arrested, sent to escort an Auxiliary under arrest for robbery back to Dublin. Despite Broy's attempt to protect him, he was dismissed upon returning; that same night his home was ransacked by masked Auxiliaries, suggesting that arrest was the least of their intentions. Fortunately, David Neligan forewarned him and he fled his home to commence life 'on the run'.

No further confidential information would flow from the Secret Service to the DMP, the force considered too much of a security risk. Consequently, Neligan, unless he could take drastic action, would become redundant as a spy.

However, undaunted by Broy's arrest and McNamara's dismissal and subsequent fugitive status, Neligan reacted quickly, audaciously approaching Collins, suggesting his only way to remain of use was to join the Secret Service. Collins, with no alternative, agreed. A few days later Neligan approached Assistant DMP Commissioner Denis Barrett – successor to gunned-down William Forbes Redmond and himself frequently in IRA crosshairs – with his request to join. Soon afterwards, Neligan and another G-Division detective stood before Andy Cope, both men's police files on his table. Cope asked them why they wished to join. Neligan's answer, voiced in his strong Limerick accent – 'for bigger pay' – was uncomplicated and believable.[14] Then, after further discussions, during which Neligan's charisma and dry wit won him over, Cope told Neligan and his colleague to submit their police resignations in an ordinary manner, then to present themselves to Major Leslie Stokes of F Company Auxiliaries and the Secret Service. When they subsequently did this, both were told by Stokes that they had been 'strongly recommended as good men'. Neligan was then 'initiated into the signs and hand grips of the Service and later learned how to use secret inks and similar artifices', before being assigned to the Dalkey, Dún Laoghaire and Blackrock district with a curfew pass signed by Gen. Boyd.[15]

Collins, meanwhile, continued operating on a knife-edge, with Dublin Castle bent on his capture. Christy Harte of Vaughan's Hotel was arrested and interrogated as to Collins' whereabouts and habits. Revealing nothing, Harte's interrogators adapted: he was brought into a long, dark room in the Castle to hear a voice peal out and boast of 'the grip which the British now had on the rebel organisation'.[16] Harte was then offered £5,000 for information.

He still divulged nothing but was told the reward stood and, should he wish to receive it, to call 'Dublin Castle, Extension 28', reciting the code words: 'The portmanteau is now ready.'[17] Soon afterwards Gen. Macready proposed rewards of £10,000 for information leading to the arrest of Collins, Brugha and Mulcahy, and £3,500 for Cosgrave, MacDonagh, O'Sullivan and Stack.[18] The measure proved fruitless.

Another occasion illustrated Collins' astonishing luck. He was staying at a safe house, 23 Brendan Road, Donnybrook, home of his secretary Susan Mason. Batt O'Connor, who lived in nearby No. 1, had built a secret compartment into No. 23. When a nearby address, among a lengthy list from the area, was raided, the officer in charge rummaged through a box of love letters belonging to a girl there. When she protested at the intrusion the officer apologised and, embarrassed, realised then that he had mislaid the list of addresses still to be raided. He telephoned Dublin Castle from the house, only to be berated by his commanding officer and told that the list could not be repeated over the telephone. He and his men then left the house, unable to continue their raids without the list, but the girl found it, read it and saw that the next address on it was 23 Brendan Road.

Collins had enjoyed similar luck during a recent search by a drunken Auxiliary. The cadet failed to find £16,000 of Dáil Loan money Collins was carrying.[19]

Collins' bewildering workload was added to by his membership of the executive committee of the White Cross, along with the still imprisoned Griffith, as well as Cosgrave, Childers and others including Lord Mayor O'Neill. Kathleen Clarke, wife of executed 1916 leader Tom, was also a member. Chaired by Quaker James Douglas, the recently established organisation's remit was to act as an alternative to the Red Cross – the vast international organisation hamstrung with officialdom – and distribute funds collected primarily in the USA to ease hardships among the tens of thousands rendered destitute by the Irish war. Irish domestic charities and philanthropic organisations were by now overwhelmed by the challenges of increasingly rampant poverty.

The White Cross, by distributing its funds, facilitated the American Committee for Relief in Ireland (ACRI) founded in December 1920. The ACRI had strong political, legal and commercial backing, and acted as a conduit for funds collected in the USA. It had been set up by Dr William J. Maloney – a former British Army doctor – five days after the burning of Cork. Seven committee members had recently arrived in Ireland, where 'they were initially given a frosty reception by Frederick Dumont'.[20] The US consul cautioned them that they were there with the permission of the British government, the only authority he recognised in Ireland. Despite this, their first meeting was a luncheon with De Valera, much to the chagrin of Macready, whose similar invitation was declined in favour of a later secret meeting with Sir John Anderson, which Macready also attended. During the latter meeting, both Anderson and Macready baulked at Collins' involvement in the White Cross, citing this as rendering the organisation a mere front for Sinn Féin. Macready forbade the £50,000 recently transferred to Ireland by the ACRI from being used by the White Cross in martial law areas, given that such areas were in an open state of rebellion. However, he later conceded that funds could be used directly 'for reconstruction of damaged or destroyed plant and equipment' in such areas.[21] A commission was set up to ensure this.

More than $5 million was eventually sent from the USA, following a report revealing that ninety-five villages and towns had already been badly damaged or completely destroyed during the war. Among the beneficiaries in the capital were hard-pressed St Ultan's and Temple Street Hospitals. However, the vast majority of funds were spent in Belfast, Connaught and Munster. They were well received; civilians were suffering terribly. Collins went to great pains as a White Cross executive member to ensure that the IRA saw none of its funds. Its executive was strictly non-partisan and it gained tremendous respect as a transparent organisation.

Collins also had his hands full as director of intelligence, a burden aggravated by the continued presence of formidable IRA nemesis Eugene Igoe, who had been promoted to head constable. Ned Kelliher was one of several intelligence operatives recently detailed to trail Igoe. Numerous ambushes had been prepared for Igoe's unit. All had failed, and one almost resulted in the combined members of the Squad and intelligence unit being enveloped by a large military foot patrol near Thomas Street.[22] Igoe was astute and constantly altered his routine. When his unit departed the Phoenix Park depot for the Castle, they used either motor transport or a tram. In the former case, routes were constantly changed; in the latter they alighted at different stops and, if necessary, caught a subsequent tram or walked in their subtle but effective formation.

Kelliher had been discreetly monitoring both the park and the Castle, noting the comings and goings of cars and their occupants as traffic flowed between both bastions. Eventually, a particular car caught his attention, a Ford containing four plain-clothed RIC officers. Kelliher's attentions focused on them because they seemed to conduct most of their business outside the Castle. Each time they arrived there, they quickly left and walked to a restaurant on Ormond Quay. Kelliher relayed his suspicions to his superiors and was ordered to maintain observation on them. Their continuing pattern reinforced his initial suspicions, although their behaviour did not match that of Igoe's unit; creatures of habit, they dined in the same restaurant daily at 1 p.m. For three of them, this was a fatal mistake. Kelliher was convinced, despite their habitual behaviour, that they were Igoe's men. The order was given to eliminate them.[23]

Kelliher met up with James Slattery. They scouted the route from the Castle to the restaurant, seeking the best location to shoot the detectives. The hotel itself was ruled out owing to the proximity of congregated civilians. It also presented the prospect of enemy agents or Auxiliaries being there. The eventual choice was the junction of Essex Street and Parliament Street, the same place recently used by the ASU.[24] However, given the hazards of operations so close to the Castle, plus the fact that their targets were assumed to be dangerous enemies, they marshalled the entire Squad for the job. By now the Squad's operational centre was in Moreland's; Seville Place was drawing far too much heat. Moreland's was only a few minutes' walk from Parliament Street.

At 12.30 p.m., Wednesday 23 February, GHQ driver Patrick Kelly pulled up in a car on East Essex Street. Jimmy Conroy and fellow recent Squad recruits Bernard Byrne and Mick Reilly alighted and stood casually close to the red-brick Dolphin Hotel at the junction of Crane Lane. Kelly parked nearby. Their job was to shoot the four expected RIC men. On the western side of Parliament Street, at its junction with Essex Gate, stood Kelliher wearing a bowler hat, which would be raised to signal that they were passing. Veterans Vinny Byrne, James Slattery and Tom Keogh and new recruits Paddy Griffin and Frank Bolster fanned out, with several others in covering positions.

Then, at 1 p.m., Kelliher observed three of his four targets walking down Parliament Street's eastern side. Alarmed that one was missing, he scanned the pedestrians behind them but saw no sign. The three Det. Consts – twenty-seven-year-old Martin Greer, thirty-two-year-old Daniel Hoey (sharing his name with an earlier gunned-down detective) and twenty-four-year-old

Edward McDonagh, the former pair on motor dispatch duties, the latter an office orderly – were about to die because of improper background checks by IRA intelligence.

The three unfortunate policemen stepped onto the cobblestones to cross East Essex Street, the hotel where they expected to dine just 200 yards away across Capel Street Bridge. Kelliher raised his bowler hat. Byrne, Conroy and Reilly observing, strode into Parliament Street in pursuit, their hands working their pistols, chambering rounds. They closed the distance. Safety catches clicked off. Seconds later they opened fire. Hoey and Greer were hurled forwards by the impact of the bullets, crumpling helplessly to the pavement, both killed instantly. Once again Dublin's city centre echoed to the sounds of semi-automatic fire and screams and shouts from terrified civilians as Greer, despite being wounded and stunned, bolted towards Wellington Quay with the assassins just behind.[25] Desperate to escape, Greer had made it as far as Horan's tobacconists when the gunmen opened fire again. Their shots struck home. Three .45 calibre rounds tore through his back, exploded out through his chest and into the plate glass shop window through which he then followed. He fell dead in a bloody heap on the shop floor, covered in smashed glass.[26]

The shooting continued. Military sentries concealed behind a canvas tarpaulin at City Hall opened fire into Parliament Street.[27] However, they quickly ceased fire due to scattering civilians, who facilitated the Squad's escape. The three killers were collected by Patrick Kelly and driven away. The supporting Squad members strolled from the scene in pairs back to Moreland's. Soon afterwards, an ambulance transported the three bodies to King George V Hospital. Parliament Street soon filled with military and Auxiliaries.

The shots that killed the three policemen were audible inside City Hall. The same day saw the courts-martial there of Frank Flood, Patrick Doyle, Thomas Bryan, Bernard Ryan and Dermot O'Sullivan of ASU section one. Ludicrously, the shots had rudely awoken some presiding officers from dozes, one of whom was fully asleep.[28] Each court generally consisted of five high-ranking officers together with the judge advocate.[29] As the initial cracks and much closer return fire rang out, officers reached for revolvers, some already laid out on their desks. A rescue attempt was feared. However, it was quickly revealed that some policemen had been shot. Security tightened.

The five defendants were charged with 'levying war against the Crown, contrary to the Treason Act of 1351', a charge usually reserved for martial law areas.[30] However, Macready had insisted that charges carrying capital punishment be applied to deter others.[31] Travers Humphreys and Sir Roland Oliver prosecuted.[32] DMP Sgt Singleton, the first prosecution witness, testified to having seen each of the defendants skulking around Clonturk Park before the 21 January attack. Singleton was followed by 'Tiny' King and John Reynolds of F Company; the latter having to testify to protect his cover.[33] Section Leader Charles Thomas and Cadet Frederick Ashard of I Company then testified. Towards late evening the hearings concluded, the presiding officer announcing that the court's decision 'would be promulgated in due course'.[34] The five prisoners were transported to Kilmainham Gaol, deemed secure again. Sgt Singleton was quickly moved to England for his own safety.

The following night the five convicted men were assembled in a large cell. A military officer entered and sombrely handed each an envelope. Opening them apprehensively, each man then read that, having been found guilty, 'the sentence of the court was death'.[35] The following day they were transferred to Mountjoy.

Meanwhile, Gen. Crozier was creating a stir in London. In two newspaper interviews, he claimed the British government had hindered his attempts to instil discipline into the Auxiliaries. Worse followed: Crozier claimed that Major Mills, soon to resign, had told him that the Black and Tans had opened fire in Croke Park on Bloody Sunday without provocation. He then stated that when he revealed this to his superiors, he was silenced and marginalised. Liberal newspapers called for Hamar Greenwood's resignation.

However, Crozier's claims did not go unanswered. He was accused of being as ruthless as his men, the only exception being his insistence on a less unruly approach to the same ultimate objective – enemy destruction. Crozier's successor, fifty-five-year-old Brig. Gen. Edward A. Wood, looked on as *The Times* commented: 'We have long known that the Auxiliary Division was designed for a purpose which we have regarded as foolish and immoral, and that the very nature of its employment renders discipline in its ranks almost impossible.'[36] This statement coincided with a barrage of castigations of the behaviour of the forces mandated to suppress the insurrection, including an assertion in *The Daily News* that the Black and Tans regarded the Irish as mere wild beasts. More acerbic was the recently published Labour Commission Report, which stated:

Irish Volunteers are fed and harboured by people who, three years ago, were certainly not Sinn Feiners, and some of whom were Unionists. So great has been the provocation by the forces of the Crown that eighty per cent of Irish men and women now regard the shooting of policemen and throwing bombs at lorries with the same philosophic resignation that Mr Lloyd George displays towards arson, pillage, and the shooting of civilians at sight in the presence of their wives and children.[37]

The apathetic reaction to the Parliament Street shootings further vindicated this statement. Gens Macready and Jeudwine looked on with growing disillusion. Jeudwine submitted a memorandum to the government arguing again for martial law as a means to unify command and, once and for all, reel in their paramilitary police forces – over 6,000 strong set beside 7,000 regular RIC – and enforce order in a harsh but necessary manner that would, he argued, rapidly restore order, instil respect and, ultimately, pave the way to their ultimate goal: 'a self-governing Ireland in close federation with Britain'.[38] Sir Warren Fisher backed him; the head of the civil service was back in Ireland to report on the effects of the changes to the Irish executive he had overseen the previous year. Fisher decried the unproductive rivalry he witnessed between the military and police.

As February closed, Dublin quietened – unlike Cork. There, the same day the three detectives were shot in Parliament Street saw the killings of Pte James Knight and Lance Corp. Herbert Stubbs in Bandon. Both belonged to the Essex Regiment, singled out for its notorious brutality. Its troops repeatedly tortured and shot prisoners and conducted house burnings under instruction from its intelligence officer, Major Arthur Percival. The previous Wednesday, 16 February, had seen four captured IRA men – Con McCarthy, John McGrath, Timothy Connolly and Jeremiah O'Neill – shot dead by the regiment at a roadside in Kilbrittain. On the night of 23 February, IRA flying column members from the 3rd West Cork Brigade filtered into Bandon to gun down any Essex soldiers they found. Knight and Stubbs were in the wrong place at the wrong time, a pattern to be repeated imminently in the city twenty miles east.

There, between 8 and 8.30 a.m. on Monday 28 February, six IRA members – 2nd Lt Thomas O'Brien, Daniel Joseph O'Callaghan, John Lyons, Timothy McCarthy, Section Commander Patrick O'Mahony and John Allen – were shot by firing squad in Victoria Barracks. The chaplain claimed that each man faced death without cowering. The first five had been sentenced on 8 February by courts martial following their capture at Dripsey; Allen had been court-martialled on 7 February for possession of a revolver and ammunition. The volleys were heard by a huge crowd gathered outside the barracks to pray, foremost among them Elizabeth MacCurtain, wife of the late lord mayor killed by the RIC at his home in Cork in March 1920.

Retaliation was swift. That night six British soldiers – Pte Albert Whitear, Signaller George Bowden, Pte Thomas Wise, Pte William Gill, Lance Corp. Edward Beattie and Lance Corp. Edward Hodnett – were shot dead in Cork city by an IRA unit with orders to shoot on sight. One of the soldiers ran into a shop to escape. He was found crying in a corner beside the counter by unit members before they shot him dead.[39] Five more troops were wounded.

However, the ramifications from Dripsey were not yet done. Two days before the Victoria Barracks executions, a letter was dropped outside the barracks by an IRA dispatch rider. Addressed to Gen. Strickland, it stated that the IRA had recently captured two informers – sixty-year-old Maria Lindsay and her chauffeur and butler, fifty-four-year-old James Clarke – who, they had since discovered, alerted the 1st Manchesters to the ambush. Both were apprehended at Lindsay's home, Leemount House in Coachford, on 17 February. A separate letter within the same envelope, written by Lindsay herself, implored the general to use his influence to prevent the executions, stating that, otherwise, her life would be forfeit.

Strickland had conferred with Macready. However, both concluded that the executions should proceed as the IRA would draw the line at shooting an elderly woman given the negative public relations ramifications. The possible repercussions had been illustrated by the execution by firing squad of Edith Cavell in Belgium by the German Army in 1915, which caused international condemnation. However, Macready and Strickland were wrong. Within weeks Lindsay's home was burned to the ground and she and her chauffeur shot dead, albeit without sanction from IRA GHQ, who feared the potential effects of such a precedent on the multitude of women spying for and stashing arms for the IRA. Women currently faced arrest like their male counterparts, and also public humiliations such as hair shearing – a horrific practice inflicted by both of the war's sides – as well as the prospect of the sexual violence prevalent in all wars. To date, however, neither side had carried out executions of women during Ireland's independence struggle. Nevertheless, the killing of another female IRA prisoner in Cork quickly followed Lindsay's execution, when forty-five-year-old Bridget Noble was shot for spying.

Lindsay's captors' O/C, Frank Busteed, spoke highly of her, describing her as a stubborn die-hard loyalist, contemptuous of the IRA, but stoic and fearless. She lost over a stone in weight during her bleak period of captivity in the frigidly cold early Irish spring. Her coat hung loose when she stood unflinching over her three-foot deep grave to be shot. Busteed's descriptions of James Clarke were less flattering.[40] House burnings, such as that of Lindsay's, would be systematically repeated across the country wherever similar 'big houses' were suspected of harbouring loyalist informers or facilitating the enemy. They would also be burned in revenge for reprisals. Republicans, to prevent collaborating owners thinking they could simply sell up and leave the country if they foresaw trouble for themselves, also placed a ban on the sale of such properties.

January and February 1921 saw no let-up in attacks, ambushes, reprisals and executions throughout Ireland. Places such as Cratloe, Kilkee, Kilfenora, Connolly, Sixmilebridge, Poolagoond and Feakle in Clare; Ballina in Mayo; Castlegar, Dunmore, Moycullen, Rosshill and Headford in Galway; Tureengarriff, Glencar, Ballymacelligott, Clonlara and Tralee in Kerry; Navan in Meath; Athlone, Kilbeggan and Rochfortbridge in Westmeath; Drogheda and Dundalk in Louth; Ballinalee and Clonfin in Longford; Mallow, Enniskeane, Millstreet, Meelin, Rosscarbery, Ballyvourney, Coolavocig and Ballinhassig in Cork; Abbeyfeale in Limerick; Cornafulla in Roscommon; Warrenpoint in Down; Belfast; Lusk in Dublin; Nenagh in Tipperary; Kilkenny city; and Maynooth in Kildare, all witnessed such episodes. There were fatalities from shootings in Ballykinlar and a vast military sweep involving over 2,000 British troops in Co. Donegal, to add to reprisals in Donegal town itself. At one point a shootout even developed between the RIC and the Ulster Special Constabulary, when the latter looted a pub in Newtownbutler, Armagh. Added to this were countless minor engagements.

An tÓglách was vocal about the incalculable value of pinprick attacks happening daily against crown forces. Meanwhile, the *Irish Bulletin* fully exploited the propaganda value of continuing reprisals. However, it was less outspoken about the manifold young Irish men flouting the Dáil's emigration ban. This had been introduced the previous summer to harness Irish manpower for the republican cause. Attempts were made by the separatists to disrupt boarding houses used for stopovers, and travel agents who failed to check exit permits deemed mandatory by the Dáil's Home Affairs department were threatened. Such checks were considered critical after Col Winter recently guaranteed money and safe passage from the country to informers. Volunteers who fled were labelled as cowardly deserters. Ironically, many of those who fled bolstered the republican propaganda campaign, relaying stories of horrors being visited upon Ireland to hungry newspaper reporters. Others fell under suspicion and police scrutiny.

The same two months saw escalating IRA arson attacks throughout Britain, particularly in London, with the IRA taking the fight to homes and areas associated with the Black and Tans and Auxiliaries, their addresses revealed following the post office raids in Ballsbridge and Balbriggan. IRA intelligence operatives, who by now infested the post office, also furnished such information.

Also in IRA crosshairs again was the British cabinet. The recent discontinuance of shielding patrols with hostages had been fortuitous for Westminster. The Dáil's response that they would hold cabinet members responsible was no bluff. As well as escalating operations, the London IRA mobilised intelligence officers to follow cabinet ministers and, if necessary, abduct them along with other senior government officials. They would then be held hostage at safe houses and killed as retribution for Dáil members lost as hostages. Frank Thornton was dispatched from Dublin, alongside Seán Flood and George Fitzgerald, as intelligence liaison. Fitzgerald had gained much experience of tailing and even engaging with British politicians, including Hamar Greenwood, the previous year. In London the three worked with Sam Maguire, London IRA chief intelligence officer, and London Brigade O/C Reggie Dunne, one of Vincent Fovargue's soon-to-be killers. Over the next few weeks their eyes widened at the extravagant personal lives of those they stalked.[41] Eventually, they compiled a list of twenty-five politicians. Plans were drawn up against each of them.

However, to Thornton's relief, the cessation of hostage-taking back home saw the perilous mission eventually abandoned, but not before an astonishing near miss. On one occasion, as Thornton and Flood raced each other through a London Underground station, Flood turned a corner, quickly followed by Thornton, who then found his comrade flat on the floor next to a middle-aged man he had just careered into and knocked over. Flood stood up, apologised and dusted himself and the older man down. That older man was the prime minister. Thornton was shocked. Lloyd George's bodyguards drew pistols. However, Lloyd George saw no need and calmly told them to put them away.

When the guards protested that they were facing Irishmen, Lloyd George retorted: 'Well, Irishmen or no Irishmen, if they were out to shoot me I was shot long ago.'[42] Thornton and Flood apologised again and made their way to the nearest tube train, travelling one stop and alighting, ensuring they were not pursued. With the overall mission abandoned, Thornton, Fitzgerald and Flood returned to Dublin. However, Thornton soon returned to London to work alongside Maguire and Dunne on another assassination attempt.

Cathal Brugha, meanwhile, was also planning operations in London. To ratchet up recent pressure there, he proposed simply assassinating British cabinet members, bypassing the need to apprehend them beforehand. Brugha had spearheaded a similar but fruitless enterprise in 1918 during the conscription crisis, as well as authorising another in September 1919. Collins, who, with Tobin and Fitzgerald, had surveyed the feasibility of the latter operation, lashed out at these proposals, instructing Brugha: 'You'll get none of my men for that,' to which Brugha rasped: 'That's all right Mister Collins, I want none of your men. I'll get men of my own.'[43] This did nothing to lessen the entrenched animosity between them. At this point the issue relating to arms purchases accounts still remained an open sore, with Collins compelled to apologise to Volunteer officers in tones of despair at ensuing supply shortages.[44]

One of those summoned by Brugha for the proposed operation was Seán Mac Eoin. He arrived in Dublin from Longford and made straight for Brugha's offices at Lalor Candles, 14 Lower Ormond Quay, where Brugha asked him to volunteer for the mission. Joe Sweeney, O/C West Donegal Brigade, had already refused, citing the proposal as immoral. Mac Eoin accepted, but afterwards spoke to Collins. Both men felt huge mutual admiration, having known one another since 1917, when Collins spent time in Longford. When Collins met Mac Eoin in Dublin, however, he was horrified; one of Ireland's most wanted men, Mac Eoin would be a sitting duck in the city. He dispatched Mac Eoin to see Mulcahy, who instantly countermanded Brugha's instruction and ordered him back to Longford. Mac Eoin complied but sent word of his return beforehand via a female messenger, who subsequently told her uncle – a retired RIC officer – who then contacted his former colleagues.[45] Mac Eoin was arrested at Mullingar by local RIC officers, reinforced with Black and Tans, and savagely beaten. When he then tried to escape he was shot through the lung. When he was eventually fit to be moved, transport was arranged for

Comdt Seán Mac Eoin, commander of the North Longford flying column, summoned to Dublin by Cathal Brugha to participate in a controversial operation to assassinate senior British politicians. *(Courtesy of the National Library of Ireland)*

him to be brought to King George V Hospital in Dublin. He had been charged with murdering Dist Insp. Thomas McGrath on 7 January 1921 in Longford. McGrath was among a raiding party at a safe house used by Mac Eoin when Mac Eoin shot him dead.

On 3 March, several Squad members, having received information of Mac Eoin's pending transport to the hospital, boarded a tram to Lucan to intercept it. Vinny Byrne and Tom Keogh detailed the men to positions around the Spa Hotel, where they waited for several hours, planning to hijack his ambulance, but to no avail. Fearing their own capture given the time spent waiting, they then held up a passing car owned by a former British Army officer, ordering him to drive them back to the city – none of them were drivers. However, he refused. Eventually, Byrne and the others, except for Keogh, managed to stall, swerve and splutter the vehicle as far as Islandbridge with the former officer held at gunpoint. Keogh chose to walk rather than place his life in their hands. At Islandbridge, Byrne ordered the officer to get out but reassured him that his car would be left in Parkgate Street. The officer, despite insisting he would not drive the car for them, had, knowing better, sworn not to resist or inform on them.

While the Squad had waited in ambush in Lucan, Dublin's quaysides echoed to grenade explosions yet again as five men from sections one and two of the ASU struck. The day's targets were court-martial officers returning from Dublin Castle in three Ford cars to Irish Command HQ, Parkgate Street.[46] Innovative tactics were employed. As the cars turned left from Capel Street Bridge into Ormond Quay, Tom Flood and Christopher Fitzsimons attacked first, hurling grenades at the last car. Further along the quay James Cahill and Seán Quinn rushed from a side street and threw two bombs at the middle vehicle, while fifty yards ahead Patrick O'Connor threw a grenade that exploded under the lead car's bonnet.[47] Luckily for the three vehicles' occupants, they were able to nurse them further up the quays, stuttering and backfiring. The ASU dispersed with typical speed. Several court-martial officers were wounded. Noteworthy during this attack was the reaction of civilians. It struck Flood that just before the attack, as he innocently perused books at a stall while keeping watch, the streets had quietened as if the civilians had learned to detect warning signals and make themselves scarce. As the five bombs had detonated, any lingering civilians had thrown themselves to the ground almost like soldiers, accustomed to the risk of injury of death not just from the blast proximity, but from their ability to hurl shrapnel causing significant injury up to forty yards.[48]

A few days after this ambush, three more Castle cars followed the exact same route. Tantalisingly, intelligence was leaked that Igoe Gang members would be passengers.[49] The result was an almost identical attack from the same ASU members bolstered by Ned Breslin, Jim Gibbons, George White, Joe Carroll, Mick White and Capt. Flanagan. The initial attack concentrated on the second and third cars, which, though severely damaged, limped on. Grenade fragments showering the quay also wounded Seán Quinn.[50] When the undamaged lead car slowed to allow the two behind to catch up at Arran Quay, beyond the Four Courts, Flanagan struck with four men from section three. Suddenly, out of nowhere, Gibbons and George White threw their grenades at the lead car and opened up with revolvers on the two behind.[51] The cars pressed on, only to then pass abreast of Mick White and Carroll, who lobbed bombs into their path causing the three vehicles to swerve violently just as Flanagan opened fire with his pistol. Several members of the Igoe Gang were badly wounded in the attack and the cars damaged.[52]

Soon afterwards another grenade attack was launched on a military lorry next to Findlater's church in North Frederick Street. Three grenades landed on target, badly damaging the truck, their thunderclap explosions succeeded by the screams of the wounded. The attackers knew better then to hang around counting enemy casualties.[53]

The aftermath of these attacks saw sixty-nine bicycle repair shops in Dublin raided by the military, convinced many of them were manufacturing munitions. The result was paltry: one Mills bomb and two bullets. Officers in charge of raids were berated by senior commanders for their troops' lack of imagination when conducting searches and were implored to think like rebels rather than soldiers.[54]

By 7 March, the day Frank Flood met Dermot O'Sullivan again in Mountjoy Prison for the first time since Kilmainham, almost 2,000 men had passed through Dublin Castle's 'Knocking Shop' and experienced why Col Winter had earned the nickname 'the Holy Terror'. Since Bloody

Sunday arrests had increased and, in turn, helped ramp up the operations of Winter's CRB. By now this number had been whittled down to roughly 200 prisoners detained in the capital, in Mountjoy, Arbour Hill, Kilmainham, and Marlborough and Royal Barracks. Their number added to over 2,000 internees spread throughout Ireland in camps such as Ballykinlar, Bere and Spike Islands in Cork, the Curragh, and Collinstown and Dollymount, the latter both serving as temporary holding camps for Dublin.

When they met, Flood's first words to O'Sullivan were: 'I am for the condemned cell.'[55] After further subdued exchanges, O'Sullivan went to his cell and prepared his own prison 'bundle' in anticipation of a similar transfer. Soon afterwards, however, he was taken instead to Gov. Charles Munroe's office. There, a military provost officer informed him that he would not face the hangman; due to his young age his sentence had been commuted to life imprisonment. Then, just as the officer spoke again, O'Sullivan interrupted, unexpectedly protesting that he sought no such preferential treatment and insisting on sharing his comrades' fate.[56] His protest was disregarded. O'Sullivan was escorted back to his cell.

Four days later, the next meeting of Dáil Éireann took place in Alderman Cole's house, 3 Mountjoy Square. This was against a backdrop of the looming Mountjoy executions, the aftermath of a spectacular IRA victory, further losses, the killing of another lord mayor, and the first coordinated attack on the British military in Mayo since 1798.

The victory was six days earlier, when a 100-strong composite IRA unit from Cork and Kerry under Comdt Seán Moylan killed fifty-three-year-old Brig. Gen. Hanway Robert Cumming, military governor of Kerry, in Clonbanin. The IRA ambushed the general's convoy of several trucks packed with troops from the East Lancashire Regiment, and a Rolls Royce armoured car, employing snipers and a Hotchkiss machine gun from defilades. The general was shot in the head during the three-hour engagement. The IRA withdrew without loss. British casualties were four dead, including the general, and several wounded, their casualties mitigated by the armoured car. Killing the general – whose subsequent funeral cortège along Dublin's quays en route to London was typically grandiose – was a boost for IRA morale, particularly in Munster.

Less conducive to morale was the loss of six men killed on the same day the Dáil sat, when a composite force of Auxiliaries and infantry from the

Bedfordshire and Hertfordshire Regiment surrounded and wiped them out at Selton Hill, Leitrim. Two informers alerted the combined crown forces to the IRA presence in the area. Among the dead was Comdt Seán Connolly, a close associate of Seán Mac Eoin. Connolly had been dispatched to the north midlands area as a GHQ trainer and organiser. Both informers soon paid the price, one with his life, the other leaving the country to preserve his. The previous day had seen four captured Volunteers shot dead in Nadd, Cork, their capture also due to an informer.

Limerick city witnessed, on 7 March, the killing of George Clancy, the city's forty-year-old lord mayor, along with his predecessor, Michael O'Callaghan, and city clerk Joseph O'Donoghue. Plain-clothed Auxiliaries shot the three. The subsequent military inquiry into their deaths ruled otherwise, claiming that 'extreme republicans who disapproved of their attempts to limit violent action' killed them.[57] Meanwhile, the same day saw eighteen British soldiers disarmed after an ambush in Kilfaul, Co. Mayo, that claimed the life of an NCO and wounded several others. A large quantity of arms was seized. Reprisals followed.

The Dáil meeting on 11 March was productive. Foremost on its agenda were the pending elections. It was, after some deliberation, confirmed by De Valera that Dáil members on an abstentionist platform, similar to December 1918, would contest the elections in the six partitioned counties. Elected TDs would recognise Dáil Éireann, not the new Parliament of Northern Ireland. Michael Collins designated £4,000 in badly needed funding for Sinn Féin's Belfast election campaign, risking accusations concerning the separation of powers between the Sinn Féin party and the Dáil. Three policemen and a civilian were shot dead in Belfast's Church Street that day.

Collins then spoke favourably of the advent of the White Cross having offset the necessity to raise another Dáil Loan, with the inevitable complications of secreting funds in bank accounts and fictitious companies, and even more unorthodox concealment strategies, such as using coffins and secret vaults. Collins had also been hatching a plan to divert Irish income tax away from the British Exchequer since the previous September. Strategies against latest enemy methods – described by Seán Hayes TD as 'terrorism' – to counter this and enforce income tax collection were formulated.[58]

Cumann na mBan were then singled out for praise in helping enforce the Belfast Boycott, tributes being paid to their having set up almost 200 boycott committees. Nevertheless, finding alternative sources for goods was proving problematic for northern counties. The boycott of English goods was also cemented; England being seen as a country waging war against Ireland. Kevin O'Higgins spoke favourably of rates revenue continuing to stream upwards, but reinforced the necessity to convey the consequences to those who steadfastly recognised the Custom House as their centre of local government.

De Valera then spoke on propaganda matters. It was felt that the *Irish Independent* and *Freeman's Journal* were far too moderate in their editorials. Measures would be taken to force their editors to row in behind the Dáil once and for all, whilst simultaneously increasing circulation of the *Irish Bulletin*. De Valera also defended Erskine Childers' recent appointment as propaganda director, parrying further criticisms over his position as neither TD nor Dáil director; De Valera insisted Childers was acting as nothing more than a senior civil servant.

Economic matters then took centre stage. Unemployment was to be tackled by public works projects. Initially, however, a more immediate strategy was rolled out to force farmers to employ labour to increase tillage; refusal to comply would see a withdrawal of Dáil protection. Landlords and banks were next, with increases in rents or mortgage interest to be forbidden until further notice.

Most noteworthy, however, was a measure many considered long overdue. De Valera asserted that the Dáil was 'hardly acting fairly by the army in not publicly taking full responsibility for all its acts'.[59] Brugha, however, reasoned that to do so might be misinterpreted as providing no similar retrospective support to the IRA. De Valera countered that this could be offset by an explanatory preamble, blaming circumstances for any such confusion.

The motion was vociferously supported by most. Notably, Liam Mellows suggested it should not be seen as a declaration of war, but an acceptance of war wrought by the enemy on Ireland. Austin Stack stirringly advocated accepting the 'army as being the Army of the Republic which came under their control in January, 1919. It was a legacy from the men who fought in 1916, and the development of it and the way it conducted itself ever since they gave it assistance, was a credit to them.'[60] Richard Mulcahy, on the other hand, opposed the motion; he argued that if ministers were now caught they would have 'a rope tied around their necks', having accepted responsibility for the war.[61]

The motion was passed, however, and a statement drawn up to announce it. Matters concluded with a noteworthy motion regarding the provision of substitute cabinet ministers in the event of their arrests. It was argued by, among others, Count Plunkett, that 'the Government should be left to the Military Body when the membership of the Dáil was reduced to a certain figure. It was usual to substitute military dictatorship in countries invaded; and instead of the House appointing substitutes, it should be left to the Volunteers as a Military Body.' Such a body, he argued, should be authorised to establish a provisional government.[62] De Valera suggested that if the cabinet fell to five in number, the army should take control. Ultimately the proposition that a provisional government would be declared in such an event was accepted.

The move to officially take the IRA under the Dáil's wing was a shot in the arm to its Volunteers. In eight days Cork would be back in the headlines having delivered an even bigger shot. It was also hoped, vainly, that the move would provide belligerent status to members captured by the enemy and bring further pressure upon its current policy of executions. That enemy policy was, in three days' time, to see Dubliners take to the streets in their tens of thousands to protest and demonstrate the power of the popular will, and organised labour, to loosen Britain's grip on Ireland's capital.

10

EXECUTIONS, MAYHEM

'Kill and burn and loot'

Late on the frigidly cold night of Saturday 12 March, the front gate of Mountjoy Prison opened. An armoured car rolled inside. Four passengers alighted, hangman John Ellis and three assistants, recently arrived in Dublin.[1] They were taken to the prison's hospital wing, their quarters for the next three nights.

The weather had not improved by 4 a.m., Monday 14 March, when, with a thin layer of snow on the ground and faced with a biting wind, a 'silent mass of humanity', defying curfew, lurched silently towards Mountjoy to pray for the six condemned men due to be hanged: Paddy Moran, Thomas Whelan, Patrick Doyle, Bernard Ryan, Thomas Bryan and Frank Flood.[2]

Few Dubliners reported to work that day. Moran was president of the Irish National Union of Vintners', Grocers' and Allied Trades' Assistants.[3] Consequently, the ITGWU, backed by the Labour movement, had called a half-day general strike in the city in protest. Dublin came to a standstill, with no trams, trains or ferries running. Shops and pubs closed.[4] Even hotel guests would have to fetch their own breakfasts.[5] Volunteers patrolled to ensure compliance. The Dáil also called for a day of mourning. It became the worst day of fatalities in Dublin since Bloody Sunday.

The Squad was hunting Ellis. IRA intelligence singled out the Gresham as his accommodation and expected him to be collected there at 5 a.m., an hour before the first scheduled executions. The Squad – also defying curfew – planned on beating his escort to the hotel.[6] However, the enemy was a step ahead, and the Squad dispersed with heavy hearts at their mustering point, Oriel Hall, at 4.30 a.m., when Liam Tobin and Tom Cullen told them they had been duped; Ellis was already inside the prison.[7]

By 5 a.m., with dense swelling crowds outside Mountjoy, the short roadway from North Circular Road to the prison gate was lit by a procession of people holding flickering candles sheltered by hands numbed with cold, clasping rosary beads and other religious relics. Troops in greatcoats, deployed to ensure order, looked on, subdued, loath to interfere.

At 5.15 a.m., Paddy Moran and Thomas Whelan, scheduled to be hanged first, knelt in the prison chapel for a service presided over by Canon John Waters of the Holy Cross College. It was the day after Moran's thirty-third birthday. He and Whelan were close friends. Auxiliaries flanked them, one kneeling. Forty minutes later, following the service, Ellis and his three assistants entered Moran's and Whelan's D Wing cells and tied their hands behind their backs. Both stood defiantly erect. They were then led – with Ellis and his men behind – by several more guards along short silent corridors to the hang-room within which stood the governor, the provost marshal and the prison's medical officer, Dr Batt Hackett. The sombre procession halted outside the hang-room, where Canon Waters spoke some final words. Ellis then stepped up beside both men and quickly placed hoods over their heads and faces. Both were then grabbed by Ellis and his assistants and jostled inside. There, a huge timber scaffold – composed of a beam set into the whitewashed gable walls – with large chains suspended, stood imposingly beneath a skylight. Within seconds both men stood side by side on a creaking double-leaf pattern trapdoor.[8] Ellis, his movements menacingly

Thomas Whelan, A Company, 3rd Battalion, Dublin Brigade, hanged in Mountjoy at 6 a.m. on 14 March 1921, flanked by two prison guards. Whelan, like his fellow condemned prisoners, struck up surprisingly cordial relationships with prison guards. He and Paddy Moran also became good friends before they were hanged side by side. *(Courtesy of Kilmainham Gaol Museum OPW, KMGLM 19PD–1A18–14(1))*

Capt Paddy Moran, D Company, 2nd Battalion, Dublin Brigade. *(Courtesy of the National Library of Ireland)*

efficient, placed and tightened a noose around each man's neck, each attached to the chain above, the rope's slack precisely calculated by a scientific measuring formula known as the 'Drop Table' based on the victims' weights, which were estimated by Ellis. This ensured a sufficient fall to break the neck and spinal cord, ensuring the victim did not suffer, but not too much of a drop, which could lead to decapitation. He then took two steps back and drew a long bolt, then a lever, opening the trapdoor with a cold, dismal thump. Both men disappeared from sight to the wrenching sound of their plunging bodies and the sudden cracks of breaking necks beneath the trapdoor. It was 6 a.m.

Mountjoy's bell had tolled to mark Kevin Barry's hanging four months earlier, also by Ellis.[9] A similar toll was expected. However, when silence took its place, rumours spread like wildfire among the crowds outside that the six men had been reprieved.[10] It was a vain hope.

Louisa Doyle, wife of Patrick – next to be hanged – held their twin baby daughters, one desperately ill, close to her chest, while their three-year-old daughter clung to her skirt. They had walked from their home in nearby St Mary's Place following a sleepless night preceded by her final visit to her husband. She prayed the rumours were true.

So too did Thomas Whelan's mother, her mind a kaleidoscope following her final visit to the son she did not yet realise had just died and her similarly sleepless night. She cursed the family's move to Dublin from Clifden in Co. Galway, reasoning that none of this might have transpired had they stayed; however, the war was also about to hit Clifden. Her son's execution would be answered in two days with the shootings dead of two policemen there, followed by the shootings of two civilians and the burnings of sixteen houses in reprisal.

A hundred miles away from Mountjoy, in Crossna, Roscommon, Paddy Moran's frail mother – hosting an all-night vigil with her equally frail husband at their home in the knowledge that the parish priest, some relatives and his girlfriend had visited her son – suffered no such delusions as the gathered crowds. She quietly asked her guests to go home, sensing correctly that her son was dead.[11] Police killings in Roscommon quickly followed.

Patrick Doyle, a twenty-nine-year-old carpenter, had, two years earlier, participated in the Collinstown raid – the 'Dublin Brigade's first high-priority offensive operation since the Dáil's inauguration'.[12] He had fought with F Company, 1st Battalion, before his skill and commitment marked him out for the ASU. He was brother to Squad member Seán.

At 6.15 a.m. in the chapel, Doyle knelt next to twenty-year-old Bernard Ryan – to be hanged alongside him – for a service by Fr MacMahon. Ryan, an apprentice tailor from nearby Royal Canal Terrace, was also from F Company. His family, for which he was the breadwinner, stood shivering outside the prison, having also visited the previous night.

Dawn was breaking. False hopes soared when the passing of 7 a.m. was similarly uninterrupted by the prison bell. The atmosphere electrified. However, Ellis had by then already carried out the second grim ritual and dispatched both men. Witnesses were struck by their serene calmness as they were led to their deaths.[13]

Thomas Bryan and Frank Flood's families had also visited the previous night. Bryan's twenty-one-year-old wife, Annie, was already heartbroken from the loss of their newborn baby three days earlier. Bryan had written a letter to Annie's father as his execution approached, expressing deep concerns for Annie, while acknowledging: 'It's the women who suffer the most.'[14] He was subdued during his final moments. Flood was more spirited, defiant when his family spoke of a late reprieve. He ordered two bottles of stout for his Auxiliary guards as a last request, citing their decency to him.[15] Both men's families stood among the crowds outside as their turns came to have their hands tied following their chapel service, for which, astonishingly, both men had to be awoken from deep slumbers.

Bryan, twenty-four-years-old, from 14 Henrietta Street, was a respected IRA veteran. He had spent time in Mountjoy in 1917 during Thomas Ashe's

Left: Patrick Doyle, IRA ASU, hanged in Mountjoy at 7 a.m. on 14 March 1921. *(Courtesy of the National Library of Ireland)*

Right: Bernard Ryan, IRA ASU, hanged in Mountjoy at 7 a.m. on 14 March 1921. *(Courtesy of Finín Ó Cheallacháin)*

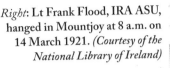

Left: Thomas Bryan, IRA ASU, hanged in Mountjoy at 8 a.m. on 14 March 1921. *(Courtesy of the National Library of Ireland)*

Right: Lt Frank Flood, IRA ASU, hanged in Mountjoy at 8 a.m. on 14 March 1921. *(Courtesy of the National Library of Ireland)*

hunger strike and been incarcerated alongside Dick McKee in Dundalk Gaol and later became McKee's orderly. He had been employing his skills as an electrician among senior IRA officers in the Dublin Mountains the previous September, detonating experimental explosives, before an Auxiliary ambush that saw forty comrades arrested and one killed. He and his officers had escaped.

Frank Flood had been a close friend of Kevin Barry's, both members of H Company, 1st Battalion, both UCD students. Flood was granted a scholarship from O'Connell's School in North Richmond Street – a school with a long list of prominent republicans among its former students.

Bryan and Flood were taken by Ellis, his men and their prison guards to the hang-room, where, at 8 a.m., they too, hooded and silent, were sent plummeting through the creaking trap door to their deaths, confirmed like the others, after they had hung for a short time, by Dr Hackett, who employed portable steps on the floor beneath to verify their deaths, following which the same steps were used by Ellis' assistants to remove the bodies.

At 8.30 am. the prison gate opened. The excited crowd in the roadway surged forward, anticipating news of a reprieve. However, the daunting sight of the same armoured car that had delivered Ellis and his accomplices halted their surge. A military officer then appeared and pinned a notice to the door. It read: 'The sentence of Law passed upon Thomas Whelan, Patrick Moran found guilty of murder and Francis Flood, Thomas Bryan, Patrick Doyle and Bernard Ryan found guilty of high treason by levying of war, was carried into execution this morning.'[16] The news was greeted with gasps and thousands blessing themselves.

The six bodies were placed in coffins assembled by prisoners in the prison workshop and buried in pairs in the order of which they had been hanged, next to where Kevin Barry had been interred the previous November. Dermot

205

O'Sullivan sat dejected in his cell. The rest of the prison's inmates reflected silently as priests, prison staff and military quietly saw to the burials. An *Irish Independent* reporter approached Canon Waters. Waters spoke of the six men 'walking to the scaffold like lions'.[17]

The crowd outside numbered more than 40,000 and included defiant Cumann na mBan members, among them Charlotte Despard, sister of Lord French, who did not share her brother's loyalties. North Circular Road and the surrounding streets were thronged. News of the executions spread fast, resulting in a hum of protest and prayer that lasted several hours until, eventually, the crowd dispersed. Family members of the executed made their way home, none more morose than Louisa Doyle, whose tragedy then unexpectedly multiplied – her sick baby died in her arms as she tramped, exhausted, along Berkeley Road.[18]

John Ellis and his three assistants were whisked to Dún Laoghaire that night to catch the overnight ferry. The following day saw Ellis back in his Rochdale barber shop, cheerfully cutting hair.

GHQ's reaction was instantaneous – authorising a general assault on crown forces. Mirroring Cork, orders were sent to city and county battalions and the ASU – desperate for revenge – to shoot enemy forces at any available opportunity, irrespective of whether armed or not.[19] Units deployed in force. The British, however, sought no such repetition of Cork and confined most soldiers and police to barracks.

At 7 p.m., Capt. Peadar O'Mara relayed GHQ's orders to B Company, 3rd Battalion, ordering attacks on any enemy forces in the Great Brunswick Street area. Following this they were to return to battalion HQ at St Andrew's Catholic Club, 144 Great Brunswick Street. There, they would eventually hand their weapons over to comrades under 2nd Lt James 'Kruger' Smithers, his job to deploy along the nearby railway line, cover its bridges and adjacent streets, and engage enemy targets of opportunity.[20] Brunswick Street, a mile long, ran parallel to the River Liffey, linking Ringsend and the south dock area to the city centre.

O'Mara deployed thirty-seven men into Brunswick Street. His second in command, Lt Seán O'Keefe, took charge of sixteen, dividing them into two sections, one of which O'Keefe commanded himself, while delegating the other to seventeen-year-old Seán MacBride. MacBride, son of executed 1916 leader John MacBride, had been raised in Paris and spoke with a French accent, much to his comrades' amusement. He joined the IRA in 1919, lying about his age. Armed with a Mauser pistol, he and O'Keefe patrolled Brunswick Street's southern side and its adjacent streets. O'Mara split his remaining nineteen men into two sections, taking seven himself, assigning twelve others to Section Commander Thomas Carass, both to patrol the wide street's northern side, initially east to west, with cyclists maintaining contact between O'Mara's and O'Keefe's men.

Soon afterwards, O'Mara, patrolling close to Lombard Street in the darkness, spotted the headlights of a distant car outside the central police station. Suspecting police or military, he ordered his unit forward, dispatching orders to Carass to follow at a distance but to remain on Brunswick Street as O'Mara's own unit turned right into Tara Street to wheel back around from Hawkins Street and trap the vehicle from behind.[21] O'Keefe's and MacBride's men would, meanwhile, remain further back on Brunswick Street's opposite side as the trap was sprung.

O'Mara cursed when his and Carass' pincers converged ten minutes later around the police station to find the car gone. ASU member Seán Dolan – seconded temporarily to his former company – suggested to O'Mara that he throw a grenade through a police station window to draw out the enemy.[22] O'Mara agreed. He positioned men covering both sides of Brunswick Street, detailing Carass' section to prepare a hasty retreat.

Dolan pulled the pin on his Mills bomb, let go of its striker lever and hurled it at the window. The result was disastrous; it missed, rebounded from the wall and landed on the pavement next to him.[23] Dolan darted backwards onto the road, directly into the path of an oncoming tram, which knocked him sideways and ran over his leg just as the grenade exploded, its blast amplified by the police station's granite façade. Dolan, momentarily delirious, was raked by red-hot shrapnel. O'Mara and several others rushed to his aid. Firefighters from the adjacent Tara Street station, a hotbed of republicans and sympathisers, sped on foot to the scene and summoned an ambulance – many of whose drivers felt similar sympathies – to spirit Dolan to Mercer's Hospital, half-a-mile away, where his mangled leg was amputated.[24] The incident was reported to Dublin Castle from the police station.

Following the setback, O'Mara and his section rejoined Carass' unit, returning eastwards. O'Mara then ordered Carass to position sentries on Brunswick Street's junctions with Sandwith and Erne Streets as cover.[25] He reported back to HQ and sent a runner to O'Keefe with instructions to report in and commence the weapons handover to Kruger's men.

Less than mile away, at 8.30 p.m., alerted by the central police station, sixteen F Company Auxiliaries under Dist Insp. Crang were dispatched there in two Tenders supported by a Rolls Royce armoured car operated by a crew of three Tank Corps personnel. The waspish cadets carried out final kit checks before climbing on board each vehicle. Lee Enfields were charged, two five-round clips pressed firmly by thumbs into each box magazine. Revolvers were loaded, as were semi-automatics. Waistband holsters were worn to facilitate quick side arm release once in action.[26]

Within minutes they were at the station. Platoon Commanders Fryer and Weber rode in the back of the armoured car. With no sign of the enemy, Crang ordered them onwards to No. 144, aware that it was an IRA building. Approaching, engines purring, their headlamps picked out several moving figures to its front. The small convoy accelerated. Forty-one-year-old David Kelly, president of the Sinn Féin Bank and brother of the lord mayor, seeing their approach, rushed towards No. 144 to warn its occupants. Then, pandemonium erupted.

The three vehicles sped through the junction at Sandwith Street and pulled over, the armoured car's brakes screeching under its weight. To their front and right stood No. 144, a two-storey townhouse two doors before the Carnegie Library. Streetlamps around the building were doused. Suddenly, the Auxiliaries came under withering fire from the junctions of Lower and Upper Sandwith Street to their rear, Lower and Upper Erne Street to their front, and from No. 144 itself. O'Mara and Seán MacBride were among those firing, the latter having been dispatched to No. 144 at this point with his men by O'Keefe in anticipation of O'Keefe's own men following – as per the order relayed by O'Mara's runner. Pistols resounded in the darkness. Muzzles flashed. Civilians rushing home for curfew threw themselves to the pavement.

The lead Tender bore the brunt of the sudden onslaught, grenade blasts amplifying the cacophony. Twenty-six-year-old Section Leader Bernard Beard and Cadet Francis Farrell, twenty-seven-years-old, fell from the Tender, both mortally wounded. Three of their comrades, Richard Dentith, Edmund Riordan and Sydney Dawson, slumped to its floor, hit by pistol rounds. Bullets pinged relentlessly off the armoured car's twelve-millimetre-thick steel plating, behind which Commanders Fryer and Weber and Inspector Crang, shot their pistols in the direction of the enemy muzzle flashes. Fryer, amid a barrage of expletives, shouted to the car's machine gunner to open fire. The chaos was then compounded by the dry staccato of the car's Vickers machine gun spewing rounds at a rate of ten per second. David Kelly was riddled by its bullets.[27]

Thomas Traynor, thirty-eight-year-old 1916 veteran, delivering a loaded pistol to HQ, was caught up in the shooting. He turned the weapon on the Tenders and armoured car while running along the street's northern side towards Sandwith Street. However, his pistol jammed as he passed the armoured car. As Traynor slowed, struggling to unjam it, Weber leapt from the car and rugby-tackled him.[28] Crang then helped pin Traynor down.

By now the Auxiliaries in the second Tender had dismounted and brought rifles to bear, shooting eighteen-year-old Leo Fitzgerald through the head. MacBride, his close friend, looked on from inside No. 144. The Vickers fired several more bursts, hitting David Kelly's prone body, causing it to jerk grotesquely in its surrounding pool of blood. O'Keefe and Carass, seeing no choice, withdrew their men under rapid rifle fire into Upper Sandwith Street. Erne Street still rang with pistol cracks, as did No. 144, which Capt. O'Mara ordered evacuated through its rear. Fire was maintained from the blacked-out building's front door to cover their retreat, as the armoured car belched out rounds to ricochet from brick and concrete and smash glass. Bullets flew wildly, landing randomly having expended their kinetic energy in flight.

Bernard O'Hanlon was still firing from the front of the HQ. He moved to enter the building, then suddenly collapsed on its steps, mortally wounded. Three doors away, John Donnelly, seventeen years old, was hit four times as the Vickers sprayed bullets all around him. He collapsed and passed out, gravely wounded.[29]

The Volunteers at Erne Street, now powerless, escaped into both sides of the street to regroup. The armoured car's turret, distinctively sloped at its sides, swivelled as its gunner maintained short bursts.

The ten-minute engagement then ended, but sporadic sniper fire was maintained by 3rd Battalion, harassing the remaining Auxiliaries around their shot-up vehicles. The armoured car soon sped to Dublin Castle with Thomas Traynor under pistol guard. It returned afterwards to Brunswick Street, accompanied by ambulances to take the dead and wounded to King George V Hospital. Pools of blood stained the ground where they had lain. Ragged fire was maintained by IRA units from houses in the area, as well as from towards Ringsend, until 3 a.m., when the area quietened, allowing the Auxiliaries to ransack No. 144.

Civilian casualties were also removed. There were several, including three dead: Mary Morgan, seventy years old, killed by a stray bullet; Thomas Asquith, sixty-eight years old, shot in the abdomen; and Stephen Clarke, a twenty-four-year-old former soldier, shot dead outside his home at 111 Brunswick Street while dragging a woman to safety. Clarke had been under suspicion of informing by B Company intelligence. The death toll in Dublin for 14 March 1921 was fourteen. Astonishingly, John Donnelly survived, regaining consciousness the following night.

The next day's newspapers sensationalised both the hangings and the Brunswick Street shoot-out. Interpretations of the former event differed significantly. The unionist *Irish Times* lent little weight to the executions. The *Irish Independent,* on the other hand, berated the authorities for hanging two men with unassailable alibis – Moran and Whelan – as well as four others, claiming their actions had not even so much as wounded a policeman. It reasoned that such blatant injustice – the result of trying civilians by courts martial – would merely drive more moderates into the IRA's arms. It referred to indignation at British rule being at its highest for forty years.[30]

Such indignation counted for little that day in Dublin Castle, where the courts martial of Edmond Foley, Patrick Maher and Michael Murphy commenced, the three charged with murdering two RIC officers at the Knocklong rescue in Limerick on 13 May 1919 during which Seán Hogan had been rescued from a train under police guard. A previous trial under civilian law saw a hung jury, prompting the authorities to charge the men under the ROIA, providing for their courts martial. If convicted, they too faced death.

Frank Thornton, meanwhile, was back in London, this time hunting Major Percival of the Essex Regiment. Thornton had recently lost his brother, Patrick, after he was severely beaten by Black and Tans in Drogheda and left to die in the street.[31] There was little time to mourn him. When word reached IRA intelligence that Percival was on leave at Dovercourt in Essex, Thornton was ordered to London following a meeting in Kirwan's pub, alongside Tadhg Sullivan of the 3rd West Cork Brigade, Patrick Murray of Cork City ASU, and Bill Ahearne. In London, Thornton once again contacted Sam Maguire and Reggie Dunne. Together they laid plans, only to find,

An RIC officer (left) with Major A. E. Percival. Percival was detested by the IRA. *(Courtesy of Mercier Archive)*

frustratingly, that Percival was well protected in Dovercourt Barracks. However, when word was received that he would board a train at London's Liverpool Street for his return trip on 16 March, a trap was laid. But then, as Thornton lay in wait at the station with his fellow assassins, he noticed Maguire discreetly beckoning him over to a newspaper stand fifteen minutes before Percival's expected arrival. This struck Thornton, as Maguire rarely ventured out in such a way. Maguire warned Thornton that a Scotland Yard contact had leaked word of a counter-ambush – the station was about to be surrounded by the enemy. The IRA men quickly fled. Percival was returning to Cork, where his regiment would soon suffer a bruising defeat. Thornton and Sullivan left their travelling companions in London and made their way to Liverpool, where Thornton boarded a coal boat for Dublin and Sullivan one to Cork, where, in just over a month, he would be shot dead by Percival's men.[32] Several weeks later, 'Hoppy' Hardy was also followed to London, where a plot to kill him was similarly scuppered.

St Patrick's Day 1921 was subdued in Dublin. The same, however, could not be said for Richill train station in Armagh. That day the IRA destroyed the station and burned a huge amount of rolling stock. The day also saw Collins musing over his position in Dublin. The unrelenting spat with Brugha, particularly over the arms accounts, had driven him to write to Michael Staines in Mountjoy that he was considering abandoning Dublin to take to the hills with the Cork IRA.[33] His correspondence also expressed grief over the recent hangings and admiration for their six executed comrades. Staines' reply implored Collins to dismiss the idea of leaving the city, suggesting he simply humour Brugha. Collins persisted, citing the fact that Brugha was pestering him to account for 'every sixpence' at a time of incessant pressure from police and military. Brugha remained deeply suspicious of Collins' IRB status and continued to feel supplanted in his role as defence minister by Collins' towering prominence.[34] Richard Mulcahy was sickened by the worsening rift, at one point telling De Valera that should it continue he 'could no longer accept the responsibility for the morale and *esprit de corps* of the staff' if measures were not taken by the president to muzzle Brugha.[35]

Cork then returned to the headlines. Tom Barry's flying column delivered a stunning result against the Essex Regiment at Crossbarry, twelve miles south-west of the city. Approximately 100 IRA saw off a series of attacks by more than 1,200 troops and RIC. During the hour-long engagement – described afterwards as the first from the British perspective that resembled a conventional battle during the war – Barry's men, almost surrounded and with just forty rounds per man, fought off repeated multi-directional assaults before successfully escaping the encirclement, leaving ten enemy soldiers dead and a dozen badly wounded, for the loss of three IRA killed. Weapons and ammunition were also seized, and two enemy trucks destroyed. The victory was tarnished by the death of Brigade O/C Charley Hurley just hours before, shot dead by the British attempting to flee a safe house where he had been recuperating from wounds received at Upton. Nevertheless, the engagement's scale, the audacious tactical performance of Barry's column and the resultant embarrassment to the military was an enormous boost to the IRA, and bestowed legendary status on Barry as a column commander. The Essex Regiment had, instead of employing its huge numerical advantage with a single overpowering blow, launched a series of staggered, disjointed attacks. Barry, initially fearing disaster given enemy strength, had skilfully manoeuvred his men to face each attack in turn, thus convincing the British they were facing far greater numbers. *An tÓglách* heralded the victory as a sure sign of the IRA's military prowess that dispelled accusations of its ranks being mere assassins or bushwhackers.

Two days later, more news came from neighbouring Kerry, when, at Headford Junction railway station, the 2nd Kerry Brigade flying column, under thirty-year-old Comdt Dan Allman, ambushed a train transporting thirty infantrymen from the Royal (London) Fusiliers. This time the IRA equalled their number and knew the enemy would be vulnerable to attack switching trains. During a furious close-quarter assault, the Fusiliers lost eight dead and thirteen wounded. The IRA lost two dead, among them Comdt Allman. Three civilians were killed in the frenetic crossfire that eventually led to column members using grenades against desperate soldiers seeking cover beneath the train. The arrival of British reinforcements on another train saw the column eventually retreat. Andy Cooney, twenty-three-year-old Bloody Sunday participant, had recently been assigned by GHQ to Kerry as an organiser to assist in the formation of flying columns. The success at Headford Junction, hot on the heels of Gen. Cumming's killing at Clonbanin, indicated that his assignment was reaping dividends. The Crossbarry battle also illustrated an unanticipated dividend of martial law – IRA members, their resolve stiffened, would fight to the death or escape; surrender was out of the question.

Back in Dublin, the evening of 18 March saw an army lorry attacked by D Company, 2nd Battalion, at the North Frederick Street/Dorset Street junction, as it lumbered there from Rutland Square. Company members were eager to strike back following the hanging of Paddy Moran, former O/C, since replaced by Capt. James Foley. Two sections were detailed to attack the vehicle from both sides with pistols and grenades. The assault was brief and frenetic, and concluded when a support lorry sped to the scene. Five IRA men were wounded, three superficially, by return fire. Motionless soldiers, lying in pools of blood, were spotted in the lead lorry's cargo area. Military convoys travelled through the city ensuring distance between vehicles, enabling rearmost vehicles to react and provide rapid support fire without suffering a surprise attack themselves – this threat was left to lead vehicles to endure. At Dorset Street the effective return fire came from the support vehicle.[36]

Two days after the Dorset Street attack, James Cahill was strolling along Sackville Street with three of the attack's participants. Several military lorries pulled up. Soldiers jumped out. The four quickly split up, but Cahill was singled out and wrenched into the back of a lorry. There, he was accused of being among the men who had 'murdered their men in Dorset Street'.[37] Then, just after a soldier and an NCO had argued over who would get to keep Cahill's watch while they threw him into the Liffey after curfew, he was transferred to another lorry which sped off, with Cahill's head now held to its floor with a rifle butt. For two hours he cursed the bumpy cobbled streets as floorboards battered his face. Eventually, the truck stopped on Bachelors Walk. Cahill braced himself for his involuntary swim in the freezing, polluted river. Then, unexpectedly, the soldiers all stepped out of the truck, but left a rifle close to Cahill. He sensed a trap, suspecting that as soon as he reached for the weapon he would be 'shot trying to escape'. Soon afterwards, a whistle was blown and the soldiers remounted the vehicle. Tellingly, Cahill then saw a soldier load the rifle.[38] Cahill was taken to Portobello Barracks, Kilmainham Gaol, Royal Barracks and Dublin Castle, suffering repeated interrogations, but was eventually released to rejoin the ASU.

Meanwhile, Dublin's 'Dardanelles' was seeing almost daily attacks against crown forces with grenades and pistols. Traders in the area, recognising IRA members from A Company, 3rd Battalion, patrolling the area between Camden and Dame Street, weary of attacks and repercussions, frequently approached them requesting that suspected ambushes be launched from elsewhere. Brugha went so far as to issue a directive that no attacks should take place in the area on Saturday afternoons due to the number of shoppers and traders. Nonetheless, when IRA men were wounded, traders sped to their rescue, fearing they would be hung if captured.

IRA patrols in the area were led by an advance party of two unarmed Volunteers, followed by several armed comrades, an armed officer, more armed men behind the officer and, finally, two unarmed men taking up the rear. Officers mapped out patrol routes. Enemy contact, whether to front or rear, was signalled by the unarmed men to their comrades and relayed to the officer. Patrols moved constantly with strict orders, similar to those for the ASU, to avoid prolonged actions. Ominously, they were ordered not to assist other patrols unless as part of larger directed operations.

The 3rd Battalion rotated company patrols. G Company successfully disarmed twenty Military Police on Westmoreland Street during one such patrol, seizing enemy side arms and ammunition, and wounding a sergeant in the process when he drew his weapon. B Company members under Seán MacBride attacked a lorry in Brunswick Street carrying tar and road-making material from Ringsend to the Black and Tans' training depot and deployment hub in Gormanston. The truck was shot at along the entire length of Brunswick Street, eventually stopping outside Tara Street fire station to unload the wounded, then turning right into Tara Street, its remaining passengers still firing. Then, when an army lorry passed Tara Street at Butt Bridge and its cargo of soldiers incorrectly assumed the shooting was coming from an IRA unit, they opened fire on the Tans, who, in the chaos, returned fire.

At Dartmouth Road in Ranelagh, a grenade attack was launched by C Company at the military from the railway bridge above the road. The unit, under Séamus Kavanagh, had a lucky escape when a Volunteer named Graham threw his grenade, only for it to bounce from the railway lattice back amongst his comrades. Luckily, Graham reacted quickly, picking the hissing bomb up to throw it again. It exploded in mid-flight. Attacks were regularly launched from railway bridges, given the cover and elevated vantage they afforded.

E Company lured a military convoy into Nutley Lane when Capt. Noel Lemass fired upon it initially with a Mauser rifle. The ambush area favoured small arms over rifles and 'a first-class fight ensued'.[39]

Meanwhile, F Company Auxiliaries were mimicking IRA city patrol tactics, sending out squads in mufti, distinctive caps concealed in pockets, which they would place back on their heads to identify them once they engaged the enemy. Armed gangs such as the Squad, ASU, Auxiliaries and the Igoe Gang, constantly stalked one another in the city's streets.

Outside the capital the fighting and killing continued. On 22 March, the homes of fourteen USC members were attacked in Roslea, Co. Fermanagh, by the IRA's 1st Battalion, Fermanagh Brigade. Two constabulary members were killed. On 23 March, six IRA members of Cork No. 1 Brigade were shot dead Having been captured by RIC and Black and Tans while sleeping in a barn at Clogheen. The killing went both ways that day; a British military unit paid a heavy price for not following recent transport protocols – illustrated recently during the Dorset Street attack – when a lone truck was ambushed by the IRA at Scramogue, Roscommon. Four soldiers were killed, several more captured. Two Black and Tans, having been under arrest by the British military, were also captured and later shot dead, despite offering to show their IRA captors how to operate a Hotchkiss machine gun. Among the IRA unit were several British Army Great War veterans, recruited to the IRA by Ernie O'Malley. Notably, the previous evening had seen an announcement by Black and Tans in Dundalk that twenty IRA men would be executed for every policeman or soldier shot or attacked. The following day, Louis Darcy, O/C of Galway's Headford Battalion, captured by Tans two days earlier, was shot dead, his body then dragged for three miles by a Black and Tan lorry before being dumped in a wood.

Good Friday, 24 March, saw the Squad, including William Stapleton, combing Dublin unsuccessfully for 'Hoppy' Hardy. Stapleton later attended a meeting to discuss rescuing Seán Mac Eoin from Mountjoy by blowing several holes in the prison's outer wall and storming in. Afterwards, Stapleton was detailed to drop weapons at the Charles Street dump. He then made for 35 Mountjoy Square, home of Fred Schweppe, section commander of Stapleton's 2nd Battalion company, bringing his own revolver en route for protection as it was after curfew. He fell asleep, exhausted, on a couch, his pistol beside him. Several hours later, Capt. Hardy, the house having been raided, rudely awakened him. Stapleton reached for his pistol, only to find it gone. Half asleep, he cursed having searched the city for ten hours only to find his quarry standing above him – hunted now hunter. Stapleton feared Hardy had discovered the Squad's attempt to locate him and was seeking retribution.

Fortunately for Stapleton, Schweppe, forty-five-years-old, had stashed his pistol while he slept. Hardy stomped around the house, deriding framed photographs of executed 1916 leaders and swearing in front of the children, for which Schweppe berated him. Hardy quietened. Schweppe told Hardy that Stapleton was his son, Michael, just returned from Glasgow for Easter. Both were arrested, Stapleton with the keys to both the Charles Street dump and the Squad car still in his pockets. Luckily, he managed to conceal them in the military truck en route to Dublin Castle. Next stop was the 'knocking shop' for interrogation. They were then transported to Arbour Hill. Stapleton found the conditions there particularly disagreeable; a single slop bucket provided toilet facilities for each cell and was only emptied daily at 4 p.m.[40] He took part in several identity parades and reflected quietly on the nearby burial plots of the executed Easter Rising leaders. Ned Broy's cell was opposite.

Stapleton and Broy exchanged small talk when the opportunity arose, as did the soldiers guarding them. Arbour Hill was a military prison and soldiers were responsible for cleaning its corridors. Both found most to be 'decent, straightforward Englishmen who were much better behaved towards the prisoners than were one or two Irish soldier-warders'.[41] One of them smuggled a letter from Stapleton – written using the name 'Michael Schweppe' – and addressed to Glasgow. The letter complained of his wrongful arrest and would lead to his eventual release in time for an even more audacious attempt to rescue Seán Mac Eoin.

Rescue plans were discussed also with Broy during prison visits by his solicitor, Philip O'Reilly, an associate of Michael Noyk. O'Reilly was not recognised for republican affiliations, which would have been detrimental to Broy. However, Broy insisted that he was not yet in serious danger; therefore, he did not want others risking their lives for him, particularly in such a heavily guarded prison. During evening exercise, Broy was introduced to 'Tiny' King and Lt Hinchcliffe, both remanded there separately from republican suspects pending courts martial for the recent Drumcondra killings. Broy sized up King, impressed with his physique, although less so with his relentless self-pity. King, trusting Broy as a police colleague, castigated their political masters for using them as mere pawns and mused on the likelihood of his own hanging as a means for the government to display impartiality.[42] Broy humoured him, suspecting, correctly, a different outcome for King than the business end of a hangman's rope. By then, charges against their accomplice, Capt. Welsh, had already been dropped.

The day after Stapleton's arrest saw Section Commander Gus Murphy become the next ASU member to die in Dublin. Murphy, from Wicklow, was en route to the section's Dolphin's Barn Brickworks HQ with the members' wages. Murphy, accompanied by Alec O'Toole and Patrick Rigney, noticed troops raiding shops as they walked up Clanbrassil Street.[43] Despite carrying on to avoid attention, three drunken soldiers accosted them, striking them with rifle butts, then searching them. When a soldier placed his hand into Murphy's pocket containing the wages he resisted. A struggle ensued. Murphy grabbed the soldier's rifle.[44] Then, a shot rang out. Murphy collapsed, clenching his abdomen. An ambulance was summoned and Murphy rushed to the nearby Meath Hospital, where he perished. When Rigney and O'Toole reported the incident, word spread to the entire ASU, who demanded reprisals.[45] Capt. Flanagan was quick to emphasise that victory would constitute their revenge, but there would be no reprisals.

The same could not be said for Westport the following day, 26 March. The picturesque Mayo town was badly damaged by enraged RIC officers following the recent killing of a local police sergeant. Numerous homes were also burned in the surrounding area.

Meanwhile, March drew to a close in Dublin with another clinically executed Squad killing. The victim, forty-seven-year-old Capt. Cecil Lees, aristocratic French-born Boer War veteran and top-rate intelligence officer, had served as a fingerprint and identification officer with the Chinese Labour Corps during the Great War. Lees initially drew the attention of IRA intelligence in March 1920, when the contents of a letter were leaked from Col Hill-Dillon's office addressed to Lees' London superiors and stating that, having recently arrived, he had found things in Dublin 'in a fearful mess' but suggesting he would be 'able to make a good show'.[46] The hunt for Lees had then commenced. However, he had subsequently returned to England, only to return again to Dublin in July. His return quickly became known in Crow Street. Lees was infamous as a brutal interrogator. Marked for assassination on Bloody Sunday, he was absent from his lodgings on intelligence work. Since the DDSB had been handed over to Col Winter, Lees' official position was 'police clerk'.

By late March 1921, Dan McDonnell had been trailing Lees for a month, gathering every snippet of information he could, nicknaming him 'The Frenchman' and tracing him to St Andrew's Temperance Hotel on Exchequer Street, from where he departed each morning between 9 and 9.30 a.m. for Dublin Castle.[47] It was the hotel's headed paper in Lees' leaked letter the previous year that drew McDonnell to it. McDonnell's comrades began to circle. However, Lees vanished for two weeks, leaving behind rumours that he was involved in the recent unsanctioned killings of captured Volunteers in Munster.[48]

When Lees' return to Dublin was relayed to Liam Tobin, the Squad received instructions to '"Oggs" him' – he was to be executed.[49] McDonnell and Charlie Dalton surveyed the hotel and surrounding streets for suitable spots to shoot him, a tall order given the hotel's proximity to the Castle from which Auxiliaries could deploy within minutes. Tom Keogh scouted with the pair one morning and saw Lees make his morning journey, standing out at well over six feet tall. Keogh ordered every Squad member to study the area over subsequent mornings. Plans were then formulated based on their appraisals.[50]

Finally, minutes before 9 a.m. on Tuesday 29 March, twelve Squad members deployed in force owing to the perilous location, gathering around Exchequer and Wicklow Streets. McDonnell and Dalton accompanied the unit.[51] Dalton stood with two members outside the International Bar at the junction of St Andrew and Wicklow Streets, the hotel entrance fifty yards to their right on Exchequer Street's southern side. Four Squad men took up covering positions across the narrow junction on South William Street. Keogh stood near the crossroads. The two shooters, Bernard Byrne and Frank Bolster, accompanied by McDonnell, stood at the junction of Drury and Exchequer Streets, 100 yards west, between the red-brick hotel and South Great George's Street – beyond which was the Castle.[52] Vinny Byrne and three others covered McDonnell and the shooters. There would be no escape for 'The Frenchman'.

Lees stepped out of the hotel at 9.30 a.m. and paused momentarily. Dalton and Keogh nodded to one another, pulses quickening. McDonnell nodded to Byrne and Bolster. They glanced to their right and saw Lees, his height and lengthy gait marking him out as he strode away. Mick O'Reilly, positioned in South William Street, noticed Keogh disappear from sight into Exchequer Street – the job was on. Two of his accomplices sprang into action, darting up South William Street to cover Cattle Market, connecting South William and Drury Streets.

Lees quickly passed three unfamiliar men in conversation at the corner of Drury Street, taking no notice as they feigned similar indifference while hands surreptitiously reached into pockets for pistols. Lees stopped again, casually putting on gloves. Byrne and Bolster pounced. Two shots rang out as two bullets tore into the victim, one lodging in his brain, killing him instantly, the other entering his back, exploding through his heart and out his chest. He fell dead in a hideous mess. Two more shots were fired. Civilians scattered.

McDonnell, Byrne and Bolster sprinted into Drury Street, leading perpendicularly away from Exchequer Street, alongside Vinny Byrne and his covering unit. At Cattle Market, 100 yards into Drury Street, they linked up with Mick O'Reilly's two men. From there they escaped up South William Street towards Stephen's Green. Keogh, O'Reilly, Dalton and the remaining two followed them up South William Street, covering them. An ambulance was summoned for the victim, lying in a pool of blood surrounded by horrified onlookers.

Paddy Daly, meanwhile, was back in Dublin following his unlikely release from Ballykinlar. Daly had taken instruction from Michael Collins to strenuously deny he was an IRA man, and with perseverance and guile, convinced the camp authorities he was simply a widower and father of four young children with no interest in republican politics.[53] All Squad and intelligence members were under the same instruction: under no circumstances were they to align with tactics such as hunger strikes or disturbance – they were too important.[54] Daly's strategy irked fellow internees, who systematically refused to cooperate with their captors. Leo Henderson, commander of the camp committee, was further discommoded when Daly failed to await his sanction for this ruse.

As soon as Daly had returned to Dublin, Collins informed him that he intended putting him in command of the Squad. Keogh, it seemed, had allowed indiscipline to creep in and unit members were drinking heavily, the strain taking its toll. Mick McDonnell, meanwhile, was still suffering from nervous exhaustion. Keogh, however, had made tactical changes to the twenty-strong unit.[55] As seen during the most recent operations, he focused more on pre-operational reconnaissance. The value he placed on his men's feedback about ambush positions and escape routes, and his use of increased numbers of covering shooters, had earned their respect.

When Collins told Keogh of his plan, Keogh protested strongly, practically refusing to relinquish command.[56] The decision was then put to the Squad during a heated meeting. Squad members echoed Keogh's protests, some threatening mutiny.[57] A subsequent Squad/ASU meeting to plan a concerted ambush also revealed to the ASU members that trouble was brewing in the Squad. Oscar Traynor became aware of the situation.

Col Winter, meanwhile, horrified and angered by Cecil Lees' killing, given the officer's proven calibre, was no less aghast at the killings of forty-seven-year-old RIC Head Const. Edward Mulrooney and forty-one-year-old Sgt Michael Hallissy on 30 March.[58] Both were part of a four-man unit returning to Lucan, having cycled to Bluebell to investigate a burning military lorry recently captured by the IRA. GHQ had instructed Volunteers of the detrimental financial cost to the enemy of destroyed vehicles, as well as the obvious tactical and strategic costs of their wholesale destruction. Some IRA men were also targeting mules and horses in the city for the same reason, to widespread revulsion. The policemen were fired on by section four of the ASU from a railway bridge in Ballyfermot. Another policeman was wounded before the ASU melted away.[59]

By now the Ballyfermot/Inchicore area mirrored Dublin's 'Dardanelles', with frequent sniping attacks from the railway line and works. Young Fianna members, among them seventeen-year-old Michael Molyneux and his sixteen-year-old brother James, looked after the local arms dump, ensuring weapons were cleaned, oiled and ready. They and other teenage Volunteers, such as Seán O'Connor, Jack Fogarty and Tommy Ward, occasionally accompanied their older comrades, armed with revolvers. They also took part in sniping and 'were all more or less instinctively good shots'.[60] By spring 1921 almost any military truck passing the nearby Oblate church was fired at, with casualties inflicted from shots fired from as far as 400 yards. Eventually, the British conducted a sweep through the area, with 300 troops combing through the red-brick terraces of houses and railway yards.[61]

Winter's CRB, meanwhile, had been relentlessly carrying out raids alongside the military. Among locations targeted towards the end of March were 100 Seville Place, Harcourt Street railway station, where a Lewis Gun and 6,000 rounds of ammunition were discovered, and an arms dump in Mountjoy Square, one of several run by Mick McDonnell, yielding six rifles and thirty-five revolvers.[62] Also targeted was Eason's bookshop. The landmark Sackville Street retailer was suspected of selling *An tÓglách*. Auxiliaries attempted to burst in on Easter Monday. However, their intelligence was clearly lacking. The shop was shut for the bank holiday, its shutters closed. By chance, next door in 84 Middle Abbey Street, an IRA GHQ meeting, chaired by Diarmuid O'Hegarty, was under way to discuss IRA strategic repositioning, attended by a host of senior figures from throughout the country, including Liam Deasy, adjutant of the 3rd West Cork Brigade and recent participant at Crossbarry. The meeting's other attendees, including Frank Henderson – the former 2nd Battalion commandant with GHQ – prepared to shoot their way out as soon as they were alerted by Cumann na mBan member Leslie Price of the Tenders outside, but breathed a collective sigh when they observed cadets remount their vehicles having kicked Eason's shutters in frustration.[63]

Another even more staggering close call was suffered in 3 Crow Street. A convoy of Auxiliary vehicles filled the entire 200-yard length of the narrow street. Those inside – Liam Tobin, Frank Saurin, Charlie Byrne, Joe Dolan, Charlie Dalton, Joe Guilfoyle and Frank Thornton – made ready with tins of paraffin, stockpiled for such a purpose, to set fire to the office, while Dalton and Guilfoyle prepared to defend the building with grenades. Then, 'a sort of armed truce appeared to exist for about a half an hour', until, to the amazement and relief of all inside, the cadets remounted and drove away.[64] It was later discovered that one of the Auxiliary officers, a major, had simply been collecting a watch from a nearby jewellery shop.

More effective intelligence had, however, led to a significant find on 26 March – the Molesworth Street offices of the *Irish Bulletin*; the British had finally unearthed it. All office contents were seized. Typewriters and printing presses were brought to the London and North Western Railway Hotel on North Wall Quay, as was the *Bulletin*'s 900-strong distribution list. The hotel was, five days earlier, designated HQ for the Auxiliaries' recently formed Q Company. The move inspired Capt. William Darling, author – alongside Basil Clarke of Dublin Castle's Public Information Department – of the police gazette the *Weekly Summary*, to employ the machinery to fabricate bogus *Bulletin* copies, subsequently dispatched to the captured mailing list's addresses. The plot, however, backfired. Testimony was secured from an expert, Richard Foley, that the forged copies were produced on the captured equipment very unprofessionally.[65] The uncovered stunt was ridiculed in the *London Times* and the Commons. The genuine *Bulletin* quickly sourced a new office in Exchequer Street alongside the Dáil local government department, and increased distribution, heralding: 'That the headquarters of the British Government should be forced by circumstances to adopt forgery in an attempt to sustain its authority is an evidence of how completely that authority is repudiated by the people.'[66]

Meanwhile, as casualties among crown forces increased to levels unseen in Ireland since Easter 1916, Éamon de Valera finally made public Dáil Éireann's position on the IRA, issuing a declaration:

> From the Irish Volunteers we fashioned the Irish Republican Army to be the military arm of the Government. The army is, therefore, a regular state force, under the civil control of the elected representatives, and under officers who hold their commissions under warrant from these representatives. The Government is, therefore, responsible for the actions of this army. These actions are not the actions of irresponsible individuals or groups, therefore, nor is the I.R.A., as the enemy would have one believe, a praetorian guard. It is the national army of defence.[67]

De Valera went on, describing crown forces as invaders while dismissing critics of IRA guerrilla tactics:

> Protected by the most modern war appliances, they swoop down upon us and kill and burn and loot and outrage – why should it be wrong for us to see that they will not do these things with impunity? If they may use their tanks and steel-armoured cars, why should we hesitate to use the cover of stone walls and ditches? Why should the element of surprise be denied to us?[68]

De Valera's statements were timed to concur with the national reorganisation of the IRA into sixteen separate divisions, overriding existing brigade structures according to county, an overhaul welcomed in some quarters, ridiculed in others. Tom Barry considered the move futile given the prevailing lack of arms and ammunition with which to supply such forces.

The move also coincided with further machinations in London. Six days earlier, the Privy Council, the crown's body of advisors, met there and deemed 19 April appropriate for the government to issue Orders in Council for the coming into force on 3 May of the Government of Ireland Act, paving the way for general elections. Southern unionists were appalled at the prospect of pending elections since the pledges made in December about restoring order had proven hollow, and correctly sensed that, consequently, no candidate in their right mind would stand against Sinn Féin, but protests were wasted on

Hamar Greenwood and Lloyd George. Greenwood insisted that they 'would not be deflected from their purpose by murder gangs'.[69] Lloyd George plotted a steady course, wanting the Ulster question to be settled before addressing the remaining twenty-six counties. The recent step-downs of Long, Carson and Bonar Law had relaxed 'the diehard stranglehold on Irish policy'.[70] Additionally, Lloyd George's influential and similarly unyielding private secretary, Philip Kerr, would also soon step down. Nevertheless, the prime minister still had to maintain harmony among remaining Conservative ministers. Once the six counties were secured, he would then have room to manoeuvre.

Gen. Macready had conveyed to Lloyd George, yet again, the necessity for martial law. Notably, however, he proposed a truce as an alternative. Failing this, Macready strove to increase the efficacy of military operations, planning to exhaust the IRA before the following autumn. Despite this, he had fewer than 40,000 operational troops, sailors, and airmen available, almost 8,000 below establishment for the country, with the British Army still cutting back. Furthermore, Macready was forced to waste five infantry battalions guarding prisoners. Then, on Friday 1 April, Irish Command was ordered 'to earmark ten infantry battalions for use in Britain, where the industrial crisis was once more allowing Sir Henry Wilson to prepare a crusade against Bolshevism'.[71] Four were eventually sent, two being maintained on standby for a month, with no fresh units sent to Ireland for another two months. Irish Command was bolstered somewhat on 24 March with the decision to arm RAF aircraft in Ireland with machine guns, particularly in Munster. Nonetheless, this was seen as a token gesture given communication difficulties in the air, a fact laid bare when IRA units still occasionally fooled pilots into dropping enemy mail into their own 'dropping circles'. Thirty-three-year-old Brigade Major Bernard Law Montgomery of the 17th Brigade in Cork, cousin of the Hugh mortally wounded on Bloody Sunday, berated the fact that RAF aircrews 'knew nothing whatever about the war, or the conditions under which it was being fought'.[72] Using aircraft offensively also incurred increased risk of civilian casualties.

Back in Dublin, Castle authorities, yet again, came within a hair's breadth of capturing Collins in an incident involving another of his female facilitators. On 1 April, Auxiliaries raided Patricia Hoey's home, shared with her mother at 5 Mespil Road. Collins had used their home as an office since 76 Harcourt Street was raided in November 1919. When they found a loaded revolver,

Hoey was arrested and interrogated. However, she kicked up such a fuss, protesting that her work as a journalist would ensure the world would know how her captors treated Irish women, that she was returned home.[73] However, Collins, Tom Cullen and Collins' finance secretary, Alice Lyons, were due at the house at 9 a.m. the following morning, and the Auxiliaries, suspecting Collins' imminent arrival, were preparing a trap.

Hoey needed to act fast. She persuaded her mother to feign a heart attack, unsuccessfully at first. However, perseverance led to a female doctor being summoned to the house, not their usual family doctor, a unionist, but a stranger. Nevertheless, the doctor, sensing something was askew, lent herself to the plot, insisting the Auxiliaries left them while Hoey's mother was examined. As a result the doctor was warned of the trap being set for Collins. She was given an address to deliver a message to: 68 Lower Leeson Street – the Land Bank.[74] She delivered the message to Volunteer John McCluskey there just in time for IRA scouts to be positioned at both ends of Mespil Road and nearby Sussex Terrace to stop Collins, Cullen and Lyons. However, the raiders did not leave empty-handed, a valuable haul of documents being captured. Collins said afterwards, when he realised the extent of their findings: 'The raid was much worse than I thought. Practically the entire record is gone.'[75] David Neligan was incensed – Collins still seemed to find it impossible to dispose of potentially catastrophic files. Patricia Hoey, like Eileen McGrane, was arrested again and subjected to 'shocking ill-treatment'.[76] Her mother 'recovered'. Less critical of Collins than Neligan, ironically, was Tom Jones, deputy cabinet secretary, who wrote, almost in his admiration: 'The tenacity of the IRA is extraordinary. Where was Michael Collins during the Great War? He would have been worth a dozen brass hats.'[77] He was correct about IRA tenacity; by now it had lost thousands to internment, with little effect.

Patricia Hoey was not the only one making April fools of the enemy that night. Bernard Nolan, thirty-two years old, of E Company, 4th Battalion, was arrested in Rathfarnham during an Auxiliary/military raid alongside his twenty-three-year-old comrade Christopher Reynolds. When the military departed, the Auxiliaries drove them to Rathfarnham RIC Barracks. As the prisoners were leaving for the Castle, Nolan was told by a cadet: 'Nolan, you had better attempt to escape to-night.'[78] When the Auxiliary added that the inevitable consequences would at least save him from the gallows, Nolan scoffed, insisting he would take his chances in the Castle.

Once on their way, the Tender stopped outside Rathmines church. It was pitch dark. The Auxiliaries dismounted, surrounding the truck, leaving Nolan and Reynolds seated against its side boards. Both were then ordered to stand up. Reynolds stood. Nolan quickly warned him to sit back down. They clasped hands in prayer, fearing the worst. Then, following a second order to stand up, both slowly stood. A similar tactic was being employed to that used unsuccessfully against James Cahill. This time, however, Nolan, seeing the enemy rifle, reached for it. He and Reynolds were cut down in a hail of gunfire.

Nolan came round several minutes later, face up on the pavement outside the church, to hear a voice say, 'That so-and-so is not dead yet.'[79] Another shot rang out. Nolan blacked out. Incredibly, he regained consciousness again soon afterwards, to find a torch being shone in both his and Reynolds' faces. Nolan feigned death, sensing the torch's glare through closed eyelids. Both men were then thrown like carcasses into the back of the truck. Nolan remained conscious as it then sped to King George V Hospital. On the way an Auxiliary stuck his bayonet through his coat sleeve, pinning his body to the floor while the Auxiliary smoked his pipe.

When they arrived at the hospital's guardroom it was a gruesome scene, several bodies of police and Black and Tans already lying there. Reynolds and Nolan's blood-soaked bodies were laid out on stretchers next to them. They heard their captors claim that they had been captured during an ambush and shot trying to escape. Nolan remained still, afraid to breathe but in excruciating pain. He assumed his comrade was dead.

When the Auxiliaries left the guardroom Reynolds stunned both Nolan and their military guards by suddenly opening his eyes, groaning loudly. Nolan did likewise. The dumbfounded guards, fearing nonetheless that both were on the brink of death, sent for Fr Francis Farrington from nearby Aughrim Street. Farrington had overseen the burials of the executed 1916 leaders five years earlier and was known to the military. Doctors were summoned. However, hearing the commotion, several Auxiliaries re-entered the guardroom, pistols drawn. This, in turn, prompted the soldiers to reach for their rifle rack. Rifles were quickly loaded and presented, the soldiers warning the cadets they would fire, adding: 'These two men, dead or alive, Sinn Féiners or whatever they are, are in our charge, and the man who will attempt to harm our prisoners will pay for it.'[80] Reynolds died the following morning, but not before both he and Nolan made statements and Fr Farrington administered the Last Rites. Six bullets were removed from Nolan's back and arm. Incredibly, none had caused severe damage. He felt deep gratitude for the guardroom soldiers.

Two Auxiliaries were shot soon afterwards in Rathmines. They had occupied Lissonfield House, adjacent to Portobello Barracks at the junction of Blackberry Lane and Lower Rathmines Road. Pádraig O'Connor shot one from the roof of Rathmines church as the cadet sat on a child's swing in the house's garden; the other was shot by ASU Section Commander Michael Sweeney, who cycled past and shot an Auxiliary on sentry duty.[81]

By April, plans to form the IRA into divisions were advanced. Ernie O'Malley's importance to GHQ was underscored when he was placed in charge of the IRA's 2nd Southern Division. Notwithstanding criticisms of the strategy, it made more sense to GHQ to coordinate sixteen divisions rather than scores of brigades. Dublin Brigade came under the umbrella of the 2nd Eastern Division. The brigade comprised seven battalions, the 6th covering south-east Dublin from Booterstown to Bray and across to the Dublin Mountains, the 7th extending west from Templeogue to Blessington. Richard Mulcahy delivered a rousing call to arms in tandem with De Valera's recent proclamations. Mulcahy heralded to his force: 'The stand you have made, that you are making now and that you mean to make right through … [is] one of the most memorable things in the history of the world.' As other countries realise what is happening in Ireland, 'many a tyranny in many a land will begin to tremble and totter. Ireland will once again be the teacher of nations.'[82] Ironically, Gen. Boyd spoke with even greater admiration of Mulcahy than Tom Jones had of Collins. Boyd, off the record, told Carl Ackerman – the American journalist, now back in Dublin – that if Mulcahy cared to join the British Army he would appoint him chief of staff, adding that Mulcahy knew more about 'organising and directing forces than anyone he knew'.[83]

Ackerman was back for another interview with, among others, the man he had been advised by Basil Thompson to consider the real Irish leader – Collins. Collins' previous interview with Ackerman had seen him portray an unyielding stance. Collins had, when Ackerman introduced the idea of dominion status, derided the idea, claiming the true goal – a republic – was attainable with equal effort. Ackerman was, like Thompson, well attuned to such remonstrations. Yet, in spring 1919, Collins had, with Harry Boland, given George Creel, another prominent American journalist, the distinct impression that dominion status 'would reconcile the Irish question'.[84]

Newspaper articles in the USA that followed the publication of the first Ackerman/Collins interview had heralded that 'Dáil Éireann was not the real power in Ireland ... Michael Collins was', and that 'the British military authorities considered him the field marshal of the Irish Army and they feared him'. Papers had dubbed Collins the 'Republican War Minister' and 'Commander-in-Chief of the Irish Army'.[85] Such imaginative captions had reaped significant rewards for their collective enemies, nurturing the growing divisions between Collins, De Valera and Brugha, as well as De Valera and John Devoy.

Now, on 2 April, Collins provided written answers to questions posed by Ackerman. Collins' responses were similarly unwavering. He stood by the Republic, dismissed compromise and scoffed at the idea of placing faith in the same British government that had put to death innocent men like Paddy Moran and Thomas Whelan.[86] He asserted that IRA morale and efficiency were improving, boasting: 'It is only a question of time until we shall have Ireland cleared of Crown Forces ... We are going on until we win.'[87] He insisted on an undivided Ireland, while assuring northern unionists of security under such an arrangement.

Ackerman also sought out Arthur Griffith to discuss peace proposals. He met him in prison. Griffith, looking particularly dishevelled, differed radically to Collins in his response, telling Ackerman dismissively that a conference which Lloyd George had the power to call at any time was the appropriate forum for such discussions.[88]

Ackerman had also asked De Valera for terms under which a meeting with Sir James Craig – Northern Ireland's prime minister-in-waiting – could be arranged to discuss the six counties. De Valera's answer was that he was prepared to meet Craig or any other Irishman, and insisted Ireland's quarrel was with England. He asserted that with England gone, internal differences could be resolved amicably.

Collins' responses to Ackerman were subsequently forwarded to Macready. Macready, in turn, forwarded them to Lloyd George. Ackerman later wrote: 'For the first time in over a year of confidential conversation, a real leader of the Republic had answered, in writing, questions upon which the British Government could formulate a peace policy.'[89] Under-Secretary for Ireland Sir James MacMahon dismissed Collins' hard-line stance as having been expected, suggesting there was room for compromise. Macready had also derided

Collins' trenchant stance the previous August to Ackerman as a typically Irish negotiation tactic.

Conspicuously, five days later, 7 April, Basil Thompson, the Scotland Yard chief highly regarded by Ackerman as a pragmatist, subtly 'nudged Lloyd George towards negotiations', suggesting the IRA were far from beaten; a sentiment echoed by a conference held by the Irish Unionist Alliance on 2 April in Dawson Street, during which prominent delegates clamoured for dominion status, seeing it as the best of a bad lot of possible options.[90] This was set against the noisy backdrop of an IRA gun and bomb attack on the military in nearby York Street. Meanwhile, Andy Cope set about arranging a meeting between De Valera and James Craig.

Basil Thompson was indeed a realist. He could sense Britain's hold on Ireland's capital, and the country itself, was slackening to the sound of gunshot, explosion, the whipping crack of the hangman's noose and the backdrop of tentative peace proposals and subtle political manoeuvrings. Meanwhile, many Dubliners, weary of war, endlessly vexed with hunger, coal shortages, unemployment, and disorder, but instilled with a growing sense of pride at witnessing what was once deemed impossible – successful resistance to the British empire – welcomed the onset of spring with hope, emboldened by the audacity of the Dáil and the IRA. The people, inspired by their sacrifices, were, by and large, resolved to see the fight to its conclusion. It was a resolve they would need – victory and peace remained, for now, a distant hope.

Frustration, Pressure and Disaster for Dublin Brigade

'My cigarette case I leave to the mess'

During April's first week, Oscar Traynor informed Harry Colley about the proposal discussed by the Army Council three months earlier to attack either Beggar's Bush or the Custom House. The pair met at Dublin Brigade HQ, 6 Gardiner Row, known as 'The Plaza'. The plan to attack the Custom House, by burning it, was by then well advanced. Since tasked with assessing its feasibility, Traynor had visited the majestic neoclassical eighteenth-century structure, its three-storey-over-basement Portland stone façade dominating the Liffey, carrying a large envelope with the letters 'OHMS' (On Her Majesty's Service) stamped on it, suggesting he was there on official business. Marvelling at the building's magnitude he observed initially that there was little of a flammable nature there, until he entered its offices, where, to his satisfaction, he found that each was ringed with wooden cupboards and shelves holding bundles of papers and files.[1] Burning the building was, he concluded, viable.

He exited through its public entrance into Beresford Place, facing north into Gardiner Street, where there was a large, grassy, semi-circular concourse. Concrete bollards linked by chains ringed its perimeter with an entrance gap for vehicles. Trees also skirted it. He studied the topography, recording details such as the various directions from where the enemy might converge once an attack commenced and, consequently, which roads would need to be blocked and manned to impede this. He subsequently detailed Comdt Ennis to plan and oversee the operation, briefing him on its strategic importance. 'The Manager' then paid the Custom House a similar visit, carrying a similar official envelope, after which he reported to Traynor that the mission could, indeed, be accomplished.

During their meeting, Colley, chosen because he had previously worked in the Custom House, was given the same envelope, ordered to survey the building and report back with his own findings about what tactics could be best employed in its burning. Colley did so, reporting several factors. First was its accessibility, with all entrances except Beresford Place reserved for staff, albeit with a small public post and telegraph office just inside its quayside entrance. Secondly, he reported that barricades erected previously by the public entrance were unmanned.[2] The military had been withdrawn from such public buildings following the previous year's successful King's Inn's arms raid by the IRA; soldiers guarding public buildings were feared unreliable and their arms a tantalising prize to the enemy. The only crown forces on site were patrolling DMP. Colley also noted the messaging system, as well as the location where foot and cycle dispatchers stood by awaiting calls, and that each room contained telephones. The stairways were all stone, balustrades were iron and the building's many passageway floors flagstoned, except the top floor which was timber.[3] Preparations continued.

Meanwhile, on 4 April, Thomas Traynor's court martial convened in City Hall. Traynor, a veteran Volunteer originally from Carlow, was wounded in the Grand Canal railway yards in 1916 and subsequently deported and imprisoned. Upon his return in 1917, he had opened a shoe repair shop a minute's walk from Crow Street, while undertaking intelligence and courier work for the IRA. Following his capture on 14 March in Brunswick Street, he suffered a vigorous interrogation by Head Const. Igoe. He was charged with the murder of Cadet Farrell.

Michael Noyk appointed barrister Nolan Whelan to defend Traynor. The case was vigorously contested, with both Gens Boyd and Macready called upon by Whelan to testify that a state of war existed in Dublin, so Traynor should be treated under the Hague Convention. Neither general turned up. The prosecution dismissed this argument, referring to the convention's insistence on belligerents carrying arms openly and displaying insignia.[4] Traynor protested that he was not an active Volunteer, merely a 'proper person to do a message'.[5] He insisted that his business and his ten children rendered active duty impossible, but freely admitted having fought with the Volunteers in 1916 and professed to still being available if necessary. He claimed, however, that he had not yet been called upon again to fight, and that he had simply been in the wrong place at the wrong time, delivering a pistol and ammunition to 144 Great Brunswick Street, when the fighting broke out on 14 March.

Arguments flowed. Auxiliaries Weber and Crang testified that Traynor had shouted, 'For God's sake shoot me now', when they had pinned him down, while asserting in the armoured car following capture that he, like them, was a soldier.[6] Whelan castigated both men for not having cautioned Traynor under arrest before questioning him, while claiming that Traynor had only requested a quick death to avoid a similar fate to Dick McKee or Peadar Clancy, whom he cited were 'tortured and butchered in the Castle'.[7] Traynor had been found with four bullets in the seven-round clip of his semi-automatic, another in the chamber, indicating he had fired twice. He had an additional clip in his pocket. However, evidence provided by the prosecution that Traynor had admitted to firing the pistol that night was contradictory.

The court president, also O/C Dublin Castle – Brevet Lt Col Francis Montague-Bates of 2nd Battalion, East Surrey Regiment – had convicted the late Paddy Moran despite overwhelming evidence indicating otherwise. Consequently, Traynor's legal team had objected to him presiding in Traynor's case, citing bias. Notably, when evidence was introduced by the prosecution that was unlisted in the Summary of Evidence, protestations over such procedural irregularity were ignored.[8] At 6.20 p.m., Montague-Bates found Traynor guilty – he would hang.

Edmond Foley and Patrick Maher would also hang, both found guilty. Their cases, prosecuted by William Wylie, who had also prosecuted the executed 1916 leaders, lasted five days. Michael Murphy was acquitted. Foley had acted as a scout at Knocklong, but Maher 'had neither hand, act nor part in it'.[9] Nonetheless, both men 'stated publicly in the courtroom that they were proud to be called on to die for Ireland'.[10] The latitude the ROIA afforded the prosecution struck witnesses in City Hall.

Also during early April, Comdt Tom Ennis received orders from Brig. Traynor to attack an enemy position foremost in both men's minds due in no small part to its proximity to the Custom House – the London and North Western Railway Hotel. The fact that bogus copies of the *Irish Bulletin* were rolling out from behind its red-brick, four-storey façade was of little concern set against the real threat posed by the building's cadre of Q Company Auxiliaries. Q Company consisted of former naval officers and merchant seamen, as well as transferees from other companies with similar experience. Their specific detail was harbour surveillance, searching arriving and departing ships for arms, documents and personnel. Naval expertise rendered these cadets ideal.

Thirty-one-year-old Major Thomas Ryan was in command at the hotel, where the rooms were shared with a handful of O Company cadets detailed to similar duties before Q Company's arrival. Q Company cadets wore distinctive skull and crossbones, or crossed anchor patches on their caps. Their impact was immediate, quickly adding to the haul of captured arms and ammunition.

The hotel was ideally situated, overlooking the Liffey and close to the city and its docks. A gangway ran to the adjacent railway station, both ends of which were locked. The hotel's security strategy was still being formulated when Ennis began planning his attack. A sentry stood at its entrance day and night, and the pavement at its front was kept clear at all times. Passing pedestrians risked arrest simply by walking too close to the hotel.

Ennis' plan was for a frontal assault by E Company, 2nd Battalion, to coincide with the 8 a.m. dockworkers' shift change. His men would mingle with workers until, reaching the hotel, they would break into four sections. The first would deal with any enemy at the hotel's central main entrance, facing the road. The second and third would also assault the building's front, to either side of the first section, with pistols and grenades, as well as newly formulated chemical bombs – small bottles with a solution of phosphorous in carbon bisulphide. James O'Donovan, GHQ director of chemicals, manufactured these specifically for this assault.[11] The fourth section, covered by the third, would attack the hotel's front and place a large mine, delivered initially to the quayside by handcart – these were used widely in the city and, therefore, inconspicuous – and subsequently carried to the door. E Company ambitiously planned on corralling the enemy at the front using the chemical bombs, and then detonating the mine when they converged there to escape, causing massive casualties. As E Company moved into position, D Company, armed with rifles, would disable the swivel bridge linking Spencer Dock and Sheriff Street, and take up positions dominating the hotel's rear from its north, east and west. Then, on North Wall Quay, Garry Holohan – released from internment due to an error – would incapacitate the drawbridge leading from the quay to Spencer Dock. Disabling both mechanical bridges would isolate Q Company from reinforcements.

The operation commenced at 7.50 a.m., Monday 11 April, when Capt. James Foley and three D Company members under his command closed Spencer Dock Bridge. Foley threw the key into the dock before moving towards the hotel's rear.[12] Another D Company section manned elevated defilades on

Upper Sheriff Street with clear fields of fire to the hotel. Meanwhile, Holohan entered the North Wall drawbridge cabin through a trapdoor beneath, nervously awaiting Comdt Ennis' signal that the attackers were ready for him to seal the quay. There was a separate draw on the bascule bridge for each direction of road traffic. The signal soon came. Dockers rushing to work then looked on curiously; boats did not usually enter Spencer Dock on Monday mornings. Holohan cursed when, having opened one bridge ramp easily, he had to hand-crank the other, a slow, arduous process. He then took the bridge's fuses and dumped them 'into the gulley in the street'.[13]

Ennis and his men mingled innocently with dockworkers. The hotel sentry, twenty-eight-year-old Cadet Gerald Body, noticed nothing untoward among the crowds walking hastily along the quay, or the handcart with the mine. Inside the hotel, meanwhile, Auxiliaries slept following night patrols, others relaxed before retiring, and those preparing for day duty ate breakfast. Major Ryan had just made his report and was briskly assigning duties to Section Leader Owen Latimer, recently transferred from K Company.[14] Latimer had held the military rank of lieutenant colonel and commanded K Company during December's burning of Cork.

At 8.a.m., all hell broke loose. Cadet Body suddenly saw six men to his front, left and right, step out from the crowd and run at him, pistols drawn. He sprang into action, raising his rifle. Shots rang out. He collapsed, hit in the leg. Frantically seeking cover, dockworkers stampeded.[15] Body, fuelled by fear, dragged himself inside the hotel, shouting that it was under attack. Bullets sending splinters flying from the doorway conveyed the same warning. Shouts erupted: 'Alarm!' Auxiliaries grabbed their weapons. Those not in uniform reached for the nearest Balmoral caps. Cadets woken from sleep rushed to battle in pyjamas.

Ennis' left and right sections hurled a dozen grenades and gas bombs through the hotel windows on the ground and first floors. Shattering glass added to the cacophony. Cadets smashed windows with rifle and shotgun butts and pistol handles to return fire. Shards cascaded. Battle was joined by D Company as Foley's men shot at the hotel's rear windows; rifle bolts worked feverishly while spotters directed fire with field glasses. Q Company was surrounded.

The gas bombs took effect, caustic fumes wafting throughout the huge building. Major Ryan, overpowered, scrambled down the staircase to be hit in the head by a flying grenade knocking him sideways. His cap tumbled from his head as his watering eyes fell upon the grenade rolling on the floor next to him. He braced himself, but that grenade, like so many, failed to explode. Others did, rocking the building's inner walls. Within seconds, Ryan was back on his feet barking orders to the backdrop of more shouts, explosions and small arms cracks. Cadets upstairs, gasping, took to the hotel roof. Shots ricocheted from chimneys and slates as D Company riflemen sought them out.

Ennis made his final move – the mine. Volunteers rolled huge barrels to cover their advance, crouching, towards the building.[16] Eighteen-year-old Peter Freyne, his blood up, broke from cover momentarily to hurl a grenade. An Auxiliary fired from a downstairs window. Like a wild-west gunslinger, Colt .45 in one hand, Webley revolver in the other, he cut Freyne down, hitting him in the chin. The bullet blew out the back of Freyne's head.[17] He lay twitching and dying in a forming pool of blood and tissue on the cobblestones. The assault party with the mine reached the hotel door, lit its fuse, then ran for their lives, shot at from the hotel windows by cadets, faces covered with cloths to mitigate the noxious smoke and fumes, thickened by plaster dust. The mine failed to explode.

The Auxiliaries counter-attacked. Ryan barked at his men to pour fire from the windows to cover a section bursting from the front door, guns blazing. Ennis looked on, cursing as he realised the bomb had failed. At 8.20 a.m., he blew a whistle to call off the assault, realising the better-armed enemy would

Auxiliaries in action, 11 April 1921. *(Courtesy of the National Library of Ireland)*

Auxiliaries standing outside the pockmarked walls of the London and North Western Railway Hotel following the IRA assault. *(Courtesy of the National Library of Ireland)*

The imposing façade of the London and North Western Railway Hotel, scene of a daring IRA assault that misfired, 11 April 1921, with Auxiliaries standing outside. *(Courtesy of the National Library of Ireland)*

quickly gain the advantage. His men disengaged. With sections providing a rearguard, they broke off, speeding into the railway station, through nearby buildings and along railway lines, pursued briefly by Auxiliaries. Back at the hotel, ambulances were summoned for two wounded civilians, plus Cadet Body, his leg strapped up, and Peter Freyne, who died upon admission to hospital. His brother, James, was among the attackers. Military engineers were also summoned to ensure the mechanical bridges were not rigged with mines.

Garry Holohan was soon once again risking his neck to circumvent Q Company's stranglehold on Dublin's docks. He, along with Joe Dolan's brother, acted as engineers on the *City of Dortmund* trawler. Under the direction of Liam Mellows, the trawler was used for 'running stuff from the German boats'.[18] By now, the IRA had an enterprising arms procurer, twenty-six-year-old Robert Briscoe, stationed in Berlin with a mandate to procure munitions left over from the Great War. Holohan and his crew ran a Royal Navy gauntlet to provide the IRA with much-needed weapons and ammunition following rendezvous with German ships at sea. Meanwhile, Mellows, along with Joe O'Reilly, Gearóid O'Sullivan and Diarmuid O'Hegarty, were acting in conjunction with Harry Boland in the USA, hatching ambitious plans to smuggle several hundred recently invented Thompson sub-machine guns to Ireland. Boland and Joseph McGarrity, leader of Clan na nGael and an ally of De Valera during the recent split in the Irish-American camp, would, if successful, oversee a monumental tactical shift in favour of the IRA.[19]

Meanwhile, on blustery 14 April, the funeral took place of Dublin's Archbishop Walsh, a ceremony that saw 200,000 civilians line Dublin's streets to pay their respects; businesses closed to allow employees to attend. The seventy-two-year-old archbishop, who had died five days earlier, had been a strong supporter of Home Rule as well as the land reforms of the late nineteenth century, frequently flying in the face of his Vatican overseers, not to mention IRA leadership the previous November when he had vocally supported Archbishop Gilmartin's plea for a truce. Not to waste an opportunity, Col Winter plotted the arrest of the Sinn Féin leadership at the funeral. The public relations ramifications of this – considering the lengthy list of public dignitaries expected to attend – appalled John Anderson and Andy Cope, who vetoed the plan. Mark Sturgis, equally horrified, derided Winter's plot to 'bait the mousetrap with the dead Archbishop and then promote a battle over the corpse'.[20] By now, Winter was gaining a disconcerting reputation among his overseers, particularly Macready. Four of those under his charge had committed suicide. However, Macready had time for few of his allies in Ireland, and Winter's reputation among his enemies remained formidable.

Macready was asked not to attend the funeral, as was Lord French and any military representatives. Nevertheless, Macready ordered flags to fly at half-mast in respect and confined troops to barracks for its duration. Lord French was later told that his letter of condolence had arrived alongside Richard Mulcahy's. French's response was revealing, coming hot on the heels of Gen. Boyd's recent expression of esteem for the IRA chief of staff – French referred to Jan Smuts, the formidable Boer War commander who had crossed swords with the empire using both conventional and guerrilla tactics, as having once been 'described as a bloodthirsty murderer ... just as Mulcahy is today'.[21] Smuts had since fought as an ally of Britain against Germany and commanded the British Army in East Africa. Notably, South African Prime Minister Smuts would soon enter Ireland's stage.

The day of the funeral also saw 'Tiny' King's field court martial commence in City Hall, along with that of Lt Hinchcliffe. There was a marked difference in the weight lent to evidence presented on their behalf to that afforded against them. Lt Commander Fry, who had witnessed Patrick Kennedy's and James Murphy's beating in the lower Castle yard before their deaths, testified, as did both DMP constables who witnessed their car being driven back to the city centre from Drumcondra following the shots they had heard. Murphy's detailed deathbed statement was deemed inadmissible. A plethora of fabrications from, among others, Capt. Hardy, provided the necessary alibis to ensure speedy acquittals, which were rebuked by the *Irish Independent*. The newspaper drew readers' attentions to far weaker evidence having seen Paddy Moran and Thomas Whelan hanged. *The Irish Times* remained conspicuously silent.[22] King was nominally transferred from F Company to the newly formed R Company, whose duties included guarding prisoners at Mountjoy and the North Dublin Union, but he spent most of the assignment on leave. He was subsequently transferred to command D Company in Galway.

On the day of the verdict, 16 April, fifty-four-year-old Capt. Patrick O'Neill, a former Auxiliary who had served just three weeks as a cadet before resigning the previous November, was shot through the shoulder by a lone gunman at his basement flat in 38 Heytesbury Street.[23] His landlady, Alice Wilson, answered the door at 9.40 a.m. to a man in a grey Mackintosh coat and cap asking for O'Neill. When she woke O'Neill he became suspicious and asked her to tell the caller to return later. When she returned to the front door the man was standing at the small garden gate leading to the basement on his right. Unfortunately for O'Neill, the stranger could see him standing at the window. When asked his name by the landlady, he replied, 'My name is Jack', pulled out a revolver and shot Wilson through the window, hitting him in the shoulder, before running away.[24] O'Neill died the following morning in King George V Hospital.

Later that day, in Kerry, Auxiliary Lt John MacKinnon, twenty-nine years old, was shot dead playing golf near Tralee. The shooter, James Healy, was a former British Army sniper and was accompanied by three comrades with shotguns. MacKinnon had developed a notorious reputation. He had been shadowed for two weeks by Healy, who finally scored two head shots from a Lee Enfield. That night and the following days saw a host of reprisals across Munster, including the burning and destruction of Michael Collins' childhood home, Woodfield, between Rosscarbery and Clonakilty. His brother, Johnny, lived there with his family and was interned on the same day on Spike Island. That day also saw the IRA, under Frank Busteed, kidnap thirty-one-year-old Major Geoffrey Compton-Smith of the Royal Welch Fusiliers outside Blarney in Cork. The major, also an intelligence and court-martial officer, would be used as a hostage for four IRA members awaiting execution in Cork. Like Gen. Lucas, taken hostage in Cork a year earlier, Compton-Smith developed a surprising rapport with his captors, conversing about history, politics and song, the major even learning a rebel song. Unlike Lucas, he did not escape.

Back in Dublin attacks continued. On 17 April Capt. James Foley took charge of six comrades: Lts Arthur Beasley and Peadar O'Farrell, and Volunteers Richard McGrath, Michael Kelly, Patrick Swanzy and Morgan Durnin, and led an attack against Q Company cadets travelling to North Wall Quay from Dublin Castle in an open-topped car.[25] The attack was launched just as the car turned onto Eden Quay, its approach signalled from O'Connell Bridge. A soldier who had stopped to ask the two IRA men about to launch the attack for directions inadvertently helped, making them look less suspicious as the car approached.[26]

Just after the car turned onto Eden Quay the Volunteers hurled their grenades and opened fire. The bombs did little damage, but as the car sped on it came under a deluge of pistol fire. One Auxiliary who stood to shoot back was hit in the chest and almost slumped out of the car. His comrades struggled to hold him while returning fire. They then came under further pistol and grenade attack from Marlboro Street, but escaped and pulled over near the Custom House to secure their wounded comrade before rushing him off for treatment.

Next day a grenade attack on an Auxiliary Tender saw three civilians wounded on Grafton Street.[27] This was hot on the heels of an attack near Portobello Barracks during which a British rifleman, positioned in a lorry, caught an incoming grenade in mid-air, before casting it away to explode out of harm's way.[28] Then, at 7 p.m. on 19 April, Volunteers from E Company, 3rd Battalion, attacked a convoy of six Crossley Tenders and a Ford car with pistols and grenades on Sandford Road, Ranelagh, wounding three Auxiliaries before the seven-man IRA patrol was chased into Hollybank Avenue to escape through nearby houses. The 'Patrol Report', written up subsequently by the company commander, detailed the IRA attack positions on both sides of Sandford Road, enemy strength, direction of travel and time. It listed two grenades and nineteen rounds of ammunition expended.[29] Such reports were routinely compiled and studied to improve their ambush tactics.

On the same evening in Ballyboughal in north Co. Dublin, RIC Sgt Stephen Kirwan was shot dead in a yard outside O'Connor's pub by an IRA unit under Capt. Peter White. Kirwan, a father of nine from Wexford, and three plain-clothed colleagues were ambushed leaving the pub by White's unit, which had been in the area preparing a separate ambush. Kirwan was shot in the temple and just above the heart. Nevertheless, he kept firing his pistol as he perished, mortally wounding thirty-three-year-old White from nearby Richardstown.

Plain-clothed RIC men had also been attacked two nights earlier in Castleconnell, Limerick, in the bar of the Shannon View Hotel. However, this time their attackers were Auxiliaries, also plain-clothed. Three fatalities occurred during this chaotic shootout: an RIC member, an Auxiliary and the hotel owner, Denis O'Donovan, shot six times.

Also from Wexford and about to die at IRA hands was thirty-four-year-old Const. William Steadman, a dispatch rider between Dublin Castle and Phoenix Park, who made the fatal mistake of taking a regular route with only minor alterations. At 11.30 a.m. on 21 April, he was shot by two ASU members under Tom Flood at the Jervis Street/Mary Street junction. A four-man covering party, which took the mortally wounded constable's pistol, backed them up. The unit had lurked for several days in the area. Eventually, a Daimler Guinness lorry had crossed the policeman's path and slowed his motorcycle enough for his ambushers to pounce. However, he survived for six days in King George V Hospital and provided detailed descriptions of the gunmen before he died.[30]

Seventy-five miles south-west of Dublin that day, the Carlow flying column was decimated when one member was killed and eight captured following a pursuit by fifteen Black and Tans and military in two Crossley Tenders. Following the pursuit, outside Ballymurphy, three more column members were captured at an arms dump and brutally killed with shotguns and bayonets. Parts of one IRA man's hands and several of his teeth were found scattered where he had been killed. He was Michael Fay, a Great War veteran.

Cloghran in North Dublin saw the death of another veteran, on 23 April, this time acting for the crown. Dist Insp. Michael Cahill was one of several RIC members travelling to Dublin from Gormanston when his driver misinterpreted a military halt signal. The soldiers opened fire, killing Cahill and wounding others.[31]

Another RIC district inspector, thirty-three-year-old Gilbert Potter, was being held hostage by the 3rd Tipperary Brigade flying column under Dinny Lacey's command. Potter had driven into the aftermath of an ambush the previous day and been taken prisoner, having been recognised despite wearing mufti. Among his captors were Seán Hogan and Dan Breen. By now Thomas Traynor's death sentence had been promulgated by Gen. Macready and was scheduled for 25 April. In an attempt to prevent it, Lacey 'sent a special courier to Dublin to propose an exchange of prisoners'.[32] The proposal was refused.

Traynor was being held in Mountjoy's D Wing, where he had befriended Seán Mac Eoin, awaiting court martial, and others including Joe Guilfoyle, incarcerated following a round-up. The day before Traynor's execution, his entire family was rotated in and out in small groups to bid him farewell in the condemned cell, comprising two cells converted into one with a fireplace at each end. Prison staff assisted sympathetically. Traynor was in good spirits. At one point, blowing smoke rings from a Sweet Afton cigarette, he joked: 'Imagine, one of those will be around my neck tomorrow.'[33] He professed to bear no ill will and wrote: 'Fight on; not for vengeance but for freedom.'[34] His

Thomas Traynor, executed in Mountjoy at 8 a.m. on 25 April 1921. *(Courtesy of Mercier Archive)*

wife, Lizzy, was the last family member to see him. As she stepped away he stood and saluted her.

The following morning was clear and sunny, markedly different to that of the previous Mountjoy hangings. Again, thousands converged around the prison. Cumann na mBan members paraded, leading renditions of the rosary from 7 a.m. Traynor's execution was scheduled for 8 a.m. Canon Waters and Fr MacMahon once again ministered beforehand. During a service Traynor knelt, flanked by kneeling Auxiliaries, to receive communion.

He then handed his watch, shirt-collar and necktie to Fr MacMahon with a final request to deliver them to his family. His hands were then tied and he was led on the short sombre route to the hang-room. John Ellis, back in Dublin with his assistants, then adjusted the neck of Traynor's shirt, saying: 'Look at me please – we won't hurt you.'[35] A hood was placed over his head and he was led to the scaffold. Standing on the trapdoor, a noose was placed around his neck and tightened. Then, the bolt was drawn, the lever pulled, the trapdoor swung downwards and Traynor fell. The rope suddenly tightened to the sound of a crack. It remained taut, the lack of subsequent movement indicating the hanging's instantaneous effect.

The prison's wicket gate was soon opened and a note announcing that sentence had been carried out was torn angrily from the warder's hand. As

Crowds outside Mountjoy during Thomas Traynor's execution, 8 a.m. on 25 April 1921. *(Courtesy of Mercier Archive)*

the murmur of prayers was amplified by the news of his death, Traynor's wife, among the crowds, collapsed, overcome with grief. A taxi was summoned to bring her home.[36] The surrounding crowds eventually dissolved. Following confirmation of his death, Traynor was laid to rest in a grave alongside his seven previously executed comrades.

Dist Insp. Potter was shot dead two days later when confirmation was received of Traynor's execution. He was buried in a shallow grave near Rathgormack in Waterford, having been shifted from place to place before being killed. Potter made an impression on Dan Breen, who considered him 'a kind and cultured gentleman and a brave officer'.[37] Breen forwarded his personal effects to his family.

After Traynor's execution, De Valera called upon Joe O'Connor and requested he join him in visiting Traynor's family. De Valera remembered him from 1916. O'Connor reminded De Valera of how Traynor had been wounded during a pivotal bayonet charge. O'Connor was deeply saddened by his loss. He had hoped that the most recent peace feelers might have forestalled his execution, particularly given his large family. O'Connor was aware that secret unofficial talks had just taken place between De Valera and Edward Stanley, 17th Earl of Derby. O'Connor considered that others had 'rushed into print' and made what he asserted were 'impossible suggestions or proposals'.[38] It would appear that this was a reference to Michael Collins' recent unyielding responses to Carl Ackerman.

De Valera had met with fifty-six-year-old Conservative MP Lord Derby on 21 April at former IPP MP and Sinn Féin TD for Kilkenny South James O'Mara's home in 43 Fitzwilliam Place. Lord Derby had travelled under the pseudonym 'Mr Edwards' for secret discussions with De Valera, who arrived by bicycle.[39] Derby had met Cardinal Logue before De Valera, a fact that irked the latter, particularly when the cardinal had refused to accept clandestine requests relayed by De Valera via an intermediary asking that Logue announce that only elected Dáil members were empowered to profess what the Irish people would settle for. Logue, however, chose otherwise. De Valera suspected Lloyd George was using Derby to drive a wedge between Sinn Féin and the church, using Logue on foot of his support for the unhelpful overtures announced by his fellow clergymen the previous December that had helped illuminate divisions between separatist factions, leaving the British feeling confident of the upper hand.

During the meeting, De Valera, recognising the similar danger of appearing at odds with Collins' professed position to Ackerman, maintained ostensible hostility to the idea of dominion status for Ireland, despite the fact that he had, the previous year, publicly suggested while in the USA that Ireland could, effectively, remain a protectorate of the United Kingdom. Lloyd George was fully aware of this. After Derby's return to Westminster, De Valera received a letter from Derby containing the outline of a speech Lloyd George would soon make in the House of Commons. Derby asked De Valera if the prime minister should announce in the speech that Sinn Féin refused to parley on anything other than complete independence. De Valera – sensing he was being lured into the trap of either answering yes and appearing inflexible, or answering no and contradicting Collins – countered tactically with his own question, asking if Lloyd George was only willing to discuss peace based on the surrender of Irish demands for full independence.

Lloyd George, reading between the lines, saw room to manoeuvre. Within two weeks – despite announcing on 27 April that there would be no truce – he would declare his willingness to meet Sinn Féin leaders without preconditions on either side. This momentous decision came in the wake of a meeting with former governor of New York and newspaper owner Martin Glynn, arranged with the assistance of Carl Ackerman. Glynn, forty-nine years old, implored Lloyd George to recognise the war's negative impact on Britain's relationship with the USA, striking a resonating chord with the pragmatic prime minister. A foundation stone was being laid towards negotiations.[40] Notably, Glynn had for many years been a vociferous supporter of Ireland's cause in the USA and had written editorials containing 'unabashed support' for De Valera.[41]

Meanwhile, the killing continued. 28 April saw the executions by firing squad in Cork's Victoria Barracks of twenty-four-year-old Patrick Ronayne, eighteen-year-old Thomas Mulcahy, twenty-four-year-old Lt Patrick O'Sullivan and twenty-six-year-old Maurice Moore, the former pair captured at Mourne Abbey in February, the latter at Clonmult. Consequently, Major Compton-Smith was shot two days later. Before he was killed he wrote two letters, the first a loving letter to his wife bequeathing keepsakes to her and his father. Notably, he left his watch to one of his killers, whom he referred to in the letter as a gentleman for whom he bore no malice. The second letter was to his regiment. He implored his Fusiliers to forgive his killers, stating that he would 'die like a Welsh Fusilier, with a laugh and forgiveness for those who are carrying out the deed'.[42] He asked that his death lessen rather than increase the bitterness between England and Ireland. He wrote of the kindness with which he had been treated while captive, and professed to 'regard the Sinn Féiners rather as mistaken idealists than as a murder gang'. He then wrote: 'My cigarette case I leave to the mess.'[43] He had carried it in his pocket throughout the Great War. He died with it in his tunic breast pocket, his letters placed in it beforehand. He then stood above his shallow grave, lit a cigarette and instructed his executioners to carry out their duty when he stubbed it out. When he did, he was shot in the head. The cigarette case was then removed from him and forwarded to GHQ intelligence. Major Compton-Smith was buried in a bog in Donoughmore, Cork. Richard Mulcahy was later impressed with what he had written in his final letters.

Back in Dublin, April ended in disaster for the Dublin Brigade. Gen. Boyd congratulated his officers on capturing, since 23 March: '3 machine-guns, 16 rifles, 97 revolvers, 356 grenades, and over 10,000 rounds of ammunition'.[44] Two days later brought worse news, when 'a machine-gun, 14 rifles, 54 revolvers, and 12,442 rounds of ammunition' were found in a raid on a Baggot Lane arms dump.[45] Then, on Friday 29 April, fifty-three members of 1st Battalion were arrested in a swoop on Colmcille Hall near Blackhall Place. Colmcille Hall was where 1st Battalion had mobilised on Easter Monday 1916 and was known to Dublin Castle. Auxiliaries and military from the 24th Brigade raided from several directions, the former overtaking and arresting a watching IRA cyclist speeding to warn his comrades, then storming the building, overpowering sentries while barring any escape routes. A large haul of small arms was also discovered, dumped inside by IRA members recognising they were hopelessly outgunned, not wanting to be caught bearing arms given the consequences. Papers were also discovered, leading to yet more raids.[46]

The war also continued to take its psychological and physical toll. Mick McDonnell, at the forefront of Dublin's guerrilla campaign from the outset, soon left Ireland for sunny California, assisted by Michael Collins. McDonnell's physical and mental health had been deteriorating under the strain of his position. This was aggravated by his affair with a policeman's daughter, Eileen O'Loughlin, after McDonnell had separated from his wife, Ellen O'Toole. The affair had caused serious problems for Squad members, flabbergasted and horrified at its potential security ramifications.

McDonnell's nemesis, Lord French, the man he had tried time and again to eliminate in 1919, only to be confounded by French's cunning and astonishing luck, also departed Ireland, on 27 April. French, despite surviving numerous assassination plots, had gradually recoiled from public life since the attack at Ashtown in December 1919, a close-run tactical failure but notable strategic success. Despite French's survival, his manifold reactions had backfired spectacularly. He had first brought Dist Insp. Forbes-Redmond to Dublin from Belfast to stiffen G-Division's resolve; Redmond lasted three weeks. His gruesome assassination all but finished G-Division. French had then introduced internment, only to trigger mass hunger strikes in response. His subsequent acquiescence to the hunger strikers utterly demoralised the police and military at the same time that the Black and Tans had entered the fray. Macready had written in his diary after Ashtown that he suspected he would be asked by Lloyd George to take military command of Ireland – a country he loathed. He was right.

French's departure came three years after his typically brash arrival, his exit far less cocksure. He was replaced by sixty-five-year-old Edward Fitzalan-Howard, appointed as Viscount Fitzalan upon arrival, the first Catholic lord lieutenant of Ireland since 1685. Fitzalan-Howard was a unionist but was far less coercive than French, his appointment seen as an olive branch to Sinn Féin and the Catholic Church. A senior member of the former quipped sardonically at the gesture: 'A Catholic hangman would be as welcome.'[47]

Oscar Traynor too was beginning to succumb to the pressures of his role, Dublin's war reaching unprecedented levels of intensity in recent months. Others, meanwhile, such as Frank Henderson, suffered with the 'Volunteer Itch', an irritating and painful skin condition believed to be caused by the stress of being 'on the run', high tension from chronic overwork and constant changing and sharing of sleeping quarters.[48]

April's closing days saw, to Comdt Ennis' further exasperation with his own engineers, another meticulously planned operation fall apart because of ineffective mines. Three were laid on the railway line at Killester, three miles north-east of the city centre, primed to explode as a northbound military munitions train was passing. Fifty IRA men were mobilised for the operation, including sections one and two of the ASU, and the Squad, whom Ennis had authority to call up when necessary. As well as a multitude of pistols and grenades at hand to press home the attack – delivered by Vinny Byrne in a covered pony and trap – Ennis' men had commandeered a petrol tanker.

Incredibly, they planned on hosing the train with petrol from the bridge in Killester above the railway line having first exploded their mines, creating an inferno and detonating the munitions cargo. They would then unleash a torrent of small arms fire and grenades upon the enemy. The plan came to nothing when, yet again, their mines proved ineffective. Vinny Byrne was then charged with returning the IRA munitions haul, including the mines, back to a dump in Dorset Row.

It was a nerve-wracking trip. Added to Byrne's fears of carrying unreliable explosives were the close calls suffered with military and Auxiliary checkpoints en route. He eventually made Dorset Row, only to find he had no key for the dump. He made his way to brigade HQ, parked his transport outside nearby Barry's Hotel, and then noticed several Crossley Tenders pull in just behind him. Auxiliaries were raiding the hotel. Byrne innocently asked a cadet if he wanted him to move out of his way, then did so and casually strolled into HQ two doors away to procure the key.

Christopher Fitzsimons took part in the failed Killester operation. Afterwards he and his ASU comrades settled instead for a Leyland military lorry, which they commandeered in Fairview at pistol point, brought to the adjacent sloblands and set alight at a corporation dump, before pushing it into the sea with the help of three unarmed soldiers who had been in charge of it. They rewarded the soldiers' assistance with tram fares back to the city.[49]

Dublin, like elsewhere in the country, was 'a wilderness of mirrors in which nothing is what it seems' in terms of espionage and suspicion.[50] Dan McDonnell was still acting as liaison between Michael Collins and David Neligan. To maintain contact, McDonnell moved to 42 Mulgrave Street in Dún Laoghaire. He met Neligan regularly and commuted to Dublin by tram relaying information. Neligan put McDonnell in touch with two Secret Service agents named Fever and Ashe. McDonnell posed as a civilian tout and regularly met them. They were not recognised as competent agents, so it was decided not to neutralise them for fear of their being replaced by more effective agents. McDonnell fed them insignificant information – that fed back being valuable. Nevertheless, his own imparted information resulted in raids and arrests that, notwithstanding their overall lack of value to the enemy, were not without risk to McDonnell, considering 6th Battalion, like its sister battalions, had its own intelligence staff. McDonnell's ruse was so convincing that he had been 'followed and under observation to be shot by local I.R.A. companies'.[51]

The killing of suspected civilian spies, collaborators and informers was at fever pitch in Ireland. By 30 April 1921, the IRA had killed more than 120 since hostilities commenced.[52] Roughly half were ex-British servicemen, some former RIC and a small handful of less dedicated IRA members shot for betraying information to the enemy, in some cases simply to save their own families and villages from reprisal. On 16 April, the IRA shot another woman, forty-year-old Kate Carroll, at Aughnameena, Co. Monaghan. Her body was found with her hands bound behind her back, shot in the head. A card was found pinned to her clothing, which, as in so many other cases, said, 'Spies and informers beware. Convicted. I.R.A.'[53]

Incredibly, despite the plethora of agents and touts circulating, Dublin Brigade HQ was never discovered. Nonetheless, a close call was suffered during a raid soon after Vinny Byrne's visit. In anticipation of such an event, a buzzer warning system activated by a hall switch had been installed. When the raid occurred, the alert provided adequate time for staff to conceal brigade papers in a wall cavity and resume the appearance of trade union workers.

Brigade staff had another ace up their sleeve that day: Emmet Dalton. He was working for GHQ as director of training after his brother Charlie had recommended him for the role following his release from internment. The recent overhauls within the IRA structure had seen Emmet's predecessor, 'Ginger' O'Connell, appointed to deputy chief of staff. Oscar Traynor had interviewed Emmet following Charlie's recommendation and was greatly impressed. So were the enemy on the day of the raid. Dalton carried himself like a typical British officer, 'very neat, debonair, small fair toothbrush moustache, and spoke with a kind of affected accent'.[54] He was visiting Traynor and his brigade adjutant, Kit O'Malley, when they struck, and simply adopted his former army officer persona, indicating to the raiders that he was there on army business and 'engaged in work about which the least said would be in the interests of all'.[55] Traynor and O'Malley were untroubled as they left.

May 1921 kicked off with a daring mission carried out successfully under the enemy's nose by K Company, 3rd Battalion. The British military had almost completed construction of a steel pillbox on the Loop Line Railway Bridge overlooking Beresford Place. A machine gun there could command the railway line itself, both sides of the Liffey, Tara Street and Beresford Place. The IRA men, under cover of darkness on the night of Sunday 1 May, climbed onto the bridge, dismantled the half-finished structure, loaded it on bogeys and pushed the bogeys to a safe place to dump the steel.[56] Richard Mulcahy forwarded a letter of commendation to the company for their initiative. Given what was being planned at an advanced stage, the last thing the Dublin Brigade wanted was an enemy pillbox adjacent to the Custom House.

Action two days later saw Christopher Fitzsimons and Tom Flood also complimented for initiative. They had waited opportunistically for enemy vehicles to pass North Frederick Street. When three army trucks passed slowly at 5 p.m., the two let fly with grenades at the second and third trucks. Both scored direct hits, inflicting several casualties.[57]

Meanwhile, the planned attack on the Custom House had seen the building's blueprints acquired by Liam O'Doherty, O/C of 5th Engineer Battalion. O'Doherty had procured them from a contact in the Board of Works.[58] This had led to additional visits by Harry Colley, Tom Ennis, Oscar Traynor and O'Doherty. Eventually, the daunting scope of their task became clear. The building was 180 yards long, sixty-eight wide, with three floors and a basement to contend with, numerous corridors, hundreds of offices and a staff complement of hundreds. The precise number of telephones was unknown, but they had discovered that the building had a direct emergency line to Dublin Castle.[59] Ennis and Traynor's minds were etched with the building's layout. Plans were prepared and revised relentlessly, tweaked if a flaw was detected or additional information received. Eventually, Traynor was ready to submit the attack plan to an Army Council sub-committee.

Sunday 1 May saw this sub-committee meet at 6 a.m. at 'The Plaza'. Traynor, accompanied by Ennis, outlined the plan to Mulcahy, Collins and 'Ginger' O'Connell. Ennis would take command of the attack, which would be executed by the 2nd Battalion – the target within their operational area – supported by both the ASU and Squad. Paraffin would be used as an accelerant. Dick McKee had issued such a directive the previous year following horrific injuries to Volunteers owing to petrol's explosive properties.[60] An oil company and its staff would be held hostage for several hours to allow their paraffin supplies to be transferred from their storage tanks to petrol tins. A commandeered lorry would then transport the tins to the Custom House.[61]

At one point, as Traynor drew breath, Collins, to Traynor's surprise, objected to the Squad's involvement. Ennis voiced his authority to commandeer them, insisting they took part owing to their experience, ruthlessness and proven abilities. Ennis had been one of the unit's first members, joining on the night

Dick McKee had formed it, and had participated in its first killing. Collins relented but demanded they act as a single unit during the operation. Ennis agreed, assuring Collins that the Squad and some of the ASU would be put in charge of prisoners and manning the Custom House's entrances and exits. Traynor then continued, explaining that an additional 2nd Battalion unit, combined with the remainder of the ASU, would provide protection to comrades within the building from Beresford Place, Loop Line Bridge, Butt Bridge and Custom House Quay, focusing their attentions on the various routes leading to Beresford Place and the Custom House. 5th Battalion engineers would sever all telephone lines leading to and from the Custom House at the last minute, to avoid arousing suspicion, while also entering the structure as the attack commenced to control or disable any additional communication points.[62] By now Garry Holohan had submitted a survey of electrical cables, telephones and junction telephone poles in the immediate area.[63]

To provide indirect support, 1st, 3rd and 4th Battalions would occupy fire stations in their respective areas to prevent Fire Brigade deployment before the fire had taken hold. Additionally, utilising similar tactics to McKee's 1918 plans, covering forces with mobile barricades assembled in respective battalion areas would be ready for deployment close to the city's military and Auxiliary barracks. Snipers and other riflemen would cover these as a delaying tactic in the event of enemy emergence from barracks during the operation. This prompted Collins to intervene again and criticise this idea, claiming such barricades could senselessly suggest a general uprising.[64] Traynor, exasperated, contended that he wanted the men inside the Custom House protected by a ring of barricades.[65] He emphasised that there were plenty of men available, and that the 'covering force was not meant to hold ground indefinitely', as in a rising, 'but to delay the enemy long enough to allow completion of the raid and withdrawal of the friendly forces. After a pre-determined signal, the covering force would retire and disperse into the city.'[66] Collins retorted that if the operation was not feasible without such a precaution then 'it should not be carried out at all'.[67]

The sub-committee eventually sided with Collins; there would be no covering force, a decision that would prove costly. Traynor reluctantly agreed, then continued to explain that the attack itself was to last no longer than twenty minutes and would commence at 1 p.m. on its chosen date – when most staff would be off-site taking lunch and numbers of visitors inside the building would be minimal. Timing was critical, Traynor emphasising that if the timetable was rigidly maintained then casualties could be minimised. Critically, however, he stated that if the enemy had time to effectively react it could cost them 130 of their most experienced Volunteers.[68] The meeting's attendees baulked at this but, nonetheless, approved the plan. Traynor and Ennis were instructed to maintain preparations while the plan was put to the Dáil for approval. Several days later the plan was approved and the date was set for the attack – 25 May.

Traynor's next step was to apprise Dublin Brigade's senior officers of the plan. Further meetings took place over ensuing days as it developed with their input.[69] Capt. James Foley was Ennis' deputy.

The ASU was back in action four miles west of the city centre on the late afternoon of 5 May, when ten section four members took positions around the Halfway House pub in Walkinstown, planning to ambush a truck on its return journey to Baldonnell Aerodrome after it dropped a contingent of civilian workers to the city. Several days earlier, two trucks and a car on the same inward journey were hijacked and driven to the Wicklow Mountains after the civilians were ordered off. A subsequent pursuit by an RAF spotter plane saw the car burnt out and the trucks abandoned in Glencree, where the army later recovered them.[70]

In response, the military mixed armed guards among the civilian workers for the ride back to the city, the extra cargo necessitating three Leyland lorries. When the civilians were dropped off, all the guards were transported back in a single vehicle, while the two others were secured in the city overnight. This returning truck became the ASU's target.[71] Each member was briefed in advance of the attack. Section Commander Michael Sweeney and Jimmy McGuinness would strike first with grenades from a public toilet adjacent to the Halfway House on the left-hand outward side of the Long Mile Road, along which the truck would travel having passed the pub. Patrick Rigney, Tom Lillis and George Nolan took covered positions 200 yards west on the road's opposite side behind a low wall at Lansdowne Valley Road leading to Drimnagh Castle. They carried Mauser and Luger pistols and were ordered to shoot the driver and any front passengers as the truck approached following the initial grenade attack.[72] Opposite them, and to Sweeney's left, concealed in a ditch, were Joseph McGuinness, Simon McInerney, Jim Harpur, Patrick Collins and Alec O'Toole. They carried Mausers, revolvers and grenades, and were to close off the attack. Once everyone was in position, they waited tensely, checking their equipment to focus their anxious minds.

Fifteen minutes later they heard the truck's slow approach from Drimnagh Road. The sixteen guards sang as it jolted along the bumpy road. Sweeney and McGuinness primed themselves. Sweeney's grenade was a No. 9 model, McGuinness carried a lighter Mills bomb.[73] Both grenades carried shortened fuses to explode on impact. Timing would be critical.

The truck came closer, the singing grew louder. Then, as it passed the pub, Sweeney and McGuinness walked away from the toilet, into the road, and hurled their grenades. McGuinness' landed on target, Sweeney's did not. To his horror, the grenade hit the truck's side, bounced, and landed at his feet. McGuinness wrenched his comrade back from the blast, which threw both men to the road, reeling from the shock. Sweeney caught the blast in his abdomen and legs. His face was also cut with shrapnel.[74]

The other grenade had exploded among the guards with devastating effect, their singing replaced by the cries of the wounded as the three-man section behind the wall at Lansdowne Valley Road stood up, firing, wounding the driver's arm. A subaltern next to the driver was hit by a bullet and shards of glass from the windscreen as rounds smashed through it. The truck jolted, swerved and stalled, its men sitting ducks for the remaining ASU members in the ditch opposite, who raked it with fire. Harpur and Collins jumped up from cover and threw grenades. Both landed on target, their blasts absorbed by the prone bodies they landed among, injuries catastrophic. Only one soldier returned fire. The remainder groaned in agony or lay mangled and still. Ruthlessly, the ASU closed in, intent on capturing weapons and ammunition. Just then, however, the driver, in desperation, cranked the engine to life again. Gears crunched. The truck lunged off, accelerating before slowing, then zigzagging, until stalling a mile away when the driver lost consciousness.[75]

Sweeney was tended by Jimmy McGuinness as the rest of the unit made their escape towards them. Harpur, Rigney and O'Toole then sped on foot to Walkinstown House, where they knew there was a car and a chauffeur employed.[76] When they arrived, however, the chauffeur refused to assist them. Angrily, they returned to the ambush scene, concerned that enemy forces would be speeding there. Luckily, a team of workers from Blessington Steam-Tram works then approached on bicycles. Seeing the IRA men's predicament, they offered these to them.[77] Jimmy McGuinness took one bicycle and his comrades helped Sweeney onto his saddle as pillion. McInerney cycled beside them, his hand on Sweeney's shoulder for support. They cycled to a safe house in Kimmage, from where Sweeney was taken to the Mater Hospital. At 2 a.m. the following morning, RAF personnel from Baldonnell, heavily armed, faces blackened, burned the Halfway House to the ground in reprisal.

Sections one and two of the ASU, meanwhile, planned a similar attack in Dorset Street. Three military trucks transported civilian workers each day to and from the city. However, they varied their routes, thus scuppering the attack plans. Several days later, a less successful strike by F Company, 4th Battalion, took place when they attacked a three-truck convoy to the west of the Long Mile Road at the Red Cow Inn. The attack's timing and execution was poorly coordinated and resulted in a Volunteer being shot in the leg by a comrade.

The day of the Long Mile Road attack saw De Valera finally meet with James Craig at the house of solicitor Thomas Greene, 8 Howth Road in Clontarf. Andy Cope had called upon Archbishop Fogarty to help set the meeting up. Craig had travelled to Dublin ostensibly to meet Lord Fitzalan. He was driven to Greene's home by 'three of the worst looking [sic] toughs' he had ever seen.[78] Both participants claimed they had been led to believe the meeting was requested by the other. Nonetheless, it showcased a starting point – an agenda agreeable to Craig and, consequently, Westminster. Craig's solution was: 'no republic for the South; no change in Ulster's [sic] status', fiscal autonomy for the south so long as free trade was maintained, and continued equitable payments made to the National Debt.[79] Both De Valera and Craig knew the latter would face serious blowback if word leaked about the meeting being about anything other than Craig imploring De Valera to work in accordance with the Government of Ireland Act; therefore, it was painted as a fruitless affair. Nonetheless, Craig invited De Valera for a subsequent meeting. When Craig suggested it take place in an Orange Hall, both were highly amused.[80] The meeting was just one of the clandestine moves made that early summer by Cope, cautiously navigating his own 'wilderness of mirrors' within which to seek common ground and, occasionally, like Dan McDonnell, risk his own life. Now assisted by Under-Secretary MacMahon – reeled back from enforced marginalisation the previous year – Cope moved feverishly between protagonists from the warring camps.

At this point some solution was essential to Dublin Castle. The Government of Ireland Act was in force and elections imminent. Cope's own government vacillated between parley and subjugation. Given recent successes, opinions swayed to the side of maintaining unrelenting pressure on the IRA, at least for now. However, an expected uncontested election victory for Sinn Féin would present a conundrum; Sinn Féin's anticipated strategy of boycotting the proposed southern parliament would leave Westminster with no option but to impose crown colony government in conjunction with martial law in the twenty-six counties. Macready and Sir Laming Worthington-Evans were fearful that pacification would require two years, but the cost and the longer-term prospects of maintaining this were forbidding. Politically the cost looked yet more daunting. In the meantime, despite increasing pressure, military and police casualties increased. Something had to give.

Cope's Castle contemporaries, shielded from the bigger picture, detested his cavalier associations with men they deemed murderers. He was under surveillance both by IRA and Castle intelligence. Robert Jeune considered 'drastic action' against him, only to find out to his shock the positions of those pulling his strings.[81] Hamar Greenwood, among them, hoped that Craig and De Valera's meeting would result in a settlement. At one point Cope nonchalantly told William Wylie, as he left the Castle dressed in a natty grey suit, a Panama hat and swinging a walking stick, that he was 'off to contact Michael Collins'.[82] On 9 May he intervened to release Erskine Childers following his arrest, to the exasperation of Dublin Castle. Under-Secretary MacMahon employed a host of connections to facilitate Cope, whose pluck and intriguing also saw him accumulate such a level of connections that Mark Sturgis described him as 'an Octopus, grasping everything with its tentacles'.[83]

Such prowess as an intermediary was scoffed at by Sir Henry Wilson, who dismissed peace feelers, boasting: 'We are having more success than usual in killing rebels and now is the time to reinforce and not to parley.' His counterparts, writing in *An tÓglách*, dismissed peace moves as a sign that the enemy was worn out, heralding that 'For us the one order, the great and serious duty of the moment is: "Get on with the war".'[84]

Rescue Attempt, Brutal Killing and Elections

'Ruthlessly and disgracefully laid waste'

Getting on with the war was what the IRA intended to do. As well as in Dublin, the first two weeks of May saw ambushes, attacks, counter-attacks and reprisals in, among other places, Shraharla, Clonakilty and Piltown Cross in Co. Cork; Cork city; Arva and Cootehill in Cavan; Lackelly and Athea in Limerick; Tourmakeady and Ballindine in Mayo; Rathmore and Castleisland in Kerry; Mountfield in Tyrone; Monard and Annacarty in Tipperary; Ballinacarrigy in Westmeath; Belfast; Newcastle in Down; Greenore and Carlingford in Louth; Glendown and Clonmany in Donegal; Galway city; Kilmanagh and Tullaroan in Kilkenny; and Inch in Wexford.[1] Despite thousands of internments, almost 4,000 from Dublin alone, and relentless harassment and raids, the IRA was proving accurate Tom Jones' statement in April about its tenacity.

However, less accurate were their grenades. Dublin's Grafton Street area, on Thursday 12 May, witnessed another such attack in which fourteen civilians and a policeman were wounded when three were thrown at an Auxiliary Tender, the first in Johnson's Place, close to Mercer's Hospital. It detonated but caused no casualties. But when the Tender drove into Grafton Street, thronged with civilians, two more were thrown. They missed, but exploded, badly injuring, among others, four children. Panicked civilians scrambled for cover or threw themselves to the ground as shots followed the thundering detonations. After the attackers fled, horrified Auxiliaries used first-aid kits to treat the wounded. Some were transported to the Mercer's Hospital, others walked there. The floor of its accident room was smeared with blood. The porch of St Teresa's church in Clarendon Street resembled a casualty clearing station, as did the Grafton Picture House, from where ambulances ferried the badly wounded to hospital.[2]

Section four of the ASU later attacked a military foot patrol from Portobello Barracks as its men turned right from Grove Road onto Sally's Bridge near Harold's Cross. Jimmy McGuinness, commanding, ordered the unit to fire from a field between Mount Jerome Cemetery and the Grand Canal as soon as the patrol rearguard reached the bridge's brow.[3] Instinctively, upon coming under fire, the entire patrol dropped to prone positions but began firing in the opposite direction. Buildings at the junction of South Circular Road and Clanbrassil Street were raked with indiscriminate rifle fire.[4] The ASU withdrew unscathed.

At 6 a.m., Saturday 14 May, Charlie Dalton, looking out from behind a lace-curtained drawing-room window overlooking the corporation abattoir in Aughrim Street, observed a Peerless armoured car enter the abattoir yard escorting two meat trucks that collected meat there for daily delivery to the city's military barracks and hospitals. The house was the official residence of IRA Comdt Michael Lynch, also the abattoir superintendent. Lynch was on the run, but his wife and children lived there. Dalton noted the armoured car's five-man crew, particularly their discipline, before leaving the house and cycling to Moreland's to alert the Squad. Their daring plan, Lynch's brainchild, was to hijack the armoured car – Number 18 Peerless – later that morning, after it had departed and then returned for resupply, and drive it to Mountjoy Prison. There, Emmet Dalton and Joe Leonard would, disguised as British officers, furnish forged papers to rescue Seán Mac Eoin, claiming to be bringing him to Dublin Castle for interrogation. High-risk prisoners such as Mac Eoin were always transported by armoured car.

Dalton had been ordered, three weeks earlier, by Liam Tobin and Michael Collins to monitor the abattoir and see if such a plan was feasible.[5] Initially horrified at the huge number of rats infesting the area, he reported that it was, sketching typical vehicle positions as they entered and left, but nonetheless, warning of challenges: the armoured car's crew rarely left the car and, unless they did so, the job would be impossible. Collins, with considerable experience in prison escapes, attuned to opportunity and desperate to rescue Mac Eoin, directed that they press ahead, suggesting that as the crew had already alighted the car on occasion up to that point, they would likely do so again. He was right. As the days passed, the car's crew became increasingly lackadaisical. Dalton relayed this, and for several mornings before 14 May, the Squad gathered 'unostentatiously in the neighbourhood of the abattoir', only to find, to their frustration, most of the crew following standing orders and staying in the car while the trucks were reloaded with meat.[6] Meanwhile, Mac Eoin, alerted to the escape plan by a warder named Breslin, had made it his business to report to Gov. Munroe on the same mornings, between 10 a.m. and noon, anticipating his rescue and masking his daily visits by presenting daily demands and complaints about Auxiliaries and warders.

Then, on 14 May, observing all five crew members leaving the armoured car upon their initial 6 a.m. arrival and appearing lacklustre, Dalton sensed the moment was ripe. He mounted his bicycle and alerted the Squad, standing by in Moreland's. It was hoped that the warm weather would see the crew behaving similarly recklessly upon their return. The Squad quickly mobilised, soon taking familiar positions around the abattoir. One hid behind a wall within sight of Dalton's window and, when alerted by a signal – a raised window blind – would summon his comrades to strike.

The armoured car and trucks re-entered the yard shortly after 9.30 a.m. Dalton watched, his pulse quickening, knowing each postponed rescue attempt brought Mac Eoin a day closer to hanging. Then, several minutes later, to his delight, he looked on as all five crew members stepped out of the vehicle and neglected to lock its door. They joked, laughed and lit cigarettes. Three stepped away. Dalton signalled with the blind, then waited with bated breath. It took two minutes for the Squad, having donned corporation caps in disguise, to walk from their positions along an entry he could not see from his vantage point. If the crew re-entered the car in that time and detected them they could be massacred on foot of his own signal. Then, to his relief, he saw Tom Keogh step briskly towards the two remaining crew members, pistol drawn. The rest of the Squad, among them Paddy Daly – in command – and Vinny Byrne, closed in, seizing their revolvers. Then, as they stood, hands raised, Pat McCrea and William Stapleton changed into overalls they had brought matching those of the drivers, relieving the latter of their caps and replacing their own corporation caps with them. Other Squad members entered the abattoir to subdue the rest of the soldiers, who had stepped inside. Seeing this, Dalton implemented his next step. His host and her children were locked into a room to enable them to deny complicity. He then cycled to a house in nearby Ellesmere Avenue to find Emmet Dalton and Joe Leonard, hearing pistol shots as he left but not looking back. When he found them, they looked the part of British officers, both wearing Emmet's pressed old army uniforms.

Emmet wore his Great War medals and decorations. Charlie told them: 'Come on, the car will be along any minute.'[7] He left them and sped off, seeing the armoured car leaving the abattoir as he passed it on Aughrim Street on his way to Moreland's to inform Collins of developments. Collins was buoyant, but wary. The operation's first part had clearly gone to plan, but he cautioned, 'I hope the second part will be as successful.'[8]

Peerless crews generally consisted of one NCO, a driver, and two gunners ranked as privates. In this case Lance Corp. Whetstone was in command. Despite having been warned days earlier by his section sergeant, named Walker, of whisperings about such an attack, Whetstone and his crew – two RASC drivers, Ruck and Harvey, and Gunners Whelan and Jordan – had disregarded protocols by leaving the Peerless in such a manner. They were not alone in their negligence; Sgt Walker, travelling in another truck, had gone into the abattoir kitchen without his sidearm.

Pte Jordan was ambling from the latrine when he heard a sharp 'Hands up!' command followed by shooting. Pte Albert Saggers, a truck passenger, fell on his back, mortally wounded having stepped out of the abattoir and reaching for his weapon. Jordan raced towards the Peerless to man its gun but was shot in the chest. Corp. Whetstone, hearing the shots, raced back out, drew his sidearm, then felt a revolver barrel press into his ribcage from behind. His pistol was taken. Then Pat McCrea, seeing Pte Harvey reach for a pistol, told him: 'It's not you we want, it is your tin can.'[9] The other soldiers were lined up. Jordan was carried, groaning, to a meat shed. Pte Ruck was forced to show McCrea how the car operated. Ruck did so, but failed to report a fuelling problem, humouring McCrea nonetheless by warning that the vehicle was past its best. When the Peerless was started up again, with the help of Ruck, who hand-cranked the engine at gunpoint, McCrea and Stapleton were joined by Keogh, Peter Goff and Seán Caffrey, the latter pair acting as gunners.[10] McCrea then drove out of the yard to collect Emmet Dalton and Leonard, who were waiting on the North Circular Road. They sat in the back of the car. McCrea soon realised the car was in bad shape; by the time they reached nearby Hanlon's Corner its radiator was overheating and Mountjoy was still a mile away.

Vinny Byrne and several other Squad members remained at the abattoir for fifteen minutes after their comrades' departure to ensure no alarm was raised, fearful of the close proximity of Marlborough Barracks. They kept the soldiers under watch while Pte Jordan was treated. When the telephone rang in the abattoir's office, Mick Kennedy picked up the receiver to hear a caller at the other end from 5th Division HQ in the Curragh place a meat order. Kennedy calmly asked him to call back in twenty minutes, which was agreed. 'He then cut the telephone cord.'[11]

Paddy Daly, seeing everything was under control at the abattoir, took a bicycle and cycled to Mountjoy Prison to assist if necessary. Daly had initially sought Leonard's place accompanying Emmet Dalton inside the prison. He and Leonard both knew the prison well. During a meeting in Kirwan's pub, while the attack was being planned, however, two friendly prison warders had warned Daly that this would be reckless.[12] Gov. Munroe knew Daly from his incarceration there in 1919, as well as his most recent stint. Joe Leonard had been imprisoned alongside Daly in 1919, but Daly, unlike Leonard, had interacted directly with the governor while seeking parole following the death of Daly's wife in March 1919. The warders argued that Leonard, at least, would have some chance of fooling him.

Seán Mac Eoin, meanwhile – prompted by Warder Breslin each time his rescue was imminent – having succeeded on two previous consecutive mornings to access Gov. Munroe's office, was, frustratingly, confined to his cell, as was the entire C Wing where he had recently been moved. An unforeseen change of guard was taking place and the prison's Auxiliary commander, not trusting the warders – the reason they themselves had been drafted into the prison – wanted to familiarise his cadets with each prisoner in their cells. C Wing was in lockdown. The plan was unravelling.

Shortly before 10.30 a.m., the Peerless turned left off North Circular Road into Mountjoy's short driveway and pulled up at the main gate. Dalton quickly

Mountjoy's short driveway, situated between the pillars, leading to its main entrance with its huge chimneys on either side. *(Courtesy of the National Library of Ireland)*

waved a large OHMS envelope. The outer gate opened and McCrea, with little clearance on either side, drove the car through. It closed behind 'with a clang'.[13] Two more gates opened into a yard. McCrea, struggling with the heavy steering, nursed the car back around in a way that prevented the two inner gates from being closed and left the Peerless facing out towards the main gate, its 6.76-litre four-cylinder petrol engine still running, arousing suspicion. Dalton and Leonard 'jumped smartly out of the car and posted Tom Keogh, dressed in British dungarees and a Tommy's uniform cap, outside the main entrance door' to cover their rear or raise the alarm if necessary.[14] They then stepped into the prison, passing a saluting sentry, just as some warders descended a nearby staircase, one of whom, seeing Leonard, involuntarily gasped, saying, 'O Jesus, look at Leonard', then 'clapping his hand over his mouth, dashed back upstairs, knocking down all the warders descending'.[15] Moments after, Leonard and Dalton were brought into Gov. Munroe's office and initially made welcome. Next to Munroe sat Dep. Gov. Meehan and Dr Hackett. Two warders stood nearby. Dalton, employing his well-honed officer's persona, handed Munroe the papers claiming Mac Eoin was required at Dublin Castle for questioning.[16] The cordial tone of their meeting changed suddenly, however, when Munroe reached for the telephone to call the Castle for confirmation. Leonard and Dalton then sprang, Leonard smashing the telephone, Dalton drawing his revolver on the warders. Rope and a penknife were produced from pockets. Leonard quickly tied up the three prison officials and warders, while Dalton searched for a prison master key, keeping his pistol trained.

Outside the prison Paddy Daly had arrived. So too had Áine Malone, as well as Seán Doyle and Frank Bolster of the Squad, and intelligence officer Jack Walsh.[17] Malone convinced the sentry to open the wicket gate, pretending she had a parcel to deliver. Doyle, Bolster and Walsh stood nearby. When the gate opened the three rushed it as she turned and walked away. Suddenly, a shot rang out. A rooftop sentry, seeing them, had shot Walsh's hand. Tom Keogh pulled his pistol and shot him. His rifle crashed to the cobbled roadway below. Keogh also shot and wounded the sentry at the inner gates.[18] An uneasy silence followed for several seconds. Pat McCrea stood ready, the overheating Peerless engine ticking over. Then, just as the alarm bell sounded, Leonard and Dalton reappeared, shouting, 'Who the hell started shooting'?[19] Realising the rescue opportunity was gone, everyone rushed for the car, climbing inside, jumping on the back or standing on running boards.

Joe Leonard, before climbing on board, picked up the sentry's fallen rifle and aimed at several onrushing soldiers, shouting at them to get back. They turned and fled. Leonard then leapt onto the back of the car as it was driven out the re-opened main gate.[20] The Peerless trundled away under continuous fire. Leonard fired back. Daly beat a retreat.

McCrea turned left onto North Circular Road, then made for North Richmond Street, half a mile east. Doyle, Bolster and Walsh jumped off en route, disappearing into side streets, Walsh nursing his wounded hand. Joe Hyland waited in North Richmond Street to spirit Dalton and Leonard away in a touring car, safer now given the recent lifting of motor restrictions. He looked on as the Peerless slowly made its way towards him at fifteen miles per hour, steam emanating from its bonnet, clearly in trouble. Nevertheless, it arrived and he quickly drove the two 'officers' to Howth, Leonard leaving the captured rifle in the Peerless.

The owner of Cassidy's pub in Howth eventually provided Dalton and Leonard with two suits. The pair refreshed themselves in their scenic surroundings before catching a tram back to the city, their officers' uniforms later dispatched to Dalton's Drumcondra home.

The armoured car's remaining five occupants were less fortunate. The car's engine packed in two miles away on Malahide Road, opposite Clontarf Golf Club. Despite a plan to drive the vehicle to Fingal for use against Gormanston Camp, its occupants had joked about driving into the city instead, turning its two Hotchkiss guns on any enemy they saw. Instead, both guns were removed after McCrea parked it under a tree. Ammunition was left in the car and they then fired shots into the petrol tank. Taking Leonard's captured rifle too, they stashed the three captured weapons in a field along with their overalls, before making their way through the nearby O'Brien Institute in Marino, and eventually to Fairview, where they entered a pub for drinks.

The stolen Peerless was a source of both anxiety and embarrassment to the military. It was feared its IRA drivers would indeed rampage through the city. Consequently, all armoured cars were confined to barracks while a spotter plane was deployed to detect the stolen one, which it did that evening, concealed under the trees and almost invisible from the air. Meanwhile, its army crew faced court martial.

Mac Eoin was compelled to maintain appearances inside Mountjoy when he eventually had his time with Gov. Munroe, now pointless. When he returned to his cell he found Auxiliaries searching it. Warder Breslin discreetly reassured Mac Eoin that his attempted rescuers had, at least, got away. Taunting the Auxiliaries, Mac Eoin warned them to go easy on his cell, lest they themselves fall foul of the car's occupants. His cell was then left alone.

The same Saturday night saw the shooting dead of forty-three-year-old Robert Redmond, a member of the Auxiliaries' Veteran and Drivers Division based at Beggar's Bush. Redmond was shot at 10.15 p.m. while at home on leave with his wife and son in Frankfort Cottages, Killarney Street. Curfew was then at 10.30 p.m. given the longer daylight hours. It was only after his killing that his wife discovered he had been a widower with seven children from a previous marriage.[21]

That night, fifteen Auxiliaries' homes were targeted in London and Liverpool. Five relatives were injured and one killed. Widespread round-ups of suspects followed.[22] These attacks came hot on the heels of IRA plots to blow up bridges in Glasgow, arson attacks in Manchester, and the wounding of a policeman and the killing of a suspected IRA member during a raid on an Irish club. Reports appeared in newspapers of IRA personnel booking hotel rooms before setting them on fire, and of a campaign of window smashing and acid being poured into postboxes.[23] Attacks were also reported in Tyneside, where a recently formed IRA unit had set fire to dozens of farms and an RAF shed.[24] The newspapers also painted a grim picture of Ireland the same week, where the highest crown forces casualties in a single week were suffered since 1916. This included another suicide, when forty-two-year-old Auxiliary Colville Crabbe shot himself. Civilians also continued to suffer; on 17 May, another grenade attack on an Auxiliary lorry in North Frederick Street wounded seven.[25] Three nights later, a Tender carrying Auxiliaries from I Company to the North Dublin Union was attacked next to Bolton Street College by Volunteers from C Company, 1st Battalion. A grenade landed among the cadets, blowing one of them, John McDonald, clear of the Tender. McDonald's comrades tended to him while others, fuelled with hate, rushed through nearby side streets seeking the enemy, who had, typically, vanished from sight.

As the war approached its climax, suspected civilian spies were increasingly targeted, both in Dublin and elsewhere. On the evening of Thursday 19 May, forty-one-year-old bachelor Arthur Bardon, a timekeeper in the Guinness Brewery, was shot several times in the head outside Newtown House, Landscape Road, Churchtown, by 6th Battalion members.[26]

Worse came the following day, when Capt. Frank Daly, B Company, 1st Battalion, received orders from Dublin Brigade HQ to arrest suspected informer John 'Hoppy' Byrne and take him to a recently established ASU HQ at 17 Great Strand Street for interrogation. 'Hoppy', like Capt. Hardy, walked with a limp – hence the nickname. A shoemaker, he lived in 44 North Brunswick Street.[27] Eventually seizing Byrne, Daly and two comrades delivered him to HQ, where, following interrogation, ASU intelligence officer William Doyle and another brigade intelligence officer concluded he was indeed an informer. Daly was ordered to execute Byrne. That evening he and his men, backed up by two ASU members, walked Byrne to nearby Jervis Street. Byrne was then shot. He collapsed, badly wounded, but remained alive as the IRA men fled from the scene. A passing civilian ran to Jervis Street Hospital to summon help. Byrne was rushed inside.[28]

The next day, Saturday 21 May, George White heard from a hospital porter that Byrne still lived and planned on informing the police about his interrogation and attempted assassination.[29] The potentially dire consequences were clear to White, who quickly discovered which ward he was in – St Joseph's. This was quickly relayed to Capt. Flanagan, who immediately alerted Brig. Traynor to the danger. Traynor's response was instantaneous. He was to be killed.

Flanagan gathered Jim Gibbons, William Doyle and James Browne. At 2.15 p.m. the four entered Jervis Street Hospital from Abbey Street, two holding the porter at gunpoint, the other two commandeering a stretcher and making straight for St Joseph's Ward posing as hospital staff.[30] Byrne, taken in, complied with their subsequent requests to lie on the stretcher to be taken for an X-ray. He was carried back the way they had come, until they detoured into a yard next to the hospital's dressing room. Two shots echoed in the confined yard, resonating throughout the hospital. The killers quickly departed with their accomplices. Hospital staff rushed to find Byrne's bloody remains on the stretcher, two bullet holes in the front of his head, one between the eyes, surrounded by powder burns. Two empty shell casings lay nearby.

Uproar ensued; hospital administrators throughout Dublin secretly demanded the removal of all wounded IRA personnel within twenty-four hours.[31] Michael Collins was furious with Flanagan. Nonetheless, after much effort, he eventually smoothed things over with the hospital authorities, assuring them that nothing similar would ever occur again.

The same night saw fifty-eight-year-old RIC Sgt Joseph Anderson shot dead by four IRA men in Balbriggan. Then, at 6 p.m. on Sunday 22 May, the body of twenty-four-year-old Peter Graham of Patrick Street, Dún Laoghaire, was found by horrified onlookers lying face down opposite St Matthias' church in Killiney on a pathway leading to the nearby golf course. The body had five bullet wounds to the head and body, and a note pinned to its navy tweed jacket saying, 'Convicted spy. Tried and found guilty by I.R.A.'[32] His hand held a religious picture. His 6th Battalion killers, having struck, escaped by car towards Dalkey. Graham had been seen walking calmly to the scene of his death with his executioners shortly beforehand by witnesses who assumed the small group were taking a shortcut to the golf course.

As Graham's bloody remains were removed to Cabinteely RIC Barracks, a military cordon was surrounding Richmond Hospital on North Brunswick Street. At 3 p.m. that day, Leslie Frazer, former Irish Guards soldier, employed ostensibly as a clerk at the Royal Barracks, was shot twice by an IRA unit having left Walsh's pub at the junction of Stoneybatter and North Brunswick Street, 100 yards from his home at 9 Blackhall Parade. He was rushed to the nearby hospital and when word reached Dublin Castle that he had survived, its intelligence offices buzzed with activity. Several truckloads of soldiers sped to the hospital, some posted to his ward to offset a repetition of the Jervis Street killing. Anyone visiting the hospital was challenged.

The Sunday newspapers published a letter written officially by Pope Benedict XV but drafted by Archbishop Mannix in Rome. The letter, sent alongside a donation to the White Cross, was viewed with exasperation by the British, who perceived it as putting 'HMG (Her Majesty's Government) and the Irish murder gang on a footing of equality'.[33] It also horrified Sir Henry Wilson, who assumed it represented a mere taste of a potential Vatican backlash to the implementation of wholesale martial law. The letter stated:

> … we do not perceive how this bitter strife can profit either of the parties, when property and homes are being ruthlessly and disgracefully laid waste, when villages and farmsteads are being set aflame, when neither sacred places nor sacred persons are spared, when on both sides a war resulting in the deaths of unarmed peoples, even of women and children is carried on. We exhort the English as well as the Irish to calmly consider … some means of mutual agreement.[34]

The previous week had seen horrific reprisals following an ambush in

Ballyturn, Galway on 15 May, during which a local RIC district inspector, his female companion and two British Army officers were shot dead by the IRA. Indiscriminate machine-gun fire that night saw the RIC kill one of their own officers. Widespread burnings in the area led to newspaper accounts of civilians fleeing their homes, one description reading: 'the scene in the neighbourhood was like a sunset glow, the horizon being fringed with the flames from burning houses'.[35] Four days later, neighbouring Mayo saw the IRA defeated following an ambush they had laid for an enemy convoy in Kilmeena. The result was a two-hour firefight during which the military and police counter-attacked, forcing an IRA withdrawal. The result was one policeman killed, five IRA of 1st West Mayo Brigade, 4th Western Division, killed, and several more wounded and captured. Later, however, the IRA dead and wounded were thrown out in the street outside Westport RIC Barracks, causing widespread revulsion.

Meanwhile, with the upcoming Custom House attack now imminent, 5th Battalion Volunteers were being deployed in its surrounding area. Disguised as telephone linesmen they went unnoticed by the DMP and civilians as they sat working around manholes or climbed telegraph poles. Night after night they patiently traced cables and wires leading to the target building.[36] Eventually, all were traced and double-checked, with one crucial exception – the direct line to Dublin Castle. GHQ intelligence desperately sought its whereabouts from contacts. Soon successful, they informed the engineers that the line was connected to a sixty-foot-high pole outside Store Street police station.[37] Engineer Michael Cremin climbed the pole and traced the cable.

At the same time Capt. Kilcoyne commandeered a paraffin tanker from the White Rose oil company and stashed it in D Company's dump at Dorset Street's junction with North Circular Road.[38] Kilcoyne also led a raid on the Shell Trading Company's yard close to North Wall to procure additional paraffin, subsequently transferred to over 100 two-gallon petrol tins Capt. Foley had scavenged.[39] The tins were then stashed in the stables of Brooks Hotel. Additional empty tins were procured from Broadstone railway station, as were rope ladders in case it became necessary to escape from the Custom House's upper floors.[40] Foley also persuaded the Typographical Institute in Gardiner Street to hand over two huge bales of cotton waste, ideal tinder.

Dublin Brigade's feverish preparations coincided with the much-anticipated general elections in both Ireland's six and twenty-six county areas, the first under the Government of Ireland Act. The Dáil had decided during February to treat these elections as a mandate for the second Dáil, declaring later that this was to facilitate the expression of the will of the people.[41] As in 1918, an agreement was hatched that the IPP and Sinn Féin would not contest the same seats in unionist dominated Ulster areas. Austen Chamberlain, Bonar Law's successor as Conservative leader, had expressed fears that electioneering by Sinn Féin would see a vocal resurgence of the party's commitment to the Republic, hamstringing potential negotiations. This, however, did not transpire. Instead, De Valera issued a speech on 1 May seen by Dublin Castle as 'less bellicose and uncompromising than the Sinn Féin manifesto of 1918'.[42] De Valera also professed a willingness to provide local autonomy within a united Ireland to the six of the Ulster counties about to officially become known as Northern Ireland, knowing this would be scoffed at by Sir James Craig and the Conservative Party, but also aware that such an offer, in tandem with his 1 May statement, would have a positive effect internationally.

Of 128 seats in the twenty-six counties, 124 were returned unopposed to Sinn Féin. The remaining four, all in Dublin University, contested by independent unionists, were also returned uncontested. Accordingly, wide nationalist control was consolidated at the expense of diverse minority opinion, including farming and labour interests, which were 'thus effectively stifled'.[43] Contrarily, Sinn Féin won just six of fifty-two seats in the six northern counties. The election's aftermath saw further high-level discussions in Westminster about the prospect of crown colony government in tandem with wholesale martial law.

The day after the election saw testing take place of the first consignment of Thompson sub-machine guns recently smuggled into Ireland in advance of several hundred planned to follow. Two former US Army officers, Major James Dineen and Capt. Patrick Cronin, accompanied the consignment to provide training on their use. Lectures were given to selected Dublin Brigade members, consisting of 'taking the gun asunder, becoming acquainted with the separate parts and securing a knowledge of the names of these parts, the clearance of stoppages', as well as their causes.[44] However, their first firing in Dublin was slapstick. When Tom Keogh got his hands on one in Moreland's during the third week in May, he loaded its fifty-round ammunition drum magazine, then attached it to the gun. His wary comrades were careful to stand behind him as he began to 'fidget around' with it, until, suddenly, there was a burst of fire.[45] Having scrambled to avoid ricochets, ears ringing, the gathered Squad looked on in awe at the damage the gun had done with its .45 calibre rounds in such a short burst; it had nearly drilled through a brick wall.

Similarly impressed with the weapon's more official testing on 24 May were Mulcahy, Collins, Gearóid O'Sullivan, 'Ginger' O'Connell, Pat McCrea and James Slattery. They congregated at Marino's Casino along with Byrne and Keogh for a test firing by Dineen and Cronin. Also present was Tom Barry. Testing took place in a tunnel beneath the Casino. Mulcahy and Collins, half-deafened, were 'delighted at the results'.[46] The Thompson or 'Tommy Gun' was an ideal weapon for urban and rural guerrilla combat, with an ability to shoot fifteen rounds per second, an effective range of 164 yards and excellent stopping power. It was easily controllable in short bursts and its removable walnut stock made it easy to conceal.[47] The testing stopped when a Christian Brother appeared from the nearby O'Brien Institute warning that the gun's distinctive staccato report could be clearly heard and would draw trouble.

Tom Barry's visit to Dublin saw him perplexed at the reckless abandon with which senior IRA personnel appeared to move through the city, as if they were businessmen – particularly Collins. Following the testing, when a car they were being driven in happened upon an Auxiliary checkpoint, Barry assumed he was experiencing his final moments. Collins, however, typically cavalier, quietly told him to act drunk as they stepped out of the car. Barry then witnessed Collins' legendary ability to bluff. He joked with the Auxiliaries, fell about the place and soon had them all laughing and joking. When they drove off, Barry berated Collins for neglecting to send forward an advance guard. Collins' response was to call Barry a 'windy West Cork beggar', before explaining that acting this way was the 'only way they could survive in the city'.[48]

The day rounded off with a grenade attack by K Company, 3rd Battalion, on an Auxiliary Tender in Merrion Row resulting in several casualties.[49] However, this attack, mirroring the countless others occurring in the capital, was about to be overshadowed by the largest Dublin Brigade operation in over five years.

Later that afternoon, with the Custom House attack drawing closer, Harry Colley undertook a final internal reconnaissance. Reporting to Ennis and Traynor at Gardiner Row, he drew both men's attentions to the Will Room on the ground floor, situated beneath the building's huge green dome. This, Colley asserted, was the only part of the building capable of forming a large fire. With the dome above acting as a chimney, he suggested the area could be used as a central core for an inferno, facilitating the destruction of the entire interior.[50] Traynor and Ennis took note as the trio tweaked final attack plans.

Two-dozen engineers were to be deployed in Beresford Place at 12.45 p.m. – just enough time to establish themselves before cutting the building's communications as its assailants were about to enter. A section would then be added to the perimeter cordon, while others joined the attack.

The Squad would divide into two ten-man sections – contrary to Collins' insistence that they remained one unit – one under Paddy Daly manning the doors, the other under Tom Keogh to assist Capt. Flanagan and twenty-five ASU men under Tom Flood in rounding up and guarding civilian workers. To accomplish this, the Squad and ASU would enter at 12.55 p.m. via Custom House Quay and the western entrance facing Liberty Hall. These routes would be controlled by the time the main force arrived. Eight engineers accompanying the main force would then assist Flanagan's ASU detailed to the post office to seize the telephone system.

The initial mustering point for 2nd Battalion would be Oriel Hall, at noon. Axes, bolt cutters and sledgehammers, procured by Assist Quartermaster Thomas Mahon, would be distributed as a precaution in the event of men becoming trapped in burning rooms, to access locked rooms, desks, safes and cabinets, and to break up furniture for burning. Each man detailed inside would be armed with a revolver and six rounds. At 12.58 p.m., the sixty-strong main force would enter from Beresford Place, where Tom Kilcoyne would park the truck loaded with filled paraffin tins. Each 2nd Battalion Volunteer would grab two tins as he went in. Once inside, individual officers and their men were to be allocated specific landings and offices.[51] Others, carrying extra ammunition, would exit the building again to form pickets around Loop Line Bridge.

James Foley was in overall command of the building's ground floor, Tom Ennis of its upper floors. The top floor, far smaller in area and protruding upwards from the building's centre, was pivotal; as well as being wooden-floored it also housed the Income Tax Arrears Office.[52] Once the offices were doused in paraffin and strewn with cotton, paper and wood – and windows closed to initially contain the fire pending evacuation and prevent escaping smoke from alerting passing police or military – each officer would report to Ennis that his job was done. Then, as soon as the fires were lit, Ennis would give a long blast on his whistle – the signal for the men to descend to the ground floor. In turn, once satisfied the top floors were vacated, Foley would order the firing of the ground floor.[53] Finally, two sharp whistle blasts by Ennis would signal the order to assemble in the building's main hall before evacuation. The two-dozen strong remainder of the ASU, acting under Pádraig O'Connor, armed with pistols and grenades, would patrol Eden Quay, Custom House Quay and control Butt Bridge from both sides, monitoring its eastern approach for Q Company Auxiliaries based in their recently assaulted hotel a mile away.

Harry Colley drew Traynor's attention to a pressing concern – the lack of peripheral cover for the men involved.[54] Traynor told him of the objection raised by Collins and subsequently ratified. Nevertheless, he and Ennis had improvised where possible by bolstering overall defences: 1st Battalion would position men at Liberty Hall, Lower Abbey Street and Gardiner Street. In addition, a Lewis gun crew, also with grenades, would be deployed on the railway bridge. He lamented that this was far from adequate but would simply have to do, given the constraining directive. He then added that all such covering units would be issued orders not to attack enemy troops if they appeared to be on routine patrol. If, on the other hand, things appeared otherwise, they were to open fire – the need for stealth clearly moot at such a point. Additionally, all city battalions were to take and hold their local fire stations for the operation's duration. Approximately 150 Volunteers would provide indirect support.[55]

Participating Volunteers were to wear work clothes to avoid arousing suspicion before or after the attack. From outside the Custom House it was to appear initially like a normal business day. Volunteers setting fires would commence within the building at 1 p.m. and take no more than twenty minutes to accomplish their tasks. Traynor would oversee the operation from Beresford Place.

Later that warm, bright evening, following company parades, Volunteers were told that they were required for an important job the following day. Squad and ASU members were ordered to report to their respective HQs at Moreland's and Great Strand Street the following morning for briefings. Traynor, Ennis and Colley spent a long night nervously hoping they had covered every contingency. Only time would tell.

13

Custom House Attack

'There is going to be sport here today'

Wednesday 25 May 1921 was warm, sunny and breezy. Dublin continued to bake in the dry, early summer heatwave – perfect conditions for the perilous task ahead for 2nd Battalion and their brigade comrades.

Upper Sackville Street buzzed with pedestrians, trams and carts that morning as James Foley, Patrick Swanzy and 2nd Lt Peadar O'Farrell stood outside the sixty-foot-wide frontage of Findlater's shop on its eastern side, close to the Parnell Monument. Savouring the aroma of its produce – everything from confectionery to coffee to whiskey – they smoked cigarettes, training their eyes every few seconds on a three-ton Austin lorry unloading shop supplies nearby.[1] Foley then approached the driver, telling him he needed to commandeer the truck for a few hours. The driver, quickly recognising he was dealing with the IRA, cooperated.[2] Fifteen minutes later it was parked outside D Company's dump to be loaded with tins of paraffin and cotton waste.

Tom Kilcoyne, still scavenging paraffin, commandeered a van from Hampton, Leedon & Company chemists and oil distributors in Henry Street. He and several comrades then filled it with empty petrol tins and drove it to the Great Northern Railway yard in Sheriff Street to fill the tins with paraffin.[3] The yard was well stocked. However, to their disbelief, as they filled the cans a truckload of Auxiliaries entered the yard to collect petrol. Fearing an encounter that could scupper their plans, Kilcoyne's accomplices dispersed. He drove the van back out, heading straight for Brig. Traynor to alert him to their presence, which posed an additional problem; the muster point for the imminent attack, Oriel Hall, sat next to the yard. Traynor improvised, changing this to Seán Connolly Hall at the Summerhill/Portland Row junction. Couriers sped, panting, through the streets with revised instructions.

Then, at 12.15 p.m. in Seán Connolly Hall, 2nd Battalion Volunteers chosen for the operation and the Squad – who mustered initially at 35 Lower

Gardiner Street, serving as temporary operational HQ – were briefed on its finer details by Comdt Ennis. At 12.20 p.m., Capt. Foley pulled up outside the hall in the commandeered lorry with Lt O'Farrell and Patrick Swanzy, and handed its keys to Tom Kilcoyne. A mile away, the ASU had been issued their final instructions in Strand Street.

Harry Colley, conducting final reconnaissance outside the Custom House, observed trucks and cars enter and leave its grounds, as was routine. He circled the building. Everything seemed normal.[4] He reported to Traynor shortly before 12.50 p.m., 5th Battalion's engineers loitering around manholes and deploying ladders as Colley passed en route. Michael Cremin prepared to climb the sixty-foot pole in Store Street to neutralise the line between the Custom House and Dublin Castle.

Tom Ennis left Seán Connolly Hall at 12.35 p.m., leading a lengthy trail of nervous Volunteers in small groups and Squad members taking alternate routes to the objective a mile away, the latter by a quicker route. Capt. Flanagan's ASU arrived on Eden Quay and Lower Abbey Street. Traynor and his staff, following Colley's report, entered Beresford Place from Gardiner Street. Capt. Seán Prendergast and twelve Volunteers from C Company, 1st Battalion, armed with pistols and grenades, spread out between Liberty Hall, the railway arches opposite and Brooks Thomas at Abbey Street's Beresford Place junction.[5] Similarly armed, seven men from G Company, 1st Battalion, under thirty-two-year-old Robert 'Bob' Oman, deployed between Gardiner Street and Store Street, a terrace of five Georgian houses to their rear facing the Custom House.

South of the Liffey, at a house in Fitzwilliam Street, Richard Mulcahy met with Cathal Brugha and Éamon de Valera. There, they positioned themselves at a fourth-floor window, looking north, anticipating a cloud of smoke appearing soon above the city's rooftops.[6] Ensuring their leaders would not be disappointed, Volunteers from all four city battalions seized fire stations, disabling engines. A Leyland was driven from Thomas Street station to Crumlin to ensure it could not be used to combat the anticipated inferno.[7]

The Squad and ASU, positioned along Eden Quay, Store Street and Lower Gardiner Street, primed and on edge, awaited the commencement signal. Engineers readied themselves, allocated cables within reach, pliers to hand. Michael Cremin climbed the telephone pole in Store Street and attached his earth cable to the line. Michael Stack climbed a similar pole outside Liberty

Hall, ready to cut the line to the Custom House's telephone exchange.[8] Ennis, just arrived, looked on as his men assembled. Again, disregarding Collins' instructions regarding the Squad owing to the situation on the ground, he approached William Stapleton, ordering him to the Marlboro Street/Talbot Street junction to command a 2nd Battalion covering unit there. Then, finally, following weeks of planning, observing Tom Kilcoyne's truck approach from Gardiner Street, he checked his watch – 12.58 p.m.

Ennis issued the attack signal.

Seeing this, the Squad and sections one and two of the ASU under Lt Flood, walked briskly towards the Custom House, an engineer section joining them as they then broke into groups to enter. As anticipated, lunchtime pedestrian activity was building, allowing the IRA to blend in. ASU sections three and four, under Pádraig O'Connor, deployed to both ends of Butt Bridge to cover the area's approaches from Eden, Custom House and North Wall Quays. The building's quayside entrance was also secured. Paddy Daly and Jimmy Conroy stood guard there. James Slattery then approached a policeman guarding the western doorway facing Liberty Hall, pulled his pistol and ordered the perplexed officer inside with him.[9]

Traffic flowed around Beresford Place, drivers and passengers of cars, trucks and carts oblivious to what was happening as engineers cut cables. Capt. Flanagan's men rushed into the Custom House, his men fanning out on the massive ground floor to secure entrances and exits. Two engineers secured the post office telephone system. Staff looked on, exasperated, confused and frightened as pistols were pulled from pockets.

Tom Kilcoyne hit the brakes on his truck at the rear of the Custom House facing Gardiner Street. He, O'Farrell and Swanzy jumped onto the back. Ennis, observing, issued another signal. Seeing it, Volunteers converged on the truck from Abbey Street, Gardiner Street and Store Street. Engineers, their specialised work done, stood up from manholes, wiped their sweaty brows and headed for the truck. Parties of men, moments earlier laughing, joking and chatting, wore determined scowls as they approached the truck. Kilcoyne and the two others began feverishly handing out paraffin tins, along with hatchets, sledgehammers, cutters and cotton waste. Volunteers, adrenalin pumping, hands full, made for their allocated north- and west-facing entrances, each following officers and section commanders.

Traynor, Colley alongside, took up a field post between Gardiner Street and

Abbey Street. Colley then took a section of men further back into Gardiner Street to guard its Talbot Street junction.[10] Adjacent to the Custom House, other sections, having carried paraffin inside, deployed in positions around the Loop Line Bridge arches and pillars, linking up with ASU members there. On the railway above, the movement of armed Volunteers went unnoticed by civilians directly below.

Within the Custom House's thick walls, terrified civilians were being rounded up. Volunteers rushing through the building brushed past them carrying paraffin tins, cotton waste bales, tools and implements. Orders were loudly barked to the sounds of vociferous protestations from civil servants such as Daniel McAleese. He had, moments earlier, been sitting among three colleagues in the ground-floor dining room, close to the Beresford Place entrance, when the drone of lunchtime chit-chat was suddenly disturbed by abrasive, determined commands from the door, shouting, 'Up! Up!', referring to their hands.[11] Three well-dressed young men pointing revolvers ensured compliance, and the staff were led from the dining hall to where others were being herded along the ground floor's southern corridor.

Ennis and Foley, having both entered the main hallway, issued a succession of orders. Amid the growing chaos and protests, frightened gasps and tirades of expletives, Ennis spotted Tom Keogh, James Slattery and Vinny Byrne. Ennis asked Keogh if he could use Byrne on the second floor; he was short of men there. Keogh agreed.[12] Byrne then raced upstairs behind Ennis, who directed him to an office. Byrne pushed open its door to find a middle-aged man and woman sipping tea at a table. Byrne, typically deadpan, told them to leave as he was about to set fire to the room. The startled response, 'Oh, you can't do that!', saw Byrne tell them to get out at once or be burned alive, showing them his pistol. They soon left to join the chaos below.[13]

Daniel McAleese had been permitted to return to his workstation to fetch his belongings. There, he found a male colleague still working. When McAleese told him to grab his hat and coat quickly, explaining his fear that the building was about to be set alight, his colleague laughed in disbelief. At that point two strangers rushed in carrying petrol tins, one pointing a pistol at them, arresting his laughter. The other stranger doused the window frames with paraffin, while McAleese and his astonished colleague quickly headed for the ground floor.[14]

By now ASU members inside controlled the Custom House's quayside doors and windows, and were marshalling staff in advance of evacuation using an inner courtyard positioned to the structure's eastern side employed five years earlier to marshal 1916 Rising prisoners. The yard also formed part of the planned escape route for the 1921 batch of Dublin's revolutionaries.[15] Once the firing of the ground floor signal was given, a set of gates would be opened, allowing egress from the courtyard through a set of railed concrete arches beyond.

Throughout the building 2nd Battalion worked breathlessly and noisily, closing windows, smashing cupboards, piling papers and files into heaps in offices, soaking tables, other furniture, paper piles, cotton and anything that would burn in paraffin. Soon the smell of the accelerant permeated the building.

Tom Ennis acted as a fulcrum on the first and second floors. Once an office was primed for ignition, Volunteers reported to section commanders and officers. They, in turn, reported to Ennis. Foley performed similarly on the ground floor. Outside, workers arrived in droves to lounge on the Custom House's parched lawn and thoroughfares.[16] The men above on the railway line did their best to remain concealed.

William Oman, twenty-one-year-old Easter Rising ICA veteran serving alongside his uncle 'Bob' with G Company, 1st Battalion, sat in a doorway near Store Street, eyes peeled for the enemy. When a DMP inspector strolled past, heading for the nearby station, William alerted Bob, suggesting they capture him. Bob ruled otherwise; he was not interfering with their mission.[17] The oblivious policeman entered the station moments later, just as a constable and sergeant left and walked to the Custom House. William monitored their every move. When he saw them turn around suddenly just before entering he primed himself, as did his uncle. A Volunteer outside the Custom House pulled a pistol to apprehend them, but they resisted. Bob ordered William to assist. He darted across. There, he warned the policemen to comply or he would 'plug' them.[18] They were then led inside the Custom House. Oman returned to his post.

Back in Store Street station, suspicion grew that trouble was stirring. At 1.10 p.m., a call was placed to Dublin Castle informing of a suspected raid at the Custom House. Castle authorities reacted instantly. A Peerless armoured car was dispatched, while thirty-two-year-old Dist Insp. Richard Caparn, successor to 'Tiny' King, mobilised his F Company cadets in two Tenders which quickly followed. One minute later, reinforcements in the form of Dist

Insp. Crang, Caparn's deputy, and another Tender full of Auxiliaries sped out the Castle gate in their wake, followed in turn by a Rolls Royce armoured car.

Simultaneously, to the city's east, Q Company in North Wall received orders from the Castle to speed to the Custom House. Dist Insp. Thomas Fox, Major Ryan's recent replacement there, dispatched twenty-eight-year-old Herbert Towse with ten cadets in a Tender, while he and twelve others quick-marched.

Back inside the Custom House, Ennis, glancing along corridors and into offices, constantly checking his watch, ordered the fires lit on the first and second floors, issuing a long whistle blast. He then descended to the ground floor as his order was relayed, joining Foley below as the captain waited for his order to torch the ground floor.[19] Rags and papers were lit upstairs and thrown onto paraffin-soaked piles, quickly igniting. Crucially, however, in the tense confusion some Volunteers mistook the whistle blast for the evacuation command, descending staircases before their allocated rooms were alight. Officers and section commanders, breathless from running around the huge building, approached Ennis with reports, one highlighting the mistake. Ennis feared that the top floor might suffer only partial damage, so, with the tax arrears office foremost in mind, he ordered the officer to finish the job, sending others to assist, wary of the tight schedule.[20] Rushing back up, these men quickly succeeded. Then, with smoke filling the top-floor corridors from the spreading flames, they worked their way back down.[21] The lost minutes were about to prove costly; the enemy was closing in.

Paddy Daly left the Custom House by its quayside exit to make for the other entrances and check developments, figuring it was quicker this way given the pandemonium inside. Spotting him in Beresford Place, Traynor called him over to report. Daly told him 'that everything was going on perfectly as far as I could see'.[22] Traynor checked his watch – 1.20 p.m. This concerned him, with no sign of evacuation or fire. Then, suddenly, 'smoke and flames were seen to be issuing from one of the top corner windows nearest the railway line'.[23] Passing civilians, caught by the spectacle, were then discreetly warned to move on by Volunteers outside. Lounging workers looked on curiously, some sensing trouble and leaving the area.

Sections three and four of the ASU spread out in pairs between Liberty Hall, Butt Bridge and westward into Burgh Quay on the bridge's southern side as far as the Tivoli Theatre. Jimmy McGuinness, adjacent to the Tivoli, seeing the smoke, pointed, alerting his comrades. Fires could be seen engulfing the top floor behind the half-dozen windows facing the river.[24] McGuinness jubilantly heralded to Pádraig O'Connor: 'This thing is going to come off without a shot being fired.'[25] O'Connor was less optimistic. He had highlighted earlier to Capt. Flanagan the disconcerting lack of outer cover for the operation. Just then, as if to prove him right, George Nolan shouted in alarm to look left towards O'Connell Bridge. There, the recently dispatched Peerless car turned ominously onto Eden Quay, lumbering slowly towards the Custom House, heaving on its creaking suspension.

The ASU men readied themselves, eyes fixed on the armoured car, which soon halted outside Liberty Hall, turrets rotating, its Hotchkiss gunners scanning for the enemy. ASU members there had bolted into Old Abbey Street, a laneway behind Liberty Hall. They and their comrades looked on, helpless against its might as it sat there, like a monster, arrogant in its invincibility. It then suddenly lurched on, the Custom House's Palladian pillars to its left, the river to its right behind a wall of beer barrels, its turrets still swivelling, until, suddenly, an ASU member stepped out from the Custom House to conduct a quick quayside patrol. He saw the Peerless, instinctively pulled his pistol and fired. Shots pinged from its armour. The Volunteer sprinted towards North Wall Quay, stopping to shoot again.[26] The ASU on Butt Bridge waited apprehensively for an inevitable burst of machine-gun fire to mow their comrade down, but then, to their surprise, a British officer jumped out from the car to pursue him on foot.[27] Pádraig O'Connor and Simon McInerney stealthily crossed the bridge northbound, expecting the action to start. Their comrades emerged from Old Abbey Street. Just then, however, Dist Insp. Caparn's two Tenders also turned right into Eden Quay from O'Connell Bridge, following the Peerless, followed soon afterwards by Crang's Tender and Rolls Royce armoured car. Seeing this, William Stapleton ordered his unit on Marlboro Street to make for the Custom House, concluding the enemy was about to pounce there.

Less than a minute later, the first two Tenders swung left into Beresford Place from Eden Quay, stopping Oscar Traynor and Paddy Daly in their tracks as they suddenly spotted them. IRA covering parties made ready, anticipating that the next few seconds would either see the enemy pass through without a shot, or all hell break loose. Civilians, already alerted by the recent shots on the quayside, dispersed cautiously in all directions. The Tenders continued slowly towards the railway arches, making for Store Street. For a brief moment it appeared as if they would keep going until, suddenly, a cadet stood up, revolver in hand, pointing towards the smoke and flames clearly visible from the Custom House's top windows.[28] The lead Tender screeched to a halt in front of Daly and Traynor. Just then a single shot rang out and ricocheted from its bonnet. Daly shouted to Traynor, 'Run!'[29] Both men bolted, as did others nearby. However, the second Tender quickly swung around the first and came abreast of Traynor, just as he was making for Gardiner Street, its occupants shouting 'Hands up!' and pointing their weapons. With no choice, Traynor threw his hands up. Dublin's IRA was about to lose another brigadier when seventeen-year-old Dan Head of D Company, 2nd Battalion, from Ballybough, stepped out from his covered position at the bridge supports and lobbed a grenade into the Tender.[30] A blast followed. Capitalising on the diversion, Traynor took flight towards Abbey Street with Daly as the cadets were blown off their feet, some tumbling to the road. IRA covering parties joined the fray, revolvers firing furiously. Beresford Place became a battle zone. Civilians scattered wildly, desperately seeking cover.

Crang's Tender entered Beresford Place. He shouted 'Halt!' at the driver. He then watched in horror as several bombs were dropped from the railway line ahead and above, those ahead directed at the leading Tenders, those above at his own. Small blasts resounded in the wide thoroughfare. A Lewis gun erupted from the bridge, then stopped, having jammed, shattering the IRA's chance of levelling the playing field. Crang's men quickly gathered themselves at Liberty Hall, opening fire in response. The Rolls Royce armoured car then sped into Beresford Place, turret swivelling, its Vickers gun hosing the area with .303 calibre rounds which whined and ricocheted as Volunteers and civilians threw themselves down or fell, among them Dan Head. Five bullets tore into him, dropping him face down on the pavement, blood oozing as he perished, his forage cap still in place. Auxiliaries added to the cacophony with the abrasive thud-thud-thud of their own Lewis guns.

Desperate to assist, Pádraig O'Connor fired at the Auxiliaries around Liberty Hall, ordering his men to advance on them. IRA revolvers and semi-automatics unleashed a torrent of fire at the cadets. Responding, Crang's well-trained men, some lying prone, others kneeling, changed the direction of fire, meeting the assault head on, prompting Joseph McGuinness to hurl a Mills bomb at them. The subsequent blast subdued the Auxiliaries, presenting a tantalising opportunity for the ASU to charge and engage at close quarters, nullifying the use of enemy Lewis guns and rifles, until the Peerless car to their right ground its gears and whined towards them, spraying the 100-yard long bridge with rapid bursts.[31] The ASU reeled rearwards, bobbing up and down from behind the bridge's concrete balustrades to fire again as the gunners reloaded the guns' metal ammunition belts.[32]

Caparn's men, further into Beresford Place, struggled to deal with the weight of enemy fire. Seán Prendergast shouted at his men to show no mercy. The Auxiliaries dashed for cover behind the bridge pillars from which sparks flew wildly as ricochets rang from them.[33] Moments later, however, the Rolls Royce car put paid to Prendergast's efforts, forcing him and his men into Abbey Street, shots gouging cement and brick from walls as they ran for cover.

The armoured car's covering fire prompted Caparn to order his Tenders on towards Gardiner Street. As soon as they reached its junction, Bob Oman's unit opened fire, using the Georgian houses' steps for cover. Harry Colley's men also fired from Talbot Street, but it was too great a distance for accuracy with pistols. Nonetheless, the Auxiliaries halted momentarily until, yet again, the Rolls Royce tipped the balance. Volunteers cursed profusely at the sight and sound of its engine's distinctive purring before being driven back under its relentless fire. Civilians bolted for their homes in panic as shots flew the length of Gardiner Street. Others, unable to resist, risked the danger to view the spectacle. The battle could be heard from miles away, including Fitzwilliam Street – where the distant din suggested to De Valera, Brugha and Mulcahy that things had gone awry. Colley realised there was nothing further his unit could do. He ordered his men back to HQ to secure weapons and ammunition there.

Squad and ASU members inside the Custom House had opened fire on the Auxiliaries from doors and windows at the first opportunity.[34] James Slattery, firing from the door facing Liberty Hall, had shouted to Tom Flood, 'There is going to be sport here today.'[35] Flood laughed and fired a salvo of shots before ducking when the Rolls Royce sprayed their section of the building with rounds. Staff and civilians inside, horrified, threw themselves down as bullets broke windows and thudded into walls and furniture. Some became hysterical, their panic aggravated by the rapidly growing staccato of further gunfire and explosions.[36] The smoke from upstairs, starting to waft downstairs, worsened their predicament. The smell of paraffin presented additional terror, as if they were about to be trapped inside an inferno. ASU members, themselves jumpy, reassured them that they would be released imminently as they corralled them slowly along the building's southern side towards the courtyard.

Ennis, realising he was moments away from losing control, acted as soon as the men sent back earlier to fire the top floor returned. Seeing Slattery, he ordered him to shut and lock the door he had fired from, then ordered the fires lit on the ground floor. Shouts and screams escalated as more windowpanes shattered under rifle and machine-gun fire to the building's north and west, to be answered by semi-automatic Mausers and Colts from offices containing Volunteers. Inevitably, civilians were killed. An incoming round killed Mahon Lawless, local government clerk and nephew of Sinn Féin TD Frank Lawless, as he inched along a corridor. Jimmy Conroy shot Francis Davis, the building's sixty-three-year-old caretaker, when he had tried to raise the alarm.[37] He died later. Outside, fifty-year-old labourer and father of five James Connolly was shot in the back by the Rolls Royce's Vickers gun as he fled home to 26 Lower Gardiner Street.[38] Twenty-seven-year-old poultry retailer John Byrne from Killarney Street was shot twice in the back and killed by rifle fire as he cycled through Beresford Place concourse on his way home for lunch.

Back at Butt Bridge, the Peerless car was driven to its northern end, its machine guns then opening fire again towards the ASU at its southern end, forcing Pádraig O'Connor to order a retreat eastwards to George's Quay.[39] Bullets whipped the ground around their ankles as they sprinted. O'Connor then spread the unit out along the southern quay, drawing further fire, ordering some men to guard their flanks around Tara Street, Sir John Rogerson's and Burgh Quays in case of further enemy attacks.

Less than five minutes after Caparn's cadets had driven onto Beresford Place, Insp. Towse's men arrived on Custom House Quay from North Wall Quay, followed by Dist Insp. Fox and his dozen men on foot. O'Connor's men furthest east on George's Quay opened fire on the Tender. Its cadets jumped off the back, rushing for cover behind Guinness barrels, followed by their comrades.[40] Their onslaught of rapid return fire ricocheted along George's Quay. The Peerless then returned past the Custom House's quayside entrance to cover Q Company from the Custom House itself, its machine guns trained on its windows.[41]

Ennis, still inside, gave two blasts with his whistle – the evacuation signal. Shouts and commands erupted as the smoke relentlessly thickened. Civilians, coughing, shook in terror. Flames crackled. Eyes watered. The temperature rose.

Volunteers looked fearfully at the idea of running the gauntlet of machine-gun and rifle fire on Beresford Place or Custom House Quay, but at this point the choice was either that, burn, or surrender and risk summary execution or the hangman's rope. Most covering parties had been driven away or captured by now. James Slattery, Seán Doyle and half a dozen others, knowing that for them capture meant certain death, ran out the Beresford Place exit, guns blazing and under ragged covering fire, rushing for Gardiner Street.[42] When they were halfway across the concourse a sudden burst of machine-gun fire sent several dozen bullets whizzing around them. Tufts of dusty dry earth erupted like geysers on the lawn. Slattery cried out and cursed as a round shattered his hand, just as Seán Doyle fell sideways.[43] Doyle staggered back up, disorientated, blood trickling down his chin, shot through the lung. He persevered, Slattery pushing him on under further fire as he gasped and gulped for air, his strength depleting with every step. Both eventually made it across and into cover. Doyle collapsed. A local woman rushed to his aid, hiding him in her nearby home before treating him as best she could. Slattery, in agony, made for HQ.

Joseph Byrne of the Squad bolted towards Abbey Street from the Custom House with Johnny Dunne of the ASU and another dozen men. Bullets flew from all directions, until the Auxiliaries around Liberty Hall, one firing a Lewis gun from his shoulder, slamming shots into and around the Custom House, were driven to cover themselves as William Stapleton's unit, approaching from Eden Quay, pumped shots at them.[44] This suppressed their fire long enough for their dozen escaping comrades to reach safety, at which point Stapleton's unit was itself driven back to Marlboro Street by the Auxiliaries, their return fire sending civilians scurrying for cover around O'Connell Bridge. Back around Marlboro Street, Stapleton's unit re-engaged, firing harassing shots every few seconds, but beyond effective pistol range.

Tom Ennis, having shouted out repeated orders to commence the evacuation of civilians and then ordered everybody else out, joined another group escaping, knowing he too could not afford capture. Charging across Beresford Place, pistol in each hand, he was hit in the groin and collapsed. He fired as he fell, only to be shot again in the leg. Despite this, he dragged himself back up and staggered into Abbey Street, disappeared momentarily into Brooks Thomas and eventually made Marlboro Street via a prearranged escape route to find a two-wheeled horse-drawn cart there. Summoning his remaining strength, he clambered up on it. The driver, seeing this, clicked his tongue to move the horse and get the wounded stranger to safety. William Stapleton looked on, knowing it was time to get his unit out of Marlboro Street.

Meanwhile, F Company Auxiliaries edged relentlessly closer to the Custom House, shouting for those inside to surrender, only to be answered with pistol rounds. Many civilians, whom the chaos afforded opportunities to escape, were too terrified to leave owing to the gunfire. Squad member Patrick Lawson took action. He marshalled one such group and ordered them out. Then, with shouts of 'Don't shoot! We are staff!' and hands raised in the air, they tentatively made their way outside into Beresford Place. Auxiliaries trained their rifle sights on them, fingers on triggers. Lawson, raising his own hands, joined the group and was marched with them to Abbey Street, where they were ordered to lie on the ground alongside other terrified civilians ordered to do likewise, Auxiliaries suspecting they were IRA. Lawson threw himself down, then cursed quietly, realising he was still carrying two revolvers.[45] Daniel McAleese, among the group, lay terrified as cadets strode along the line of their prone bodies swearing profusely, threatening to shoot anyone who moved. McAleese's eyes moved slowly towards a young man next to him. He thought he was a colleague, only to realise otherwise. The young man, to McAleese's astonishment, lit a cigarette. A cadet rushed over, shoving a pistol into his neck and, crouching with his face inches from the youngster, 'swearing that if he moved a muscle again he would blow his head off'.[46] McAleese was more dumbfounded when the youngster blew a puff of smoke into the cadet's face in response.

Back amid the chaos at the Custom House, Vinny Byrne made for the building's quayside exit seeking escape. He saw Q Company engage his comrades across the river, and the Peerless car. Realising this way was barred, he turned around and made for Beresford Place. When an Auxiliary, closing in, appeared out of nowhere at the entrance there, Byrne fired his Mauser, only to draw a hail of return fire. A Lewis gun rattled outside. Windows shattered as rounds smashed through and embedded in the walls and furniture around him, sending fine clouds of plaster and wood splinters flying, the former adding to the still thickening smoke. Luckily for Byrne, the wall of sandbags at the disused barricade to his front saved him.

More Auxiliaries appeared in the doorway. Byrne fired again; then, the pistol clicked harmlessly, out of ammunition. Byrne, cursing, threw it away and walked towards the door, hands raised, expecting to be shot. Instead, however, he was slapped, kicked and punched several times, struck on the head with a rifle butt and marched across to Abbey Street, next to Brooks Thomas. On the way he saw four fallen comrades – twenty-six-year-old 2nd Battalion Quartermaster Capt. Paddy O'Reilly, his nineteen-year-old brother, Assistant Battalion Adjutant Stephen, twenty-three-year-old E Company Section Commander Edward Dorins, and Dan Head – as well as civilian John Byrne strewn across Beresford Place. Beneath the railway arches he spotted captured Squad and 2nd Battalion members, hands raised, under heavy guard.

Back across the river the fight continued. However, Pádraig O'Connor's men, almost out of bullets, began withdrawing into Tara Street train station, firing sporadically as they went. They were not, however, out of grenades. O'Connor considered ordering them across the railway bridge to drop them on the enemy. However, he could hear that the rest of the firing had died down, bar odd bursts.[47] Huge sheets of flame and plumes of smoke were undulating skyward from the Custom House's upper windows, smashed by gunfire. O'Connor was satisfied there was nothing more they could do. He looked at the Custom House's south-facing clock, situated under its green roof dome, above which stood the majestic Statue of Commerce, witnessing for the second time in five years the flames of open revolt. The clock read 1.50 p.m.[48] He dismissed the unit. Its men dispersed into the streets.

The lack of fire from south of the river allowed Q Company to concentrate their efforts on the Custom House itself. Cadets fired in, shots answered by sporadic return fire from Tom Flood's ASU men, still determined to fight, but time was running out. They were converging in and round the inner courtyard, to where the remaining civilians had by then been ushered. James Harpur was still shooting his pistol from the smoke-filled stationery office when Tom Keogh shouted at him jubilantly 'that the job was going to be a huge success, that nothing would stop the fire'.[49]

Despite Keogh's jubilation, however, they were hopelessly surrounded. He and Capt. Flanagan, with no other option, issued orders to their comrades to dump weapons and mingle with staff, the battle clearly over. Several comparatively calm minutes later, shouts of 'Surrender and come out with your hands in the air!' in British accents were heard from outside, much to the relief of the civilians.[50] The yard gates opened to an uneasy silence, until, seconds later, civilians and staff, Squad, ASU and 2nd Battalion Volunteers filed slowly out through the railed concrete arches between them and the enemy, hands raised high. Flanagan, upon exiting, spotted an unexpected opportunity, a donkey and cart parked close to the burning building. He watched the enemy become distracted by the numbers exiting after him and made his move, calmly walking to the donkey and grabbing its reins. His plan worked. A cadet, spotting him, ordered him to take himself and his cart and 'Get the hell out of that'![51] Flanagan obliged. Also spotting escape opportunities were Squad members Mick Reilly and Jimmy Conroy. They disappeared over the Port & Docks Company's adjacent wall and hid.

Insp. Fox quickly realised he had a problem. Among his captives he could not distinguish attacker from staff, and no one seemed interested in helping his men identify the former. Caparn, however, had by now rounded up Custom House officials to identify staff, sending some to assist Fox, among them the departmental assessor of taxes, Mr Hogan.[52] He stood next to an Auxiliary on the quayside, the pair at the head of a gauntlet of cadets every captive there had to pass through, allowing Hogan to pick out staff. Tom Keogh, James Harpur, Tom Flood, Ned Breslin, Seán Burke, Mick Dunne, Christopher Fitzsimons and a handful of others were separated and questioned. Dunne, with guile and perseverance, convinced his captors he was a respectable businessman and was freed.[53] Burke also bluffed his way out. Then, when the questioning was over, the remainder were marched next to the bridge arches on Beresford Place

The Custom House on fire. *(Courtesy of Mercier Archive)*

with the rest of the captured Volunteers and civilian suspects. At the side door facing Liberty Hall, Charles Grant of the Local Government Board and Local Government Inspector Frank McCauly also identified Custom House staff as they were led there at gunpoint.[54]

Units from the Wiltshire Regiment soon arrived on trucks from Royal Barracks to secure the area. Medical assistance was provided to the wounded, including several civilians, plus six Auxiliaries, four severely wounded. Ambulances rushed in.

Vinny Byrne, standing among others awaiting identification, noticed an army major standing with two well-dressed civilians at the entrance to Brooks Thomas' yard. A queue was formed within which Byrne observed individuals being segregated as they reached the three men. Civilians were sent into the yard, while soldiers escorted his comrades back alongside the bridge arches. Seeing an opportunity, Byrne inched his way warily into the line. Then, realising his hands stank of paraffin, he took cigarettes from his coat pocket, spat on them, and rolled and rubbed them vigorously into his hands to conceal the smell. When his turn came soon afterwards, he innocently asked the army officer if he could go home. The officer asked: 'Why are you here?' Byrne, a joiner, told him he had been there to buy timber and showed him a carpenter's rule and scraps of paper with timber measurements on them. Squad members habitually carried such means of feigning innocence under enemy questioning. The ruse worked. The officer, eyeing him up momentarily, told him: 'Get to hell out of this.' He was free.[55]

When Daniel McAleese was questioned, he stood next to the young Volunteer who had blown smoke in the Auxiliary's face. McAleese was amazed at his pluck. When a slip of paper was removed from his pocket and read with interest by the Auxiliaries, the young Volunteer was asked, 'So you were in the Custom House.' He replied, 'Yes', to then be asked, 'What were you doing in the Custom House?' He stood straight, clicked his heels and smartly replied, 'On duty.'[56]

As the flames licked and scorched the building's outside walls and huge plumes of smoke shot skyward, IRA units who had taken command of the city's fire stations dispersed. Telephones at stations buzzed with emergency calls. Volunteers who had taken control of Tara Street fire station were given spare uniforms and told to mount fire trucks to escape as the station was raided by crown forces, suspicious because no fire tenders had arrived on scene,

An Auxiliary with captured civilians outside the Custom House, 25 May 1921. *(Courtesy of Mercier Archive)*

An Auxiliary examining the body of a man killed. *(Courtesy of Mercier Archive)*

despite repeated summoning.[57] Joseph Connolly, ICA member, drove several IRA men to safety before making for the Custom House, where, alongside his republican Fire Brigade colleagues, he would do everything within his power to ensure the operation's continued success.[58] Firemen smashed in its

Interior of the Custom House after the burning. *(Courtesy of Mercier Archive)*

windows and opened doors fully, ostensibly to access the building, but instead of tackling the flames, they probed around inside. Fireman Michael Rogers and several others then purposely spread the flames and left again as sucked-in air supercharged the growing inferno. When four IRA men were discovered hiding in a small area not yet affected by the fires, Rogers sped to Tara Street to fetch spare firemen's shirts and caps to disguise them and whisk them to safety.[59]

Thousands of civilians surveyed the blazing spectacle from O'Connell Bridge and the Liffey's quayside walls. On Fitzwilliam Street, Brugha, De Valera and Mulcahy looked on as the smoke rose higher into the sky, blocking the bright afternoon sun.

Back at temporary HQ, runners came and went with reports and dispatches. Paddy Daly and Harry Colley stood next to Oscar Traynor, the latter with a bullet hole in his coat, as one such message for 'Mister Blake' – Traynor's codename – detailed the badly wounded Tom Ennis' current whereabouts – Croydon Park House, Marino. Traynor and Daly sped there by bicycle. Arriving fifteen minutes later, Traynor patched Ennis up while Daly sent for Batt Hyland, Michael Collins' driver, who, rushing there, subsequently delivered Ennis to 62 Eccles Street, the nursing home operated by Geraldine O'Donel as a secret IRA hospital.[60] Ennis survived his wounds, thanks in no

Huge plumes of smoke rising from the burning Custom House, 25 May 1921. *(Courtesy of the National Library of Ireland)*

Flames devouring the ground floor of the Custom House. *(Courtesy of the National Library of Ireland)*

small part to Traynor's first aid. As he was treated, he heaped praise on the conduct of the units who had taken part in the raid, particularly ASU sections three and four who had engaged the enemy so ferociously.

Traynor then returned to 'The Plaza' on Gardiner Row. Colley and the staff who had been detailed to the temporary HQ had by now returned there and listened intently as Traynor read out the operation's preliminary reports. Four Volunteers were dead, three wounded and seventy captured, including the majority of ASU sections one and two; this particularly unwelcome news was mitigated, however, by Capt. Flanagan's escape. Brigade staff waited for Traynor's overall reaction; it was instantaneous: he issued orders for Dublin Brigade to be in action wherever possible that evening and night as a gesture of defiance.[61] Traynor had already instructed battalion commandants to anticipate such orders. Additionally, daytime operations were to be immediately ratcheted up. Colley would oversee recruitment to re-establish the ASU at full strength; finding no shortage of Volunteers, he completed the task within a week. Dublin Brigade quickly recovered, assisted in no small part by Seán Russell's organisational and logistical abilities.

Traynor then sent Colley with Christopher O'Malley back to the Custom House to report. Arriving in Beresford Place soon afterwards, they had to force their way through the thick gossiping crowd feverishly embellishing stories of dozens having been killed during the fighting with scores more incinerated inside. The pair laughed when they observed one of the firemen hosing the pavement but not the building, completely engulfed, a tactic mimicked by his colleagues to assist the destruction. An Auxiliary cursed profusely at the fireman, commanding him to get closer. He refused.[62]

Dublin had not witnessed such devastation since 1916, nor had it witnessed such a weight of machine-gun fire ripping into buildings, sending stray bullets in their hundreds flying and ricocheting throughout the city, or so many Volunteers captured at once and, by then, secured behind the walls of Arbour Hill, Kilmainham and Mountjoy.

In the same crowd of onlookers were Joseph Byrne, Johnny Dunne and Michael Collins. Collins had been eager to survey the operation's results. Byrne and Dunne, having cleaned themselves up following their earlier escape, escorted him there and mingled with the crowd. When Collins saw the engulfed building he smiled before they moved off.[63]

That night, the city's skyline was lit up as the conflagration was visible for miles. The building burned for ten days. Dublin's, and Ireland's, fight, as De Valera had predicted, again became the focus of world attention. 'From England to France, Philadelphia, New York, even as far as New Zealand, the attack was international news.'[64] That evening the *Belfast Telegraph* carried the headline: 'Another insurrection in Dublin'.[65] A frenzy of speculation built up among city dwellers as to when the Custom House's clock would stop working and the flames would finally devour the structure.[66] James Gandon, the building's eighteenth-century architect, had built it well. The clock told perfect time for several days, but became the boast of Dubliners who claimed to have witnessed the final moment when it finally stopped.

Crown forces examining a captured revolver following the Custom House attack. *(Courtesy of Mercier Archive)*

14

PEACE FEELERS AMID WAR, FORMATION OF

DUBLIN GUARD

'Thank God Sister, the fight goes on'

The Custom House's destruction finally relieved the crown's Local Government Board of any lingering influence in Ireland. This was music to the ears of William Cosgrave and Kevin O'Higgins, whose Dáil Local Government inspectors, conversely, increased in number by fifty per cent in May.[1]

Capt. Flanagan and Jim McGovern and Pádraig O'Connor of the ASU's section four were back in action the following day, sniping at Auxiliaries from Skipper's Row. O'Connor observed from the cadets' reactions – shooting wildly from the quay walls as he and his comrades escaped towards Thomas Street – that they appeared jittery.[2] Section four also ambushed a touring car full of Auxiliaries running the gauntlet of the 'Dardanelles' from Rathmines. Three Auxiliaries slumped forward, wounded, in the vehicle when it was riddled with bullets.

On the evening of 26 May, Harry Colley attended St Agatha's church on North William Street in North Strand for a requiem mass for Capt. O'Reilly. After most mourners had left, Tom O'Reilly, another brother, quietly called Colley to the coffin, raising the lid. Colley saw a bullet hole in the body's face, next to the nose, which clearly showed scorching, indicating the shot had been fired with the gun held right at his face.[3] Colley attended the church again the next night in a service for Tom O'Reilly's other brother, Stephen.

James Slattery and Seán Doyle were treated in adjacent beds in the Mater Hospital, undetected by the enemy, Slattery's hand completely shattered, Doyle's life slipping away. Eventually, his eyes sunken, his face deathly white, and wheezing with each breath, Doyle turned to a nun next to his bed, quietly asking: 'Are the boys beaten?' The nun had no time to answer; the thuds of distant grenade explosions from another attack sounding out. Hearing them,

Doyle turned to her and whispered: 'Thank God, Sister, the fight goes on.'[4]He then joined his brother, Patrick, in death.

The fight was also going on in the political sphere. The day after the Custom House attack – which had demonstrated that the IRA 'could operate at will and were capable of striking at any target they chose including major government centres in the heart of Dublin' – saw the Irish Situation Committee meet in Westminster.[5] Notably, its chairman, Austen Chamberlain, advocated a 'new offer of peace' with 'a larger offer of self-government than that envisaged in the Better Government of Ireland Act', betraying a far less vociferously unionist stance than his predecessor, Bonar Law.[6] Lloyd George, nonetheless, at this point, remained wary of steering towards dominion rule given his Conservative cabinet majority. Hamar Greenwood, at odds with Chamberlain, insisted: 'The Government will go on with patience and courage until the last revolver is plucked out of the hands of the last assassin in Ireland.'[7]

The uncertain military situation, notwithstanding Greenwood's posturing, was discussed, Gen. Macready declaring ominously: 'The present state of affairs in Ireland, so far as regards the troops serving there, must be brought to a conclusion by October.' Failing this, he warned that most troops, commanders and staff would need to be relieved. Macready was deeply concerned about the recent upsurge in IRA attacks nationwide, his predicament worsened by the realisation that replacements would require training for Irish conditions and time-consuming reorganisation into larger more conventional formations.[8] Secretary for War Worthington-Evans was even more worried. He wrote to cabinet warning of a stalemate culminating eventually in a winter period of 'decisive advantage to the rebels'.[9] He recommended taking full advantage of the summer heatwave to ratchet up military activity, stripping home garrisons for deployment to Ireland. However, continuing unrest at home limited this initiative. Ultimately, crown colony government and martial law, to commence on 12 July if the southern parliament did not operate, was recommended. The army was to be reinforced by at least sixteen battalions, with enhanced naval assistance.[10] However, no public announcement was to be made – a doorway to peace negotiations would remain ajar.[11]

Stepping into one such doorway on 28 May was Patrick Moylett, when he entered Frederick Dumont's office at 14 Lower Sackville Street, to be told by the consul, following typical courtesies, that the British were 'very anxious to meet De Valera'.[12] Moylett humoured him, until Dumont's subsequent admission that he had been acting as a 'political agent' – far beyond his official brief – on behalf of the British, momentarily floored him. Dumont professed that if his Washington superiors knew this he 'would never serve them another day'. When Dumont showed him a file of correspondences from Sir John Anderson within which was a letter asking him to 'bring the British authorities and De Valera together', Moylett realised he was serious.[13]

Moylett dispatched word via William Cosgrave to De Valera, who was presiding over a cabinet meeting that night. De Valera, initially wary of a trap, eventually agreed to Moylett entering Dublin Castle on 30 May at 11 a.m., but warned Cosgrave to report him missing if he did not return to his company's office in Fleet Street by 2 p.m. The following morning Moylett approached Dumont, who then arranged the visit. Both walked to the Shelbourne Hotel, where, in the basement lavatory, an unexpected meeting took place. Moylett, to his further perplexity, met Gen. Brind, the latter's face 'as red and as round as a well-shaped tomato'.[14] There, Brind, ensuring there was no one else within earshot, convinced him their motives were genuine.

After they had left, Stephen's Green became a battle zone. An Auxiliary Tender from C Company was attacked with grenades from Cuffe Street, with simultaneous pistol fire from within the Green. Storming into the Green, the cadets captured IRA member Leo Fox, while observing a novel enemy tactic; IRA men throwing themselves down like civilians during gunfights, then opening up on unsuspecting individual cadets. The tactic was reported to Dublin Castle.[15]

Michael Collins, troubled by the capture of Squad members at the Custom House, also became red-faced following a raid on his finance office in 22 Mary Street on 26 May. This followed an earlier raid on another of his Mary Street offices, No. 5, just a week earlier, during which Joe O'Reilly had a narrow escape, forced to climb out the rear of the building and escape precariously across rooftops. During the later raid, Mary Street was sealed off from Liffey Street to Capel Street as Auxiliaries ransacked No. 22. O'Reilly, again escaping by a hair's breadth, left just as the raid commenced and rushed to warn Collins. Another of Collins' couriers, Bob Conlon, was arrested. Collins was scheduled to be there at the time, but yet again, his incredible luck held. Having eaten lunch in Woolworth's Store, he and Gearóid O'Sullivan went for a drink instead in Bannon's pub, 41 Upper Abbey Street, before being intercepted by O'Reilly as they were making their way back towards Mary Street. Collins'

British Army raid on Sackville Street. By early summer 1921 raids in Dublin, fed by increasingly effective intelligence, were endemic. *(Courtesy of Mercier Archives)*

secretary, Alice Lyons, escaped the premises using pluck. Having been questioned forcefully by an Auxiliary as to Collins' whereabouts, she removed her hat and coat and simply walked out of the building while the raiders were preoccupied searching for documents, discovered among which were the late Major Compton-Smith's belongings, as well as a note written by Collins lamenting the loss of so many men at the Custom House. Lyons subsequently became a fugitive. The same day saw Austin Stack's Molesworth Street office raided. Collins, highly agitated, sensing the enemy had infiltrated and were closing in, repeated hopelessly that evening in Batt O'Connor's Donnybrook home: 'There's a traitor in the camp.'[16] Collins subsequently moved his Mary Street operation to 9 Upper Sackville Street.

Patrick Moylett finally entered Dublin Castle at 11 a.m. on Monday 30 May, leaving William Cosgrave, 'with his quiff of hair', and several others looking warily after him as he walked through the lower gates for a meeting with Andy Cope, still being treated like a traitor by many in the Castle.[17] Moylett was escorted by a DMP officer who quietly pointed out where McKee, Clancy and Clune had been killed, giving Moylett the shivers as the gates closed ominously behind him. He then saw several Auxiliaries firing revolvers into small barrels filled with clay, their shots echoing in the enclosed courtyard. He was led through an archway to the upper yard and to his right, where, in an apartment, he was introduced to Cope. Offering cigars, Cope spoke of wanting to meet De Valera. Moylett, refusing a cigar, responded by sardonically suggesting he should place an advertisement in the newspapers, before asking him to explain why. Moylett listened, momentarily astonished, as Cope elaborated: 'We are willing to acknowledge that we are defeated. There is nothing else for us to do but to draft into this country four hundred thousand men and exterminate the whole population of the country, and we are not willing to do that.'[18] Then, pressed for a proposition for De Valera by Moylett – who, as an aside, suggested the British would have no problem with such a strategy if they thought the world would stand for it – Cope continued, pledging that the British were prepared to withdraw their entire establishment 'from the lowest policeman to the highest judge', albeit with guaranteed access to the country's ports during wartime. Trade, currency and economic issues were discussed. Cope insisted these would be left solely to Ireland, as would politics. He then added that he had direct authority from Lloyd George to make peace, above the heads of both the lord lieutenant and chief secretary if necessary. Leaving at 1.30 p.m., Moylett met Cosgrave, much relieved with his return to Fleet Street and buoyant with Moylett's account of the meeting.[19]

. May 1921 featured a series of attacks by the IRA's 6th Battalion in South Dublin. Operations had ratcheted up in April with several attacks launched simultaneously in Bray. Its coastguard station, its courthouse, housing Black and Tans, its lighthouse, and the Royal Hotel, full of military, were attacked in lengthy skirmishes. Black and Tans opened fire from the courthouse's steel-shuttered windows with Lewis guns, spraying Main Street with bullets. Several Tans were later wounded in the picturesque seaside resort during continued fighting.

Another skirmish took place in Wyattville Road, Ballybrack. Bridges were blown up in Shanganagh, Sandyford and Bride's Glen, while another engagement took place with the military during a trenching operation in Shanganagh. Dundrum RIC Barracks was attacked. Each Volunteer fired once, then withdrew. Nonetheless, trigger-happy RIC officers inside maintained fire from the building's shuttered windows for several hours. Cabinteely RIC Barracks was attacked twice during April. An army lorry was shot up in Sandyford, another on Kilgobbin Road. A Black and Tan truck was engaged on Milltown Bridge. A house in Ballycorus belonging to an Orange Order member, and frequented by British artillery and intelligence officers, became the scene of a protracted gun and grenade battle until the IRA withdrew for want of ammunition, leaving behind several enemy casualties. This house was attacked again on a later occasion, resulting in the serious wounding of Comdt McDonnell. He was treated in the IRA hospital in Eccles Street.

Volunteer activities continued to intensify. Bray RIC Barracks was attacked. On 10 May, Cabinteely Barracks was attacked again. Volunteers threw grenades from the front of a car, while their comrades in the rear fired into the building with rifles. It was attacked again on 12 May, resulting in the grave wounding of a Volunteer, and yet again on 13 May, when twenty-four-year-old Const. Albert Skeats was shot dead by a sniper. When a Very light was fired into the air to summon reinforcements, a military lorry, speeding to the scene, was shot at in nearby Cornelscourt. A huge consignment of military uniforms was set alight in Dartry dye works resulting in an inferno, which attracted several Tender-loads of Auxiliaries. They were shot up en route by Volunteers, who then escaped across the River Dodder. Dundrum Barracks was attacked with No. 9 grenades, a much-improved and steady flow of which was being sent to the battalion since their increased activities brought them to 'Ginger' O'Connell's attention. On this occasion a number of Black and Tans ran out to engage the IRA – directly into the path of exploding grenades. An RIC cycle patrol was attacked in Foxrock. A military lorry was ambushed soon afterwards.

Then, on 25 May, as the Custom House burned, following orders from GHQ, Cabinteely Barracks was again attacked, twice, and Dundrum once, along with Enniskerry and Stepaside Barracks, a military foot patrol in Stillorgan, Dún Laoghaire naval base and wireless station outposts, and a military truck on Alma Road, Monkstown. The next day, following another hour-long attack at Dún Laoghaire naval base, two military patrols converging from separate directions opened fire on each other in confusion. One soldier was killed and five wounded. The driver of an army truck was shot dead in Castle Street, Dalkey. The truck crashed and a large haul of weapons was seized by 6th Battalion before they set the truck ablaze. Kill O'The Grange then saw a sharp encounter between the IRA and RIC, but without casualties.[20] On Merrion Road, fifty-six-year-old retired colonel Reginald Dyer, nicknamed 'the Butcher of Amritsar' following the notorious massacre in the Indian Punjab province in 1919, had his escort – an armoured car, two Tenders and a lorry – ambushed as it sped to the city from Dún Laoghaire where he had just landed. Dyer escaped, as did the attackers, pursued by machine-gun fire, a bullet from which killed a civilian in his house.[21]

The battalion's recent killing of suspected enemy spies was answered on the night of 30 May with the shooting dead of twenty-two-year-old Volunteer Capt. Tommy Murphy of F Company during a raid on his Foxrock home by Black and Tans from Cabinteely Barracks. His body was discovered wearing the label 'Executed by IRA', a tactic subsequently castigated as black propaganda in An tÓglách.[22]

The battalion had its own arms supply chain from London and Birmingham, funnelled through Capt. Laurence Nugent of K Company, 3rd Battalion. Its increased activity prompted military sweeps across the Dublin Mountains, which, by drawing crown forces from the city, enabled the further actions called for by Brig. Traynor in the wake of the Custom House attack. Therefore, the number of overall IRA attacks in the city and county in May was double that since March.

On 31 May, at 4 a.m., Blackrock College was raided by a 100-strong composite force of C Company Auxiliaries and troops from the Worcestershire Regiment sent out from Portobello Barracks. The raid yielded little. The same night saw Auxiliary and military raids at 167 Emmett Road, Inchicore, 28 South Frederick Street, Nos 1 and 42 Westland Row, Moran's Hotel in Talbot Street, 18 Westmoreland Street, several addresses in Castleknock, 173 Great Brunswick Street, the Mansion House, 77 Clanbrassil Street, six separate addresses between Rathfarnham and Rockbrook, 55 Percy Place, and in the Bridewell area.[23] Night after night such raids continued to provide sustenance for the editors of the Irish Bulletin.

May ended with the killing of seven band members from the Hampshire Regiment and the wounding of twenty more by an electrically detonated mine outside Youghal, Co. Cork. The mine was constructed by filling a six-inch naval training projectile with a powdery chemical composite referred to as 'War Flour'. This was placed against a wall and covered in loose stones. The results were horrific. The band members were part of a larger convoy en route to a firing range. Two of them, Boy George Simmons and Boy Frederick Heisterman, were fifteen years old. Boy Frederick Evans, also killed, was seventeen.

June commenced on a similarly bleak note for the British authorities when a police cycle patrol was ambushed outside Castlemaine in Kerry. Five were killed. In Culleens, Sligo, two RIC men were shot dead following capture. The Irish Bulletin, by then being translated into several languages, claimed they were killed in action, an inaccuracy; police and army reinforcements were pursuing their captors.[24] Consequently, the two captured policemen were shot, having been given a brief time to pray.

Incredibly, at Modreeny, Tipperary, a seventeen-man flying column took on a Black and Tan and army patrol consisting of four cars, a lorry and some cyclists. Four Tans were killed and fourteen wounded, with no IRA casualties.[25] Back in the capital, also on 1 June, a grenade was thrown into a lorry returning to barracks carrying troops from the East Surrey Regiment, following guard duty at the ruined Custom House, which was riven with looters. The driver lost a leg, while a private was killed and several others wounded.[26] Then, on 2 June, seven RIC and Black and Tans were killed and six wounded at Carrowkennedy, Mayo, by a fifty-strong IRA flying column from the West Mayo Brigade, 4th Western Division. Despite the raid being seen as payback for the IRA defeat at Kilmeena, four RIC and Black and Tan prisoners were subsequently released. A number of rifles, a Lewis gun and a huge quantity of ammunition were captured. Locals in the area fled from their homes afterwards, fearing reprisals. 'A massive sweep of the whole area from Connemara to North Mayo followed, involving a sea blockade and planes, which captured nobody.'[27]

Back in Dublin, on 2 June, as if to further prove its growing prowess, the IRA came within a hair's breadth of killing its nemesis – Col Winter. When word reached brigade intelligence that Winter would be travelling to the vice-regal lodge along Thomas Street from Dublin Castle in a touring car, Dublin Brigade jumped at the opportunity to intercept him. Section four of the ASU was immediately ordered by Capt. Flanagan to ambush him.[28]

The nine-man unit spread out between Francis Street, where a spotter was placed, and Meath Street, slightly further west. Pádraig O'Connor, in charge, positioned the remaining eight men, including himself, in pairs between Vicar Street and Meath Street to take advantage of a slight bend in the road. Soon after they arrived, Winter's car, as expected, crossed from Cornmarket into Thomas Street. The spotter watched it pass, carrying four occupants, one in military uniform.[29] He signalled his expectant comrades.

Seconds later, O'Connor and the Volunteer beside him opened fire at the rear of the car as it sped by. As the shots echoed, Joseph McGuinness and George Nolan, positioned at Wright's butchers, next to Molyneux Yard, a small entry, pointed their pistols at the car and squeezed the triggers, their weapons recoiling as they fired.[30] When Winter's men opened fire in response, bullets thudded into the hanging meat carcasses there.[31] Civilians rushed for cover. Patrick Mullen and another Volunteer joined the fray, hurling grenades at the car before firing their pistols. The driver swerved to avoid the deafening grenade blasts. Shrapnel showered shop façades and rattled against windows. The car lurched sideways as the driver wrenched the steering wheel left and right, rounds smashing into its metalwork and glass. Nolan, McGuinness and Mullen kept firing. Winter, shooting from the back of the car, then slumped forward, hit in the hand.[32] Thomas Lillis and Paddy Rigney opened fire as the car passed Meath Street, before cursing profusely when it continued on its way; 'the Holy Terror' had survived.

As more affluent Dubliners grappled with the increasing hostilities, light relief was provided by a two-day cricket match in Trinity College's park between the Gentlemen of Ireland and the Military of Ireland at 11 a.m. on Friday 3 June. A huge crowd of well-attired civilians and military ringed the cricket pitch, savouring the glorious summer weather until, at 5 p.m., Pádraig O'Connor and Jimmy McGuinness, cycling to South Leinster Street's junction with Lincoln Place, parked their bicycles at the kerbside and opened fire from the railed wall towards the players. They then sped away as startled players and spectators threw themselves to the lawn. Not to be outdone, the cricketers quickly resumed, until attention was drawn to twenty-one-year-old Kathleen Wright, who, having raised herself up, collapsed again with an entry wound in her back and an exit wound in her chest from a bullet. She soon died. A woman standing nearby was shot in the shoulder.[33] The game was subsequently abandoned. The IRA men were lambasted for having fired recklessly into the crowd. Accusations flew that they were no better than those who had shot into Croke Park on Bloody Sunday.

The same day, just as the last of the Custom House's embers died out, another huge conflagration sent massive clouds of thick noxious smoke drifting and hanging across Dublin's summer skyline. The National Shell Factory in Parkgate Street was set alight by members of E Company, 3rd Battalion, under orders from Joe O'Connor.[34] No complicated planning was required for this operation – it was sabotage. The E Company members worked there and simply left stumps of burning candles close to flammable materials before departing with their co-workers after their day's work.[35] The factory, operating as a motor repair and ordnance depot, and employing almost 200 ex-servicemen, was filled with military vehicles. Five Peerless armoured cars and thirty-five other vehicles were destroyed. Almost £100,000 worth of stores

Cleaning up in the aftermath of the huge fire, an audacious and successful act of sabotage carried out by members of E Company, 3rd Battalion, Dublin Brigade at the National Shell Factory in Parkgate Street, 3 June 1921. *(Courtesy of the National Library of Ireland)*

also went up.[36] In total, almost £250,000 worth of damage, some structural, was inflicted.[37] As huge civilian crowds gathered at Kingsbridge station to view the spectacle, military and Auxiliary units, as well as armoured cars, sped to the city's fire stations to prevent the IRA detaining crews again or commandeering fire tenders.[38] Large parts of the factory were gutted. Luckily for the military, the Fire Brigade saved most of the workshops. Nonetheless, the damage to their hard-pressed transport situation was devastating. Notably, Gen. Boyd's command issued new instructions for foot patrol tactics to be used in the city, mirroring those being used effectively in Munster and in the midlands, wherein several platoons effectively formed their own flying columns, relying only on bicycles to perform reconnaissance. Despite these adaptations, British military officers rued the further evidence of enemy adaptability and its ability to strike anywhere, at any time, and IRA morale soared.

The IRA struck again the following day, in Clontarf. At 8.45 p.m. twenty-one-year-old John Brady and twenty-two-year-old Thomas Halpin were targeted by Lt Danny Lyons and a comrade from F Company, 2nd Battalion, who approached initially on bicycles from Dollymount. Brady, a former British Army soldier, invalided following eighteen months' service, lived at 21 Hollybrook Road and was suspected of involvement with the Auxiliaries. There had also been rumours of his involvement in the sacking of Balbriggan the previous September.[39] Subsequent information gathered by Dublin Brigade intelligence led to the conclusion that he was an informer.[40] He was a marked man.

Brady and Halpin had been chatting with Mitchel Denvir, a friend of Arthur Griffith's who lived in 28 St Lawrence's Road. The three failed to notice the two approaching cyclists stop to speak briefly with a man who had been watching them. The three then made their way, laughing and joking, towards a nearby pub. Just then Lt Lyons, remaining with the observer, ordered his comrade to carry out Brady's killing. He approached the three, unnoticed, from behind, parked his bicycle against the kerb, stepped up quickly behind them and fired three shots at Brady.[41]

Brady was hit twice through the chest, one bullet tearing through his spinal column before exiting next to his collarbone, the other lodging in his chest. Halpin, twenty-two-years-old, lived in Brookside Cottages, Clontarf, and was a former Royal and Merchant Navy able seaman. He was not a target, but was shot accidentally. The bullet tore through his stomach, before ripping through his intestines and liver and lodging in his chest cavity close to the heart. He fell against Denvir, who also collapsed fearing he too had been shot, before realising he had not, despite being splattered with blood.

Horrified witnesses, seconds earlier enjoying the warm evening on the seafront, rushed to their aid as the gunman remounted his bicycle and pedalled towards the city. Brady twitched in agony, Halpin spoke a little. Pools of blood formed around them. They were soon carried to Hamilton and Long's Chemist nearby and an ambulance summoned. Brady was dead upon arrival at the Mater Hospital, Halpin died there at 11 p.m. Brady's sixty-four-year-old father, James, emphatically denied his son was involved with crown forces.[42] John was the third of four sons James had lost, the first two during the Great War. Both victims of this attack were due to emigrate the following day to the USA.

Then, on 7 June, with tensions acute in the city following two more hangings in Mountjoy, six IRA members took positions on Ha'penny Bridge, and there, lying prone, opened fire on a military lorry heading westward along the northern quays. When the soldiers on board returned fire the IRA men retreated into Eustace Street. The truck sped on, crossed Capel Street Bridge into Parliament Street and turned left into Dame Street in hot pursuit, with Auxiliaries joining them there. Shots were fired into College Green at suspected attackers, causing a stampede of civilians. No one was wounded and all IRA members escaped.[43] Civilians were less fortunate a half mile away the same day, when Auxiliaries, a grenade having just exploded in their midst as they drove past Trinity College, badly wounding five, opened fire into Great Brunswick Street, killing a sixty-year-old man and wounding five other civilians, including three women.[44] Also that day, a touring car containing five Auxiliaries was shot at entering Dublin Castle via Palace Street, the same gate through which Patrick Moylett had been led to talk peace. Four cadets jumped from the car as it screeched to a halt. Raising the alarm, they ran back out the gate with drawn revolvers towards Dame Street in search of their assailants, with other cadets following. The military appeared at both Castle gates having heard the shots, but seemed disinterested in the affair.[45]

That morning, Edmond Foley and Patrick Maher had taken their places at 7 a.m. to be dispatched by John Ellis in Mountjoy's hang-room, Maher's last words being 'I am innocent', shortly before plunging seven feet through the trap door.[46] He was thirty-two years old, Foley twenty-four. Foley wore a religious scapular from Lourdes, the Catholic pilgrimage destination in southern France, placed around his neck by an Auxiliary in an act of humanity. The prison doctor subsequently returned the scapular to the officer.[47] Numerous pleas for clemency were ignored, including one from the father of RIC Sgt Wallace, killed at Knocklong. Both the condemned men's families had visited Mountjoy the previous evening and had taken their place among the morning's crowds, several thousand strong, outside the prison for the latest and what would become the last such grim ritual under British rule. Both men urged the IRA to fight on in their last statements. A note confirming their executions was torn in anger from the prison's front gate at 8.15 a.m., as their prison-fabricated coffins were placed in the same grave as Mountjoy's eight other most recent hanging victims.[48]

Foley was spoken of with reverence five days later by the man he had helped rescue at Knocklong, Seán Hogan, who, along with Dinny Lacey and numerous other prominent IRA officers, was attending Dan Breen's wedding to Brigid Malone, with Hogan as best man. Áine Malone was Brigid's bridesmaid. The

Dan Breen's wedding party: Breen is standing centre left with Brigid Malone beside him.
(Courtesy of Mercier Archive)

wedding took place on 12 June at Glenagat, New Inn, Tipperary. Glenagat was made 'as impregnable as the South Tipperary Brigade could make it'.[49] During early morning 'trees were felled to provide road-blocks; armed guards were posted at the approaches ... If the British forces had attempted to visit the area they would have got a warm reception.'[50] The actual reception saw dancing and singing as if there were no war being fought. Outposts were maintained all night with reliefs rotated to allow all to join the merriment.

Back in the capital that night, two former British soldiers serving in the RIC, twenty-six-year-old Michael Brannan and twenty-five-year-old John Smith, were shot dead in Rainsford Street, adjacent to Guinness' Brewery, by three gunmen who quickly escaped on foot.

Seán Mac Eoin's court martial finally convened in City Hall on 14 June, but not before Pádraig O'Connor, now 2nd lieutenant in the newly established IRA 'Dublin Guard', attempted to ambush any prosecution witnesses en route.

In early June it became clear that the Squad was virtually redundant. Firstly, its numbers had been depleted since the Custom House attack; secondly, Michael Collins' information flow from Dublin Castle had all but dried up. The ASU was another story; Volunteers had flocked to join since the Custom House and it was almost back to full strength. GHQ amalgamated the Squad and ASU into a single elite fighting unit – the Dublin Guard.

Capt. Flanagan, however, was removed from command. Counter-claims had been made against him by two unit members court-martialled for refusing to participate in an operation. They had demanded that Flanagan take part and berated him for refusing. They were found guilty and suspended for three weeks, it being spelled out to them that Flanagan's position as an officer meant he made such decisions, not them, and that it was ridiculous to expect a commanding officer to participate in each and every such operation.[51] Flanagan's leadership was hailed as a success. Notwithstanding the backlash from the shooting in Jervis Street Hospital – this had seen Flanagan lambasted by Collins, who also criticised him for not assembling the unit quickly enough on another occasion when he became trapped within an enemy cordon in Charles Street – he had led the unit successfully from the front.[52] The speed with which replacements flocked to it testified to its reputation. Nevertheless, the courts martial had caused ill feeling within the unit. Oscar Traynor, therefore, reluctantly concluded that the best option was to appoint a new commanding officer.

That officer was Capt. Paddy Daly. He was appointed at a meeting in 'The Plaza' chaired by Traynor and attended by Squad and ASU members. Several, including Jack Dunne and Mick White, refused to serve under a new commander given the circumstances. They were permitted to return to their former units.[53]

Daly then addressed the men. He informed them of the new unit's title, then clarified that, similarly to both its predecessors, it would remain a full-time unit, receiving orders directly from Traynor.[54] It would divide into two half companies. Lt Joe Leonard would command the 'right half company' comprising former ASU sections one and two, and would, as before, operate on the city's north-side. Lt O'Connor would command the 'left half company' consisting of former sections three and four, operating similarly on the south-side.[55] No staff officers would be appointed; every officer and section commander was to actively seek targets or engagements at all times while on duty. Every Tan, Auxiliary or military vehicle was fair game, especially motorcycle dispatch riders, as were military provisions and laundry trucks. No individual shootings of civilians suspected as spies were authorised. GHQ and Brigade intelligence, seconded to the Dublin Guard, directed such information on suspects to Brigade HQ, henceforth the only authority on such matters.[56] Lts Leonard and O'Connor would report to Daly at Brigade HQ each morning, sometimes together, other times separately; for combined operations they would be given their orders together. They would then visit GHQ Intelligence – headquartered in the Antient Concert Rooms – to pore over collated information there, primarily on regular enemy movements, to select targets.[57] Operations were to commence immediately, the enemy to be harried relentlessly.

O'Connor subsequently oversaw the laying of mines in Palmerston to eliminate Mac Eoin's court-martial witnesses travelling to the city from the midlands in military convoys. After engineers laid the mines, Volunteers from 4th Battalion stood ready, as did O'Connor's men. They waited several days, rotating in and out of the city, trying to keep those waiting in ambush occupied. Eventually they realised their plan was futile. Despite the mines having been concealed, local farmers were seen purposely leading their horses around them.[58] It was obvious that a trap had been set and O'Connor feared the enemy would also find out and his men would be compromised.

Michael Noyk represented Mac Eoin. Noyk had initially appointed Charles Wyse Power as defence counsel. He had met him along with Michael Collins in Kirwan's to discuss the case. Wyse Power was taken aback with Collins' gift for hiding in plain sight. The most wanted man in Ireland sat calmly in a snug working through papers, engaging in banter until more serious matters necessitated a business-like demeanour, albeit from an unpolished pub table. Collins was desperate to get Mac Eoin out. A subsequent meeting in Wyse Power's Upper Mount Street flat saw Collins walk straight through a military and police cordon, first asking politely to be allowed to go to the head of the search queue due to pressing business concerns, then vociferously protesting that he had no time to waste over the misguided actions of Sinn Féiners, the well-practised tactic working for him once again. In Mount Street, Collins suggested smuggling a revolver into Mac Eoin to use in conjunction with a break-in attempt to get him. Noyk dismissed the idea as suicide; Mac Eoin was too well guarded.[59]

When Wyse Power took ill, Charles Bewley took his place. There was little Mac Eoin could say in his defence. Noyk and Bewley both recognised that in a civilian court a murder conviction would be difficult, given the dark and chaotic conditions at the time of the gunfight, with several men around firing weapons, but this was a world apart from a civilian court. Mac Eoin was led in handcuffed and remained so, flanked by two tall Auxiliaries. He was identified from the January shooting by the RIC men who had circumvented Lt O'Connor's planned ambush. Mac Eoin mounted a spirited defence and was later commended by several Auxiliaries as a chivalrous enemy, given the assistance he had afforded wounded cadets at Clonfin. He made a speech, which read:

Officers and Gentlemen of the Courtmartial,

When you opened the proceedings this morning, I told you I was an officer of the Irish Republican Army, and claimed treatment as an officer.

But Gentlemen you are here to try me – not as an officer but as a murderer; why? Just because I took up arms in defence of my native land. Defence of one's native land has ever been a privilege to the peoples of all nations, and all nations have demanded the services of their sons as a right. Be sure that the principle which is a proper principle for the Jugoslavs, the Czechoslovaks, for the Belgians, for the Siberians, is equally a proper principle for the Irish. I took my stand on that principle. That stand has been fully approved of by the people of Ireland, and I am glad to feel that in carrying out my duty to my country, I have always acted in accordance with the usages of war. The acts which were committed by me, and by the officers and men under my command, can stand any test judged by an impartial tribunal. All prisoners who fell into my hands were treated in a fair way: the wounded were treated to the best of my ability. Some of these prisoners will be called here t-day [sic] to prove this. They will be called, not in order that any punishment which you intend to bestow upon me should be mitigated, but just to show that my words are true.[60]

Mac Eoin then contrasted this with the beating he had received following his capture and wounding, treatment which subsequently continued. He detailed his account of the killing of Dist Insp. McGrath, claiming that the house he and his men were in had been approached by the enemy and that, on word of this, he had ordered his men outside to spare his elderly hosts a siege. The enemy had confronted him with weapons in the 'present' position, whereupon a gunfight had commenced with both sides firing. Three policemen had admitted to firing at Mac Eoin, just as he had admitted to firing back. Therefore, he claimed, with the district inspector positioned between the three and himself, there was every possibility that he was, in fact, shot by his own men; but in any event, he was killed in action. He then concluded:

I take the opportunity further of paying tribute to the gallantry and the loyalty of the men who have fought by my side. They stood up to superior numbers and superior equipment and every time they beat the foe. From you, gentlemen, I crave no favour. I am an officer of the Irish Army and merely claim the right, at your hands, what you would receive at mine had the fortunes of war reversed the positions. If you don't give me that right but execute me instead, then my last request is that you give my dead body to my relatives so that my remains may be laid to rest among my own people. Long live the Republic.[61]

He was sentenced to death.

Lt O'Connor's men were, quickly back in action, attacking an Auxiliary laundry truck in Lansdowne Valley, Inchicore, then burning the uniforms while distributing anything else of value to locals. Then, they targeted an enemy dispatch rider from Baldonnell making for the city. He was shot dead and his motorcycle captured. Joseph McGuinness was also hit in the hand by a ricocheting round. O'Connor was subsequently informed that the victim was Pte Snelling, who had testified against Paddy Moran.[62] The news was not unwelcome.

Back in Westminster, the Irish Situation Committee met again on 15 June. Since its previous meeting the cabinet had officially decreed on 2 June that martial law would be proclaimed throughout the twenty-six counties if the southern parliament did not function on time. Military reinforcement commenced, with two battalions per week redeploying. Despite Lloyd George continuing to favour combating the IRA with police units, notwithstanding their chronic indiscipline – much to Gen. Macready's chagrin – it was arranged that Macready, in such an event, would be placed directly under Hamar Greenwood as military governor.[63] Macready, in turn, advocated widespread employment of summary executions and the death penalty for carrying arms, rather than official reprisals, which, he claimed, were only necessary in the absence of martial law and were hated by troops, as were the current half-hearted means of conducting the campaign. Greenwood subsequently ordered all reprisals to cease.

Matters continued to accelerate. On 7 June James Craig became prime minister of the Northern Ireland parliament. It was agreed the same day to invite King George V to formally open the inaugural session of the new parliament. At this point Gen. Smuts stepped in. In London to attend the Imperial Conference as South African prime minister, Smuts encouraged the King to 'turn his speech into an olive branch for Sinn Féin'.[64] He was backed by Philip Kerr's successor, Edward Grigg. Smuts, fifty years old, wrote to Lloyd George, resting in Wales, that 'an unmeasured calamity' was destroying Britain's international image.[65] Reprisals, costly both financially and morally, had failed. Northern Ireland was secured, justifying negotiation with the rest of the country.

Meanwhile, Macready continued to clear his own path in the event of a continued impasse, predicting that drumhead courts martial of IRA members captured during operations and hangings for membership of Dáil Éireann, the IRA and IRB would see 'as many as 100 men a week' executed.[66] When questioned hypothetically by a wide-eyed Austen Chamberlain about what would happen if the army captured an entire column of 1,000 men, Macready indicated that in such a scenario only its leaders would be summarily executed but emphasised, nonetheless, that 'the time for illusions and half-measures was over'. It had to be 'all out or get out'.[67]

Trepidation was felt at the implications of such a strategy. Lloyd George had shown inhibitions about British policy being viewed both at home and abroad as the military 'reconquest of Ireland'.[68] Arthur Balfour, seventy-two-year-old former Conservative prime minister and foreign secretary, expressed fears that the announcement of such measures would be catastrophic and suggested instead the long-trodden path of transportation to remote colonies as a substitute for widespread hangings. When he asked Macready if he could see any alternative to such draconian military measures, Macready indicated no, before driving home the point that he required clarity from them no later than 7 July to commence full mobilisation if required.[69] Images of the global revulsion triggered by the German invasion of Belgium in 1914 sprang into the minds of politicians as they baulked at the daunting prospect of Ireland effectively grinding to a halt for the two years it was expected to take to subdue the country – and then what? With such a prospect in mind, Andy Cope and Sir James MacMahon shifted into overdrive. The Situation Committee's recommendations were purposely leaked to the Sinn Féin leadership. The grim picture painted was not wasted on them.

The same grim picture was made clearly visible to the British the following day in Cork. In Rathcoole, close to Millstreet, a large IRA column comprising 140 Volunteers from Cork No. 2 Brigade under Paddy Byrne ambushed an Auxiliary convoy of two open Crossley Tenders, one armoured Tender, and a Lancia armoured car. Between them they carried twenty-nine men. Four electrically detonated tubular-shaped mines were spread out, each a quarter mile apart to match the distance being maintained between vehicles in such convoys. Three detonated with precise timing, the Lancia's armour plating surrounding its engine blown forty yards away. The cadets then came under heavy and protracted fire, each vehicle's complement compelled to fight as individual isolated units for a time owing to their distance apart. The IRA had deployed in several sections along the length of the route, with riflemen, others armed with shotguns, and a Hotchkiss machine gun that jammed. Two cadets were killed and a further dozen wounded; the IRA suffered no casualties. Following the firefight, the IRA discovered over a thousand rounds of badly needed ammunition.

A military sweep of the region followed, with 2,000 troops from 6th Division and spotter planes providing support, further highlighting what potentially lay ahead on a vaster scale given the forces being marshalled and the strategies being formulated. Across the country the IRA was being harried by such formations conducting wide-sweeping drive operations. The dry weather assisted the military, as did the long summer evenings. Thousands of civilians were rounded up. Telegraph stations were closed down outside larger garrison towns to hamper IRA communications.[70] The telegraph service, like the post office, was fully recognised as a nest of republican sympathisers; indeed, Macready had been horrified to learn of the employment of Richard Mulcahy's younger brother Paddy as a post office official, citing such a situation as ludicrous.[71]

Two days after Rathcoole, Thursday 16 June, a Dublin Guard 'welcoming committee' ensured an infantry contingent from the 2nd Battalion, Queen's Own Royal West Kent Regiment, under Lt Col R. J. Woulfe-Flanagan – transferred to Dublin District from Upper Silesia in Germany and having arrived in Dún Laoghaire as part of the reinforcements streaming into the country – was provided with an equally ominous picture of what lay ahead.[72] At 8.05 a.m., as it passed slowly westward along a fifteen-foot embankment, bombs were thrown from both sides – St Patrick's Parade and St Clement's Road – at the train's first four carriages by the main Volunteer body led by Paddy Daly. Then, William Stapleton opened up with a Thompson gun 100 yards further along the track, emptying a twenty-round stick magazine before reloading to mark the first time the weapon was ever fired in action. Charlie Dalton also carried a 'Tommy Gun', which he failed initially to operate. Stapleton, having collected the weapons earlier, from Moreland's, had driven Dalton to the scene. Stapleton opened fire from a laneway at the junction of St Patrick's Parade and Upper St Columba's Road, while Dalton tried frantically to operate his, the junction sealed behind them by the car. To conceal the guns until the last moment – as per Daly's orders – both had waited at the car, its doors ajar, until, hearing the grenade blasts, they grabbed them and dashed through the short lane to fire. Dalton finally got his weapon to work, but only after the train had passed. Other Volunteers shot rounds through the train's roof from a footbridge further along on Claude Road as it passed beneath. Sleeping soldiers, heads resting against windows, were rudely awoken by the short but intense outburst.[73] Schoolboys walking to a nearby school rushed into houses upon hearing the bombing and shooting. Local residents had been warned to keep away and mind their business when the ambushers had first arrived on scene. When the train arrived in Kingsbridge soon afterwards one soldier, twenty-year-old Pte William Saunders, 'was removed from the train in a dying condition', whilst two sergeants were also wounded.[74] 'There was a large pool of blood and a substance resembling brain matter in one van. The coaches presented a wrecked appearance, windows being smashed and woodwork torn and splintered. The van next to the engine suffered particularly, being practically riddled with bullets.'[75] When the rest of the 'West Kent's' were ordered off the train, they appeared jumpy and were quickly marched away to Phoenix Park accompanied by a military band. One soldier protested afterwards: 'We were not half-an-hour in the country, when we ran up against the "Shinners".'[76] Earlier, as their train had passed through South Lotts Road, a grenade attack on an Auxiliary Tender took place, with bombs thrown from the nearby glass factory. It was stormed afterwards by cadets and Fergus de Búrca arrested.

Two days earlier, the same morning's Dublin Guard ambushers had awaited another troop train. Having removed a rail and some sleepers, they had anticipated the train's derailment, ready to attack. However, their intelligence had been faulty; a cattle train being derailed instead.[77] The following week, nonetheless, would see a far ghastlier but brutally effective example of a train derailment outside Newry, as well as an embarrassing failure following another local attempt.

Returning to London that same week from a two-day visit to Ireland was forty-year-old Col Hugh Elles, head of the Tank Corps. When he wrote to Field Marshal Wilson of his visit, Wilson was horrified at his account, which he subsequently forwarded to cabinet. Describing the military in Ireland as besieged, the note also read:

To go from Dublin to Cork, one may go by T.B.D. [destroyer] and be met by escort at the docks, or one may go – very slowly – by armed train …

On the other hand, the population moves when, where and by whatever route it wishes. This is a curious situation for a force whose *raison d'être* in the country is to maintain order.[78]

Elles then wrote of never having felt so bewildered while on liaison work. The Irish administrative system he described as confused and cumbersome, the controls on arms importation farcical. Troop morale was listless. He suggested the only remedy was the 'vigorous exploitation of martial law, with identity controls, naval blockade, and block-houses on which to base drive operations'.[79] Worryingly for the cabinet, he also suggested that, even with such repressive measures, two years would be required to restore order. He warned, ominously, that anything less than such measures would necessitate abandoning Ireland.

As if to prove Elles right in his assessment of arms importation controls, IRA Fingal and South Louth Brigades sent out units to destroy coastguard stations between Donabate and Laytown on 18 June. These stations were laid out within sight of each other and equipped with telephones and signalling equipment. GHQ, having targeted such stations since the war's commencement, ordered them destroyed as a consignment of Thompson guns was expected to land soon in the area.

Harry Boland's efforts in the USA to procure shipments of Thompson guns had already seen more than fifty reach Ireland via Liverpool. By June, 600 guns, along with over 400 spare magazines and boxes of equipment, had been surreptitiously purchased and concealed in the hold of the East-Side freighter, chartered by the White Cross to transport humanitarian aid, set to depart Hoboken in New Jersey on 17 June for Cork. Some of the weapons would then be relayed to Fingal. The plan was scuppered, however, by the consignment's discovery by the Federal Bureau of Investigation in a raid led by twenty-two-year-old John Edgar Hoover. The discovery of such a potentially devastating cargo on a White Cross vessel was not wasted on Macready.

Midnight on 18 June saw coastguard stations attacked and set alight with paraffin. Comdt Michael Rock led a successful attack against Skerries station. Balbriggan was, however, deemed too risky to attack owing to the large number of Black and Tans in the town. Rock's column had been trying to take the fight to them by numerous means. Suggestions included mounting a Lewis gun in a car to attack the train station nearest their Gormanston Camp, and spiking their drinks in a pub they frequented with croton oil; neither plot materialised. Then, in a far more sinister plot, they planned to poison their camp water supply with typhus, until this idea was subsequently ruled out by GHQ. On one occasion they came close to assassinating the camp commander when they were informed of his planned social visit to the owners of the Smyth & Co. Hosiers – whose establishment was attacked by his men the previous September alongside an adjacent factory that was completely gutted. When one Volunteer was stopped just outside Balbriggan en route by a Black and Tan, the Volunteer shot him, thus placing the town on alert, ruling out the operation. The column came within a hair's breadth another night as the commander's car approached Balbriggan from Dublin. They attempted to tie a steel cable across the road in his path and then riddle the car with bullets as it was wrenched to a halt. However, the IRA, with Michael Lynch in charge, was unable to fix the cable in time. The RIC commander shared Col Winter's luck: the car sped through the gauntlet of fire.[80]

Further carnage was seen in Dublin on 18 June, when a Wiltshire Regiment officer, five soldiers and ten civilians were wounded in a truck ambush at the junction of Ryder's Row and Capel Street. Reinforcements and Auxiliaries rushed there, followed by ambulances, just as the IRA attackers melted away into the surrounding streets, alleyways and houses. Local homes were ransacked that night, just as another shooting took place in Drumcondra. Robert Pike, who had alerted Dublin Castle to the presence of Frank Flood and his ASU men the previous 21 January, was shot several times and died of shock and haemorrhage.[81] Charlie Dalton and several accomplices waited for him to leave Fagan's pub before shooting him just after he had crossed the street on his way home. It had long since been suspected that Pike had provided the Castle with information leading to the raid at Fernside in Drumcondra the previous October, culminating in the breathtaking escapes of Seán Treacy and Dan Breen from the address. Pike had been watched ever since and once his suspected collaborations with the enemy were confirmed, his fate was sealed.[82]

The 6th Battalion, over 700 strong, continued at full tilt throughout June. Dún Laoghaire Company commander, Billy Walsh, a former British soldier with the Irish Guards, used a number of his ex-military contacts in the area to draw out information on enemy agents and touts. Volunteers were sent into the magnificent Royal Marine Hotel, 'a favourite hunting ground for gentlemen from the Castle'. Documents and pistols were stolen from pockets. Eventually, when an Auxiliary unit arrived in the hotel, the IRA, under Jim McIntosh, attacked. What ensued resembled a 'Wild West' show.[83] Shootings took place in its foyer, stairs and corridors. There were numerous casualties, including McIntosh, who subsequently died on his way to hospital.

Another Auxiliary unit, accompanying a military lorry, was ambushed on Marine Road, one Volunteer firing at their Tender with a rifle while two comrades hurled grenades, one, thrown by Joe Hudson, exploding among its cadets. The Tender, then limped into Lower George's Street, followed by the lorry, where it was attacked again by men under Billy Keenan. Escaping this gauntlet, it was attacked yet again by the Blackrock Company under Joe Flanagan. This time the lorry was also raked with fire and bullets, as well as grenades that were manufactured in Blackrock. An armoured car later returned to Blackrock, where there was further fire. A policeman was wounded when Dún Laoghaire train station was raided successfully for a large ammunition cargo en route to Rathdrum RIC Barracks in Wicklow. Bray railway station was also attacked and two army ambulances destroyed. On 19 June, twenty-year-old Lt Alfred Breeze, 2nd Battalion Worcestershire Regiment, was shot dead in Carrickmines, after the IRA held up the car he was travelling in with two ladies. Breeze, dressed in mufti, had pulled a revolver before being shot and initially wounded. A subsequent struggle saw him taken from the car and shot at the roadside.[84]

The 250-strong 7th Battalion had also joined the fray in Dublin, attacking a military post at Clondalkin pumping station, and drawing more enemy from the city centre, as well as from the 6th Battalion's operational area.

The offensive action was not, however, all one-way. Auxiliaries located and seized a large IRA arms dump in Ticknock, and the Blackrock bomb factory was forced to move to Glencullen for fear of discovery. Then, three days after Lt Breeze's death, his battalion, searching a house in Cross Avenue, Blackrock, for documents, pursued a tall, bearded man as he fled across a neighbouring back garden.[85] He was captured. Brought to Portobello Barracks, he eventually divulged his name: Éamon de Valera.[86]

On 22 June, the day of De Valera's arrest, King George V opened Northern Ireland's parliament with a speech in which he declared a deep affection for Ireland. He described the event itself as a particularly moving moment in Irish history. He spoke of his confidence that the statelet would be governed with wisdom, fairness and moderation. He paid tribute to the deeds of Irishmen during the Great War, several thousand of whom, predominantly Catholics, had since been driven from their nearby homes and jobs, rendered destitute in recent loyalist pogroms. He referred to 'the eyes of the whole Empire' being on Ireland that day. He described the Irish as 'my people', and appealed to them to 'pause, to stretch out the hand of forbearance and conciliation', and 'to forgive and forget'.[87] During the two preceding weeks, seventeen Catholics had been killed in Belfast, six by the USC. One hundred and fifty Catholics in Belfast had been burned out of their homes, and there was much more of this to come.

IRA GHQ that day issued a directive authorising the burning of houses belonging to prominent outspoken unionists in retaliation for the continued burning of homes by the forces under King George. In Cork, the earl of Bandon and his wife were taken hostage by the IRA under Seán Hales. A letter was then sent to Gen. Strickland threatening that the earl and his wife would be executed if there were any more IRA members executed in martial law areas; the most recent being thirty-four-year-old Thomas Keane, shot by firing squad on 4 June in New Barracks, Limerick, following a court martial conviction for carrying arms.

Two days after the speech, the watching empire's eyes recoiled in horror when the train carrying the King's Own Royal Escort, the 10th Huzzars, was derailed by an IRA mine at Adavoyle, outside Newry, at 10 a.m. More than a dozen coaches were derailed before tumbling down a steep thirty-foot embankment. Three soldiers were killed and more than twenty wounded, some horrifically. Eighty horses were either killed or destroyed afterwards.

In Killester, on the same day as the king's speech, the Dublin Guard mined the train tracks in anticipation of a passing enemy troop train carrying 300 soldiers. They planned to blow it up, set it alight and open up with a Thompson gun, only for the job to be abandoned after another train from the same direction, carrying civilians as well as several prominent IRA brigade staff members, was confused for the troop train by one Volunteer, who threw a grenade through a carriage window that exited out the far side before exploding on the tracks.[88] This was fortunate for the IRA; Diarmuid O'Hegarty was among the brigade staff in the carriage. Given that the enemy would soon be alerted to their presence, the job was abandoned. Meanwhile, their brigade comrades from 3rd Battalion had been busy again in Great Brunswick Street.

21 June saw six grenades explode among a party of C Company Auxiliaries and an ensuing firefight during which a cadet was shot in the foot.

The aftermath of the king's speech also saw Andy Cope, albeit from London, employing his tightrope-like skills to have De Valera released, much to Col Winter's disgruntlement. Winter was also in London, recuperating. Cope's success saw De Valera depart Portobello Barracks, somewhat despondent at having been captured, at the same time as Lt Breeze's body was being brought in. De Valera, stepping out into a city about to be plagued by further assassinations and reprisal killings – whilst parrying a tirade of verbal abuse from the late lieutenant's comrades with some choice comments of his own – was soon to be handed an unexpected letter from Lloyd George, by Cope, inviting both himself and James Craig to London to discuss, informally, an accommodation.[89] The British government were finally realising that they simply could not win. Hamar Greenwood had just announced in the Commons that for the preceding three months, the British military had failed to maintain pace with the IRA. Greenwood, completely out of touch, saw his words as a call to arms to help turn this tide; instead, they inadvertently provided an admission of the lack of the military's ability to persevere. The republicans had succeeded in making the 'price of British military victory too high for British public opinion', as well for the eyes of the empire.[90] It was time to talk peace.

15

PEACE, A CLOSE-RUN THING

'It is well for mortal man'

The British public's reaction to King George's speech was positive, and it was well received in moderate Ireland. Much of it was written by Jan Smuts and worded judiciously so as not to disparage the IRA.[1] Accordingly, Lloyd George felt he could open exploratory dialogue 'with a semblance of magnanimity rather than seeking terms with men who had been branded as murderers'.[2]

Lloyd George's letter to De Valera 'punctiliously shielded' Northern Ireland's position, referring contrivingly to De Valera as 'the chosen leader of the great majority in Southern Ireland'. James Craig was referred to as 'Premier of Northern Ireland'.[3] Craig's response was tactful, assuring Lloyd George he could count on his cooperation, but urging caution about not 'jumping in' too quickly, fearing this might suggest terms were swayed in his favour, an eventuality that could undermine De Valera's influence on those with whom they sought accord. Nonetheless, he would 'sit on Ulster like a rock'.[4]

De Valera too was not yet prepared to jump in. Responding, he protested that Lloyd George's invitation denied 'Ireland's essential unity'.[5] He summoned a conference at the Mansion House, establishing an office there, and inviting Craig, who declined, astonished with what he perceived as an impertinent response and gesture. John Andrews, Northern Ireland's minister for home affairs, dismissed De Valera, saying: 'If De Valera and his people want to give the people peace, it is up to them not us. In the interest of peace we have taken a parliament we never wanted ... If they want peace, why don't they do the same?'[6] De Valera invited Lord Midleton to represent southern unionists, as were Sir Maurice Dockrell, Sir Robert Woods and Andrew Jameson. De Valera conveyed to them that he, as 'spokesman for the nation', could learn from them 'at first hand the views of a certain section' of the Irish people. They subsequently met De Valera on 4 July and Midleton's eventual input became far more influential than mere representation of a minority.

Meanwhile, the destruction and killing continued. In Grafton Street on Thursday 24 June, twenty-seven-year-old Leonard Appleford and twenty-nine-year-old cadet George Warnes, both F Company Auxiliaries, off duty, unarmed and in mufti, were shot dead by Ned Kelliher, Paddy Rigney and three others.

A far larger operation – effectively a mass execution of Auxiliaries – had been planned for that evening.[7] Dublin Brigade and Dublin Guard units, briefed the previous evening at 'The Plaza', were to deploy in four sections along Grafton Street – each with an intelligence officer to identify targets – with additional supporting units throughout the area, one under Pádraig O'Connor. Grafton Street was a popular haunt for Auxiliaries during summer evenings. Joe Guilfoyle, Dan McDonnell, Frank Saurin and Ned Kelliher were detailed to designated street sections. Kelliher's included the Cairo Café, 59 Grafton Street, a regular Auxiliary hangout.[8] Joe Dolan was to lead an additional six-man section into Kidd's buffet, similarly popular, where they would open fire on any identified enemy. Notably, during the briefing, intelligence officers had stood on tables and identified themselves to unfamiliar comrades to ensure they did not accidentally shoot them during the operation.[9]

Ultimately, however, an unusually large number of military roadblocks that day prevented the requisite number of attackers from marshalling beforehand. Additionally, most city bridges were cordoned. This also prevented an IRA car from being driven to Grafton Street to evacuate any wounded. On the other hand, with typical pluck, Joe Leonard, William Stapleton and Charlie Dalton reached the area in a stolen army truck, Dalton in the cargo area with one of three Thompson guns on his lap, having ensured he could operate it.[10] When stopped at a military checkpoint, Stapleton stuck his head out the window and, shouting something in an imitated Cockney accent, bluffed his way through.[11] This was fortunate for the soldiers; Dalton had primed his sub-machine gun to mow them down. The three eventually took position on Duke Street. However, few of Leonard's half-company made it to the area as ordered.

Kelliher and Rigney, with several others, had shadowed their targets, Appleford and Warnes, recognising them upon their arrival in the area. Their orders were to await a 6 p.m. pre-attack signal – a shot fired into the air by Joe Dolan once his unit had commenced the slaughter in Kidd's Buffet.

On the stroke of six, however, no signal came. Joe Guilfoyle alerted Dolan just before he and his men entered Kidd's Buffet that none of his unit had made it; they were to have been Dolan's covering party. Nevertheless, moments later, at the junction of Grafton Street and Chatham Street both Auxiliaries were cut down in a storm of bullets, fired by James Tully, Joseph McGuinness – from his unwounded hand – and Alec O'Toole.[12] Appleford was shot in the chest, abdomen, right thigh, right upper arm and shoulder, left hand, and four times in his lower back and buttocks. Warnes was hit four times in the chest, and once in the back and the left thigh.[13]

Paddy Drury and John Cafferty had been alerted to Appleford and Warnes' presence by a well-dressed female contact of Drury's. However, seeing that they were in Kelliher's street section, they backed off. Their sights fell upon another plain-clothed Auxiliary. They rapidly closed in, with Simon McInerney close by. Hearing Drury call out 'there's another', the cadet turned and saw them pacing towards him among the street's scattering pedestrians, weapons drawn.[14] He raced for cover in a shop doorway. Drury and Cafferty opened fire. The cadet threw himself down, whizzing bullets smashing the shop's window.[15] Staff screamed in fright. But the cadet was lucky; IRA runners sprinted the length of Grafton Street signalling the job was off.[16] Drury and Cafferty beat their retreats, as did the others, including Leonard, Stapleton and Dalton. Hearing the shots, the three had alighted from the van and walked along Duke Street, each carrying unfamiliar-looking Thompson guns in view of astonished civilians, ready to join the fray until Frank Saurin told them what had happened.[17] They returned to the van and sped off to dump their vehicle and weapons.

Officers subsequently questioned Kelliher and Rigney as to why they and their three comrades had opened fire without hearing the signal. However, no action was taken against any of them.[18]

Late June saw Dollymount added to the list of coastguard stations destroyed. It also saw increased IRA sniping in the city, late into the drawn-out summer evenings, particularly in the Custom House area.[19] A prophetic warning was sent out to the civilian population from Dublin Castle – its surrounding area particularly affected – that persons out after curfew would be shot on sight. Night patrols increased. As the short hours of midsummer darkness descended upon the capital, its deserted streets rattled to trucks, Tenders, Castle cars, armoured cars, motorcycles and hobnailed infantry boots.

No. 30 Lower Baggot Street set the scene for the IRA's next gruesome killing. At 7 p.m., Sunday 26 June, thirty-one-year-old Auxiliary William

Hunt of R Company, who had a reputation as an aggressive intelligence officer, was shot in the Mayfair Hotel as he dined with twenty-four-year-old Q Company colleague Enfield White, their two visiting wives, Alice and Annie, and Hunt's ten-year-old daughter, Doris, staying at the hotel. White was badly wounded. Their seven Dublin Guard attackers, commanded by Lt O'Connor and described afterwards as aged between seventeen and twenty, took them by surprise. Intelligence officer Paddy Drury had gleaned information from a hotel maid about its guests. That afternoon she informed him of their presence, described both of their appearances and where they customarily sat while dining.[20]

When they turned up, O'Connor rang the doorbell four times and knocked once; a prearranged signal for the maid to answer and direct them to the dining room, the second door to their left as they entered.[21] O'Connor stepped in first, followed by Michael Stack and Alec O'Toole, then James Tully, who immediately went to disconnect the hotel's telephone.[22] The three others stood guard in the reception area as O'Connor and Stack drew weapons, O'Toole just behind them, and opened the dining room door. Hunt and White, facing them, jumped to their feet at the sight of their pistols. O'Connor and Stack fired instantly. Hunt was hit in the chest by O'Connor, the bullet tearing through and exiting, spattering the scene, his family and fellow diners with blood. He fell and lay motionless, face down. White was shot through the jaw. He spun under the shot's impact in time for Stack's second bullet to tear into his back. O'Toole watched from the door. Stack then covered O'Connor as he took both victims' guns, their wives and Hunt's daughter screaming and crying. Then, O'Connor turned Hunt over, still alive. He stood over him, said coldly: 'You are dead D.I. Hunt' and shot him again. The bullet ripped through him, then, ricocheting, grazed his daughter's leg.[23]

Stack, hands shaking, dropped two rounds reloading his gun just as O'Connor ordered him out. Stack, however, insisted he was not leaving until he found the dropped bullets. He and O'Connor searched until they found them. The delay was fortuitous. Had they and their comrades left just seconds earlier they would have stumbled into an Auxiliary convoy passing en route to Stephen's Green.[24]

O'Connor's escaping men were pursued by White momentarily until he collapsed. A hotel servant fainted in shock. White's wife rushed to fetch a local doctor, who, arriving, found White slumped at the hotel doorstep, blood smeared all over his face, seriously wounded, having left a trail of blood from the dining room. Hunt lay dead on the dining-room floor, face-up in a pool of blood, his wife and wounded daughter sobbing in disbelief among horrified guests. The pungent smell of cordite hung in the room.

The attackers rushed to a getaway car driven by Jim O'Neill in Lower Fitzwilliam Street, only to find it broken down. They escaped on foot. The police subsequently found James Tully's Webley revolver and holster in the car.[25]

The following day saw K Company, 3rd Battalion, back in action when an Auxiliary Tender was attacked at the junction of Lombard Street and Westland Row. Then, on 29 June at 5 p.m., thirty-two-year-old plain-clothed Const. Owen Hoey was gunned down by three IRA members on bicycles on St James's Walk in Rialto. Local children, playing, were rushed to safety by terrified mothers when they heard the shots.

Hoey's killing was succeeded by a devastating attack the next day by ten members of Pádraig O'Connor's Dublin Guard half company. They ambushed a Ford Model T car at Dolphin's Barn's wide junction with South Circular Road. Intelligence was received from 4th Battalion that it carried Eugene Igoe and some of his unit, and regularly travelled eastbound from Kilmainham to Dublin Castle at approximately 8 p.m. each evening.[26]

Its arrival having been signalled, the car ground to a halt in the centre of the junction as soon as it came under fire from the chapel to its front, from behind a large concrete cross to its right, and from O'Connor and Michael Stack to its rear outside a bank on the South Circular Road junction. As it was peppered with bullets, civilians, some having already dispersed once they observed armed men taking positions around the junction, scattered. Two panicked colleagues wrenched the driver, badly wounded, from his seat, his front passenger sliding across.[27] The car took off once again as its windows were shot out by O'Connor's furious fire, but there were more IRA men ahead.[28] Jimmy McGuinness, positioned 200 yards away, ran out into the road from the White Heather laundry, on a bend in the road to the car's right, and opened fire.[29] Ragged fire was returned momentarily until Joseph McGuinness emerged from Rehoboth Place, to its left, and threw a grenade, as did Thomas Lillis from the right. One bomb landed in the car, the other beneath. Two dull explosions followed and the car, lifted by the blast, halted again.[30]

Incredibly, the new driver, under further sporadic fire, his face and hands bloodied, restarted the stalled car. With smoke billowing from its engine he then nursed it to nearby Wellington Barracks, where it caught fire. Luckily for the four occupants, all seriously wounded, they were dragged out.[31] Intelligence was later received that Igoe had not been in the car, the frustrating news greeted with a tirade of expletives by the attackers.

June ended in an utterly war-weary country still simmering in a heatwave, the month witnessing ambushes, reprisals, assassinations, executions of suspected spies, kidnappings, jailbreaks and house burnings in places such as Lisacall, Frenchpark and Castlerea in Roscommon; Ballybofey, Glenties and Buncrana in Donegal; Edenderry, Ballyduff and Coolacrease in Offaly; Swatragh in Derry; Abbeyfeale in Limerick; Moylough, Milltown and Athenry in Galway; Ballyvoile and Carrigbeg in Waterford; Camlough in Armagh; Ballywilliam, Rossgreen, Knockfune and Templemore in Tipperary; Glasson, Kilbeggan and Kinnegad in Westmeath; Newry in Down; the Falls Road, Dock Street and North Queen Street in Belfast; Meelick, Corraclare, Ennis, Tulla and Newmarket-on-Fergus in Clare; Farranfore, Killarney and Listowel in Kerry; Rower, Piltown and Castlecomer in Kilkenny; Nurney and Allen in Kildare; Dundalk, Castletown and Carlingford in Louth; Ballincastle in Mayo; Sligo town and Cliffoney in Sligo; Clogher in Tyrone; Carnagh and Ballybay in Monaghan; and Kildorrery, Skibbereen, Bandon, Millstreet and, incredibly, Fastnet Rock in Cork.[32]

In North Dublin on Saturday 2 July, Comdt Michael Rock was shot twice as he cycled, unarmed, past two Black and Tan Tenders en route from The Naul to the Oldtown flying column HQ in Mooretown. Hit in the hip and arm, he collapsed on a narrow roadway. He was thrown into the back of a Tender and taken to Balbriggan coastguard station, occupied by Tans since the recent attacks on nearby stations. Dr Fulham from Balbriggan was summoned, and a priest. Local girls brought whiskey for his pain. Rock was then taken to King George V Hospital in an armoured car, part of a small convoy, an agonising four-hour journey with several stops, accompanied by Dr Fulham at the latter's insistence. Rock was operated on and, with the exception of one vitriolic nurse, treated kindly in the hospital, an aspect that struck him given that it was run by the British military. Four IRA comrades, including Thomas 'Sweeney' Newell, shot by Sgt Igoe, were also convalescing there. Rock was questioned regularly by enemy intelligence officers at the hospital about recent shootings in the Balbriggan area and warned he would probably be hanged once recovered if he refused to divulge information. He divulged nothing.[33]

Forty-five-year-old father of four Daniel Duffy fell victim to the recent shoot-on-sight curfew directive at 10.45 p.m. on 3 July. A fitter with Guinness' Brewery, Duffy was walking home carrying flowers for his wife. Called upon to halt by the military, he dropped the flowers. When he bent to pick them up he was shot dead.[34]

The following day, 4 July, saw Tricolour flags draped across the city, as well as American flags. Each flew proudly side by side above the Mansion House, Sinn Féin employing the anniversary of America's independence from Britain to highlight Ireland's continuing struggle to free itself from the same foe, and as an expression of gratitude to the country that had assisted the struggle so wholeheartedly. Among some, a sense was dawning that the war might be drawing to a close, with possible peace in the air, and that some sort of normality could return to the long-suffering city and country. For many, normality simply meant mundane poverty, hunger and premature death from disease, to which the war, at least, provided a distraction; indeed, in some cases affording them the opportunity for recognition, camaraderie and status. Those who prayed for peace remained wary, lest their hopes be dashed. They were certainly dashed in the quiet Dublin village of Lucan, where the RIC barracks was attacked that day, the attack driven off by return fire. Tensions remained palpable. Soldiers, their officers at home going to great lengths not to be posted to Ireland, and Auxiliaries, patrolled the city nervously, firearms protocols in urban areas long since disregarded. Rounds remained chambered; magazines filled; safety catches ready to be switched off in a heartbeat. Enemy gunfire or grenades were expected at any time, from any place. The last thing the city's Auxiliaries expected to be wounded by, however, were flowerpots.

That evening, when soldiers in Dominick Street removed two flags, 'an angry crowd of women and girls rushed them'.[35] They seized one flag back from the soldiers. Shots were fired into the air. The crowd scattered. Then, when the military departed the scene, several local men replaced the flag, prompting a passing Auxiliary patrol to enter the fray and tear it down. 'A further scramble took place, in which a large crowd of women, girls and young men participated.'[36] Missiles were hurled at the cadets, one struck on the head with a bottle, another on the shoulder by a flowerpot, prompting them to fire several shots, one of which wounded nineteen-year-old Lily Douglas. She was shot in the thigh and rushed to Jervis Street Hospital. Her wound was not serious.

By now Dublin Castle was feverishly laying the groundwork for peace talks. Six days earlier the suspension of raids on the homes of 'persons of political importance' was ordered.[37] That same day the southern parliament had met at the Royal College of Science in Upper Merrion Street as necessitated by the Government of Ireland Act.[38] It was a farce, the only attendees fifteen senators nominated by Lord Fitzalan, who presided, and four members for Trinity College. The parliament, with an insufficient quorum to fulfil statutory requirements, lasted fifteen minutes before adjourning.[39]

Two days later, 30 June, Andy Cope, bypassing Hamar Greenwood, secured the releases from Mountjoy Prison of Arthur Griffith, Eoin MacNeill, Éamonn Duggan and Michael Staines, and Robert Barton from Portland Prison in England, where he had suffered appalling treatment since his incarceration there over a year earlier.[40] Gens Macready and Brind cautiously welcomed the prison releases.

Barton soon crossed the Irish Sea, on the same ferry as Jan Smuts. Having first fought against the British in the Boer War, then alongside them in the Great War, Smuts was in the 'unusual position of being trusted by both sides' in Ireland.[41] Barton and Smuts arrived in Dún Laoghaire on 5 July.

Smuts, acting in an unofficial capacity as intermediary, met De Valera on the day of his arrival in Dublin. Tom Casement, brother of executed 1916 leader Roger, and an old friend of Smuts, acted as an initial go-between, having travelled with Smuts.[42]

By the time Smuts met De Valera, Lord Midleton was already preparing to act as intermediary and convey De Valera's position personally to Lloyd George, having spoken with the Dáil president at a meeting hosted by the lord mayor the previous day in the Mansion House; the barbed-wire entanglements that had for months grown like wild brambles outside noticeably absent, the Tricolour and Stars and Stripes both undulating above in the warm breeze. To reach the meeting Midleton and his three fellow unionist representatives had waded 'through a mass of cheering enthusiasts', many overwhelmed by the magnitude of change in the city and country since January 1919, when so many had gathered there in much colder weather in the midst of the Spanish Flu pandemic for the Dáil's inaugural meeting.[43]

Midleton relayed to Lloyd George that De Valera 'refused to attend a conference at which Craig was also present', denying the six-county statelet's claim to 'an equal voice with the Irish people of whom he [De Valera] was the only accredited representative'.[44] He also carried the message that De Valera agreed in principle with a suggestion that was discussed: 'that he should go to London and begin negotiations', but 'stressed the need for a truce before he would commit to talks', adding that De Valera 'did not believe negotiations could well go forward while the two sides were actively engaged in war'.[45] Midleton had undertaken to De Valera 'to secure an offer of truce from the British Government if De Valera would ensure that any arrangements would be observed by the IRA'.[46] It was agreed that he would report back to the Mansion House on 8 July.

Lord Mayor Laurence O'Neill was deeply struck by the Mansion House meeting, reflecting, following Midleton's departure, on all that had happened since 18 April 1918, a date that, despite being recent, felt like it was from a different epoch. This was when the same round table around which he, De Valera and Griffith had just conferred with the unionist delegation on matters he referred to as delicate but momentous, had been used to launch the successful anti-conscription campaign, the event which had effectively marked the recommencement of hostilities following the 1916 Rising – at least as far as the Dublin Brigade and GHQ were concerned.[47]

Meanwhile, Smuts, his expression typically straightforward and steely, signalled to De Valera during protracted talks at Dr Farnan's in Merrion Square, what he perceived as the dangers of turning domestic and international opinion against his cause if, for whatever reason, he refused Lloyd George's offer to parley. He also argued against demands for a Republic, asserting that dominion status, a far more realistic prospect, had been favourable to South Africa since its recent attainment. He highlighted 'the problems that a republic had faced in the Transvaal' and made 'the point that, when the people had been given the chance of voting for a republic, they had instead voted by a large majority for a free partnership within the Empire'.[48] De Valera remained wary, suspicious of British intentions. He and others suspected they simply wished to present the appearance of wanting to settle to appear magnanimous to their Imperial Conference delegates, including Smuts, as well as their global ally – the USA. De Valera suspected that any settlement terms offered during talks would be unreasonably weighted in favour of Britain and that, furthermore, any blame for refusing such terms – and consequently continuing the war – would land squarely on his shoulders.[49] He also saw the offer as 'a trap set to get him to recognise partition'.[50]

De Valera had already, during an interview with Swiss newspaper *Neue Zürcher Zeitung* in early May, presented the appearance that dominion status was acceptable, but suggested Britain was being disingenuous in its conception of such status by referring to examples such as Canada and New Zealand similarly as dominions. These countries, he argued, were dominions by their own free will and had the right to secede from the empire should they choose. Britain was not offering Ireland such a choice. He argued that if this were offered, it would inadvertently represent a tacit acceptance by Britain of Ireland's status as a republic.[51] He insisted that a free choice between becoming a dominion or a republic 'must be forthcoming from Britain'.[52] De Valera had, since the *Neue Zürcher Zeitung* interview, also alluded publicly to controversial comments he had made the previous year in the USA, comparing the possibility of Ireland's future relationship with Britain with Cuba's existing one with the USA under the Monroe Doctrine – effectively a protectorate. London could declare to the world that any attempt by a foreign power to gain a foothold in Ireland would be seen as an act of aggression against Britain herself. Ireland, he had argued, could be happy to comply with such a directive should such a status accompany independence.

De Valera responded to Smuts with questions: would Lloyd George meet him without Craig, and would a truce be agreed as a precondition to such a conference?[53] Arguments continued. Smuts implored De Valera to concede ground, saying, 'As a friend I cannot advise you too strongly against a republic. Ask what you want but not a republic.'[54] Eventually, their exchange ended with De Valera pledging to try to get the Irish people to accept dominion status if it was offered. Smuts then returned to Westminster, not particularly impressed by De Valera or any of his cohorts; nevertheless, he recommended an immediate truce. Midleton also spoke favourably of sitting down with De Valera.

Lord Balfour baulked at the implications of the word 'truce', sensing it suggested dealing with belligerents as opposed to those they had considered all along to be murderers. Balfour had also contributed far more bellicose wording to the draft of King George's speech for the opening of the Northern Parliament, much of it removed.[55] Forty-seven-year-old Lord Chancellor Frederick Smith, referred to as Lord Birkenhead, reassured Balfour that murderers would be pursued regardless of any truce, making Balfour more amenable to the idea, subsequently agreed to in principle, but on the grounds that six-county Northern Ireland would not be coerced into any agreement repugnant to its unionist majority. As Lloyd George prepared to speak with James Craig to inform him of his choice to agree to bipartisan talks – based in no small part on the conviction of Smuts that he should – Smuts contacted De Valera, informing him of Lloyd George's decision, but warning him 'of the dangers of offending Lloyd George's Ulster Unionist sensitivities'.[56] Smuts emphasised that a conference of two, instead of three, should not contain language that might belittle the northern position. De Valera called a meeting with Brugha, Collins, Stack, Griffith, Count Plunkett and Eoin MacNeill 'to consider a very important decision to be made'.[57]

Back in the Mansion House, early on Friday 8 July, Lord Midleton, returned from London and, accompanied by his unionist colleagues, conveyed Lloyd George's offer of a truce to De Valera, Griffith, Duggan and Barton. The offer was subject to approval 'by the British military authorities in Ireland'.[58] Following this, at 1 p.m., Midleton and his colleagues were driven to Irish Command HQ, Parkgate Street, to seek Macready's sanction.[59] Macready – furnished by Midleton with a letter from Lloyd George stating that once De Valera was prepared to parley and 'cease all acts of violence' they themselves should 'suspend active operations' – then contacted Andy Cope and Gens Boyd and Tudor.[60] Terms were agreed that 'in the event of a truce, raiding and searching would stop; the army would confine itself to supporting the police and lift the curfew'.[61] Macready dispatched his aide-de-camp to accompany Midleton back to the Mansion House to meet with De Valera and present draft truce terms. They arrived at 4 p.m. Then, at 5 p.m., they left anxiously again for Parkgate Street, De Valera insisting on changes to the terms. Midleton, sixty-three years old, exhausted and with a night ferry to catch to London, was pressed for time. Realising this, Macready and Boyd grasped the nettle. With loaded pistols in their unbuttoned right pockets, they made their way under a small escort to the Mansion House in an open touring car, their staff telephoning ahead, oblivious to the ruthless and potentially devastating operation the IRA was putting in place in the streets their car would be speeding through.

On 29 April 1916, a forerunner of Macready's, Brig. Gen. Lowe, had parleyed with De Valera's former commander in chief, Pádraig Pearse, and demanded nothing short of unconditional surrender. Now, just over five years later, everything had changed. Macready waded through the crowds still outside the Mansion House. An elderly woman grasped his hand and kissed it. Macready was unimpressed with her ostensible sincerity. Typically cynical

General Macready, with Lord Mayor Laurence O'Neill to his right, steps towards the Mansion House through jubilant crowds, overjoyed at the prospect of imminent peace, 8 July 1921. *(Courtesy of the National Library of Ireland)*

regarding the country he despised, he castigated the fact that the same people cheering him and Boyd would, without doubt, rejoice with equal fervour their deaths at IRA hands. He also took note of firemen stewarding the crowds, with no sign of any DMP, who knew better. This was stark comparison with the Dáil's 1919 inauguration, which was closely monitored by the police.[62]

Greeted exuberantly by the lord mayor, the two generals entered and spoke with De Valera. Press reporters hovered outside. 3rd Battalion Volunteers looked on discreetly. De Valera, wary of the press, had warned his Dáil cabinet ministers present of the 'danger of committing to paper any plans or views on the present negotiations'.[63] Following initial introductions and courtesies, talks began. Then, at 8 p.m., the final truce terms were agreed. Macready returned to the Royal Hospital, Kilmainham, to telephone Lloyd George.[64] There, he was briefed about a significant attack on a train that afternoon, three miles west of his HQ, by officers who had no inkling of the bloodbath the city had just been spared.

Pádraig O'Connor's left half company, having received word that a civilian train leaving Kingsbridge at 1 p.m. would carry a detachment of enemy soldiers and their stores, had prepared an ambush in Ballyfermot next to its railway bridge. A motorcyclist was dispatched to Kingsbridge to determine which carriages the military occupied and report. A scout was also detailed to a footbridge east of the ambush point to signal the train's approach. Petrol was to be poured on the carriages from the bridge itself. Pat McCrea delivered a Thompson gun to Jimmy McGuinness in a van to the ambush scene. Shortly after 1 p.m. the motorcyclist arrived, specifying which carriages to hit. Two-dozen Volunteers stood primed to attack from an embankment to the train's left. The train tracks had been greased in an attempt to stop the train.

As the train steamed towards the scout, he signalled his comrades. An accomplice emptied a can of petrol onto the train's roof as it passed just feet below moments later. The scout then lit and threw a petrol-soaked rag on top. The carriage roof quickly caught fire but it did not spread. Seconds later, O'Connor's men opened up. Pistols chattered. McGuinness emptied a drum magazine of bullets into the train, his teeth clenched as he squeezed the Tommy gun's trigger, the weapon's stock rammed into his right shoulder, his hands clenching the handgrips to hold it steady. His ears rang. No fire was returned from the train, which kept going, slowed by its wheels spinning and skidding on the tracks. Minutes later, a badly wounded female civilian was taken off at Clondalkin station. She later lost her leg. The train then continued to the Curragh, where the military carriages were detached from the rest of the train. Reports came back to brigade intelligence of numerous enemy casualties and severe damage to the carriages, the IRA fire reported as highly effective.[65]

The arrival of the train in the Curragh was followed soon afterwards by another attack in nearby Newbridge. The IRA set fire to an army and navy canteen. The caretaker, William Dolan, and his thirteen-year-old stepson were burned alive, having fled to their upstairs lodgings above.[66]

Back in Dublin that evening, O'Connor's zealous unit prepared another ambush at Crumlin Cross, with two extra Thompson guns having been delivered to his men since the earlier attack. However, word of pending truce negotiations was sent to his men just in time to stop them. Their assembly was a small part of a wider Dublin Brigade operation ruthlessly formulated to have an even greater impact on the enemy than the recent Grafton Street misfire, Bloody Sunday, or the Custom House. Oscar Traynor was by now worn out and, on doctor's orders, on leave in Wales. Vice-Brig. Seán Murray had stepped up to the brigade helm as it prepared to unleash a torrent of killings.

The summer's long, warm and dry evenings were being exploited by large numbers of Auxiliaries strutting through city streets, brandishing weapons regardless of whether they were on duty, some swinging revolvers in one hand, their other arms linked with lady friends. Sackville Street was a recent regular venue for such romantic liaisons, with dozens of cadets gathering arrogantly on its wide boulevard. The same thoroughfare had been divided into four attack quadrants, one for each city brigade battalion, who, at 7 p.m. that Friday evening, would filter elements into Sackville Street, shoot any Auxiliaries on sight, then escape. Nassau and Grafton Streets, their cobbled roadways similarly replete with the same hated enemy eager to spend their pay-packets, despite obvious dangers, would be attacked similarly by Joe Leonard's half-company.[67] 2nd Battalion, its quadrant being Sackville Street's lower eastern side, would provide mobile vehicular support with a van driven by Denis Begley. Patrick Holohan had assigned members of F Company, 1st Battalion, such as John Kenny, to attack any enemy at La Scala cinema, a regular enemy haunt adjacent to the ruined GPO.[68] Joe O'Connor, 3rd Battalion, deployed men in Lower Mount Street and Holles Street, primed to ambush expected Auxiliary reinforcements from Beggar's Bush. 7th Battalion were brought into the city in support of 4th Battalion in the Christchurch/Dublin Castle area.[69] GHQ and Brigade intelligence had been feverishly busy gleaning information on military, police and secret service movements in preparation for the attack. Bridges into the city were to be covered by IRA snipers. Even Tom Ennis, still in hospital, plotted a 2nd Battalion attack on a Black and Tan lorry in Baldoyle. Other such attacks were planned throughout Dublin.

Any talk of truce was far from the minds of those primed to pounce throughout the city, such was the level of planning, detailed even to the point of Volunteer units rehearsing attacks with dry runs in preceding days. Many were scathing of the idea of being drawn out into the open by a truce, which they had heard rumblings of, but suspected was in any case bound to fail. Todd Andrews had dismissed talk of truces since Bloody Sunday as a British ploy to weaken IRA morale, the enemy rationale being that no IRA member would want to risk death if peace was in sight.[70] Michael Collins, marginalised for now along with other cabinet members deemed too toxic and hard-line for elected British ministers to be seen parleying with by the British public, was particularly wary of such acute dangers associated with a truce. He had written on 18 June, referring to peace talks, that:

It would be a great pity if well-meaning people queered the position by too much of this. There are always those who want to insist on shaking hands before the combat is over, and, in my opinion, we are not so near the end yet that we can afford to start the hand-shaking.[71]

Collins had also urged Volunteers discussing whisperings of a truce, to: 'Stop talking and get on with the work.'[72] He and Mulcahy were, nonetheless, acutely aware of ammunition shortages in the city. Joe Leonard and Frank Thornton baulked at the meagre ammunition dished out by IRA quartermasters to Volunteers in advance of Friday's planned mass attack.

Then, at 6.45 p.m. that Friday, as C Company, 2nd Battalion, filtered into Sackville Street between North Earl Street and Lower Abbey Street, with other battalion units following suit, and as the Dublin Guard converged on their kill zones, and Joe O'Connor's men primed themselves, while Volunteers from Bachelors Walk to Great Britain Street and from O'Connell Bridge to Rutland Square stubbed out cigarettes and readied themselves, as weapons were loaded and checked in alleys, escape routes surveyed yet again and discreet signals passed from man to man, couriers such as Séamus Kavanagh sped throughout the city with urgent countermand orders. Kavanagh cycled into Sackville Street waving a white handkerchief. His countermand – received like a 'bolt from the blue' – was greeted with dismay and disbelief, but also with relief.[73] The operation was off. Word had been rushed from the Dáil cabinet to GHQ that a truce was being agreed. Frank Henderson, in Sackville Street taking stock, noted that, for whatever reason, there were few, if any, Auxiliaries in Sackville Street. He wondered if the enemy had just received their own orders to remain off the streets and in barracks to help pave the pathway to the truce, or had, perhaps, more ominously, been alerted to their plans. Dublin remained conspicuously placid on the night of 8 July 1921, but it was close-run, and a testament to Dublin Brigade organisation and discipline that it was called off, largely, without incident.[74]

However, not everywhere escaped; no such countermand saved forty-five-year-old Dalkey tram inspector and father of four Andrew Knight, from 9 Clarinda Park East, Dún Laoghaire. Shot through the jaw by members of 6th Battalion, the suspected informer's body was found by a boy herding cattle near Dalkey. Papers were found on his remains indicating he had been paid by the British for information.[75]

The following morning, Saturday 9 July, Robert Barton and Éamonn

Duggan, both recent prisoners, met with Andy Cope and Sir John MacMahon in Dublin Castle, Cope dressed typically gleefully for the hot summer sunshine, the four blissfully ignorant of the slaughter just spared the city. Barton and Duggan declined a lift to Parkgate Street in Cope's car, both for their own safety and for optics. The four travelled instead by tram, paid for by Cope – he and MacMahon downstairs, Barton and Duggan upstairs – their fellow passengers oblivious to their current importance. Entering Irish Command HQ, they were introduced to its sentries as Cope's friends.[76] Soon afterwards, having met Gens Macready and Brind, the Truce's terms – practically indistinguishable from the terms insisted upon by the separatists via Archbishop Clune but dismissed by Westminster the previous December – were finalised and agreement signed. Winston Churchill later said, 'No British Government in modern times has ever appeared to make so sudden and complete a reversal of policy.'[77] The Truce was to become effective at noon, Monday 11 July. 5th Division were to be informed without delay.

One hundred miles south-west of Dublin, in Waterford, the Truce's agreement coincided with a horrific incident. In Kilgobnet, the IRA allowed a road trench they had dug to be filled in to facilitate the passing of a funeral. When they subsequently went to retrench it, a booby-trap bomb exploded, planted by the enemy, blowing six IRA Volunteers – John Quinn, Thomas Burke, Thomas Dahill, James and William Dunford, and Richard Lynch – to pieces.[78]

Then, on 10 July, Belfast experienced what became known as its own 'Bloody Sunday'. Shortly before midnight on Saturday 9 July, following the killing during an ambush in Raglan Street to the city's west of thirty-three-year-old RIC Const. Thomas Conlon from Roscommon, carnage erupted throughout the city.[79] Truckloads of USC rolled into Catholic and nationalist areas, as did armoured cars. Frenetic gun battles ensued, as well as aggressive sniping attacks, with civilians falling to snipers from both sides. Rampaging loyalist mobs again attacked Catholic areas. Over 100 homes were burned out. Twenty-two civilians were killed and dozens badly injured over a twenty-four-hour period. The violence lasted another week, following a brief interlude on 11 July.

The war's last major confrontation took place between Kerry No. 2 Brigade, 1st Southern Division, and the North Lancs Regiment on the evening of 10 July in Castleisland, Kerry. A large curfew patrol was ambushed on Main Street. A ferocious and prolonged firefight ensued. A machine gun swept the street. Four British soldiers were killed and three wounded, while the IRA lost five dead, among them Jack Flynn. Notably, Flynn had participated in the attack on Gortatlea Barracks on 13 April 1918 that had seen two Volunteers killed by RIC fire, the action seen by some as having effectively lit the fuse of the War of Independence.[80]

Back in Dublin the summer heatwave showed no signs of abating on the morning of 11 July. City dwellers roused themselves to witness a day few would forget. But the killing was not finished yet, at least in the country. Messengers rushed feverishly throughout Ireland conveying a dispatch from the IRA chief of staff, written as soon as the Truce was agreed. It read:

To officers commanding all units,

In view of the conversations now being entered into by our government, with the government of Great Britain, and in pursuance of mutual understandings to suspend hostilities during these conversations, active operations by our troops will be suspended as from noon Monday 11th July.

Risteard Ua Maolchata

Chief of Staff.[81]

News of the Truce was slower to reach outlying units and was generally met with shock and surprise, with some only finding out late on the night of 10 July or early the following morning. Tom Barry was informed, while manning a roadside position, by a comrade he refused to believe, until the same comrade returned with a newspaper confirming the revelation.[82] Other commanders also received word from the newspapers.

Fifty-two-year-old RIC Const. Alexander Clarke, an intelligence officer from Tipperary long since in IRA crosshairs, was shot dead in Skibbereen that morning. In picturesque Killarney, fifteen minutes before the Truce took effect, IRA gunmen in High Street ambushed two unarmed NCOs from the Royal Fusiliers; twenty-four-year-old Sgt Charles Mears was killed, his comrade wounded. Forty-eight-year-old civilian Hannah Carey was shot dead by RIC revolver five minutes later in nearby College Street in what was claimed afterwards to have been an accidental discharge.[83] In Edenderry, Co. Offaly, RIC Const. George Adam from Forfar in Scotland, with eighteen months' service, was shot at 11.20 a.m. He died of his wounds two months later.[84] RIC Sgt James King, forty-four years old and with a brutal reputation, was shot dead in Castlerea, Co. Roscommon on the same morning that also witnessed a litany of other small-scale 'pin-prick' attacks.[85] The previous day had seen countless other such small-scale actions with many killings and woundings, some grievous, others less so, such as an attack on 'a group of RIC Constables swimming in a pond' at Taghmon, Co. Wexford. They were fired upon by a large group of IRA who subsequently made off with their clothing. However, other than bruised egos, the policemen suffered no injuries.[86]

Following three days of frenetic political jousting during which scores more victims joined the ranks of those killed by bullet, bayonet, bomb and fire over the previous three years, the IRA's 'parting shot' of the War of Independence was fired from a pistol at Kingscourt, Co. Cavan, at 11.55 a.m. by a unit driving through the town. One of them fired a single shot at an RIC patrol.[87] It contrasted ironically with the shots fired at Soloheadbeg on 21 January 1919; the first significant IRA action directed towards the RIC since Sinn Féin had gained its electoral mandate in December 1918. Those shots, since having become more widely regarded as the war's first, had resonated throughout the British empire. The war's last shot was, conversely, barely met with a flinch – being mistaken by its intended target for nothing more than an engine misfire.

The Truce terms decreed that, on the British side, there would be no further reinforcements of military, RIC, Black and Tans, Auxiliaries and munitions, no further military movements other than for maintenance, and no provocative displays of armed or unarmed force. The Truce applied equally to martial and non-martial law areas. There would be no pursuit of IRA or Cumann na mBan members or their materiel. No agents would monitor, or interfere with the movements of Irish persons, military or civil, nor would there be pursuit or observance of lines of communication or connection. No searches would be conducted for the 'haunts or habits' of Irish officers and men, and the curfew would be lifted. The respite would not be unwelcome; by July 1921, thousands of homes had been raided and searched during the war in both Dublin and the country, and hundreds destroyed in reprisals.

On the Irish side, attacks on crown forces and civilians would cease, there would there be no provocative displays of force and no interference with government or private property. No actions would be undertaken to cause disturbance that might 'necessitate military interference'.[88]

The pistol shot mistaken for a backfire was succeeded five minutes later with a cacophony in Dublin, which presented a marked difference to the sound of gunfire, explosions, warnings and screams. At noon, Dublin Brigade's 5,366 serving Volunteers stood down.[89] The fleet of ships and small boats moored along the Liffey, many overlooked by the ruins of the Custom House, sounded ship horns in celebration. Barges did likewise with their whistles.[90] It was a world away from the cold and grim November day the previous year that had seen the same calm stretch of water witness military bands playing the Last Post as Union Jack-draped coffins were carried onto HMS *Sea Wolf* set against the mocking flotilla of caps drifting by on the outward tide. Today there was no such dirge, nor the displays of cruelty that had triggered the flotilla, but instead a symphony of resounding honks, hoots, hisses and whistles. Tricolour flags were strewn throughout Dublin, as well as on the boats. One flag, taken down by an angry British soldier, was immediately rehoisted by order of his officer. They were draped and waved from the windows of tenements to fashionable townhouses, pubs, shops and hotels, from horses and carts, from cars and from churches, the bells of which also rang out in celebration, their deeper tolls contrasting with the higher-pitched chiming of city trams.

Fifteen minutes earlier, elated civilians, many welling up with tears of joy, had looked on in disbelief from the streets they began to throng in anticipation of huge celebrations in the sweltering heat as 'a slow procession of armoured cars, tanks and patrols began to return to their barracks'. As the last of them disappeared through their barrack gates, they were seen off with cheers and well-wishes, as well as hoots of derision.[91]

Sackville Street filled with flag-waving crowds. Marching bands played. Street-hawkers had a field day, as did shops selling ice-cream and sweets for the armies of young children playing and dancing in the streets singing rebel songs, their parents today unconcerned about the danger of a stray bullet or grenade fragment. The trains filled with gleeful passengers making for the seaside, Auxiliaries among them in civilian clothes, some with bathing costumes rolled into towels under arms, others heading for Bray to spend the night drinking on its seafront and around its bandstands. Others stayed in the city, spilling paralytic out of the London and North Western Hotel or Dublin Castle to stagger to city haunts to toast fallen comrades and even, in some cases, their worthy IRA enemies, some of whom themselves would become similarly insensible through alcohol, a convenient means of momentarily silencing the inner tumult that had begun to grip them and tighten progressively with every pull of a grenade pin or pistol trigger. Less troubled IRA members, many of whom remained on duty, basked that day in a sense of relaxation most had not known in years. Some gazed in disbelief at some of the city's lingering ruins from 1916 and thought back to the week when the clock of revolution in Dublin had first struck; they thought too of comrades and friends they had lost then and since, whom they themselves would pray for in church pews or toast from Devlin's, Kirwan's, the Gresham and a host of other city hotels and pubs. Phil Shanahan's became packed, as did nearby Hynes', the scene of 'Shankers' Ryan's gruesome shooting, and the many other nearby public houses, such as Phil Sheeran's in Amiens Street, whose proprietors had suffered their own share of raids, shootings and close calls while oiling the machine of revolution by concealing weapons and ammunition, sustaining fugitives and relaying messages.

Cumann na mBan members took to the streets, celebrating their contribution to a war that could not have been prosecuted without their effort and sacrifice. Annie Cooney, incarcerated in Mountjoy following a raid, absorbed the momentous news with thoughts of her former sweetheart Con Colbert, executed in 1916, who had written to her before he was shot, asking her 'to pray for those of us who must die'.[92] She, along with many comrades, had heard the echoing dawn volleys at Kilmainham from a cell there, each like a dagger to their own hearts. On 11 July she heard the more welcome echoes of cheers down prison corridors from comrades, some of whom had stood in ranks close to her back in Kilmainham in 1916, when William Wylie, then a serving army lieutenant as well as a prosecutor, had 'insisted that they reflect on their future behaviour', warning them to be 'good in future, or else'; the condescending warning clearly disregarded, the result evident.[93] Warders also joined cautiously in celebrations, as did their male colleagues in Mountjoy's radial prison wings, still thronged with IRA prisoners and suspects, their own corridors and floors echoing to whoops and shouts of defiance, contrasting with quiet reflection for those they had lost, including the ten executed comrades lying buried in the prison garden. Similar cheers and taunts echoed through Kilmainham Gaol and Arbour Hill, and soon also among the country's 4,454 internees.[94]

Ambulance drivers joined in the festivities, as did firemen, labourers, professionals, priests, drunks, shopkeepers, barmen, hoteliers and the multitude of civilians, from the well-heeled to the impoverished, who had sustained the

Republican prisoners and a prison warder. *(Courtesy of Mercier Archive)*

nationwide organisation that had just achieved what seemed impossible, with the world looking on. Street parties were thrown, bonfires lit. With the curfew lifted, cinemas, cafés and theatres along with the pubs remained open well into the following morning's early hours. IRA intelligence, senior brigade staff, former Squad and ASU members, some of their nerves long since shredded with the perilous, unrelenting and frequently repugnant tasks they daily faced, let off steam in their own idiosyncratic ways, each reflecting in disbelief at how they had actually succeeded. Whilst wary of what might lie ahead, they were, nonetheless, determined to relish the day. Charlie Dalton, overcome, held back tears at the sight of Tricolour flags 'waving from every window'.[95] The day was similarly savoured by most of those, IRA or otherwise, both in Dublin and provincially, who were not as welcoming of the Truce for a variety of reasons – soon to be articulated both forcefully and otherwise – but, regardless, happy to enjoy its respite.

Black and Tan members recruited in Dublin – fourteen per cent of their entire number – concealed misgivings behind bravado.[96] RIC members looked on with anxiety, but also relief, as did their commanders, given that casualty rates among crown forces had doubled in the first six months of the year compared with the last six of 1920. Unionists who viewed the Dáil's inauguration, some mockingly, others apprehensively, took stock with both relief and trepidation, the latter sentiment underpinned by fears of ascendant Catholicism. Lord French and Walter Long, who dismissed that same fateful January inauguration day in the Mansion House when the Union Jack had been taken down in its Round Room to be replaced with the Tricolour, stating that the recently elected members would soon fall in with Westminster lest they lose their ministerial salaries, were far more reticent. Newspaper editors who scoffed at the inauguration, dispatched reports and cables to international colleagues. There were celebrations in London, Manchester and throughout Irish areas in Britain, alongside the relief throughout Ireland at large, including Tipperary, where Seán Treacy's comrades paid tribute to his huge influence on events. Glasses were also raised to Brig. McKee and Peadar Clancy, and to many others similarly toasted back in the capital and elsewhere. Irish America celebrated too; Harry Boland, still an envoy there, foremost amongst them.

Éamon de Valera – spared execution in 1916 because he was considered 'an unimportant schoolmaster unlikely to cause trouble in the future' – met Lloyd George in London three days after the Truce to commence formal discussions and negotiations.[97] Notably, Dublin Castle's *Weekly Summary*, released the same day as the Truce, referred to the IRA not as a murder gang, but as 'the Irish Army', a literary parapraxis that betrayed recognition not just for the IRA and, by association, for the political organisation it had sworn allegiance to in August 1919, Dáil Éireann.[98]

The Dáil's administrators and ministers, having endured the war with astonishing fortitude, now had to deliver the peace. The diminution of the enemy's visible might inevitably provided fertile ground for mistrust, suspicion and canniness within their own ranks, and inner divisions became amplified with the collective enemy restrained. Political realism and the prospect of having to compromise was not prominent in the minds of those looking on in the Round Room on 21 January 1919 when Cathal Brugha heralded: 'We are now done with England!'[99] But the Truce represented an admission by both camps that compromise was firmly on the table. Making this digestible to the diverse composite of interests who coalesced so successfully up to this historic point was another story.

An tÓglách's first post-Truce edition heralded bombastically: 'The guns are silent – but they remain in the hands of the Irish Volunteers. From the military point of view we remain exactly where we are; we have lost no advantage.'[100] Over that momentous Truce night, and during the ensuing days as Dublin,

A small child carries a Tricolour flag following the Truce declared on 11 July 1921. Dublin's war-weary civilians were gripped with joy at the end of hostilities. Onlookers here might have been struck by the sight of such a young child joyously transfixed with the flag of a nation whose independence was similarly youthful and, on that day, similarly blooming. However, it proved similarly fragile and vulnerable. *(Courtesy of the National Library of Ireland)*

and Ireland, strained to return to normality, as thousands of those physically, emotionally and mentally wounded and scarred grappled with the war's after-effects, as families mourned mothers, fathers, brothers, sisters, sons and daughters, some to be remembered in song and verse, others to be quietly forgotten, many from both sides pondered whether the guns would remain silent. Contingency plans were implemented by both sides in preparation for firing in anger once again, which, tragically, they would be. Only this time Irishman would fight Irishman in a brutal and costly civil war. Dublin, and Ireland, was not done with war yet.

Michael Noyk savoured his participation in a great gathering in Vaughan's Hotel soon after the Truce. Harry Boland, since returned from the USA, was there, as was Michael Collins, Gearóid O'Sullivan, Diarmuid O'Hegarty, Liam Mellows, Liam Tobin, Rory O'Connor, Frank Thornton, Ned Broy, Jim McNamara and many others. It was a joyous occasion. Collins and Mellows entertained their comrades with song. Noyk later wrote from hindsight: 'Little did we think that night of the events that were in store before another year had passed. It is well for mortal man that he cannot see into the future'.[101]

CORK CITY LIBRARIES

Epilogue

An enemy who had its heel on our throat

'The battalion was called on to supply a number of officers or suitable men to act as Liaison Officers for the purposes of the Truce. Andy Doyle, Adjutant of the Battalion, was one of those provided by the 2nd Battalion. We also received orders to parade the Companies regularly but not too ostentatiously and to perfect organisation, but not to engage in the acquiring of arms on any large scale. These orders, we were told, were in accordance with the terms of the Truce.

'The 2nd Battalion did plenty of drilling, lecturing on military matters and marching. All was done, as ordered, in an unprovocative way. There was a scarcity of arms and ammunition and, when Stephen Murphy, Captain of B. Company, reported to me that an opportunity had presented itself of importing a considerable quantity of revolvers and ammunition from England, I did not hesitate to accept a loan of £100 – arranged by Stephen Murphy also – from Mr Nagle, North Earl Street, Dublin, for the purpose. Unfortunately nothing was ever received for this money. I saw Mr Nagle later and repaid him £40 of this loan but the Civil War had broken out before the balance could be repaid. The £40 paid back on account was obtained by Stephen Murphy also.

'About mid-August each Battalion was ordered to secure a suitable place for an outdoor camp and to get all the Companies into it. Men working during the day were to go to the camp as soon as they were free, and unemployed men were to remain in camp during the day on guard duty, etc. Blankets and utensils for meals were to be provided by the Volunteers individually. Military exercises were to be practised, lectures arranged and strict discipline maintained. Accompanied by Danny Lyons, Captain of F. Company, I secured a building on lands near Kilmore owned by the Christian Brothers and close to Artane Industrial Schools. As the summer and autumn of 1921 were exceptionally fine, the camp was continued until some time in October, but before that month (as the Christian Brothers were anxious to have for harvest purposes the building occupied by the Battalion) we arranged to go under canvas in lands at Coolock owned by Mr Cullen, a dairyman.

'In addition to practising suitable field exercises, field cooking and sanitation, church and other parades, we prepared for a review of the Battalion by the Chief of Staff, Richard Mulcahy. The 2nd Battalion was reviewed by the Chief of Staff on a Sunday morning in October (1921) at the first camping site near Artane, by arrangement with the Christian Brothers, many of whom, including the local superiors, were present at the function. The Chief of Staff was accompanied by the Assistant Chief of Staff, Eoin O'Duffy, and the Brigade Commandant and his staff were present. The parade was addressed by the Chief of Staff who congratulated all the Volunteers present and, reminding them that our Government was negotiating with an enemy who had its heel on our throat, urged all to perfect themselves in every way as soldiers and to be prepared for a renewal of fighting.

'The review marked the end of the camping period which ended when the Chief of Staff had taken his departure.'[1]

Endnotes

Introduction

1. The official name of Black and Tans was the Royal Irish Constabulary Special Reserve, while the Auxiliaries were the Auxiliary Division Royal Irish Constabulary. Details regarding the formations of these units can be found in Derek Molyneux & Darren Kelly, *Killing at its Very Extreme: Dublin, October 1917–November 1920* (Mercier Press, Cork, 2020), chapters 7–13.

Prologue

1. Paddy Daly is referred to as Paddy O'Daly in his Bureau of Military Witness Statement, as he later altered his surname from Daly to O'Daly. Throughout our works, for consistency, he is referred to as Paddy Daly.
2. William Stapleton, Bureau of Military History Witness Statement (hereafter BMH WS) 882, pp. 34–6.

1 The Lead-in to Bloody Sunday

1. His remains rest today in Tyrrellspass Cemetery, Co. Westmeath.
2. Charles Townshend, *The British Campaign in Ireland 1919–1921: The Development of Political and Military Policies (Oxford* Historical Monographs, Oxford, 1975), p. 125.
3. Arthur Mitchell, *Revolutionary Government in Ireland: Dáil Éireann 1919–1922 (*Gill & Macmillan, Dublin, 1995), p. 239.
4. Mitchell, *Revolutionary Government*, p. 239.
5. Townshend, *The British Campaign in Ireland*, p. 146.
6. Anne Dolan, 'Killing and Bloody Sunday, November 1920', *The Historical Journal*, 49, 3 (2006), p. 790.
7. Molyneux & Kelly, *Killing at its Very Extreme*, p. 333. Hot intelligence comes from recently captured documents for which countermeasures could be rapidly enacted.
8. Pádraig Yeates, *A City in Turmoil: Dublin 1919–1921*, p. 186.
9. *Ibid..*, p. 187.
10. *Ibid..*
11. Harry Colley, BMH WS 1687, p. 49.
12. Michael T. Foy, *Michael Collins's Intelligence War: The Struggle Between the British and the IRA 1919–1921* (Sutton Publishing, Gloucestershire, 2008), p. 156. This page is referenced as it alludes to the fact that Richard Mulcahy never himself denied the allegations during decades of extensive subsequent writings and that his access to UCD's chemistry corridor facilitated such experiments. Mulcahy had studied medicine at UCD before his GHQ demands became too time-consuming to continue. Nevertheless, he was still granted access to its laboratories afterwards.
13. Mitchell *Revolutionary Government*, p. 209.
14. Ronan Fanning, *Fatal Path: British Government and Irish Revolution 1910–1922* (Faber and Faber, London, 2013), p. 241.
15. Richard Bennett, *The Black and Tans* (Four Square Books, London, 1961), p. 97.
16. Mitchell *Revolutionary Government*, p. 215.
17. Various, *Dublin's Fighting Story 1916–21* (Cork, Mercier Press, 2009), p. 286.
18. Foy, *Michael Collins' Intelligence War*, p. 132.
19. Lily Mernin, BMH WS 441, p. 2.
20. *Ibid..*

21. Foy, *Michael Collins' Intelligence War*, p. 121.
22. W. H. Kautt, *Ambushes and Armour: The Irish Rebellion 1919–1921* (Irish Academic Press, Dublin, 2011), p. 231.
23. Lily Mernin, BMH WS 441, p. 3.
24. Fanning, *Fatal Path*, p. 242.
25. Yeates, *A City in Turmoil*, p. 185.
26. *The Irish Times*, 27 August 2011.
27. Charles Townshend, The Irish Rail Strike of 1920: Industrial Action and Civil Resistance in the Struggle for Independence (Cambridge University Press, Cambridge, 1979), p. 279.
28. Bennett, *The Black and Tans*, p. 100.
29. James Gleeson, *Bloody Sunday* (Four Square Books, London, 1963), p. 117.
30. Frank Thornton, BMH WS 615, p. 24.
31. Gleeson, *Bloody Sunday*, p. 117.
32. T. Ryle Dwyer, *The Squad and the Intelligence Operations of Michael Collins* (Mercier Press, Cork, 2005), p. 168.
33. Patrick O'Daly, BMH WS 387, p. 43.
34. May Moran, *Executed for Ireland: The Patrick Moran Story* (Mercier Press, Cork, 2010), p. 105.
35. Dwyer, *The Squad*, p. 171.
36. Yeates, *A City in Turmoil*, p. 198.
37. Cormac Ó Comhraí & Stiofán Ó Comhraí, *Peadar Clancy*: Easter Rising Hero, Bloody Sunday Martyr (Cranny Publications, Galway, 2016), p. 161.
38. Various, *Dublin's Fighting Story 1916–21*, p. 288.
39. Paul O'Brien, *Havoc: The Auxiliaries in Ireland's War of Independence* (The Collins Press, Cork, 2017), pp. 78–9.

2 Bloody Sunday: Assassinations

1. http://www.bloodysunday.co.uk/addresses/morehampton-rd/morehampton-rd.html.
2. *Ibid.*.
3. Daniel McDonnell, BMH WS 486, p. 10; Joseph Dolan, BMH WS 663, p. 10; http://www.bloodysunday.co.uk/addresses/ranelagh-rd/ranelagh-rd.html; C. S. Andrews, *Dublin Made Me* (The Lilliput Press, Dublin, 2001).
4. http://www.bloodysunday.co.uk/addresses/eastwood-hotel/eastwood-hotel.html.
5. Bennett, *The Black and Tans*, p. 104.
6. Gleeson, *Bloody Sunday*, p. 127.
7. http://www.bloodysunday.co.uk/addresses/earlsfort-ter/earlsfort-terrace.html.
8. Dwyer, *The Squad*, p. 172.
9. Dolan, 'Killing and Bloody Sunday', p. 796.
10. Charles Dalton, BMH WS 434, p. 20.
11. *Ibid.*.
12. Caroline Woodcock, *An Officer's Wife in Ireland* (Parkgate Publications Ltd, London, 1994), p. 63.
13. Dolan, 'Killing and Bloody Sunday', p. 791.
14. Woodcock, *An Officer's Wife in Ireland*, p. 66.
15. Dolan, 'Killing and Bloody Sunday', p. 791.
16. Gleeson, *Bloody Sunday*, p. 130.
17. Dolan, 'Killing and Bloody Sunday', p. 799.
18. *Ibid.*.
19. William Stapleton, BMH WS 822, p. 29.
20. Joe Leonard, BMH WS 547, p. 12.
21. Vincent Byrne, BMH WS 423, p. 54.
22. Michael Lawless, BMH WS 727, p. 3.
23. Frank Saurin, BMH WS 715, p. 7.

24. Vincent Byrne, BMH WS 423, p. 54.
25. Thomas Duffy, BMH WS 1409, p. 1.
26. Michael Lawless, BMH WS 727, pp. 3–4.
27. Vincent Byrne, BMH WS 423, p. 55.
28. *Ibid.*.
29. Dominic Price, *We Bled Together: Michael Collins, the Squad and the Dublin Brigade* (The Collins Press, Cork, 2017), p. 166.
30. *Ibid.*.
31. http://www.bloodysunday.co.uk/murdered-men/angliss.html.
32. Dwyer, *The Squad*, p. 179.
33. *Ibid.*, p. 181.
34. Gleeson, *Bloody Sunday*, p. 129.
35. James Cahill, BMH WS 503, p. 7.
36. *Ibid.*.
37. Patrick McCormack's killing has remained controversial, since his identification as a spy was queried by his mother, Kate, in March 1922 in correspondence with Richard Mulcahy. Mulcahy, conferring with Michael Collins at the time, told Kate that McCormack had been shot because he was an enemy officer, but not necessarily a spy. However, the weight of evidence required by Cathal Brugha and the Army Council before authorising the killings requires consideration – only those with enough evidence against them were authorised as targets. Added to this was the fact that McCormack had been staying at the Gresham since September, while his family resided elsewhere in Ireland, and that his behaviour, such as the hours he kept, mirrored that of other targeted spies. Notably, McCormack had left the British Army some time previously, but his subsequent employment in Egypt had positioned him in an area known for the prevalence of British Secret Service personnel. Furthermore, Mark Sturgis' diary for 21 November 1920 refers to two British Secret Service agents killed in the Gresham. Nevertheless, his position remains inconclusive.

3 Bloody Sunday: Reprisals

1. Patrick Lawson, BMH WS 667, p. 7.
2. Price, *We Bled Together*, p. 171.
3. Frank O'Connor, *The Big Fellow* (Poolbeg Press Ltd, Dublin, 1991), p. 125.
4. *Ibid.*.
5. Patrick McCrea, BMH WS 413, p. 19.
6. *Ibid.*, p. 20.
7. Various, *Dublin's Fighting Story 1916–21*, p. 290.
8. Foy, *Michael Collins' Intelligence War*, p. 120.
9. Yeates, *A City in Turmoil*, p. 194.
10. *Ibid.*.
11. Ó Comhraí & Ó Comhraí, *Peadar Clancy*, p. 165.
12. Michael Foley, *The Bloodied Field: Croke Park. Sunday 21 November 1920* (O'Brien Press, Dublin, 2014), p. 161.
13. *Ibid.*, p. 169.
14. *Ibid.*.
15. Today known as Hill 16.
16. Foley, *The Bloodied Field*, p. 170.
17. Harry Colley, BMH WS 1687, p. 53.
18. *Ibid.*, p. 54.
19. *Ibid.*, p. 55.
20. Foley, *The Bloodied Field*, p. 179.
21. Thomas Ryan, BMH WS 783, p. 35.
22. *Ibid.*, p. 36.
23. William Stapleton, BMH WS 822, p. 30.

24. Thomas Ryan, BMH WS 783, p. 36.
25. John F. Shouldice, BMH WS 679, p. 28.
26. Terence de Vere White, *Kevin O'Higgins* (Anvil Books, Kerry, 1948), p. 44.
27. Those killed were as follows: James Burke (44), Windy Arbour, Dublin – crushed; Daniel Carroll (30), Tipperary – shot; James Teehan (26), Dublin – crushed; Joseph Traynor (21), IRA Volunteer, Dublin – shot; Tom Hogan (19), Limerick – shot; James Matthews (38), Dublin – crushed; Patrick O'Dowd (57), Dublin – shot; William Robinson (11), Dublin – shot; Mick Hogan (24), IRA Volunteer, Tipperary – shot; Thomas Ryan (27), Wexford – shot; Jane Boyle (28), Dublin – shot; John William Scott (14), Dublin – shot; Jerome O'Leary (10), Dublin – shot; Michael Feery (40), Dublin – impaled and bled to death.
28. Oscar Traynor, BMH WS 340, p. 54.
29. David Neligan, BMH WS 380, p. 9.
30. *Ibid.*.
31. Patrick McCrea, BMH WS 413, p. 20.
32. Foley, *The Bloodied Field*, p. 192.
33. John F. Shouldice, BMH WS 679, p. 29.
34. Yeates, *A City in Turmoil*, p. 198.
35. Mitchell, *Revolutionary Government* in Ireland, p. 216.
36. Foley, *The Bloodied Field*, p. 199.
37. Bennett, *The Black and Tans*, p. 107.
38. Foy, *Michael Collins' Intelligence War*, p. 150.
39. Yeates, *A City in Turmoil*, p. 198.
40. Gleeson, *Bloody Sunday*, p. 150.
41. *Ibid.*.
42. Ó Comhraí & Ó Comhraí, *Peadar Clancy*, p. 166.
43. Michael Lynch, BMH WS 511, p. 63.
44. Various, *Dublin's Fighting Story 1916–21*, p. 292.

4 Bloody Sunday: Aftermath

1. Dolan, 'Killing and Bloody Sunday', p. 798.
2. de Vere White, *Kevin O'Higgins*, p. 45.
3. *Ibid.*., p. 44.
4. Terence Brown, *The Irish Times: 150 Years of Influence* (Bloomsbury, London, 2015), p. 99.
5. Mitchell, *Revolutionary Government* in Ireland, p. 216.
6. *Ibid.*.
7. O'Connor, *The Big Fellow*, p. 126.
8. Foy, *Michael Collins' Intelligence War*, p. 66.
9. Pte Bernard Flood, Derek Molyneux's great-grandfather, formerly of the Royal Irish Rifles, is referred to in this case.
10. Patrick Moylett, BMH WS 767, p. 67.
11. https://www.irishexaminer.com/sport/gaa/arid-40086521.html.
12. Patrick Moylett, BMH WS 767, pp. 67–8.
13. Patrick McCrea, BMH WS 413, p. 21.
14. *Ibid.*., p. 22.
15. O'Connor, *The Big Fellow*, p. 127.
16. Meda Ryan, *Michael Collins and the Women Who Spied For Ireland* (Mercier Press, Cork, 2006), p. 71.
17. Dwyer, *The Squad*, p. 194.
18. Foley, *The Bloodied Field*, p. 229.
19. Yeates, *A City in Turmoil*, p. 204.
20. Foley, *The Bloodied Field*, p. 227.
21. de Vere White, *Kevin O'Higgins*, p .45.
22. Fanning, *Fatal Path*, p. 245.

23. Patrick O'Daly, BMH WS 387, pp. 49–50.
24. *Ibid.*., p. 51.
25. *Ibid.*., pp. 51–2.
26. Tim Pat Coogan, *Michael Collins: A Biography* (Arrow Books, London, 1991), p. 187.
27. *The Irish Times*, 23 December 2017.
28. Oscar Traynor, BMH WS 340, p. 33.
29. Townshend, *The British Campaign in Ireland 1919–1921*, p. 148.
30. O'Connor, *The Big Fellow*, p. 136.
31. Patrick O'Daly, BMH WS 387, p. 52.
32. *Ibid.*.
33. Townshend, *The British Campaign in Ireland 1919–1921*, p. 134.
34. *Ibid.*.
35. Patrick Moylett, BMH WS 767, pp. 71–2.
36. Mitchell, *Revolutionary Government* in Ireland, p. 220.

5 Divisions, Peace Talks, Raids and Continued Killings

1. Richard Walsh, BMH WS 400, p. 141.
2. Geraldine Dillon, BMH WS 424, p. 25.
3. Gearóid Ua h-Uallachain, BMH WS 336, p. 30.
4. Tim Pat Coogan, *De Valera: Long Fellow, Long Shadow* (Arrow Books, London, 1993), p. 203.
5. Mitchell, *Revolutionary Government* in Ireland, p. 220.
6. Coogan, *De Valera*, p. 202.
7. Denis Carroll, *They Have Fooled You Again: Michael O'Flanagan (1876–1942), Priest, Republican, Social Critic* (The Columba Press, Dublin, 2016), p. 130.
8. Mitchell, *Revolutionary Government* in Ireland, p. 221.
9. Coogan, *Michael Collins*, p. 195.
10. *Ibid.*., p. 196.
11. Bennett, *The Black and Tans*, p. 117.
12. Mitchell, *Revolutionary Government* in Ireland, p. 222.
13. Patrick Moylett, BMH WS 767, p. 76.
14. They would be kept secret for eighty years.
15. Tim Carey, ' Bloody Sunday 1920: New Evidence', *History Ireland,* Vol. 11, Issue 2 (Summer 2003).
16. Peter Hart (ed.), *British Intelligence in Ireland, 1920–21: The Final Reports, Irish Narratives series* (Cork University Press, Cork, 2011), p. 84.
17. Price, *We Bled Together*, p. 189.
18. Yeates, *A City in Turmoil*, p. 206.
19. Joseph V. Lawless, BMH WS 1043, p. 354.
20. *Ibid.*.
21. Later to become the Irish National Anthem.
22. Oscar Traynor, BMH WS 340, p. 33.
23. Thomas Newell, BMH WS 698, p. 4.
24. Price, *We Bled Together*, p. 191.
25. http://www.theauxiliaries.com/INCIDENTS/cork-burning/cork-burning.html.
26. *Ibid.*.
27. Bennett, *The Black and Tans*, p. 120.
28. Patrick McHugh, BMH WS 664, p. 22.
29. Harry Colley, BMH WS 1687, p. 58.
30. http://theauxiliaries.com/INCIDENTS/dublin-1920-dec-post/post-office-dec.html.
31. Townshend, *The British Campaign in Ireland 1919–1921*, p. 160.
32. Bennett, *The Black and Tans*, p. 121.
33. Mitchell, *Revolutionary Government* in Ireland, p. 224.

34. Bennett, *The Black and Tans*, p. 125.
35. Edward J. Kelliher, BMH WS 477, p. 2.
36. *Ibid.*; Joseph Leonard, BMH WS 547, p. 13; Joseph Byrne, BMH WS 461, p. 5.
37. https://www.cairogang.com/police-killed/o-sullivan-1921-jan/o-sullivan.html.
38. *Ibid.*.

6 Government of Ireland Act, Active Service Unit.

1. D. M. Leeson, *The Black & Tans: British Police and Auxiliaries in The Irish War of Independence* (Oxford University Press, Oxford, 2013), p. 195.
2. Linda Connolly, 'Towards a Further Understanding of the Violence Experienced by Women in the Irish Revolution', Maynooth University Social Sciences Institute, working paper series, no. 7 (Maynooth: Maynooth University, January, 2019), p. 19.
3. Bennett, *The Black and Tans*, p. 128.
4. Price, *We Bled Together*, p. 102.
5. Kathleen Napoli-McKenna, BMH WS 643, pp. 7–8.
6. *Ibid.*, p. 7.
7. Yeates, *A City in Turmoil*, p. 212.
8. Coogan, *Michael Collins*, p. 187.
9. https://www.dail100.ie/en/long-reads/eamon-de-valera-in-america/.
10. Coogan, *De Valera*, p. 196.
11. Mitchell, *Revolutionary Government* in Ireland, p. 226.
12. John Ainsworth, 'The Black & Tans and Auxiliaries in Ireland, 1920–1921: Their Origins, Roles and Legacy' (Queensland History Teachers' Association, Brisbane, Australia, May 2001), p. 4.
13. O'Connor, *The Big Fellow*, p. 141.
14. James Doyle, BMH WS 771, p. 3.
15. Coogan, *Michael Collins*, p. 166.
16. Foy, *Michael Collins' Intelligence War*, p. 139.
17. Price, *We Bled Together*, p. 189.
18. Gearóid Ua h-Uallachain, BMH WS 336, pp. 21–4.
19. Townshend, *The British Campaign in Ireland 1919–1921*, p. 159.
20. Bennett, *The Black and Tans*, p. 126.
21. Patrick J. O'Connor, BMH WS 608, p. 7.
22. James Cahill, BMH WS 503, p. 9.
23. Joseph Gilhooly, BMH WS 390, p. 4.
24. The foreign division of the Secret Service Bureau.
25. http://www.bloodysunday.co.uk/castle-intelligence/britishintelligence.html.
26. Coogan, *Michael Collins*, p. 199.
27. Mike Rast, 'Tactics, Politics and Propaganda in The Irish War of Independence, 1917–1921' (Georgia State University, USA, 2011), p. 98. Available at https://scholarworks.gsu.edu/cgi/viewcontent.cgi?article=1045&context=history_theses.
28. Kautt, *Ambushes and Armour*, p. 224.
29. Bennett, *The Black and Tans*, p. 129.
30. A quote from Frederick the Great, eighteenth-century Prussian emperor.
31. Diarmuid Ferriter, *A Nation and Not a Rabble: The Irish Revolution 1913–1923* (Profile Books, London, 2015), p. 197.
32. Eileen MacCarvill, BMH WS 1752, p. 7.
33. Eamon Broy, BMH WS 1280, p. 104.
34. *Ibid.*, pp. 106–7.
35. Bennett, *The Black and Tans*, p. 130.
36. Coogan, *Michael Collins*, p. 170.
37. Frank Thornton, BMH WS 615, p. 34.
38. James Hughes, BMH WS 535, p. 11.

39. Thomas Newell, BMH WS 698, p. 5.
40. *Ibid.*.
41. Charles Dalton, BMH WS 434, p. 24.
42. Thomas Newell, BMH WS 698, p. 6.
43. Vincent Byrne, BMH WS 423, p. 58.
44. *Ibid.*.
45. Thomas Newell, BMH WS 698, p. 6.
46. Charles Dalton, BMH WS 434, p. 25.
47. Thomas Newell, BMH WS 698, p. 7.
48. *Ibid.*.
49. Eamon Broy, BMH WS 1280, p. 107.
50. *Ibid.*, p. 108.
51. Mitchell, *Revolutionary Government* in Ireland, p. 225.
52. James Harpur, BMH WS 536, p. 5.
53. The information about where Flood would have relayed these orders comes from James Carrigan, BMH WS 613, p. 9.
54. Christopher Fitzsimons, BMH WS 581, pp. 6–7; Joseph Gilhooly, BMH WS 390, p. 4.
55. Tom McGrath, pension application, WMSP34REF21184, p. 100.
56. https://theauxiliaries.com/INCIDENTS/dublin-1921-jan-12-grenade/bomb-jan-1921.html.
57. Christopher Fitzsimons, BMH WS 581, p. 7.
58. Joseph Gilhooly, BMH WS 390, p. 5.
59. https://theauxiliaries.com/INCIDENTS/dublin-1921-jan-12-grenade/bomb-jan-1921.html.
60. Joseph Gilhooly, BMH WS 390, p. 5.
61. George Nolan, BMH WS 596, p. 4.
62. *Ibid.*.
63. James Harpur, BMH WS 536, p. 6.
64. *Ibid.*; George Nolan, BMH WS 596, p. 4.
65. Yeates, *A City in Turmoil*, p. 230.
66. Oscar Traynor, BMH WS 340, pp. 67–8.
67. The Earl of Longford & Thomas P. O'Neill, *Eamon De Valera* (Arrow Books, London, 1974), p. 123.
68. John McCann, *War by the Irish* (The Kerryman Ltd, Tralee, 1946), p. 206.
69. Oscar Traynor, BMH WS 340, p. 68.
70. McCann, *War by the Irish*, p. 206.
71. Liz Gillis, *May 25: Burning of the Custom House 1921* (Kilmainham Tales Teo, Dublin, 2017), p. 75.
72. McCann, *War by the Irish*, p. 206.
73. Maryann Gialanella Valiulis, *Portrait of a Revolutionary: General Richard Mulcahy and the Founding of the Irish Free State* (Irish Academic Press, Dublin, 1993), p. 77.
74. Oscar Traynor, BMH WS 340, p. 69.

7 Attacks Intensify, Dáil Reflects, IRA Setbacks and Successes

1. Townshend, *The British Campaign in Ireland 1919–1921*, p. 155.
2. Patrick J. Brennan, BMH WS 1773, p. 15.
3. Joseph O'Carroll, BMH WS 728, p. 4.
4. Joseph O'Connor, BMH WS 487, p. 40.
5. Dermot O'Sullivan, BMH WS 508, p. 7.
6. Joseph Gilhooly, BMH WS 390, p. 5.
7. Dermot O'Sullivan, BMH WS 508, p. 8.
8. *Ibid.*.
9. Price, *We Bled Together*, p. 202.

10. Dermot O'Sullivan, BMH WS 508, p. 9.
11. Harry Colley, BMH WS 1687, p. 63.
12. Dermot O'Sullivan, BMH WS 508, p. 9.
13. https://www.oireachtas.ie/en/debates/debate/dail/1921-01-25/4/. All following information and quotes regarding this Dáil meeting are taken from this source.
14. https://www.oireachtas.ie/en/debates/debate/dail/1921-01-25/10/.
15. https://www.oireachtas.ie/en/debates/debate/dail/1921-01-25/4/.
16. https://www.oireachtas.ie/en/debates/debate/dail/1921-01-25/8/.
17. https://www.oireachtas.ie/en/debates/debate/dail/1921-01-25/4/.
18. Coogan, *De Valera*, p. 219.
19. Coogan, *Michael Collins*, p. 200.
20. Coogan, *De Valera*, p. 201.
21. Eamon Broy, BMH WS 1280, p. 109.
22. Frank Thornton, BMH WS 615, pp. 41–2.
23. Joseph Dolan, BMH WS 663, p. 4.
24. *Ibid.*.
25. Joseph Dolan, BMH WS 663, p. 4.
26. Charles Dalton, BMH WS 434, p. 10.
27. http://www.bloodysunday.co.uk/shot-by-ira-as- spies/doran/doran.html.
28. Joseph Dolan, BMH WS 663, p. 4.
29. *Ibid.*.
30. http://www.bloodysunday.co.uk/shot-by-ira-as- spies/doran/doran.html.
31. William Stapleton, BMH WS 822, p. 37.
32. William Sheehan, *Fighting for Dublin: The British Battle for Dublin 1919–1921 (The Collins Press, Cork, 2007)*, p. 88.
33. Kautt, *Ambushes and Armour*, p. 201.
34. C. S. Andrews, *Dublin Made Me* (The Lilliput Press, Dublin, 2001), p. 174.
35. Joseph V. Lawless, BMH WS 1043, p. 372.
36. Daithí Ó Corráin, '"A most public spirited and unselfish man": The Career and Contribution of Colonel Maurice Moore, 1854–1939', *Studia Hibernica*, 40 (2014), p. 119.
37. Mitchell, *Revolutionary Government* in Ireland, p. 272.
38. Fanning, *Fatal Path*, p. 247.
39. *Ibid.*., p. 248.
40. Irish Times Limited, *1912 Ulster and Home Rule's Resistance* (Irish Times Books, 2015), p. 19.

8 Vengeance, Shoot-outs, Escape

1. http://www.millstreet.ie/blog/2014/02/01/the- execution-of-captain-con-murphy.
2. Maurice Meade, BMH WS 891, p. 27.
3. Thomas L. Flood, Pension Application, WM24SP1550, p. 34.
4. Joseph Gilhooly, BMH WS 390, p. 6; James Michael Heery, pension application, WMSP34REF3730, p. 30.
5. Joseph Gilhooly, BMH WS 390, p. 6.
6. *Ibid.*.
7. *Ibid.*.
8. Foy, *Michael Collins' Intelligence War*, p. 176.
9. Patrick Kennedy, BMH WS 499, p. 6.
10. *Ibid.*., p. 7.
11. Bernard Byrne, BMH WS 631, p. 20.
12. William Stapleton, BMH WS 822, pp. 38–9.
13. http://www.bloodysunday.co.uk/shot-by-ira-as- spies/ryan/ryan.html.
14. William Stapleton, BMH WS 822, p. 39.
15. http://www.bloodysunday.co.uk/castle-intelligence/thomson/ryan/ryan.html.

16. George Nolan, BMH WS 596, p. 12.
17. http://www.irishmedals.ie/Civilians-Killed-WOI.php.
18. Kautt, *Ambushes and Armour*, p. 202.
19. *Ibid.*.
20. George Nolan, BMH WS 596, p. 12.
21. http://www.bloodysunday.co.uk/castle-intelligence/thomson/fovargue/fovargue.html.
22. Frank Thornton, BMH WS 615, p. 49.
23. *Ibid.*.
24. *Ibid.*, p. 50.
25. Patrick Kearney, BMH WS 868, p. 6.
26. *Ibid.*, p. 7.
27. Frank Thornton, BMH WS 615, p. 50.
28. Kautt, *Ambushes and Armour*, p. 203.
29. *Ibid.*, p. 204.
30. Charles Dalton, BMH WS 434, p. 28; Vincent Byrne, BMH WS 423, p. 62.
31. Daniel McDonnell, BMH WS 486, p. 20.
32. *Ibid.*.
33. Frank Thornton, BMH WS 615, p. 50; Vincent Byrne, BMH WS 423, pp. 62–62(A).
34. Kautt, *Ambushes and Armour*, p. 204.
35. Vincent Byrne, BMH WS 423, p. 63.
36. Yeates, *A City in Turmoil*, p. 231.
37. *Ibid.*, p. 251.
38. https://theauxiliaries.com/INCIDENTS/drumcondra/drumcondra.html.
39. https://api.parliament.uk/historic-hansard/commons/1921/apr/18/lieut-commander-fry.
40. https://theauxiliaries.com/INCIDENTS/drumcondra/drumcondra.html.
41. Dwyer, *The Squad*, p. 222.
42. https://theauxiliaries.com/INCIDENTS/drumcondra/drumcondra.html.
43. Fanning, *Fatal Path*, p. 247.
44. Townshend, *The British Campaign in Ireland 1919–1921*, p. 165.
45. *Ibid.*, p. 163.
46. Derek Molyneux & Darren Kelly, *Those of Us Who Must Die: Execution, Exile and Revival after the Easter Rising* (The Collins Press, Cork, 2017), p. 23. The Bastille, in Paris, served as a prison in which both King Louis XV and XVI housed political prisoners during the eighteenth century, until it was stormed and destroyed during the French Revolution of 1789.
47. Seán Enright, *After the Rising: Soldiers, Lawyers and Trials of the Irish Revolution* (Merrion Press, Kildare, 2016), p. 154.
48. Vincent Rice, BMH WS 843, p. 6.
49. *Ibid.*, p. 4.
50. Harry Colley, BMH WS 1687, p. 60.
51. Patrick Kennedy, BMH WS 499, pp. 7–8. Kennedy erroneously refers to one of the friendly soldiers as being named Storkman.
52. Enright, *After the Rising*, p. 153.
53. Woodcock, *An Officer's Wife in Ireland*, pp. 83–4.
54. Enright, *After the Rising*, p. 158.
55. Moran, *Executed for Ireland*, p. 104.
56. Enright, *After the Rising*, p. 152.
57. Ernie O'Malley, *On Another Man's Wound* (Mercier Press, Cork, 2013), p. 335.
58. *Ibid.*.
59. Moran, *Executed for Ireland*, p. 114.
60. Niamh O'Sullivan, *Every Dark Hour: A History of Kilmainham Gaol* (Liberties Press, Dublin, 2007). This is taken from the Kindle edition, page numbers unavailable.

9 Pandemonium, Intelligence Blunders, Courts Martial

1. Moran, *Executed for Ireland,* p. 91.
2. Enright, *After the Rising,* p. 159.
3. Moran, *Executed for Ireland,* p. 111.
4. Lorcan Collins, *Ireland's War of Independence 1919–21: The IRA's Guerrilla Campaign* (O'Brien Press, Dublin, 2019), p. 211.
5. Moran, *Executed for Ireland,* p. 117.
6. Sheehan, *Fighting for Dublin,* p. 45.
7. Foy, *Michael Collins' Intelligence War,* p. 141.
8. Michael Noyk, BMH WS 707, p. 69.
9. Christopher Fitzsimons, BMH WS 581, p. 8.
10. *Ibid..*
11. Patrick O'Connor, BMH WS 608, pp. 10–11.
12. Christopher Fitzsimons, BMH WS 581, p. 8.
13. Eamon Broy, BMH WS 1280, p. 112.
14. David Neligan, BMH WS 380, p. 16.
15. *Ibid..*, p. 17.
16. O'Connor, *The Big Fellow,* p. 135.
17. *Ibid..*
18. Mitchell, *Revolutionary Government*, p. 274.
19. O'Connor, *The Big Fellow,* p. 136.
20. Mitchell, *Revolutionary Government*, p. 263.
21. *Ibid..*, p. 264.
22. Joseph Leonard, BMH WS 547, p. 19.
23. Edward J. Kelliher, BMH WS 477, p. 3.
24. James Slattery, BMH WS 445, pp. 10–11.
25. Bernard Byrne, BMH WS 631, pp. 22–3.
26. *Ibid..*, p. 23.
27. William Stapleton, BMH WS 822, p. 47.
28. Dermot O'Sullivan, BMH WS 508, p. 13.
29. Michael Noyk, BMH WS 707, p. 38.
30. Enright, *After the Rising,* p. 162.
31. *Ibid..*, p. 163.
32. Michael Noyk, BMH WS 707, p. 38.
33. Reynolds' cover was blown several months later and he was suspended from service.
34. Dermot O'Sullivan, BMH WS 508, p. 13.
35. *Ibid..*
36. Bennett, *The Black and Tans,* p. 148.
37. *Report of the Labour Commission to Ireland* (1921), Robarts Collection, Toronto, p. 8.
38. Townshend, *The British Campaign in Ireland 1919–1921,* p. 158. Regular RIC strength at this point was only seventy-five per cent of what it had been two years earlier.
39. Collins, *Ireland's War of Independence 1919–21,* p. 209.
40. https://www.historyireland.com/volume-23/the-case-of-mrs-lindsay/.
41. Frank Thornton, BMH WS 615, p. 30.
42. *Ibid..*, p. 31.
43. Coogan, *Michael Collins,* p. 179.
44. O'Connor, *The Big Fellow,* p. 141.
45. Foy, *Michael Collins' Intelligence War,* p. 254.
46. Patrick O'Connor, BMH WS 608, p. 9.
47. *Ibid..*
48. Kieran E. McMullen, *Weapons of The Irish War of Independence* (Kilmainham Tales Teo, Dublin, 2020), p. 152.
49. Patrick O'Connor, BMH WS 608, p. 10.

50. Joseph Gilhooly, BMH WS 390, p. 7.
51. George White, BMH WS 956, p. 7.
52. Patrick O'Connor, BMH WS 608, p. 10.
53. Robert Purcell, BMH WS 573, p. 1.
54. Townshend, *The British Campaign in Ireland 1919–1921*, p. 157.
55. Dermot O'Sullivan, BMH WS 508, p. 14.
56. *Ibid.*.
57. Brian Hughes, '"Make the Terror Behind Greater Than the Terror in Front?" Internal Discipline, Forced Participation, and the I.R.A. 1919–1921', *Irish Historical Studies,* Vol. 42, Issue 161 (May 2018). Available at https://dspace.mic.ul.ie/handle/10395/2444, see p. 9.
58. https://www.oireachtas.ie/en/debates/debate/dail/1921-03-11/16/.
59. https://www.oireachtas.ie/en/debates/debate/dail/1921-03-11/32/.
60. *Ibid.*.
61. David McCulllagh, *De Valera, Volume 1: Rise 1182–1932* (Gill Books, Dublin, 2017), p. 200.
62. https://www.oireachtas.ie/en/debates/debate/dail/1921-03-11/33/.

10 Executions, Mayhem

1. Gleeson, *Bloody Sunday*, p. 175.
2. Yeates, *A City in Turmoil*, p. 234.
3. Moran, *Executed for Ireland*, p. 147.
4. Yeates, *A City in Turmoil*, p. 234.
5. Bennett, *The Black and Tans*, p. 154
6. Bernard Byrne, BMH WS 631, p. 28. Byrne mistakenly calls the executioner Pierrepoint, the name of Ellis' predecessor in the job, and also the name of the executioner around the time this WS would have been recorded.
7. Moran, *Executed for Ireland*, p. 156.
8. http://www.capitalpunishmentuk.org/ireland.html.
9. Ellis had also executed Roger Casement in London's Pentonville Prison on 3 August 1916.
10. Moran, *Executed for Ireland*, p. 157.
11. *Ibid.*., p. 158.
12. Molyneux & Kelly, *Killing at its Very Extreme*, p. 72.
13. Moran, *Executed for Ireland*, p. 158.
14. *The Irish Times*, 25 July 2018.
15. Yeates, *A City in Turmoil*, p. 235.
16. Moran, *Executed for Ireland*, p. 157.
17. Yeates, *A City in Turmoil*, p. 235.
18. *Ibid.*.
19. Pádraig O'Connor, BMH WS 813, pp. 19–20.
20. Joseph O'Connor, BMH WS 487, p. 48.
21. Kautt, *Ambushes and Armour*, p. 207.
22. *Ibid.*.
23. Joseph O'Connor, BMH WS 487, p. 49.
24. *Ibid.*.; Kautt, *Ambushes and Armour*, p. 207.
25. Kautt, *Ambushes and Armour*, p. 207.
26. O'Brien, *Havoc*, p. 153. The reference in question applies to a different engagement. Nonetheless, preparations as such applied throughout the ADRIC.
27. John Donnelly, BMH WS 626, p. 3. Donnelly mistakenly calls David Kelly by the name Tom, David's brother, who was also involved in the movement.
28. *Ibid.*.
29. *Ibid.*.
30. Yeates, *A City in Turmoil*, p. 237.

31. http://www.irishmedals.ie/IRA-Killed.php.
32. Frank Thornton, BMH WS 615, p. 49.
33. Coogan, *Michael Collins*, p. 174.
34. *Ibid.*.
35. Mitchell, *Revolutionary Government* in Ireland, p. 231.
36. Kautt, *Ambushes and Armour*, p. 209.
37. James Cahill, BMH WS 503, p. 11.
38. *Ibid.*., p. 12.
39. Joseph O'Connor, BMH WS 487, p. 40.
40. William Stapleton, BMH WS 822, pp. 49–54.
41. Eamon Broy, BMH WS 1280, p. 114.
42. *Ibid.*., p. 116.
43. Augustine Murphy, pension application, MSP 1D192, pp. 54, 104.
44. *Ibid.*., p. 86.
45. Patrick J. Mullen, BMH WS 621, pp. 7–8.
46. Piaras Béaslaí, *Michael Collins and the Making of a New Ireland*, Vol. 2 (Harper & Brothers Publishers, New York, 1926), p. 96.
47. Vincent Byrne, BMH WS 423, p. 69; Daniel McDonnell, BMH WS 486, p. 13.
48. Vincent Byrne, BMH WS 423, p. 69.
49. Charles Dalton, BMH WS 434, p. 10.
50. Daniel McDonnell, BMH WS 486, p. 14.
51. *Ibid.*.
52. Bernard Byrne, BMH WS 631, p. 29.
53. Patrick O'Daly, BMH WS 387, p. 53.
54. Daniel McDonnell, BMH WS 486, p. 15.
55. Patrick O'Daly, BMH WS 387, p. 64.
56. George White, BMH WS 956, p. 10.
57. *Ibid.*.
58. Price, *We Bled Together*, p. 218.
59. Pádraig O'Connor, BMH WS 813, p. 16.
60. *Ibid.*., p. 22.
61. *Ibid.*.
62. Townshend, *The British Campaign in Ireland 1919–1921*, p. 175.
63. Frank Henderson, BMH WS 821, pp. 97–8.
64. Frank Thornton, BMH WS 615, pp. 19–20.
65. Kathleen Napoli-McKenna, BMH WS 643, p. 7.
66. Mitchell, *Revolutionary Government* in Ireland, p. 252.
67. Coogan, *De Valera*, p. 206; Bennett, *The Black and Tans*, p. 157. The passage appears in parts in both publications.
68. Bennett, *The Black and Tans*, p. 158.
69. *Ibid.*., p. 156.
70. Fanning, *Fatal Path*, p. 250.
71. Townshend, *The British Campaign in Ireland 1919–1921*, p. 175.
72. *Ibid.*., p. 171.
73. O'Connor, *The Big Fellow*, p. 143.
74. Laurence Nugent, BMH WS 907, p. 227.
75. Coogan, *Michael Collins*, p. 168.
76. *Ibid.*.
77. *Ibid.*. 'Brass Hat' is a slang term for a high-ranking military officer.
78. Bernard Nolan, BMH WS 844, p. 6.
79. *Ibid.*., p. 7.
80. *Ibid.*., p. 9.
81. Pádraig O'Connor, BMH WS 813, p. 24.

82. Mitchell, *Revolutionary Government* in Ireland, p. 277. Quotation marks are as they appear in Mitchell's text.
83. Carl W. Ackerman, 'Janus-headed Ireland', *Atlantic Monthly* (June 1922), p. 808.
84. Molyneux & Kelly, *Killing at its Very Extreme*, p. 68.
85. Mike Rast, 'Tactics, Politics and Propaganda in *The Irish War of Independence*, 1917–1921' (thesis, Georgia State University, USA, 2011), p. 128.
86. Moran, *Executed for Ireland*, p. 147.
87. Price, *We Bled Together*, p. 212.
88. Ackerman, 'Janus-headed Ireland', p. 807.
89. Meghan Elizabeth Menard, 'Reporting for the State Department: Carl W. Ackerman's Cooperation with Government during WW1' (Louisiana State University and Agricultural and Mechanical College, USA, 2015), p. 46.
90. Foy, *Michael Collins' Intelligence War*, p. 270.

11 Frustration, Pressure and Disaster for Dublin Brigade

1. Oscar Traynor, BMH WS 340, p. 69.
2. *Ibid.*.
3. Harry Colley, BMH WS 1687, p. 77.
4. https://tullowhistorian.wordpress.com/2016/11/09/thomas-traynor-1882-1921-tullows-executed-patriot/comment-page-1/#_ftnref48.
5. Michael Noyk, BMH WS 707, p. 88.
6. *Ibid.*., pp. 84, 86.
7. *Ibid.*., p. 94.
8. *Ibid.*., p. 85.
9. Joseph Kearney. BMH WS 704, p. 8.
10. *Ibid.*.
11. James L. O'Donovan, BMH WS 1713, p. 13.
12. James Foley, BMH WS 774, p. 7.
13. Gearóid Ua h-Uallachain, BMH WS 336, p. 29.
14. https://theauxiliaries.com/men-alphabetical/men-l/latimer-owrg/latimer.html.
15. O'Brien, Havoc, p. 188.
16. *Ibid.*., p. 189.
17. https://theauxiliaries.com/INCIDENTS/lnwr-hotel-attack/lnwr-hotel.html.
18. Gearóid Ua h-Uallachain, BMH WS 336, p. 29.
19. Clan na nGael was the IRB's sister organisation in the USA, founded in 1867.
20. Foy, *Michael Collins' Intelligence War*, p. 260.
21. Yeates, *A City in Turmoil*, p. 251.
22. *Ibid.*., p. 252.
23. https://theauxiliaries.com/men-alphabetical/men-o/o'neill-pj/pj-o'neill.html.
24. *Ibid.*.
25. James Foley, BMH WS 774, p. 6.
26. Michael O'Kelly, BMH WS 1635, p. 2.
27. Price, *We Bled Together*, p. 201.
28. *Ibid.*., p. 197.
29. Kautt, *Ambushes and Armour*, p. 227.
30. James Carrigan, BMH WS 613, pp. 11–12; Christopher Fitzsimons, BMH WS 581, pp. 11–12.
31. 'IRA man was gunned down on Clonard Street', Fingal Independent, 16 April 2006, available at: https://www.independent.ie/regionals/fingalindependent/news/ric-man-was-gunned-down-on-clonard-street-27766768.html.
32. Dan Breen, *My Fight for Irish Freedom* (Anvil Books, Dublin, 1989), p. 161.
33. https://tullowhistorian.wordpress.com/2016/11/09/thomas-traynor-1882-1921-tullows-executed-patriot/comment-page-1/#_ftnref58.

34. *Ibid.*.
35. *Ibid.*.
36. Yeates, *A City in Turmoil*, p. 268.
37. Breen, *My Fight for Irish Freedom*, p. 162.
38. Joseph O'Connor, BMH WS 487, p. 51.
39. Coogan, *De Valera*, p. 213. O'Mara, a millionaire businessman, remained in the USA while his home was used as a venue for the meeting. He had travelled there at the same time as *De Valera* in June 1919 and had been hugely successful as a Sinn Féin fund-raiser. However, he soon fell out with *De Valera* over the latter's management of funds.
40. *Ibid.*., p. 214.
41. Margaret Lasch Carroll, 'Martin Glynn's Newspaper Editorials: Constructing Albany's Answers to the Irish Questions, 1913–1924', *Nordic Irish Studies*, Vol. 14 (2015), p. 120.
42. https://www.cairogang.com/soldiers-killed/compton-smith/compton-smith.html. Compton-Smith's use of Welsh rather than Welch was probably due to the fact that from 1881 to 1920 the regiment was known as the Royal Welsh Fusiliers before reverting to the original Welch spelling in 1920.
43. *Ibid.*.
44. Townshend, *The British Campaign in Ireland 1919–1921*, p. 175.
45. *Ibid.*., p. 176.
46. O'Brien, *Havoc*, p. 70.
47. Bennett, *The Black and Tans*, p. 157.
48. Frank Henderson, BMH WS 821, p. 93.
49. Christopher Fitzsimons, BMH WS 581, p. 10.
50. Foy, *Michael Collins' Intelligence War*, p. 158.
51. Daniel McDonnell, BMH WS 486, p. 22.
52. Over sixty more would follow in the next eleven weeks.
53. http://www.bloodysunday.co.uk/shot-by-ira-as- spies/carroll-kate/kate-carroll.html. This wording is taken from the Derry Journal, although other papers give slightly different variations.
54. Oscar Traynor, BMH WS 340, p. 80.
55. *Ibid.*.
56. Joseph O'Connor, BMH WS 487, p. 35.
57. Christopher Fitzsimons, BMH WS 581, p. 12.
58. Liam O'Doherty, BMH WS 689, p. 6.
59. Oscar Traynor, BMH WS 340, p. 69.
60. *Ibid.*., p. 73.
61. Various, *Dublin's Fighting Story 1916–21* (2009), p. 317.
62. *Ibid.*.
63. Gillis, May 25, p. 79.
64. Oscar Traynor, BMH WS 340, p. 70.
65. *Ibid.*.
66. McMullen, *Weapons of The Irish War of Independence*, p. 77.
67. Oscar Traynor, BMH WS 340, p. 70.
68. Price, *We Bled Together*, p. 214.
69. Oscar Traynor, BMH WS 340, p. 71.
70. Thomas Lillis, BMH WS 1664, p. 4.
71. Patrick Collins, BMH WS 506, p. 5.
72. Pádraig O'Connor, BMH WS 813, p. 25.
73. *Ibid.*.
74. James Harpur, BMH WS 536, p. 10.
75. George Nolan, BMH WS 596, p. 7; Joseph McGuinness BMH WS 607, p. 14.
76. James Harpur, BMH WS 536, p. 10.
77. *Ibid.*., pp. 10–11.

78. Coogan, *De Valera*, p. 215.
79. Bennett, *The Black and Tans*, p. 168.
80. Michael Hopkinson, *The Irish War of Independence* (Gill & Macmillan, Dublin, 2002), p. 162.
81. Foy, *Michael Collins' Intelligence War*, p. 273.
82. *Ibid..*, p. 269.
83. *Ibid..*, p. 271.
84. Bennett, *The Black and Tans*, p. 168.

12 Rescue Attempt, Brutal Killing, Elections and Tommy Guns

1. http://irishhistory1919-1923chronology.ie/may_1921.htm.
2. Yeates, *A City in Turmoil*, p. 271.
3. Pádraig O'Connor, BMH WS 813, p. 27.
4. *Ibid..*
5. Charles Dalton, BMH WS 434, pp. 29–30.
6. *Ibid..*, p. 34.
7. *Ibid..*, p. 37.
8. *Ibid..*
9. Kautt, *Ambushes and Armour*, p. 214.
10. Patrick McCrea, BMH WS 413, p. 25.
11. Kautt, *Ambushes and Armour*, p. 215.
12. Dwyer, *The Squad*, p. 235.
13. Joseph Leonard, BMH WS 547, p. 16.
14. *Ibid..*, p. 17.
15. *Ibid..*
16. Price, *We Bled Together*, p. 206.
17. Dwyer, *The Squad*, p. 238.
18. Patrick McCrea, BMH WS 413, p. 30.
19. *Ibid..*
20. Joe Leonard, BMH WS 547, p. 18.
21. https://theauxiliaries.com/vets-drivers-div/t-cons-r/redmond/redmond.html.
22. O'Brien, *Havoc*, p. 218.
23. Bennett, *The Black and Tans*, p. 164.
24. McMullen, *Weapons of The Irish War of Independence*, p. 66.
25. Price, *We Bled Together*, p. 201.
26. Patrick J. Brennan, BMH WS 1773, p. 22.
27. Price, *We Bled Together*, p. 213.
28. George White, BMH WS 956, p. 9.
29. *Ibid..*
30. Pádraig O'Connor, BMH WS 813, p. 35; https://www.customhousecommemoration.com/wp-content/uploads/2019/06/Hoppy-Byrne-shot-again.jpg.
31. Price, *We Bled Together*, p. 213.
32. http://www.bloodysunday.co.uk/shot-by-ira-as- spies/graham-p/p-graham.html.
33. Coogan, *De Valera*, p. 220.
34. *Ibid..*
35. 'Burnings and panic follow Ballyturn ambush', *Galway Advertiser*, 18 October 1921, available at https://www.advertiser.ie/ Galway/article/55879/burnings-and-panic-follow-ballyturn-ambush.
36. Liam O'Doherty, BMH WS 689, p. 8.
37. *Ibid..*, p. 7.
38. Joseph Leonard, BMH WS 547, p. 20.
39. Michael O'Kelly, BMH WS 1410, p. 3.
40. McMullen, *Weapons of The Irish War of Independence*, p. 68.

41. Gillis, *May 25*, p. 82.
42. Mitchell, *Revolutionary Government* in Ireland, p. 282.
43. Hopkinson, *The Irish War of Independence*, p. 193. By facilitating Sinn Féin again, as they had done in 1919, Labour removed themselves from influence either at cabinet during autumn 1921 during the Truce negotiations, or during the Treaty vote in January 1922.
44. Oscar Traynor, BMH WS 340, p. 83.
45. Vincent Byrne, BMH WS 423, p. 49.
46. *Ibid.*.
47. McMullen, *Weapons of The Irish War of Independence*, p. 111.
48. Foy, *Michael Collins' Intelligence War*, p. 144.
49. Laurence Nugent, BMH WS 907, p. 235.
50. Harry Colley, BMH WS 1687, pp. 77–8.
51. Oscar Traynor, BMH WS 340, p. 72.
52. Harry Colley, BMH WS 1687, p. 81.
53. James Foley, BMH WS 774, p. 3.
54. Harry Colley, BMH WS 1687, p. 78.
55. Gillis, May 25, p. 82.

13 Custom House Attack

1. Joseph Leonard, BMH WS 547, p. 21; Michael Kelly, BMH WS 1410, p. 4.
2. Michael O'Kelly, BMH WS 1410, p. 4.
3. Ernest R. Jordison, BMH WS 1691, p. 16.
4. Harry Colley, BMH WS 1687, p. 80.
5. Sean Prendergast, BMH WS 755, p. 516.
6. Risteárd Mulcahy, *My Father the General: Richard Mulcahy and the Military History of the Revolution* (Liberties Press, Dublin, 2009), p. 56.
7. Yeates, *A City in Turmoil*, p. 273.
8. Michael Stack, BMH WS 525, p. 11.
9. James Slattery, BMH WS 445, pp. 15–16.
10. Harry Colley, BMH WS 1687, p. 80.
11. Daniel McAleese, BMH WS 1411, p. 1.
12. Vincent Byrne, BMH WS 423, p. 64.
13. *Ibid.*.
14. Daniel McAleese, BMH WS 1411, pp. 1–2.
15. McCann, *War by the Irish*, p. 208.
16. Sean Prendergast, BMH WS 755, p. 517.
17. William Oman, BMH WS 421, p. 15.
18. *Ibid.*.
19. James Foley, BMH WS 774, p. 3.
20. Harry Colley, BMH WS 1687, p. 81.
21. Michael O'Kelly, BMH WS 1410, p. 7.
22. Patrick O'Daly, BMH WS 387, p. 75.
23. Sean Prendergast, BMH WS 755, p. 518.
24. Joseph McGuinness, BMH WS 607, p. 17.
25. Pádraig O'Connor, BMH WS 813, p. 28.
26. *Ibid.*.
27. *Ibid.*.
28. Sean Prendergast, BMH WS 755, pp. 518–19.
29. Patrick O'Daly, BMH WS 387, p. 75.
30. Oscar Traynor, BMH WS 340, p. 74.
31. Pádraig O'Connor, BMH WS 813, p. 29.
32. *Ibid.*.
33. Sean Prendergast, BMH WS 755, p. 519.

34. Michael O'Kelly, BMH WS 1410, p. 6.
35. James Slattery, BMH WS 445, p. 16.
36. Daniel McAleese, BMH WS 1411, p. 2.
37. Price, *We Bled Together*, p. 215.
38. https://www.customhousecommemoration.com/2016/06/17/james-connolly-custom-house-burning/.
39. Patrick Collins, BMH WS 506, p. 7.
40. Joseph McGuinness, BMH WS 607, p. 17.
41. George Nolan, BMH WS 596, p. 9.
42. James Slattery, BMH WS 445, p. 16.
43. *Ibid..*, p. 17.
44. William Stapleton, BMH WS 822, pp. 78–9.
45. Patrick Lawson, BMH WS 667, p. 17.
46. Daniel McAleese, BMH WS 1411, p. 4.
47. Pádraig O'Connor, BMH WS 813, p. 29.
48. *Ibid..*
49. James Harpur, BMH WS 536, pp. 14–15.
50. Joseph Gilhooly, BMH WS 390, p. 9.
51. Joseph Leonard, BMH WS 547, p. 23; McCann, *War by the Irish*, p. 210.
52. Joseph Gilhooly, BMH WS 390, p. 9.
53. James Harpur, BMH WS 536, p. 15.
54. Gillis, May 25, p. 125.
55. Vincent Byrne, BMH WS 423, p. 67.
56. Daniel McAleese, BMH WS 1411, p. 6.
57. Yeates, *A City in Turmoil*, p. 274.
58. Gillis, *May 25*, p. 128.
59. Las Fallon, *Dublin Fire Brigade and the Irish Revolution* (South Dublin Libraries, Dublin, 2012), p. 78.
60. Oscar Traynor, BMH WS 340, p. 75.
61. *Ibid..*, p. 76.
62. Harry Colley, BMH WS 1687, p. 83.
63. Joseph Byrne, BMH WS 461, p. 9.
64. Gillis, May 25, p. 133.
65. Frank Thornton, BMH WS 615, p. 52.
66. Ernest R. Jordison, BMH WS 1691, p. 18.

14 Peace Feelers Amid Plans for War

1. Mitchell, *Revolutionary Government* in Ireland, p. 236.
2. Pádraig O'Connor, BMH WS 813, p. 30.
3. Harry Colley, BMH WS 1687, p. 84.
4. Oscar Traynor, BMH WS 340, p. 76.
5. Fallon, *Dublin Fire Brigade*, p. 76.
6. Coogan, *De Valera*, p. 221.
7. Bennett, *The Black and Tans*, p. 176.
8. Townshend, *The British Campaign in Ireland 1919–1921*, p. 182.
9. *Ibid..*, p. 183.
10. *Ibid..*, p. 184.
11. Fanning, *Fatal Path*, p. 256.
12. Patrick Moylett, BMH WS 767, p. 85.
13. *Ibid..*
14. *Ibid..*, p. 86.
15. https://theauxiliaries.com/INCIDENTS/st-stephens-green-grenades/grenades-st-stephens-green.html.

16. O'Connor, *The Big Fellow*, p. 148.
17. Patrick Moylett, BMH WS 767, pp. 86–7.
18. *Ibid..*, p. 87.
19. *Ibid..*, pp. 87–9.
20. Patrick J. Brennan, BMH WS 1773, p. 23.
21. Andrew McDonnell, BMH WS 1768, pp. 59–60.
22. Patrick J. Brennan, BMH WS 1773, p. 23.
23. http://theauxiliaries.com/INCIDENTS/RAIDS/09-1921-may/dublin-may-31/may-31.html.
24. Hopkinson, *The Irish War of Independence*, p. 137.
25. *Ibid..*, p. 122.
26. Price, *We Bled Together*, p. 217.
27. Hopkinson, *The Irish War of Independence*, p. 135.
28. Patrick Collins, BMH WS 506, p. 7.
29. George Nolan, BMH WS 596, p. 5.
30. Joseph McGuinness, BMH WS 607, p. 10.
31. Patrick J. Mullen, BMH WS 621, p. 8.
32. Joseph McGuinness, BMH WS 607, p. 10.
33. https://www.historyireland.com/18th-19th-century-history/gentlemen-ireland-versus-military-ireland-3-june-1921/.
34. Joseph O'Connor, BMH WS 487, pp. 57–8; Sheehan, *Fighting for Dublin*, p. 55.
35. Harry Colley, BMH WS 1687, p. 85.
36. Townshend, *The British Campaign in Ireland 1919–1921*, p. 186.
37. W. H. Kautt (ed.), *Ground Truths: British Army Operations in The Irish War of Independence* (Irish Academic Press, Dublin, 2014), p. 156.
38. Yeates, *A City in Turmoil*, p. 275.
39. Frank Saurin, BMH WS 715, p. 4.
40. Charles Dalton, BMH WS 434, p. 11.
41. http://www.bloodysunday.co.uk/shot-by-ira-as- spies/brady-je/brady-je.html.
42. *Ibid..*; see also http://www.bloodysunday.co.uk/shot-by-ira-as- spies/halpin-t/halpin-t.html.
43. https://theauxiliaries.com/INCIDENTS/dublin-jun-7-attacks/jun-7-attacks.html.
44. Yeates, *A City in Turmoil*, p. 276.
45. https://theauxiliaries.com/INCIDENTS/dublin-jun-7-attacks/jun-7-attacks.html.
46. David Dineen, 'Paddy Maher: A Judicial Murder', History Studies (Journal of the University of Limerick History Society), Vol. 16 (2015), p. 35.
47. http://www.limerickcity.ie/media/rebel013.pdf.
48. These men subsequently were referred to as 'The Forgotten Ten'. Following a protracted campaign to have them re-interred with a proper burial service it was decided on 1 November 2000, the eightieth anniversary of Kevin Barry's hanging, to re-inter them in Glasnevin Cemetery. On 14 October 2001 they were re-interred following requiem mass at the pro-cathedral and a state funeral. Tens of thousands of Dubliners lined the streets and applauded as the coffins, draped in Tricolours, passed. A lone piper played a lament as the cortege passed the GPO in O'Connell Street en route.
49. Breen, *My Fight for Irish Freedom*, p. 164.
50. *Ibid..*
51. Patrick Flanagan, pension application, MSP34REF445, p. 30.
52. Pádraig O'Connor, BMH WS 813, p. 35.
53. Patrick O'Daly, BMH WS 387, p. 81; George White, BMH WS 956, p. 10.
54. William Stapleton, BMH WS 822, p. 86.
55. Pádraig O'Connor, BMH WS 813, p. 36.
56. Patrick O'Daly, BMH WS 387, p. 81.
57. Pádraig O'Connor, BMH WS 813, p. 36.

58. Pádraig O'Connor, BMH WS 813, p. 38.
59. All information on Mac Eoin's legal representation and trial is drawn from Michael Noyk, BMH WS 707 pp. 74–81.
60. *Ibid..*, p. 80.
61. *Ibid..*, p. 81.
62. Joseph McGuinness, BMH WS 607, p. 9.
63. Townshend, *The British Campaign in Ireland 1919–1921*, p. 184.
64. Fanning, *Fatal Path*, p. 257.
65. *Ibid..*
66. Foy, *Michael Collins' Intelligence War*, p. 276.
67. *Ibid..*
68. Molyneux & Kelly, *Killing at its Very Extreme*, p. 229.
69. Foy, *Michael Collins' Intelligence War*, p. 277.
70. Townshend, *The British Campaign in Ireland 1919–1921*, p. 187.
71. Foy, *Michael Collins' Intelligence War*, p. 261.
72. Kautt, Ground Truths, p. 167.
73. William Stapleton, BMH WS 822, p. 82; Charles Dalton, With the Dublin Brigade: Espionage and Assassination with *Michael Collins'* Intelligence Unit (Mercier Press, Cork, 2014), pp. 183–4; https://www.cairogang.com/soldiers-killed/saunders/saunders.html.
74. Price, *We Bled Together*, p. 220.
75. https://www.cairogang.com/soldiers-killed/saunders/saunders.html.
76. *Ibid..*
77. William Stapleton, BMH WS 822, p. 81.
78. Townshend, *The British Campaign in Ireland 1919–1921*, p. 190.
79. *Ibid..*
80. Michael Rock, BMH WS 1398, pp. 23–4.
81. http://www.bloodysunday.co.uk/shot-by-ira-as- spies/pike/pike.html.
82. Charles Dalton, BMH WS 434, p. 11.
83. Andrew McDonnell, BMH WS 1768, p. 57.
84. https://www.cairogang.com/soldiers-killed/breeze/breeze.html.
85. Foy, *Michael Collins' Intelligence War*, p. 279.
86. Sheehan, *Fighting for Dublin*, p. 58.
87. http://www.generalmichaelcollins.com/life-times/treaty/kings-speech-june-22nd-1921/.
88. Patrick O'Daly, BMH WS 387, pp. 65–6.
89. Fanning, *Fatal Path*, p. 260.
90. Townshend, *The British Campaign in Ireland 1919–1921*, p. 192.

15 Peace, a Close-run Thing

1. Yeates, *A City in Turmoil*, p. 282.
2. Townshend, *The British Campaign in Ireland 1919–1921*, p. 191.
3. Fanning, *Fatal Path*, p. 260.
4. Coogan, *De Valera*, p. 227.
5. Fanning, *Fatal Path*, p. 261.
6. Bennett, *The Black and Tans*, p. 184.
7. William Stapleton, BMH WS 822, p. 83.
8. Pádraig O'Connor, BMH WS 813, pp. 39–40.
9. *Ibid..*
10. Dalton, With the Dublin Brigade, p. 187.
11. William Stapleton, BMH WS 822, p. 84.
12. Joseph McGuinness, BMH WS 607, pp. 20–1.
13. http://theauxiliaries.com/INCIDENTS/grafton%20St/inquest/grafton-st.html.
14. John Anthony Caffrey, BMH WS 569, p. 12.
15. *Ibid..*; https://theauxiliaries.com/INCIDENTS/grafton%20St/inquest/grafton-st.html.

16. William Stapleton, BMH WS 822, p. 85.
17. *Ibid.*.
18. Edward J. Kelliher, BMH WS 477, p. 5.
19. Sheehan, *Fighting for Dublin*, p. 57.
20. Pádraig O'Connor, BMH WS 813, pp. 40–1.
21. *Ibid.*., p. 41.
22. James Tully, BMH WS 628, p. 5.
23. https://theauxiliaries.com/men-alphabetical/men-h/hunt/hunt.html.
24. Michael Stack, BMH WS 525, p. 13.
25. https://theauxiliaries.com/men-alphabetical/men-h/hunt/hunt.html.
26. Pádraig O'Connor, BMH WS 813, pp. 41–2.
27. *Ibid.*., p. 42.
28. Michael Stack, BMH WS 525, p. 14.
29. Thomas Lillis, BMH WS 1664, p. 4.
30. Joseph McGuinness, BMH WS 607, p. 15.
31. Thomas Lillis, BMH WS 1664, p. 4.
32. http://irishhistory1919-1923chronology.ie/june_1921.htm.
33. Michael Rock, BMH WS 1398, pp. 25–7.
34. Yeates, *A City in Turmoil*, p. 282.
35. https://theauxiliaries.com/INCIDENTS/dublin-1921-jul-dominick-riot/riot-dominick-st.html.
36. *Ibid.*.
37. Townshend, *The British Campaign in Ireland 1919–1921*, p. 196.
38. Today the former Royal College of Science is Ireland's Government Buildings.
39. Bennett, *The Black and Tans*, p. 184.
40. Pauric J. Dempsey & Shaun Boylan, 'Barton, Robert Childers', https://dib.cambridge.org/viewReadPage.do;jsessionid=B430ABAA38A5979CEFA4C17E276CED0C?articleId=a0485&searchClicked=clicked&searchBy=1&browsesearch=yes.
41. Foy, *Michael Collins' Intelligence War*, p. 288.
42. Hopkinson, *The Irish War of Independence*, p. 196.
43. Yeates, *A City in Turmoil*, p. 282.
44. Fanning, *Fatal Path*, p. 261.
45. Pádraig Óg Ó Ruairc, 'The Anglo-Irish Truce: An Analysis of its Immediate Military Impact' (University of Limerick, 2014), p. 46.
46. *Ibid.*.
47. Yeates, *A City in Turmoil*, p. 283.
48. Coogan, *De Valera*, p. 228.
49. https://www.difp.ie/docs/1921/Moves-towards-truce/97.htm.
50. Coogan, *De Valera*, p. 227.
51. *Ibid.*., p. 223.
52. *Ibid.*., p. 228.
53. Fanning, *Fatal Path*, p. 261.
54. Coogan, *De Valera*, p. 228.
55. *Ibid.*., p. 224.
56. Fanning, *Fatal Path*, p. 261.
57. Mitchell, *Revolutionary Government* in Ireland, p. 298.
58. Ó Ruairc, 'The Anglo-Irish Truce', p. 47.
59. Yeates, *A City in Turmoil*, p. 284.
60. Ó Ruairc, 'The Anglo-Irish Truce', p. 47.
61. Foy, *Michael Collins' Intelligence War*, p. 289.
62. Yeates, *A City in Turmoil*, p. 284.
63. Mitchell, *Revolutionary Government* in Ireland, p. 298.
64. Ó Ruairc, 'The Anglo-Irish Truce', p. 48.

65. Pádraig O'Connor, BMH WS 813, pp. 43–4.
66. http://irishhistory1919-1923chronology.ie/july_1921.htm.
67. Frank Henderson, BMH WS 821, pp 118–19. Auxiliaries were paid £1 per day, Black and Tans £3.10 per week.
68. John Kenny, BMH WS 1693, p. 21.
69. James Fulham, BMH WS 630, p. 24.
70. Ó Ruairc, 'The Anglo-Irish Truce', p. 53.
71. *Michael Collins to George Gavan Duffy 18 June 1921, No. 134, NAI George Gavan Duffy Papers, 1125/20, available at https://www.difp.ie/viewdoc.asp?DocID=134.*
72. Sean Prendergast, BMH WS 755, p. 538.
73. *Ibid..*
74. Frank Henderson, BMH WS 821, p. 120.
75. Patrick Mannix, BMH WS 502, p. 4.
76. Foy, *Michael Collins' Intelligence War*, p. 289.
77. Coogan, *De Valera*, p. 218.
78. http://irishhistory1919-1923chronology.ie/july_1921. htm;http://www.waterfordmuseum.ie/exhibit/web/Display/article/316/   21/   The_Struggle_For_Freedom_In_West_Waterford_Ballyvoile_The_Kilgobinet_Booby_Trap.html.
79. Ó Ruairc, 'The Anglo-Irish Truce', p. 268.
80. Hopkinson, *The Irish War of Independence*, p. 126.
81. Ó Ruairc, 'The Anglo-Irish Truce', p. 57.
82. *Ibid..*, p. 54.
83. *Ibid..*, p. 254.
84. http://irishhistory1919-1923chronology.ie/july_1921.htm.
85. Ó Ruairc, 'The Anglo-Irish Truce', p. 145.
86. *Ibid..*, p. 151.
87. *Ibid..*, p. 186.
88. Townshend, *The British Campaign in Ireland 1919–1921*, p. 198.
89. https://www.militaryarchives.ie/collections/online-collections/military-service-pensions-collection-1916-1923/brigade-activities/brigade/1-dublin-brigade-2-eastern-division/.
90. Yeates, *A City in Turmoil*, p. 285.
91. O'Connor, *The Big Fellow*, p. 152.
92. Annie O'Brien, BMH WS 805, p. 15.
93. Molyneux & Kelly, *Those of Us Who Must Die*, p. 202.
94. Mitchell, *Revolutionary Government* in Ireland, p. 271.
95. McCullagh, *De Valera, Volume 1: Rise 1882–1932*, p. 209.
96. Ferriter, *A Nation and Not a Rabble*, p. 197.
97. Molyneux & Kelly, *Those of Us Who Must Die*, p. 198.
98. Ó Ruairc, 'The Anglo-Irish Truce', p. 51.
99. Molyneux & Kelly, *Killing at its Very Extreme*, p. 60.
100. Ó Ruairc, 'The Anglo-Irish Truce', p. 49.
101. Michael Noyk, BMH WS 707, p. 106.

Epilogue
1. Frank Henderson, BMH WS 821, pp. 120–2.

BIBLIOGRAPHY

Archives

Military Archives, Dublin, Bureau of Military History Witness Statements, 1913–1921
Military Archives, Dublin, Military Service Pensions Collection, 1916–1923

Books and Articles

Abbott, Richard, *Police Casualties*
Ackerman, Carl W., 'Janus-headed Ireland', *Atlantic Monthly* (June 1922)
Addison, RT. Hon. Christopher, *Politics From Within 1911–1918*, Vols 1 & 2 (Herbert Jenkins Limited, London, 1924)
Ambrose, Joe, *Seán Treacy and the Tan War* (Mercier Press, Cork, 2007)
Andrew, Christopher, *The Defence of the Realm: The Authorized History of MI5* (Penguin books, London, 2010)
Andrew, Christopher, & Dilks, David, *The Missing Dimension: Government and Intelligence Communities in the Twentieth Century* (Palgrave, London, 2014)
Andrews, C. S., *Dublin Made Me* (The Lilliput Press, Dublin, 2001)
Asquith, Margot, *The Autobiography of Margot Asquith*, Vol. 2 (Thornton Butterworth Ltd, London, 1922)
Augusteijn, Joost, T*he Irish Revolution 1913–1923* (Palgrave, Hampshire, 2002)
Barry, Tom, *Guerilla Days in Ireland* (Anvil Books, Dublin, 1989)
Béaslaí, Piaras, *Michael Collins and the Making of a New Ireland*, Vol. 1 (Phoenix Publishing Co. Ltd, Dublin, 1922)
—, *Michael Collins and the Making of a New Ireland*, Vol. 2 (Harper & Brothers Publishers, New York, 1926)
Bennett, Richard, *The Black and Tans* (Four Square Books, London, 1961)
Bew, Paul, *Churchill & Ireland* (Oxford University Press, Oxford, 2016)
Boyle, Andrew, T*he Riddle of Erskine Childers: A Biography* (Hutchinson & Co. Ltd, London, 1977)
Breen, Dan, *My Fight for Irish Freedom* (Anvil Books, Dublin, 1989)
Bromage, Mary C., *Churchill in Ireland* (University of Notre Dame Press, Indiana, 1964)
—, *De Valera: The Rebel Gunman Who Became President of Ireland* (Four Square, London, 1967)
Brown, Terence, *The Irish Times: 150 Years of Influence* (Bloomsbury, London, 2015)
Buckland, Patrick, *James Craig: Irish Lives* (Gill, Dublin, 1981)
Byrne, Myles, *The Memoirs of Myles Byrne*, Vol. 1 (Maunsel & Co. Ltd, Dublin 1907)
Carey, Tim, *Mountjoy: The Story of a Prison* (The Collins Press, Cork, 2000)
—, 'Bloody Sunday 1920: New Evidence', *History Ireland*, Vol. 11, Issue 2 (Summer 2003)
Carroll, Denis, *They Have Fooled You Again: Michael Flanagan (1876–1942), Priest, Republican, Social Critic* (Columba Press, Dublin, 2016)
Carroll, Margaret Lasch, 'Martin Glynn's Newspaper Editorials: Constructing Albany's Answers to the Irish Questions, 1913–1924', *Nordic Irish Studies*, Vol. 14 (2015), pp. 111–125
Clarke, Kathleen, *Kathleen Clarke: Revolutionary Woman* (The O'Brien Press, Dublin, 1991)
Collier, Basil, *Brasshat: A Biography of Field-Marshal Sir Henry Wilson 1864–1922* (Secker & Warburg, London, 1961)
Collins, Lorcan, *Ireland's War of Independence 1919–21: The IRA's Guerrilla Campaign* (O'Brien Press, Dublin, 2019)
Collins, Michael, *The Path To Freedom* (Mercier Press Press, Cork, 2019)
Column, Padraig, *Arthur Griffith* (Browne & Nolan Ltd, Dublin, 1959)

Comerford, Marie, *The First Dáil* (Joe Clarke, Dublin, 1969)

Connell Jnr, Joseph E. A., *Michael Collins: Dublin 1916–1922* (Wordwell Ltd, Dublin, 2017)

Coogan, Tim Pat, *Michael Collins, A Biography* (Arrow Books Ltd, London, 1991)

—, *De Valera: Long Fellow, Long Shadow* (Random House, London, 1993)

—, *Ireland in the Twentieth Century* (Arrow Books Ltd, London, 2003)

Corbett, Jim, *Not While I have Ammo: A History of Captain Connie Mackey, Defender of the Strand* (Nonsuch Publishing, Dublin, 2008)

Costello, Francis (ed.), *In His Own Words: Michael Collins* (Gill & Macmillan, Dublin 1997)

Cottrell, Peter, *The Anglo-Irish War: The Troubles of 1913–1922* (Osprey Publishing, Oxford, 2006)

Crowley, John, Ó Drisceoil, Donal, Murphy, Mike, & Borgonovo, John, *Atlas of the Irish Revolution* (Cork University Press, Cork, 2017)

Crozier, Brigadier General F. P., *A Brass Hat in No Man's Land* (Jonathan Cape & Harrison Smith, New York, 1930)

—, *The Men I Killed* (Createspace Independent Publishing, Amazon, 2016)

Dagg, George A. de M. Edwin, *The Road Route Guide of the Royal Irish Constabulary* (Hodges, Figgis & Co. Ltd, Dublin, 1993)

Dalton, Charles, *With the Dublin Brigade: Espionage and Assassination with Michael Collins' Intelligence Unit* (Mercier Press, Cork, 2014)

Dangerfield, George, *The Damnable Question: A History of Anglo-Irish Relations* (Barnes & Noble Inc., New York, 1999)

Dawson, Richard, *Red Terror and Green: The Sinn Fein-Bolshevist Movement* (E. P. Dutton & Company, New York, 1920)

de Burca, Padraig, & Boyle, John F., *Free State or Republic?* (Talbot Press, Dublin, 1922)

de Vere White, Terence, *Kevin O'Higgins* (Anvil Books, Kerry, 1948)

Deasy, Liam, *Towards Ireland Free: The West Cork Brigade in the War of Independence 1917–21* (Mercier Press, Cork, 2020)

Dineen, David, 'Paddy Maher: A Judicial Murder', *History Studies* (Journal of the University of Limerick History Society), Vol. 16 (2015)

Dolan, Anne, 'Killing and Bloody Sunday, November 1920', *The Historical Journal*, 49, 3 (2006), pp. 789–810

Dorney, John, *Peace After The Final Battle: The Story of the Irish Revolution 1912–1924* (New Island Books, Dublin, 2013)

Dwyer, T. Ryle, *De Valera: The Man and the Myth* (Poolbeg Press Ltd, Dublin, 1992)

—, *Eamon De Valera* (Gill & Macmillan, Dublin, 1980)

—, *The Squad and the Intelligence Operations of Michael Collins* (Mercier Press, Cork, 2005)

Enright, Seán, *After the Rising: Soldiers, Lawyers and Trials of the Irish Revolution* (Merrion Press, Kildare, 2016)

Fallon, Las, *Dublin Fire Brigade and the Irish Revolution* (South Dublin Libraries, Dublin, 2012)

Fanning, Ronan, *Fatal Path: British Government and Irish Revolution 1910–1922* (Faber & Faber, London, 2013)

Ferriter, Diarmuid, *The Transformation of Ireland 1900–2000* (Profile Books, London, 2005)

—, *Judging Dev* (Royal Irish Academy, Dublin, 2007)

—, *A Nation and Not a Rabble: The Irish Revolution 1913–1923* (Profile Books, London, 2015)

Figgis, Darrell, *The Historic Case for Irish Independence* (Maunsel & Company Ltd, Dublin, 1918)

—, *Recollections of the Irish War* (Doubleday, Doran & Company Inc., New York, 1928)

Finlay, Ken, *Dublin Day by Day: 366 Days of Dublin History* (Nonsuch Publishing, Dublin, 2005)

Finlay, Ken, & Roche, Tom, *Dublin 4: Sandymount – Donnybrook – Ballsbridge – Ringsend* (Cottage Publications, Donaghadee, 2006)

Fitzpatrick, David, *Harry Boland's Irish Revolution* (Cork University Press, Cork, 2004)

Foley, Michael, *The Bloodied Field: Croke Park, Sunday 21 November 1920* (O'Brien Press, Dublin, 2014)

Foster, R. F., *Vivid Faces: The Revolutionary Generation in Ireland 1890–1923* (Penguin Books,

London, 2015)

Foy, Michael T., *Michael Collins's Intelligence War: The* Struggle Between the British and the IRA 1919–1921 (Sutton Publishing, Gloucestershire, 2008)

Gallagher, Frank, *Days of Fear: Diary of a 1920s Hunger Striker* (Mercier Press, Cork, 2008)

Galligan, Kevin, *Peter Paul Galligan: 'One of the Most Dangerous Men in the Rebel Movement'* (The Liffey Press, Dublin, 2012)

Gillis, Liz, Women of the Revolution (Mercier Press, Cork, 2014)

—, *May 25: The Burning of the Custom House Dublin* (Kilmainham Tales, Dublin, 2017)

Gleeson, James, *Bloody Sunday* (Four Square Books, London, 1963)

Grayson, Richard S., *Dublin's Great Wars: The First World War, the Easter Rising and the Irish Revolution* (Cambridge University Press, Cambridge, 2018)

Gregory, Adrian, & Paseta, Senia, *Ireland and the Great War: A War to Unite Us All?* (Manchester University Press, Manchester, 2002)

Guevara, Ernesto 'Che', *Guerrilla Warfare* (BN Publishing, California, 2013)

Haldane, Richard Burdon, *Richard Burdon Haldane: An Autobiography* (Hodder and Stoughton, London, 1929)

Hannigan, Dave, *Terence MacSwiney: The Hunger Strike that Rocked an Empire* (O'Brien Press, Dublin, 2010)

Hart, Peter (ed.), *British Intelligence in Ireland, 1920–21: The Final Reports, Irish Narratives series* (Cork University Press, Cork, 2011)

Haverty, Anne, *Constance Markievicz, Irish Revolutionary* (Pandora, London, 1988)

Henry, Robert Mitchell, *The Evolution of Sinn Fein* (The Talbot Press, Dublin, 1920)

Herlihy, Jim, *The Dublin Metropolitan Police: A Short History and Genealogical Guide* (Four Courts Press, Dublin, 2001)

Hinkson, Pamela, *Seventy Years Young: Memories of Elizabeth, Countess of Fingall* (The Lilliput Press, Dublin, 1991)

Hittle, J. B. E., *Michael Collins and the Anglo-Irish War: Britain's Counterinsurgency Failure* (Potomac Books, Nebraska, 2011)

Holmes, Richard, *The Little Field-Marshal: Sir John French* (Jonathan Cape, London, 1981)

Hopkinson, Michael, *The Irish War of Independence* (Gill & Macmillan, Dublin, 2002)

—, *Green Against Green; The Irish Civil War* (Gill & Macmillan, Dublin, 2004)

Hughes, Brian, '"Make the Terror Behind Greater than the Terror in Front?" Internal Discipline, Forced Participation, and the I.R.A. 1919–1921', *Irish Historical Studies*, Vol. 42, Issue 161 (May 2018), pp. 64–86

Irish Times Limited, *1912 Ulster and Home Rule's Resistance* (Irish Times Books, 2015)

Jeffery, Keith (ed.), *The Military Correspondence of Field Marshal Sir Henry Wilson 1918–1922* (The Army Records Society, London, 1985)

Jeffery, Keith, *MI6: The History of the Secret Intelligence Service 1909–1949* (Bloomsbury Paperbacks, London, 2011)

Johnstone, Tom, *Orange, Green & Khaki: The Story of the Irish Regiments in the Great War 1914–1918* (Gill & Macmillan, Dublin, 1992)

Kautt, W. H., *Ambushes and Armour: The Irish Rebellion 1919–1921* (Irish Academic Press, Dublin, 2011)

— (ed.), *Ground Truths: British Army Operations in The Irish War of Independence* (Irish Academic Press, Dublin, 2014)

Kee, Robert, *Green Flag, Volume 3: 'Ourselves Alone'* (Penguin Books, London, 1989)

Keegan, John, *A History of Warfare* (Vintage, New York, 1994)

Kenna, G. R., *Facts and Figures of the Belfast Pogrom 1920–1922* (The O'Connell Publishing Company, Dublin, 1922)

Kenneally, Ian, *The Paper Wall: Newspapers and Propaganda in Ireland 1919–1921* (The Collins Press, Cork, 2008)

—, *Courage and Conflict, Forgotten Stories of the Irish at War* (The Collins Press, Cork, 2010)

Laffan, Michael, *Judging W.T. Cosgrave* (Royal Irish Academy, Dublin, 2014)

Lawlor, Sheila, *Britain & Ireland 1914–1923* (Rowman & Littlefield Publishers, Maryland, 1983)

Leeson, D. M., *The Black & Tans: British Police and Auxiliaries in The Irish War of Independence* (Oxford University Press, Oxford, 2013)

Liam, Cathal, *Fear Not The Storm: The Story of Tom Cullen, an Irish Revolutionary* (St. Pádraic Press, Ohio, 2011)

Lloyd George, David, *War Memoirs, Vol. 5* (Ivor Nicholson & Watson, London, 1936)

Lloyd George, Earl, *My Father, Lloyd George* (Crown Publishers Inc., New York, 1961)

Longford, The Earl of, & O'Neill, Thomas P., *Eamon De Valera* (Arrow Books, London, 1974)

Mac Curtain, Fionnuala, *Remember It's For Ireland: A Family Memoir of Tomás Mac Curtáin* (Mercier Press, Cork, 2006)

Macardle, Dorothy, *The Irish Republic* (Farrar, Straus and Giroux, New York, 1965)

MacLaren, Roy, *Empire and Ireland: The Transatlantic Career of the Canadian Imperialist Hamar Greenwood, 1870–1948* (McGill, Queen's University Press, Canada, 2015)

MacLellan, Anne, *Dorothy Stopford Price: Rebel Doctor* (Irish Academic Press, Dublin, 2014)

MacManus, Seamus, *The Story of the Irish Race* (Chartwell Books, New York, 2018)

Macready, General the Rt. Hon. Sir Nevil, *Annals of an Active Life*, Vols 1 & 2 (Hutchinson & Co., London, 1925)

Marreco, Anne, *The Rebel Countess: The Life and Times of Constance Markievicz* (Phoenix Press, London, 2000)

Maurice, Major General Sir Frederick, *Haldane 1915–1928: The Life of Viscount Haldane of Cloan. K.T., O.M.* (Faber and Faber Ltd, London, 1939)

McCall, Ernest, *The Auxiliaries, Tudor's Toughs: A Study of the Auxiliary Division Royal Irish Constabulary 1920–1922* (Red Coat Publishing, Newtownards, 2010)

McCann, John, *War by the Irish* (The Kerryman Ltd, Tralee, 1946)

McCarthy, Cal, *Cumann na mBan and the Irish Revolution*, revised edition (The Collins Press, Cork, 2014)

McConville, Seán, *Irish Political Prisoners, 1848–1922: Theatres of War* (Routledge, Abingdon, 2002)

McCullagh, David, *De Valera, Volume 1: Rise 1882–1932* (Gill Books, Dublin, 2017)

McDonnell, Vincent, *Michael Collins: Most Wanted Man* (The Collins Press, Cork, 2015)

McGee, Owen, *The IRB: The Irish Republican Brotherhood from the Land League to Sinn Féin* (The Four Courts Press, Dublin, 2007)

McGough, Eileen, *Diarmuid Lynch: A Forgotten Irish Patriot* (Mercier Press, Cork, 2013)

McGreevy, Ronan, *Wherever the Firing Line Extends: Ireland and the Western Front* (The History Press, Dublin, 2017)

McGuire, Charlie, *Seán McLoughlin: Ireland's Forgotten Revolutionary* (Merlin Press, Pontypool, 2011)

McMahon, Seán, *Rebel Ireland, from Easter Rising to Civil War* (Mercier Press, Cork, 2001)

—, *Great Irish Heroes* (Mercier Press, Cork, 2008)

—, *Introduction to the War of Independence*,

McMullen, Kieran E., *Weapons of The Irish War of Independence* (Kilmainham Tales Teo, Dublin, 2020)

Messenger, Charles, *Broken Sword: The Tumultuous Life of General Frank Crozier 1879–1937* (The Praetorian Press, Barnsley, 2013)

Mitchell, Arthur, *Revolutionary Government in Ireland: Dáil Éireann 1919–1922* (Gill & Macmillan, Dublin, 1995)

Molyneux, Derek, & Kelly, Darren, *When the Clock Struck in 1916: Close-Quarter Combat in the Easter Rising* (The Collins Press, Cork, 2015)

—, *Those of Us Who Must Die*: *Execution, Exile and Revival after the Easter Rising* (The Collins Press, Cork, 2017)

—, *Killing at its Very Extreme*: *Dublin, October 1917–November 1920* (Mercier Press, Cork, 2020)

Moran, May, *Executed for Ireland: The Patrick Moran Story* (Mercier Press, Cork, 2010)

Mulcahy, Risteárd, *Richard Mulcahy (1886–1971): A Family Memoir* (Aurelian Press, Dublin, 1999)

—, *My Father the General: Richard Mulcahy and the Military History of the Revolution* (Liberties Press, Dublin, 2009)

Murphy, Brian P., *John Chartres: Mystery Man of the Treaty* (Irish Academic Press, Dublin, 1995)

Murphy, William, *Political Imprisonment and the Irish* (Oxford University Press, Oxford, 2014)

Naughton, Lindie, *Markievicz: A Most Outrageous Rebel* (Irish Academic Press, Dublin, 2016)

Norman, Diana, *Terrible Beauty: A Life of Constance Markievicz* (Poolbeg Press Ltd, Dublin, 1988)

O'Brien, Paul, *Havoc: The Auxiliaries in Ireland's War of Independence* (The Collins Press, Cork, 2017)

O'Brien, Stan D., *John Joe's Story: Commandant Joe O'Brien* (Self Published, 2016)

Ó Comhraí, Cormac, & Ó Comhraí, Stiofán, *Peadar Clancy: Easter Rising Hero, Bloody Sunday Martyr* (Cranny Publications, Galway, 2016)

O'Connor, Batt, *With Michael Collins in the Fight for Irish Independence* (Peter Davies Ltd, London, 1929)

O'Connor, Frank, *The Big Fellow* (Mercier Press Cork, 2019)

Ó Corráin, Daithí, "A most public spirited and unselfish man": The Career and Contribution of Colonel Maurice Moore, 1854–1939', *Studia Hibernica*, 40 (2014), pp. 71–134

Ó Duibhir, Liam, *Prisoners of War: Ballykinlar Internment Camp 1920–1921* (Mercier Press, Cork, 2013)

O'Farrell, Fergus, *Cathal Brugha* (University College Dublin Press, Dublin, 2018)

O'Farrell, Padraic, *Who's Who In The Irish War of Independence and Civil War 1916–1923* (The Lilliput Press, Dublin, 1997)

O'Hegarty. P. S., *Sinn Fein: An Illumination* (Maunsel & Co. Ltd, Dublin, 1919)

—, *A Short Memoir of Terence MacSwiney* (P. J. Kenedy & Sons, New York, 1922)

O'Malley, Ernie, *On Another Man's Wound* (Mercier Press, Cork, 2013)

—, *The Singing Flsme* (Mercier Press, Cork 2012)

—, *The Men will Talk to Me: Galway Interviews* (Mercier Press, Cork, 2013)

O'Reilly, Terence (ed.), *Our Struggle for Independence: Eyewitness Accounts from the Pages of An Cosantóir* (Mercier Press, Cork, 2009)

O'Sullivan, Niamh, *Every Dark Hour: A History of Kilmainham Gaol* (Liberties Press, Dublin, 2007)

Pakenham, Frank, *Peace By Ordeal* (Jonathan Cope, London, 1935)

Phillips, W. Alison, *The Revolution in Ireland 1906–1923* (Longmans, Green and Co. Ltd, London, 1926)

—, *The Flame and the Candle: War in Mayo 1919–1924* (The Collins Press, Cork, 2012)

Price, Dominic, *We Bled Together: Michael Collins, The Squad and the Dublin Brigade* (The Collins Press, Cork, 2017)

Raymond, E. T., *Mr. Lloyd George, A Biography* (W. Collins Sons & Co. Ltd, Glasgow, 1922)

Regan, John X. (ed.), *What Made Ireland Sinn Fein* (Washington Press, Boston, 1921)

Ryan, Annie, *Comrades: Inside the War of Independence* (Liberties Press, Dublin, 2007)

Ryan, Meda, *Michael Collins and the Women Who Spied For Ireland* (Mercier Press, Cork, 2006)

—, *Tom Barry: IRA Freedom Fighter* (Mercier Press, Cork, 205)

—, *Liam Lynch: The Real Chief, Irish Revolutionaries series* (Mercier Press, Cork, 2012)

Scannell, James, 'DMP Casualties During the War of Independence', *Dublin Historical Record*, Vol. 61, No. 1 (Spring 2008), pp. 5–19

Sheehan, Captain D. D., *Ireland Since Parnell* (Daniel O'Connor, London, 1921)

Sheehan, William, *British Voices from The Irish War of Independence 1918–1921: The Words of British Servicemen Who Were There* (The Collins Press, Cork, 2007)

—, *Fighting for Dublin: The British Battle for Dublin 1919–1921* (The Collins Press, Cork, 2007)

—, *Hearts & Mines: The British 5th Division, Ireland, 1920–1922* (The Collins Press, Cork, 2009)

Shouldice, Frank, *Grandpa the Sniper: The Remarkable Story of a 1916 Volunteer* (The Liffey Press,

Dublin, 2015)

Stewart, A. T. Q., *Edward Carson: Irish Lives* (Gill, Dublin, 1981)

Strachan, Hew, *The First World War* (Penguin Books, London, 2005)

Taber, Robert, *War of the Flea: The Classic Study of Guerrilla Warfare* (Potomac Books Inc., Nebraska, 2002)

Talbot, Hayden, *Michael Collins' Own Story* (Hutchinson & Co., London, 1923)

Townshend, Charles, *The British Campaign in Ireland 1919–1921: The Development of Political and Military Policies* (Oxford Historical Monographs, Oxford, 1975)

—, *The Irish Rail Strike of 1920: Industrial Action and Civil Resistance in the Struggle for Independence* (Cambridge University Press, Cambridge, 1979)

—, *The Republic: The Fight for Irish Independence* (Penguin books, London, 2014)

Turner, Edward Raymond, *Ireland and England in the Past and at Present* (The Century Co., New York, 1919)

Valiulis, Maryann Gialanella, *Portrait of a Revolutionary: General Richard Mulcahy and the Founding of the Irish Free State* (Irish Academic Press, Dublin, 1993)

Various, *Dublin's Fighting Story 1916–21* (Mercier Press, Cork, 2009)

Various, *Limerick's Fighting Story 1916–1921* (Mercier Press, Cork, 2009)

Various, *IRA Jailbreaks: 1918–1921* (Mercier Press, Cork, 2010)

Various, *The Anglo-Irish War* (Belfast Historical and Educational Society, Belfast, 2010)

Various, *With the IRA in the Fight for Freedom, 1919 to the Truce: The Red Path of Glory* (Mercier Press, Cork, 2010)

von Clausewitz, Carl, *On War* (Wordsworth Editions Ltd, Hertfordshire, 1997)

von Spohn, Col, The Art of Command (Herr A. Bath, Berlin, 1907)

—, *The News from Ireland: Foreign Correspondents and the Irish Revolution* (I. B. Tauris, London, 2011)

Walsh, Maurice, *Bitter Freedom: Ireland in a Revolutionary World* (Faber & Faber, London, 2016)

Ward, Margaret, *In Their Own Voice: Women and Irish Nationalism* (Attic Press, Dublin, 1995)

Wells, Warre B., *An Irish Apologia: Some Thoughts on Anglo-Irish Relations and the War* (Maunsel & Co. Ltd, Dublin, 1917)

White, G., & O'Shea, B., *Irish Volunteer Soldier 1913–23* (Osprey Publishing, Oxford, 2003)

Woodcock, Caroline, *An Officer's Wife in Ireland* (Parkgate Publications Ltd, London, 1994)

Yeates, Pádraig, *A City in Turmoil: Dublin 1919–1921* (Gill & Macmillan, Dublin, 2012)

Younger, Calton, *A State of Disunion: Griffith, Collins, Craig, De Valera* (Muller, London, 1972)

E-books

Eddleston, John, *British Executions, Volume Four: 1916 to 1920* (Bibliofile Publishers, 2012)

Igoe, Mark, *Nemo & The White Snake* (Marco Books, 2016)

Marques, Major Patrick D., *Guerrilla Warfare Tactics in Urban Environments* (War College Series, 2015)

Theses

Ainsworth, John, 'The Black & Tans and Auxiliaries in Ireland, 1920–1921: Their Origins, Roles and Legacy' (Queensland History Teachers' Association, Brisbane, Australia, May 2001)

Biggs, Michael, 'Hunger Strikes by Irish Republicans, 1916–1923' (University of Illinois, 2004)

Connolly, Linda, 'Towards a Further Understanding of the Violence Experienced by Women in the Irish Revolution', Maynooth University Social Sciences Institute, working paper series, no. 7 (Maynooth University, Maynooth, 2019)

Leeson, David, 'The Black and Tans: British Police in the First Irish War, 1920–21' (McMaster University Ontario, 2003)

Menard, Meghan Elizabeth, 'Reporting for the State Department: Carl W. Ackerman's Cooperation with Government during WW1' (Louisiana State University, 2015)

Ó Ruairc, Pádraig Óg, 'The Anglo-Irish Truce: An Analysis of its Immediate Military Impact' (University of Limerick, Limerick, 2014)

—, *The Truce Murder, Myth and the Last Days of the Irish War of Independence* (Mercier Press, Cork 2016)

Rast, Mike, 'Tactics, Politics, and Propaganda in The Irish War of Independence, 1917–1921' (Georgia State University, 2011)

Reynolds, John, 'Divided Loyalties: The R.I.C. in County Tipperary 1919–1922' (University of Limerick)

Websites

http://1914-1918.invisionzone.com/
http://annual.capuchinfranciscans.ie/
http://hansard.millbanksystems.com/
https://irishconstabulary.com/
http://irishhistory1919-1923chronology.ie/
http://irishvolunteers.org/
https://issuu.com/
http://kilmainhamgaolmuseum.ie/
http://kilmainhamtales.ie/
www.bloodysunday.co.uk/
www.bureauofmilitaryhistory.ie/
www.caucus99percent.com/
www.communistpartyofireland.ie/
www.dublin-fusiliers.com/
www.heritageireland.ie/
www.historyireland.com/
www.irishmedals.org/
www.militaryarchive.co.uk/
www.militaryarchives.ie/
www.nli.ie/
www.policehistory.com/museum/
www.richmondbarracks.ie/
www.royalirishconstabulary.com/
www.theauxiliaries.com/
www.westernfrontassociation.com/
www.bl.uk/
www.cairogang.com/
www.irishnewsarchive.com/
www.iwm.org.uk/
www.mi5.gov.uk/history/
www.oireachtas.ie/
www.paperspast.natlib.govt.nz/
www.rcpi.ie/
www.royal-irish.com/
www.sis.gov.uk/our-history/
www.thegazette.co.uk/

Acknowledgements

Darren: To my wife Joanne and my children Aaron, Liam and Adele. Yet again I could not have done this without you by my side. Thank you for all the encouragement, support and most importantly the fun, the joy and the laughter. All I can say is I love you all.

Derek: Profound thanks, again, to my beautiful wife Lisa, and my gorgeous two girls Shannon and Catríona. You are an endless source of inspiration. Your encouragement (and frequent facepalms), love and support has once again seen me over the hurdles that come hand in hand with work such as this. Thank you again so much.

Thanks yet again to both our parents and families for your inexhaustible support. It has been amazing to continue uncovering our shared family histories relating to this period and your patience and support has been an inspiration and a godsend.

We would like to express tremendous gratitude to Pat Rooney and Paul Greene for helping us with such typical enthusiasm – thanks again – you made things so much easier. Thanks also to Marcus Howard, Jean O'Connell, Frances Howard for working alongside us. May you always retain your infectious love for Irish history; Johnny Doyle for all your help, encouragement and unsurpassed expertise, Claudine, Max and Axel Meyer, Una Molyneux, Colin Crawford, Cain and Jack, Dolores, Sarah and Ben Quinlan, Colin O'Reilly, Maurice and Alison Moran, Angela and the late Tommy Lawless, Dick and Collette Sweetman, Pam Beacom, Don Doyle, Anthony O'Reardon, Conor Forde, Derek Jones, Terry Crosbie, Larry and Gráinne Murphy, Proinsias Ó Rathaille, Joe Mooney, Sinead Crowley at RTÉ, Niall MacDonagh, Diane Butler, Jill Corish, Shane McMenamin and Greg Simons (Department of Foreign Affairs and Trade Library), Niamh McDonald, Garbhan De Paor, Tanith Conway, Robert Dooley, Jim, Yvonne, Kelly, Shane and Dean Barrett, Michelle, Vitor and Alex Gonsalves, Aidan Gorman, Pat and Andrew Little, Steve and Mia Doyle, May Moran and Finin Ó Cheallacháin; all the staff at Registry and Corporate Services – Department of Foreign Affairs and Trade, as well as everyone else in the Department for all their assistance and encouragement, especially Linda Collins, James Searson, Darragh O'Neill, Jenny McStay and Deirdre Greene; everybody at the Office of Public Works (OPW) for all your help and support, particularly Philip Early and everyone at Registry and Facilities Management and all the staff at OPW Property Management, Aoife Torpey of Kilmainham Gaol (OPW); thank you so much – again. A big thanks must go to Johnny O'Dwyer, Jimmy Sheridan, Richie Ellis, Shane Doyle,

Jim McDermott, Finnian O'Dowd, Ant Dennehy and all the players and members of Tomás Mac Curtain GAA Club East London & Essex, also to Marc and Mags Ó Dálaigh, Breda and Cormac Grannell, Conor and Caroline O'Mahony, Liam and Clare O'Leary, Martin and Siobhan McGovern and all the children at Tomás Mac Curtains Underage Hurling, Camogie and Gaelic Football, Dave and Nev from *Claidheamh Soluis*, Con and Niamh O'Connor, Wayne Jenkins, Teresa Culleton, Kevin Brennan, Bróna, Mel, Diarmuid, Bart and all the Moore Street crew, Liz Gillis, Las Fallon, Kieran and Christina McMullen, Rick and Carolyn Styron, Declan Woolhead, Maria Poole, Sinclair Dowey, Mick and John O'Brien, Paul O'Brien, Joseph E.A Connell Jnr, Lorcan Collins, Niamh Hassett and everyone from *Comóradh na nÓglach* – 'Where Tipperary leads ...' Bernie Metcalfe of the National Library of Ireland, Military Archives, Kilmainham Gaol, Petesy Burns, Liam Beattie, Stevie McLoughlin, Anne Campbell, Cathy O'Sullivan and the old Belfast Crew. Liam Ó Briain, Stef Thompson and everyone at Raw Combat International, Tommy and Billie Allen and everyone at Resistance PT, everyone at Self Protection Ireland.

Thanks so much again to all the followers of the Facebook page 'Dublin 1916 – 1923 Then and Now'. We hope to count on your continuing support and feedback which inspires us so much. Meeting with so many of you has truly enhanced this adventure. The same goes for everyone who has helped and encouraged us in our previous works and gave them such a fantastic response.

Finally, we would also like to express our sincerest gratitude to all at Mercier Press for your boundless enthusiasm. Your love for what you do sets you apart. We look forward so much to working with you in the future. We would also like to express our thanks to Con and Anna Collins, Paula Elmore, Gillian Hennessy and all at The Collins Press for helping to set us on this incredible journey some years back, and to Gill Books.

Index